P R

V

N

C

R P

W

1 9

R T

1 8

ART IN THE SERVICE OF

CONVERSATION

PORTFOLIO

DISPATCH

SCREEN

LETTER TO THE EDITOR

OUTLOOK

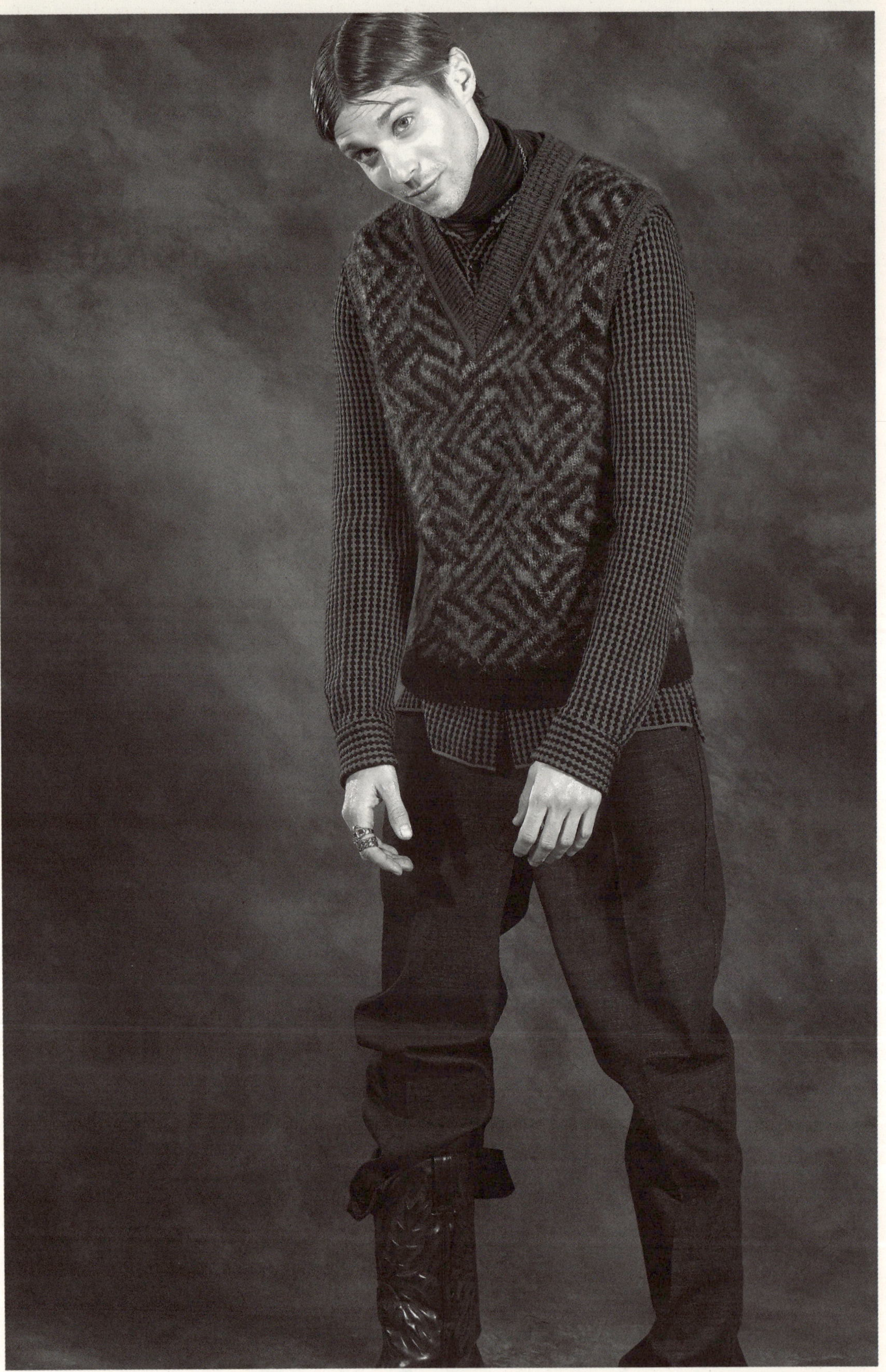

Photography Federico Reyes
Styling Nina Hollensteiner
Set Emilia Margulies
Production Greta Tettamanzi
Model Egon Thuile
HMU Maria Boman

PREFACE

While certain artistic practices of the 1990s asked how and for whom art serves, the economies of the art worlds have since changed, with new implications. Nowadays the arts are arguably more embedded within society and culture at large than ever before—witness the rise of socially engaged art, political art, financialized art, and so forth—and thus exposed to a wider field of forces with divergent interests. Along with a growing number of participants, taxes, wages, and other standards are being introduced for better or worse. That the art worlds have, in any case, always been part of the life praxis of the "real" world, overlapping in economic, social, and political structures, attests that the intensification we observe has been gradually building over years. Today's imperative, perhaps, directs our gaze ever outwards—toward arts' entanglements with other fields in functionally differentiated societies; and equally, to follow their reverberations on the shifting terrain of the artistic field itself.

The PROVENCE REPORT Autumn/Winter 2018/2019 focal point is *Art in the service of…* We look at moments when artists use their practice and skills in the service of something or someone else. In the backdrop, we are confronted with an artistic field triggering "descriptions" and suggestions like the Content Industrial Complex's false sublation of art into life or—on the other end of the spectrum—the self-abolition of all art and art workers. While the former is some sort of *Kulturindustrie* takeover, the latter is drafted as a left political practice. Paradoxically, with both comes the end of the art world. In this highly volatile period of criticism, how might a renewed interest in services comment on art's relative autonomy? As thoughts without content are empty, primary research forms the basis for this issue of PROVENCE REPORT: where possible, we have elected for conversations held or reports written by practitioners in the field.

Dominique Gonzalez-Foerster talks to Philip Pilekjær about her collaboration with Nicolas Ghesquière, involving the total redesign of Balenciaga stores worldwide. A commissioned liaison by an artist and a fashion house must be carefully framed: the interaction is precarious not only for the potential pitfalls of losing artistic autonomy, but also for the larger political, economic or psychological dynamics at play. Art school educated stylist Nina Hollensteiner directed our fashion editorial, photographed by Nadine Fraczkowski outside Paris. Rather than spotlight sundry brands, the contribution features the individual stylistic choices of gardener Éric Remba at an artist residency in a pastoral French setting. As Hollensteiner elaborates in her accompanying text, the gardener's sartorial choices embody exactly the type of idiosyncratic "everyday" inspiration exploited by the fashion industry—an inspiration reproduced, yet rarely credited.

Further on the subject of exploitation, Raphael Gygax assesses Vanessa Beecroft's early performances and art installations. Although the artist's work has been fairly widely discussed, Gygax claims that Beecroft's employment of *the other body*—that is, the function her work assigns to women, and to fashion models in particular—has drawn strikingly little critical scrutiny; in this overdue analysis, Gygax reads Beecroft's work as a trenchant critique of the powers that control the female body. In another vein, artist Emanuele Marcuccio reflects on the brute challenges of working for others. Having been employed as an assistant for fashion shoots and video productions, he realizes that—in spite of the job's gratuitous catering with salmon mini bagels—his wages inevitably fail to cover his on-the-job expenses, such as the nightly cost of his hotel room. In a Marxist sense, one doesn't get paid to have a nice life, but theoretically, capitalism keeps the labor force "alive." With a job that pays less than the cost involved simply to keep the job, this idea of reproduction begins to unravel.

Silvia Simoncelli reviews a discussion between Adrian Piper and Ian Burn on the question of value in artists' labor. Piper proposes a system of remuneration for artists beyond the walls of the gallery and the museum, underlining the need to define applicable parameters on artists' labor and artistic value; Burn, on the other hand, argues that hourly wages could instigate an even more exploitative economic reality for artists. Meanwhile, navigating the threshold between *real* and *symbolic* labor, Adam Linder's choreographic services explore relations of work and labor in the symbolic economy. Whilst conceiving formats for dance outside the theatre, Linder submits himself and his co-performers to formalized work contracts and systems of exchange. In the process, the specific qualities of dance that can neither be translated into economic value nor into theory's attempts for critical framing come to light: "If the work is reflexive, what are the aspects within which this reflexivity is nested?" Linder asks.

Inspired by the film *Karl's Perfect Day* (2017), Karl Holmqvist, Tobias Kaspar, Inka Meißner, and Rirkrit Tiravanija speak about collaboration with friends, artistic production outside the parameters of the white cube, and the difference between popular perceptions of the life of an artist and lived reality. Along this trajectory, Julia Moritz waxes poetic on Mildreds's Lane, a house in the woods that doubles as a retreat and an artistic project. The founders, participants, and public of Mildred's Lane openly adhere to a type of institution-critical practice that drops "service" as a household name.

Moritz presents Mildred's Lane as a site for contemporary artistic work at the interstices of economy, ecology, practice, and domesticity—here, "service" is collectively determined, in a broad reciprocal sense between use and value, private and public.

Interrelated with this issue's focus on service, the following conversations permit more casual forays into artistic practice. Tobi Maier talks to Jac Leirner about her inter-decade work with airline cutlery, blankets, trays, air sickness bags, stickers and ticket stubs; Anne Dressen and Shahryar Nashat discuss Virgil Abloh's Paris debut for Louis Vuitton; Inka Meißner interviews LaKela Brown on subjectivity and identity politics; Isabel Mehl and Lynne Tillman exchange ideas on Tillman's latest book *Men and Apparitions* (2018), literature versus contemporary art, and critical fictions; musician Karsten Pflum gives Cecilie Norgaard an account of his career, between the desire to make a living, the pitfalls of the music industry, and "soulful music;" last but not least, Inga Lāce talks to Katerina Gregos about RIBOCA—Riga's first Biennial for contemporary art—and its controversial financier, the *North West Fishing Consortium*.

Looking at the state of the artistic field, two tendencies are to be observed: one tendency characterizes art as an endangered species, mourning the endgames of art and cultural criticism in the age of internet fandom; the second tendency asserts that art has, for so long, been pestered by the assertion of autonomy, that dependency and arts entanglements are regarded as aberrant—a purely negative condition. To paraphrase Craig Owens, both observations lie contrary to the facts and to the extraordinary and ongoing proliferation of cultural activity, lubricated by the market: "We ought to ask the real question about why capitalism promotes this [cultural activity], and what it gains from it, and how its interests are vested in it."

PROVENCE, September 2018

RT
TH
S R

N

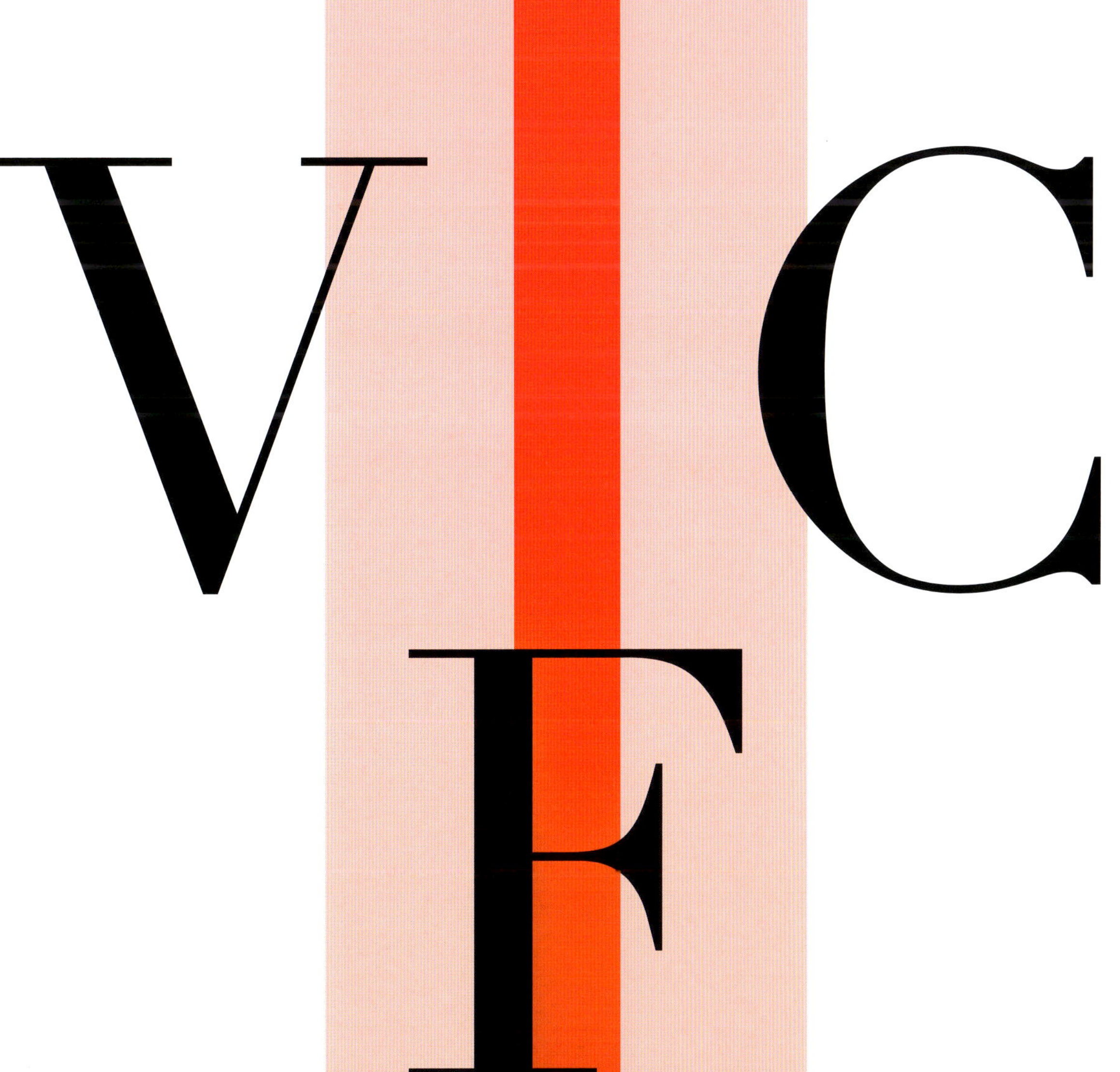

LANDSCAPES FOR BALENCIAGA

Interview — Dominique Gonzalez-Foerster
Philip Pilekjær

Photos — Gregoire Vieille
Courtesy — Poste 9

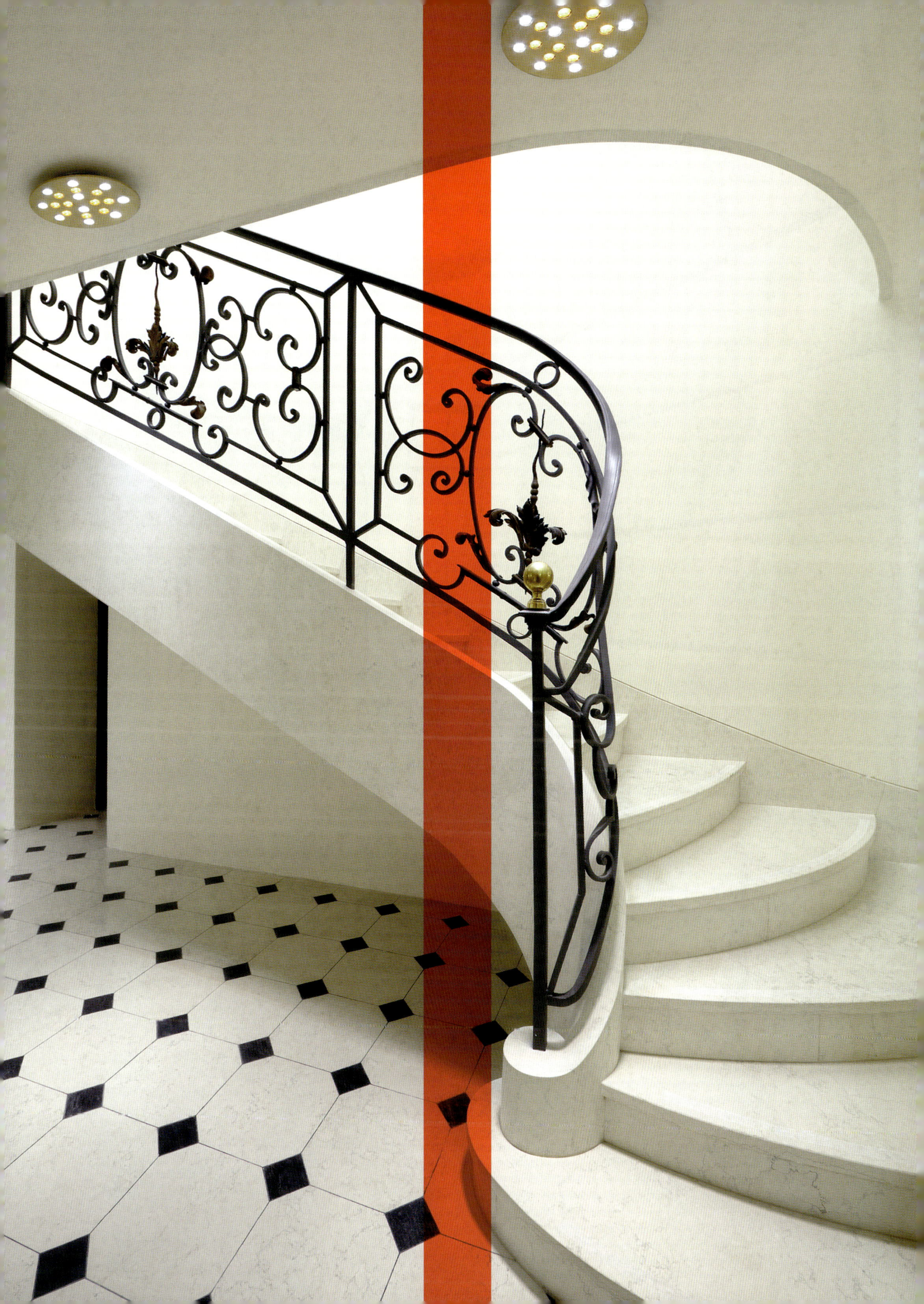

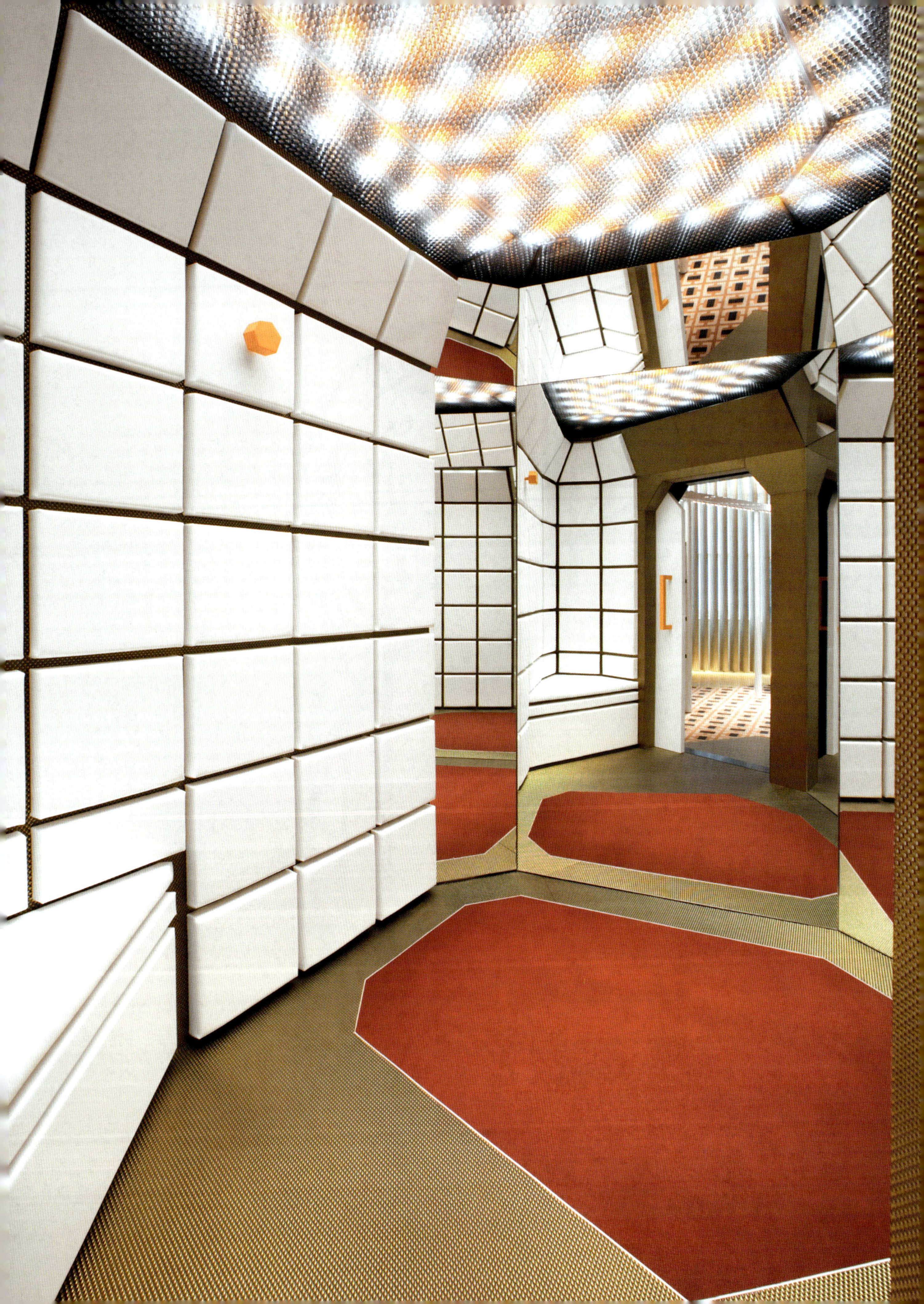

Since 2000, Dominique Gonzalez-Foerster, Martial Vieille/Galfione, and Benoit Lalloz, who form Poste 9 and take their name from Rio de Janeiro's lifeguard station No. 9, have conceived a subway station, parks, museum scenographies, light fixtures and fashion shows. From 2002 to 2012, Poste 9 redesigned all Balenciaga stores worldwide in collaboration with Nicolas Ghesquière, who, in 1997 at the age of 25 started as chief designer at Balenciaga. Instead of commissioning an architect for the project, Ghesquière invited Gonzalez-Foerster along with Poste 9 to reimagine the boutiques' entire concept. Every aspect of each boutique was reformulated, using architectural concepts based on climate and landscape, fiction and abstraction; aiming to adapt to the city's context and history.

Philip Pilekjær interviewed Gonzalez-Foerster for PROVENCE REPORT about this collaboration between an artist and a designer; a collaboration which ended in 2013 with Ghesquière's move to Louis Vuitton. Given Balenciaga's recent efforts to embrace a young Berlin-based art world, with artists working as models and shooting campaigns, Dominique Gonzalez-Foerster's collaboration with the company is of particular interest.

Philip Pilekjær: First of all, how did this project come about, and what was your motivation as an artist to take on the task of designing a line of retail stores?

Dominique Gonzalez-Foerster: It was a proposal by M/M (Paris) graphic design, and since I was very much into architecture at that time it turned into a wonderful experiment. Alongside this, I liked Nicholas' clothing very much but also his method, ways and inspirations. It was not so much about retail in my mind, more about learning and collaboration. He could have been a musician or a writer.

PP: Could you talk about how the skills that you've developed in your art practice were translated into this other field of work?

DGF: At the time lots of stores had a white cube/gallery look and I thought we should go another way and develop landscapes and more immersive spaces.

PP: Balenciaga came from a slightly stagnant position in fashion when Nicolas became director and decided to completely rebrand the house, and your stores became a vital part of this rebranding strategy. How did you work with your own agenda within this larger framework of Balenciaga's brand campaign?

DGF: There was an almost complete freedom and we agreed from the beginning that it was not about having art in stores but about developing a full language.

PP: Did it feel like a job?

DGF: It felt like a great experience, like developing videos and stage design for French singers Christophe and Alain Bashung, or like making short films that were shown in Cannes. It felt like going beyond galleries and museums, which was what I wanted at that time.

PP: All the stores are designed for their specific milieu and so there's no uniform identity, which undermines the trademarks that are usually the core aim of creating a line of fashion stores. Did you deliberately disregard these conventions?

DGF: Absolutely. That was a choice from the beginning, as a fertile reaction, and the language was developed and complexities added in different steps over more than 10 years and for about 120 spaces.

AT THE TIME LOTS OF STORES HAD A WHITE CUBE/GALLERY LOOK AND I THOUGHT WE SHOULD GO ANOTHER WAY AND DEVELOP LANDSCAPES AND MORE IMMERSIVE SPACES.

PP: Nicolas has previously talked about the "DNA of Balenciaga," which made me think that the notions of "fashion house" and "art practice" might not be so far apart. They both define a body of work, methods, tendencies, and a position within culture. Was it productive for you to engage with the "practice" of Balenciaga?

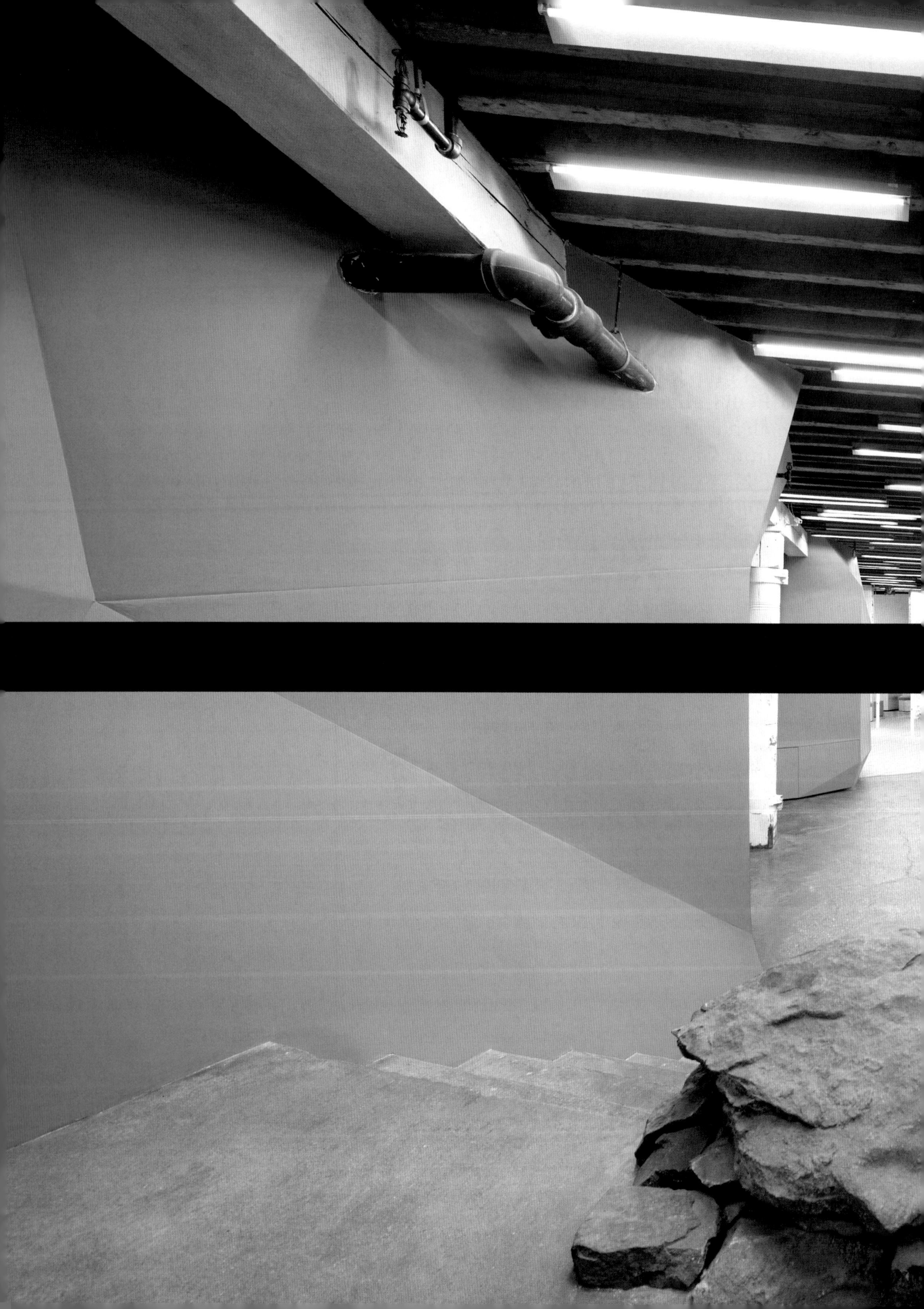

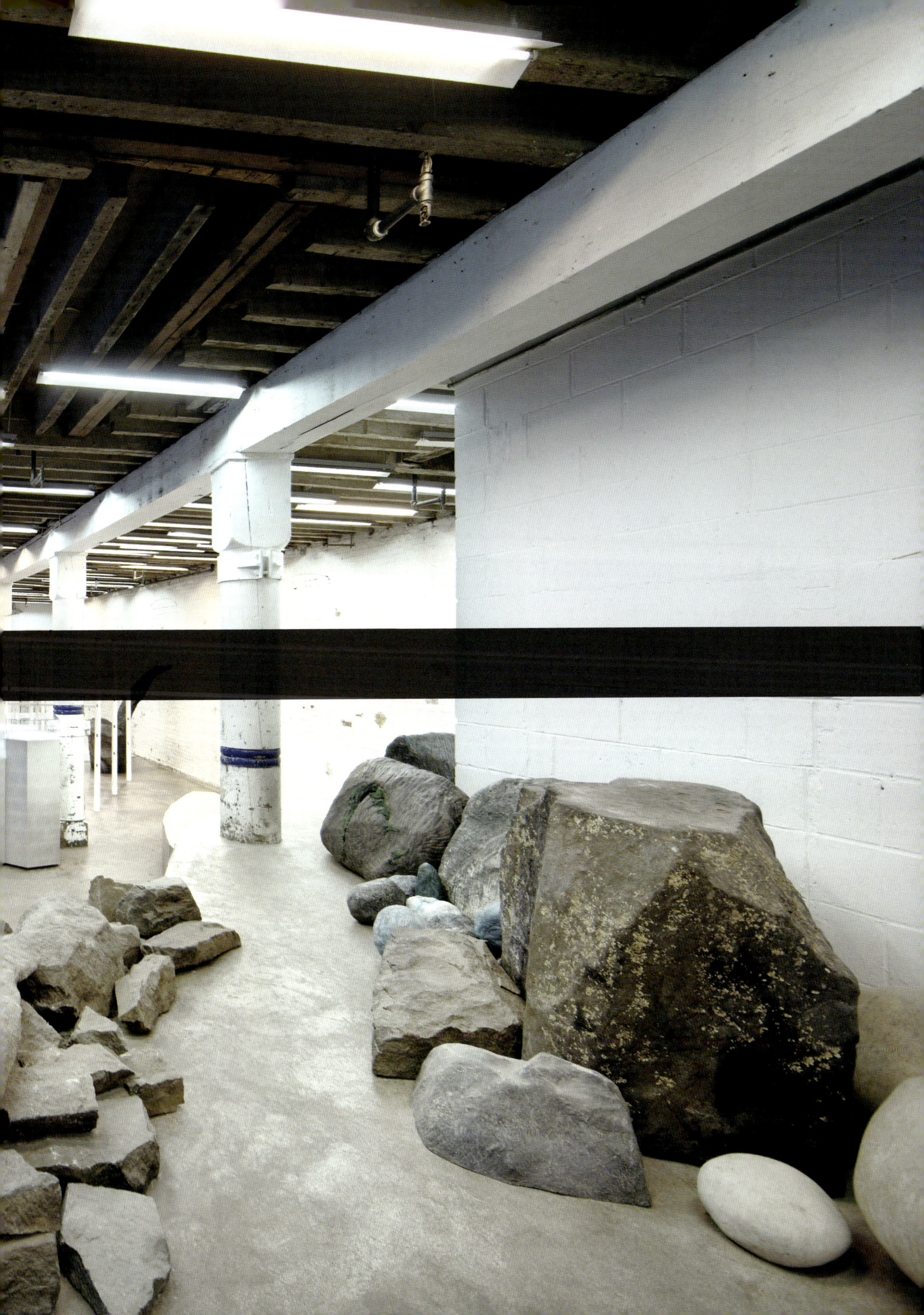

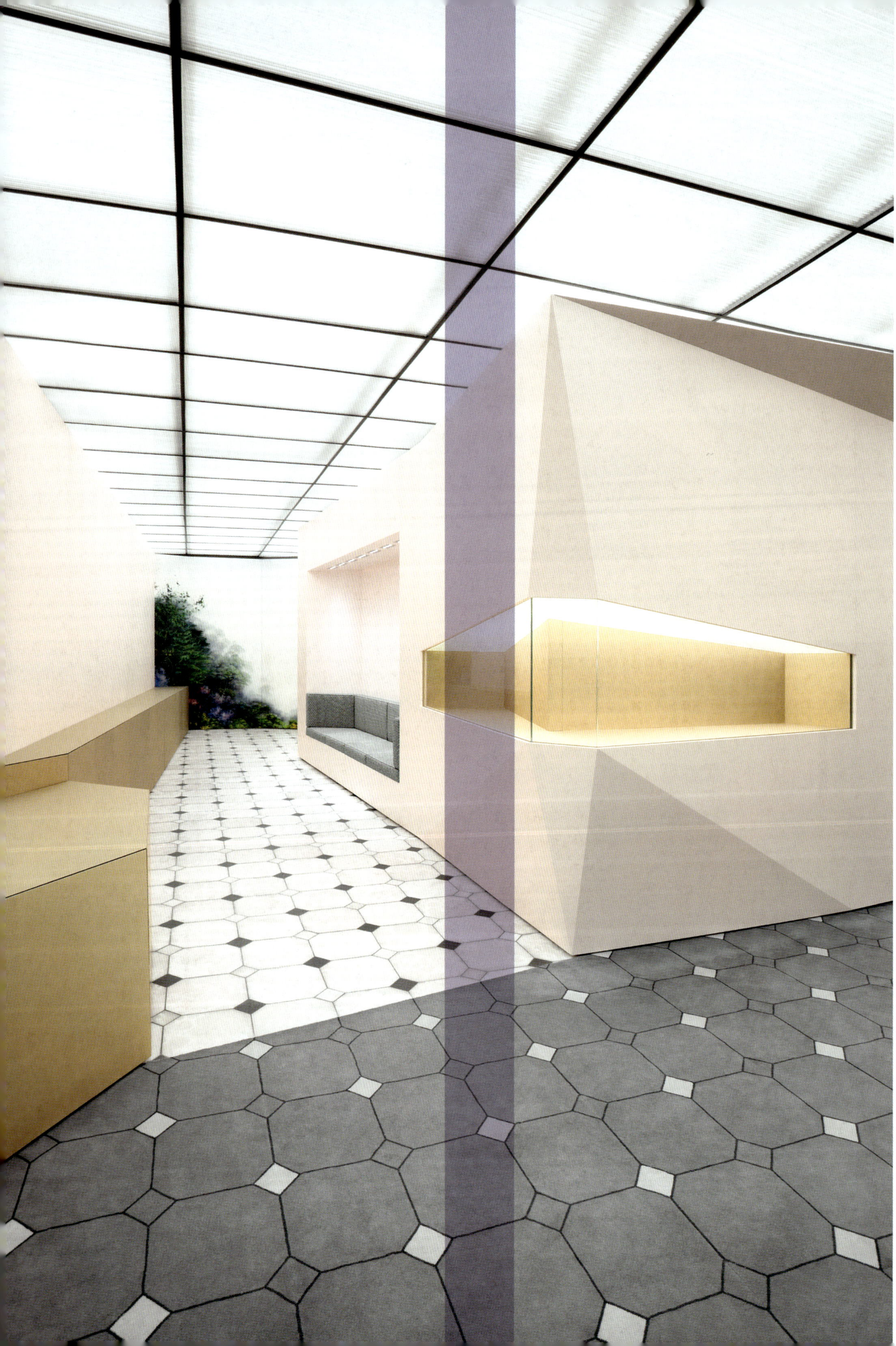

Previous spread: New York / Chelsea
This page: Paris / Avenue George V

DGF: It was much more about Nicolas than Balenciaga, or maybe Nicolas engaging with Balenciaga, but when we were addressing the historical context of Balenciaga we also worked on the archive.

PP: Your work is often described in terms of relational aesthetics and several of your projects function across the confines of art institutions and into other spaces and economies. It makes sense that you should push your work into the "real," as far as a retail store can be considered real. Did it feel like a natural progression of your work to take on this task?

DGF: I felt like Friedrich Kiesler or other artists playing in other contexts open to their ideas and questions...

PP: You ended up collaborating on these stores for more than a decade and your collaboration also spilled over into your own art. You did the show "Expodrome" at the Musée d'art moderne de la ville de Paris in 2007 with Nicolas, right?

DGF: Yes, it was great to develop *La Jetée* and *Solarium* with Nicolas for "Expodrome." We also always wanted to do a film together.

PP: Perhaps the ability to move fluently between distinct cultural spheres opens up opportunities, for better or worse, for artists to make a living from whatever skills they might have developed through their art. As an artist, letting oneself be absorbed into other economies might paradoxically be a strategy to stay part of an art world that is less commercially viable?

DGF: Yes. It can be an interesting choice, but only if the company is ready to take some risks and experiment and if the designer is brave enough to support a completely new way which is not always the case.

PP: Your work on these stores took place under the banner of Poste 9, a collaboration between Martial Vieille, Benoit Lalloz and yourself. How do you see the role of Poste 9 within your artistic practice?

IT FELT LIKE GOING BEYOND GALLERIES AND MUSEUMS, WHICH WAS WHAT I WANTED AT THAT TIME.

DGF: Poste 9 has been a brilliant collaborative and practical tool. Architecture and larger productions require different settings and frames, but Poste 9 is also a place on the beach in Ipanema... very important.

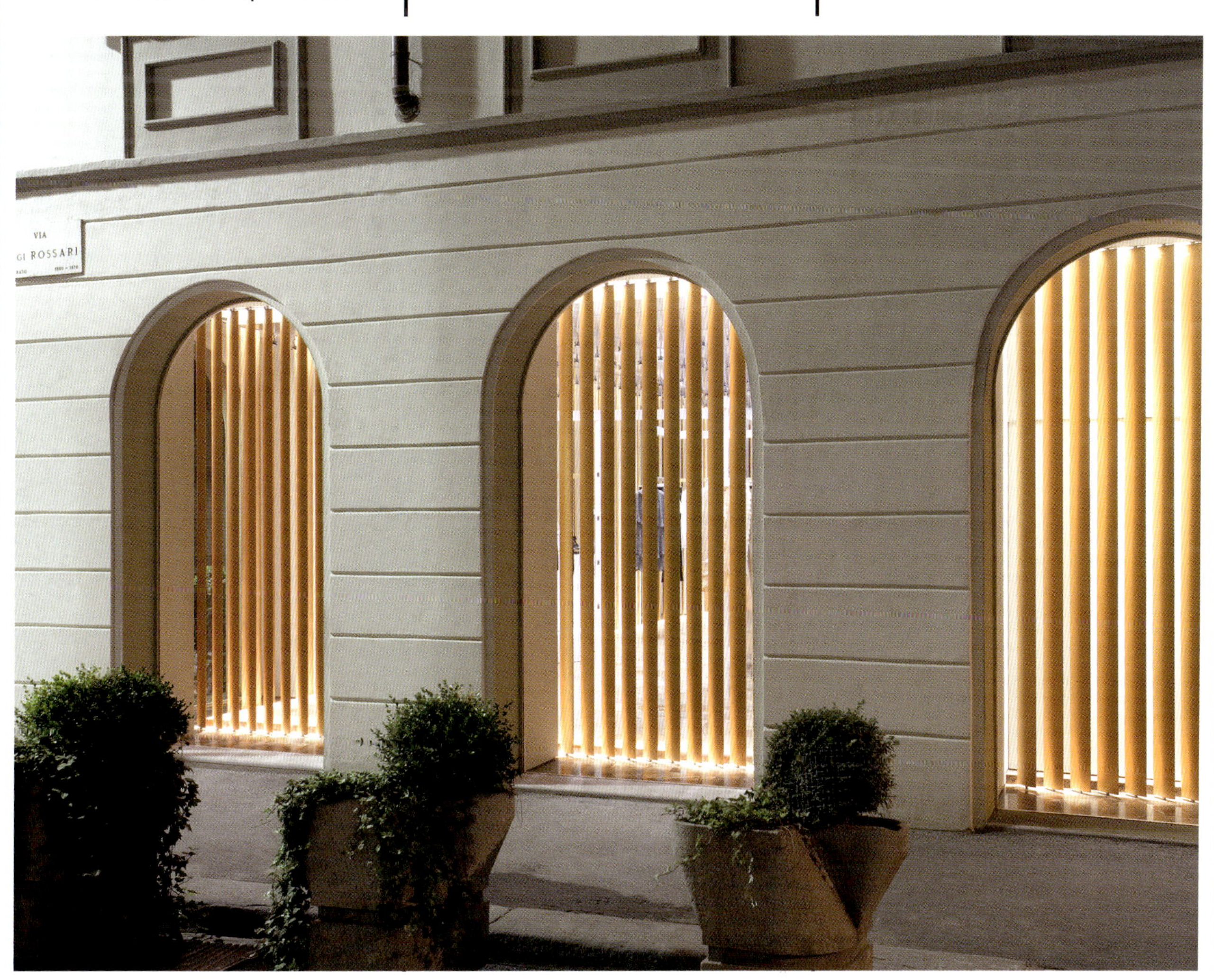

Milan

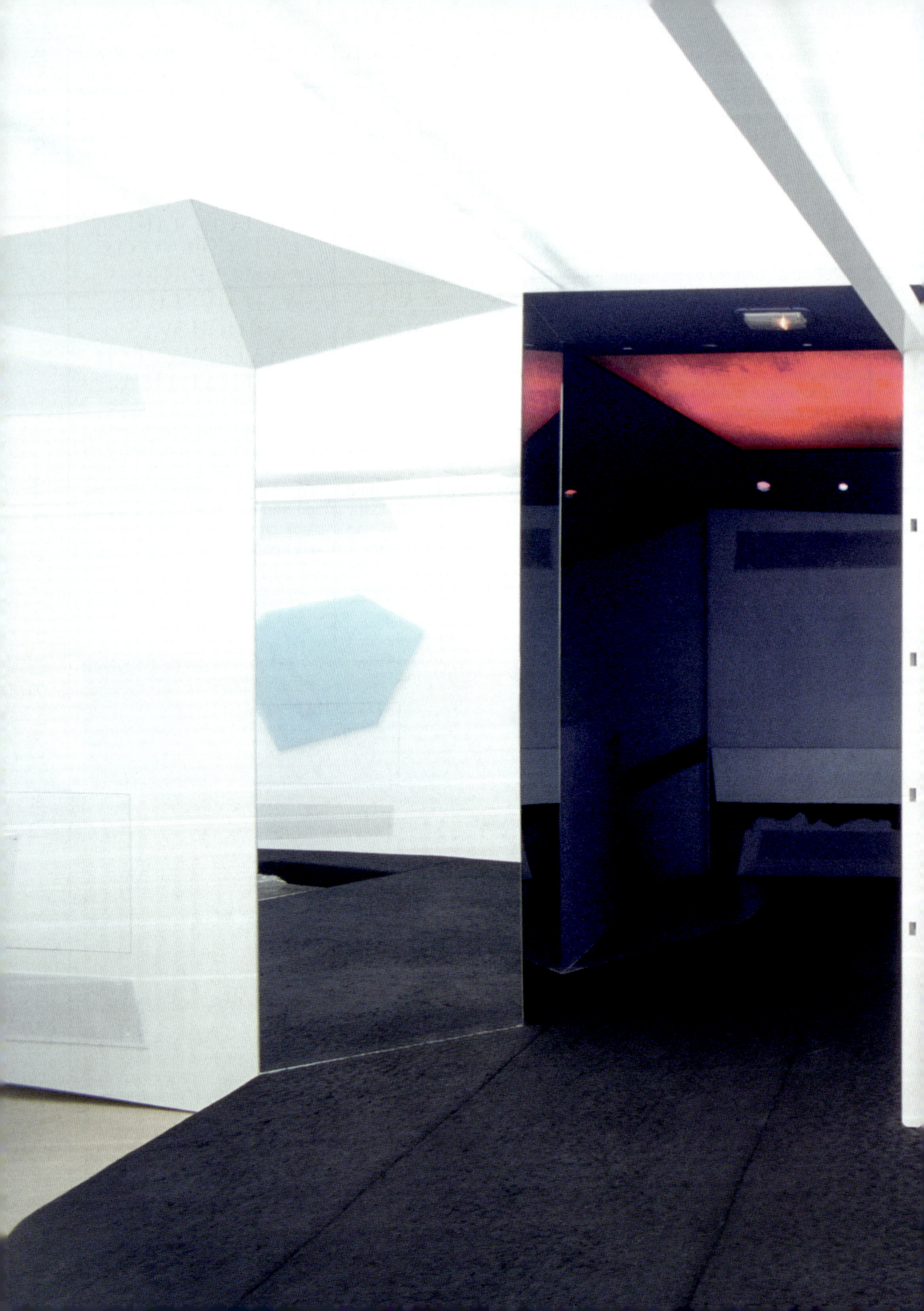

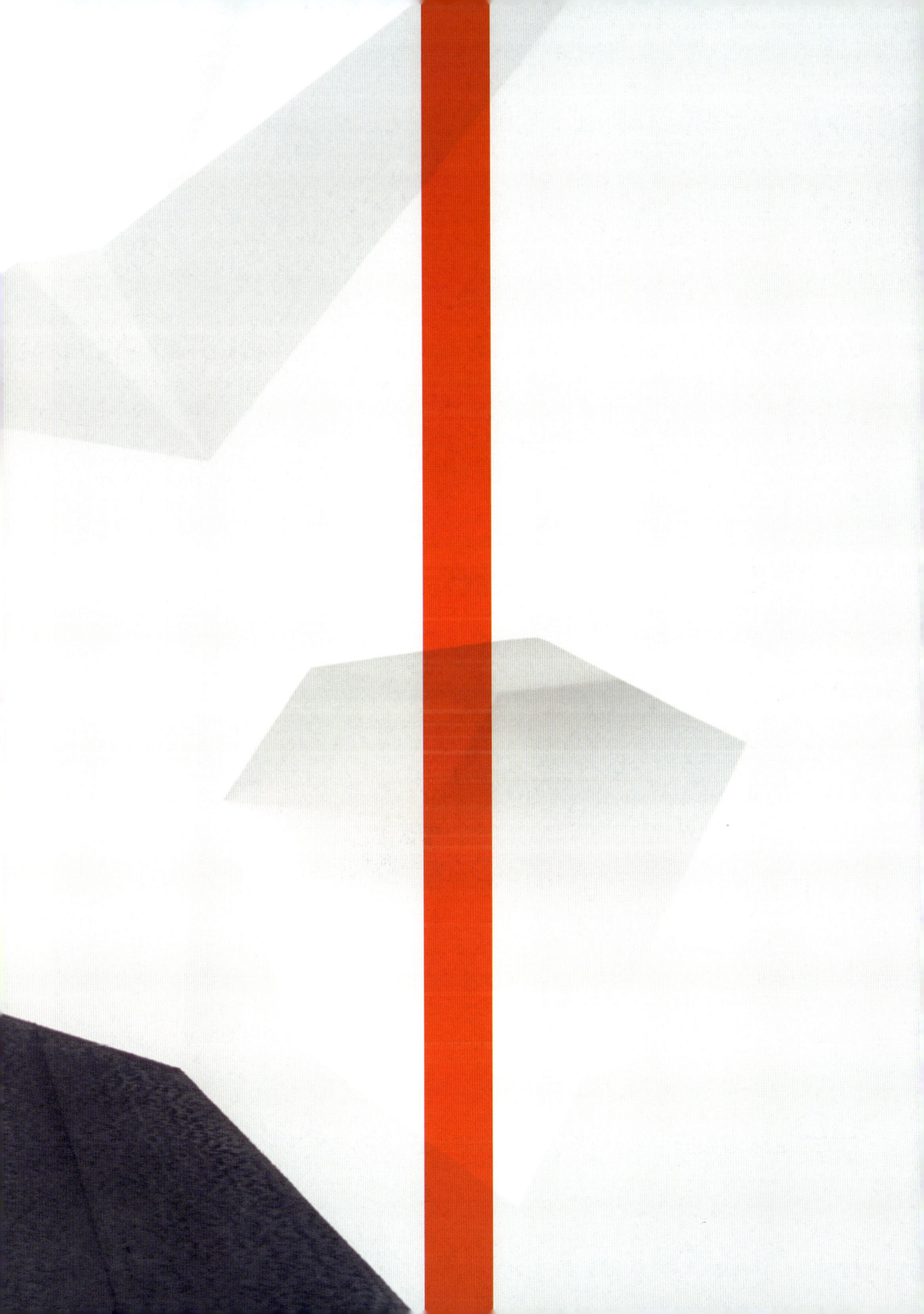

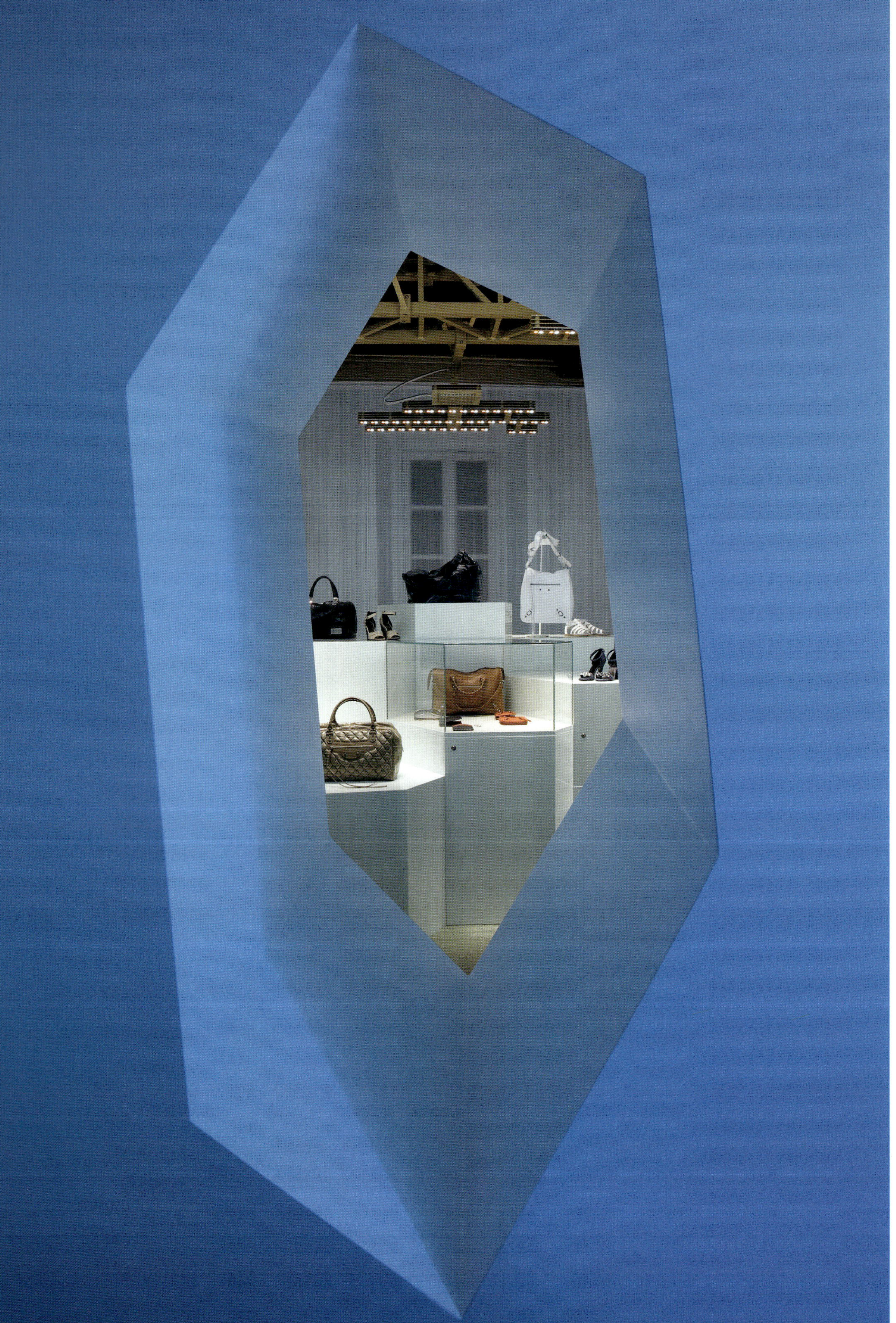

Previous spread: Paris / Avenue George V
This page: Milan

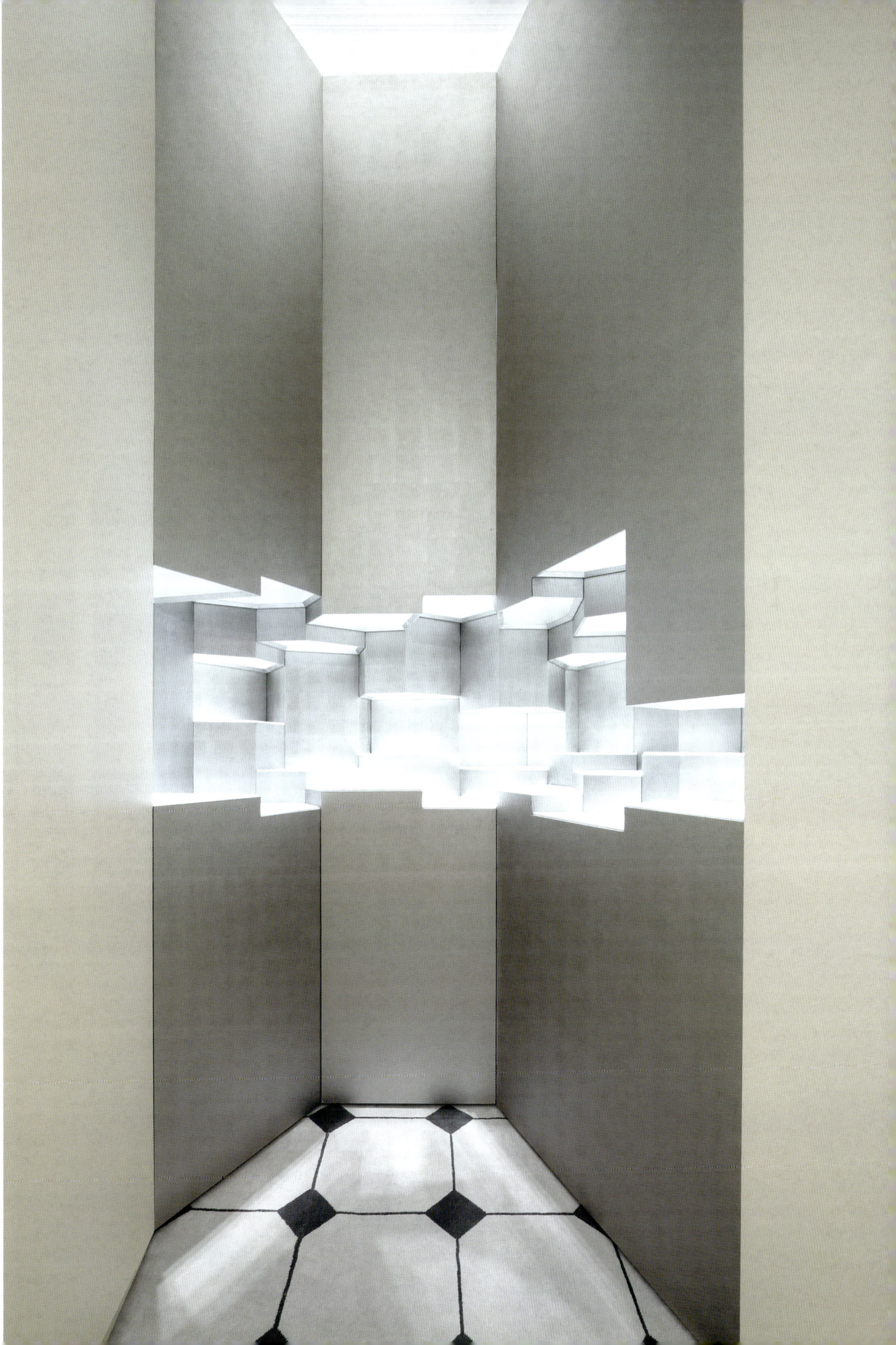

This page: Paris / Avenue George V
Following spreads: London and Milan

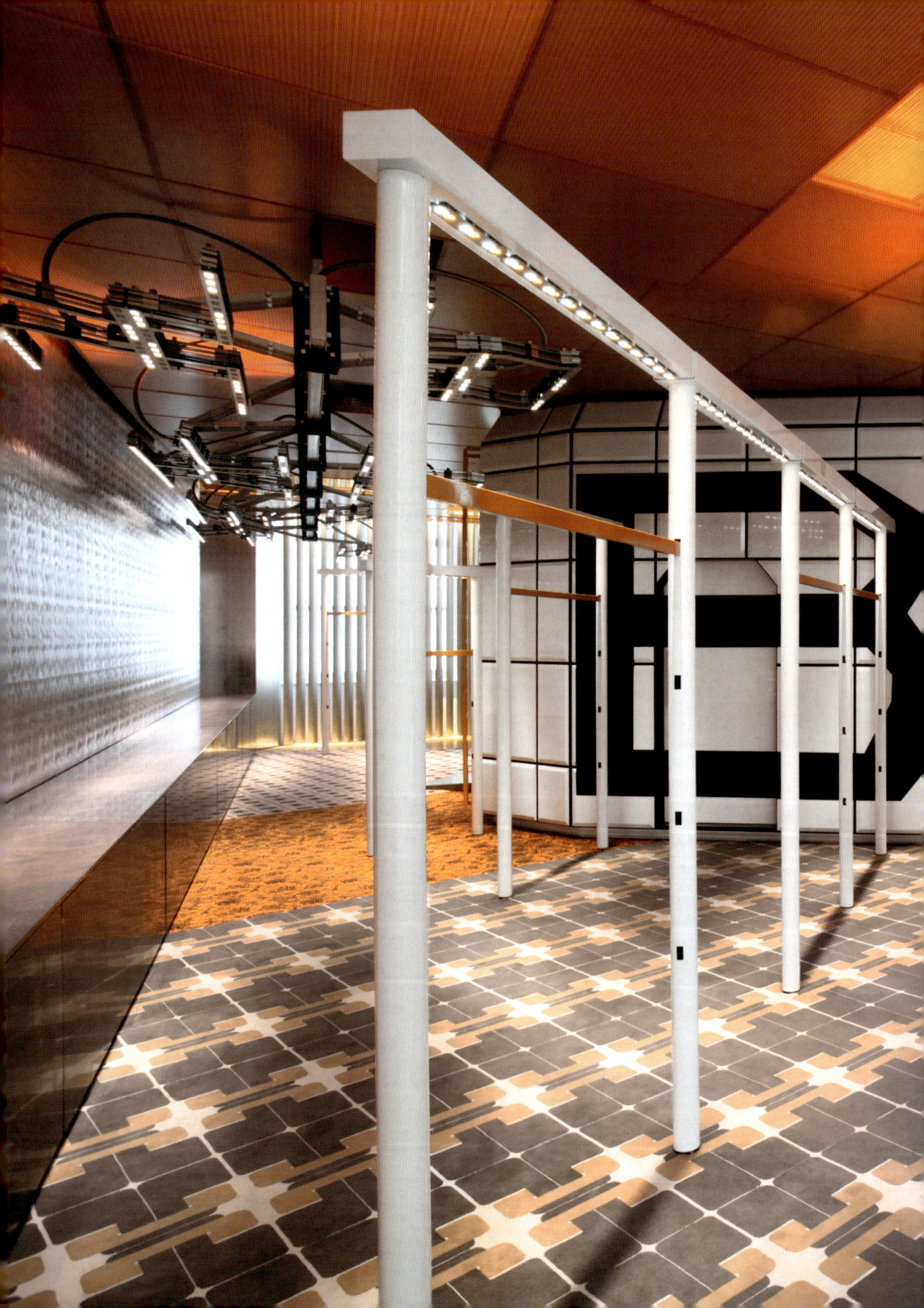

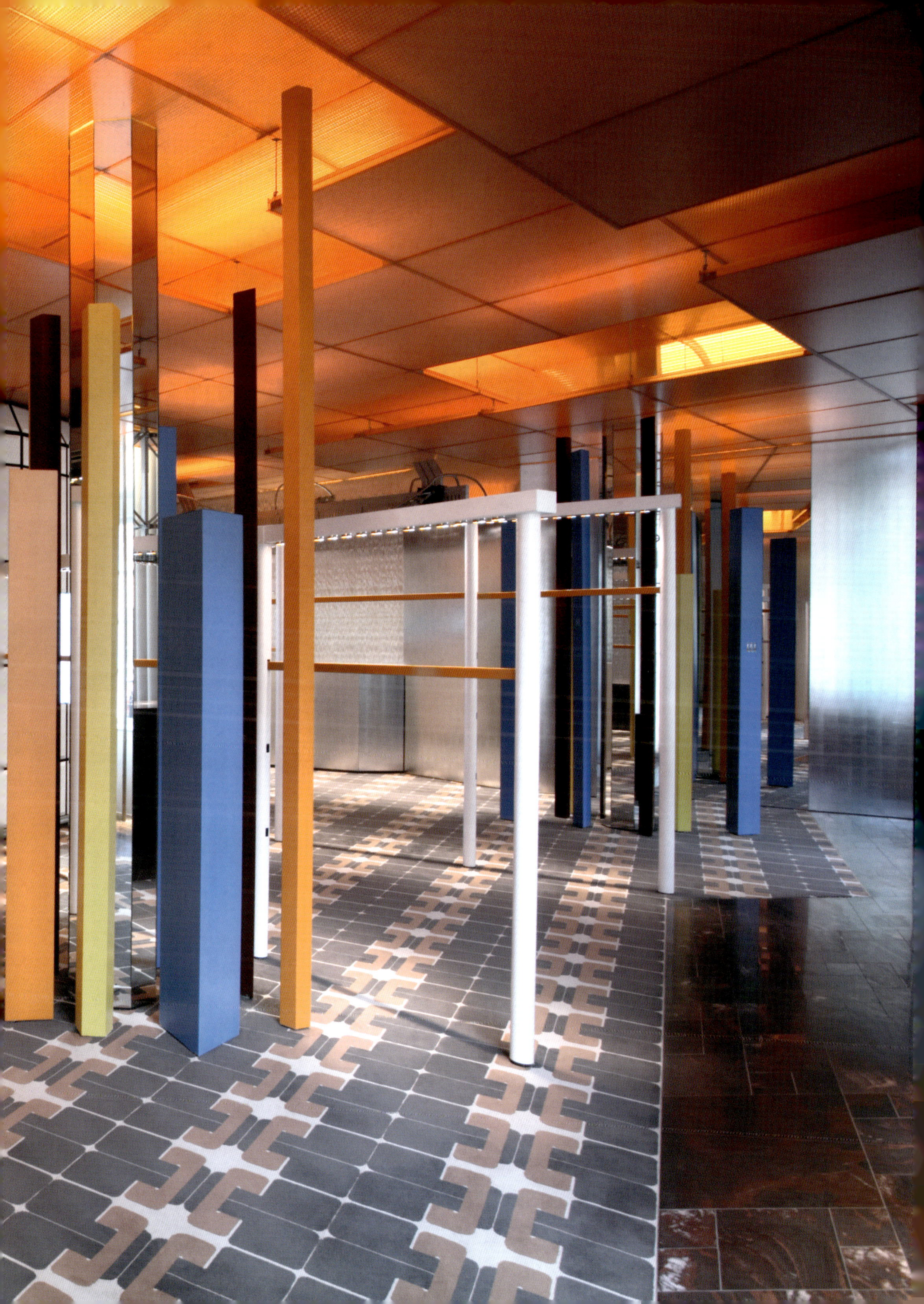

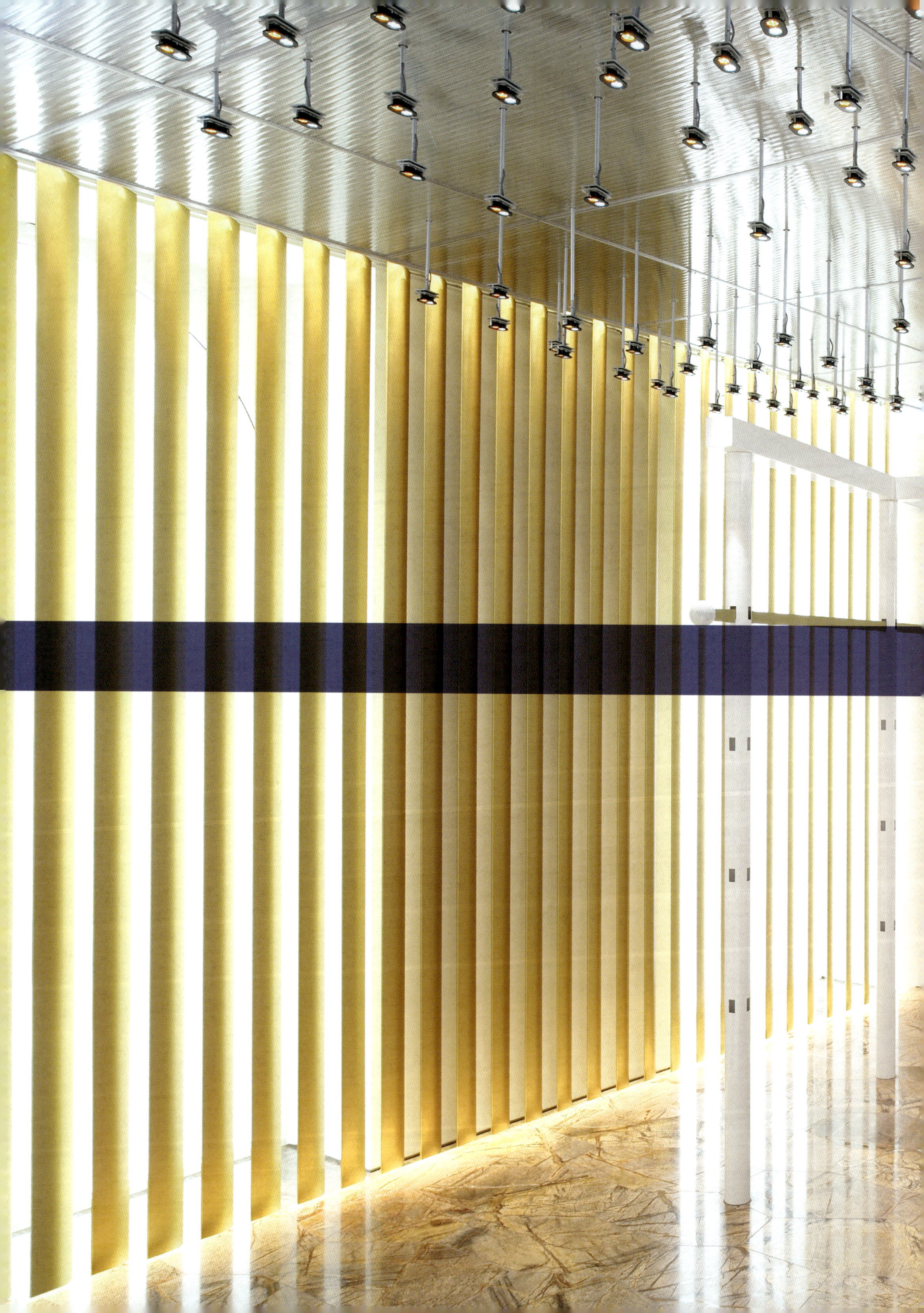

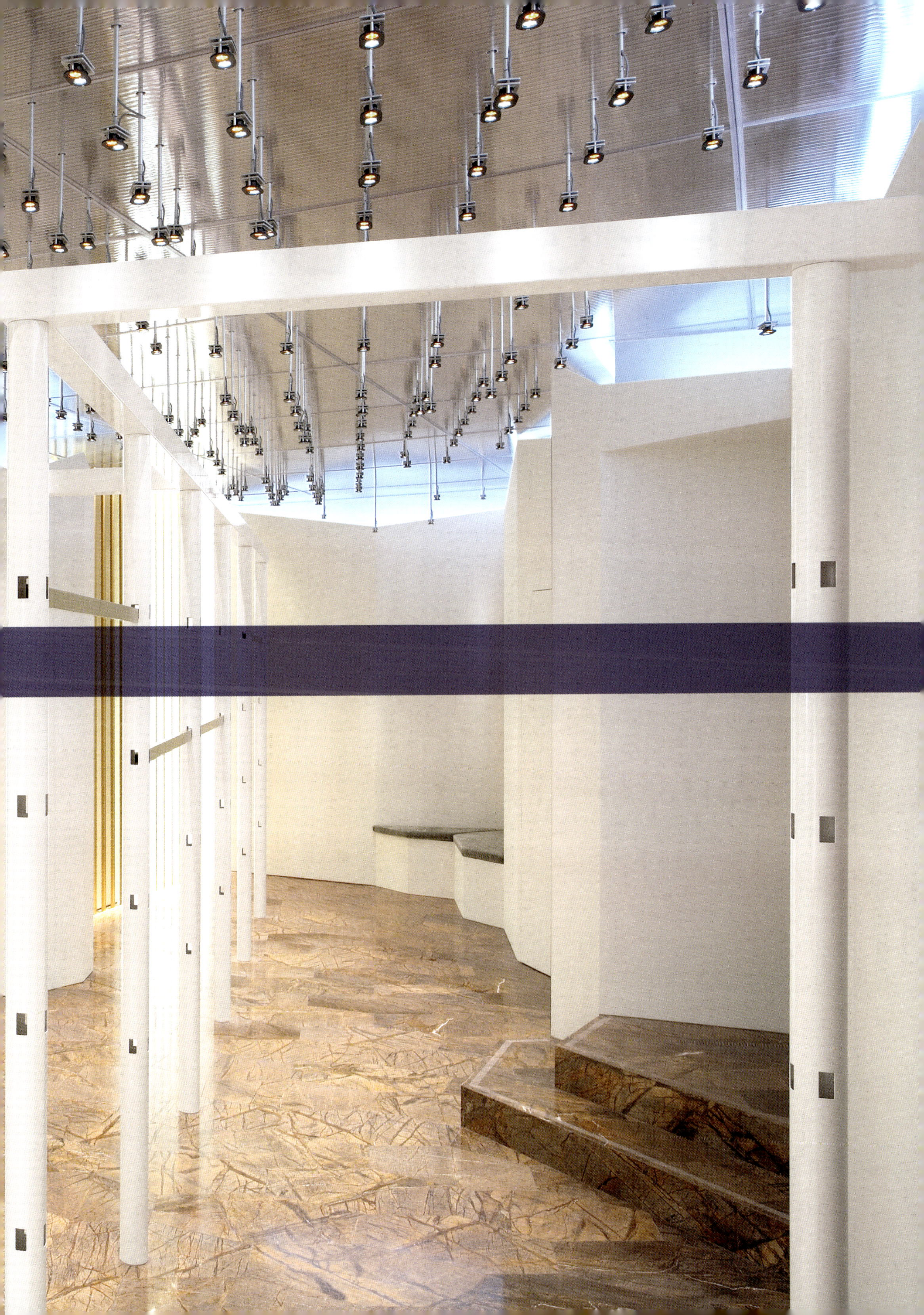

BACKSTAGE BACKSTAGE: THE GARDENER

Text and art direction	Nina Hollensteiner
Photography	Nadine Fraczkowski
Model and styling	Éric Remba

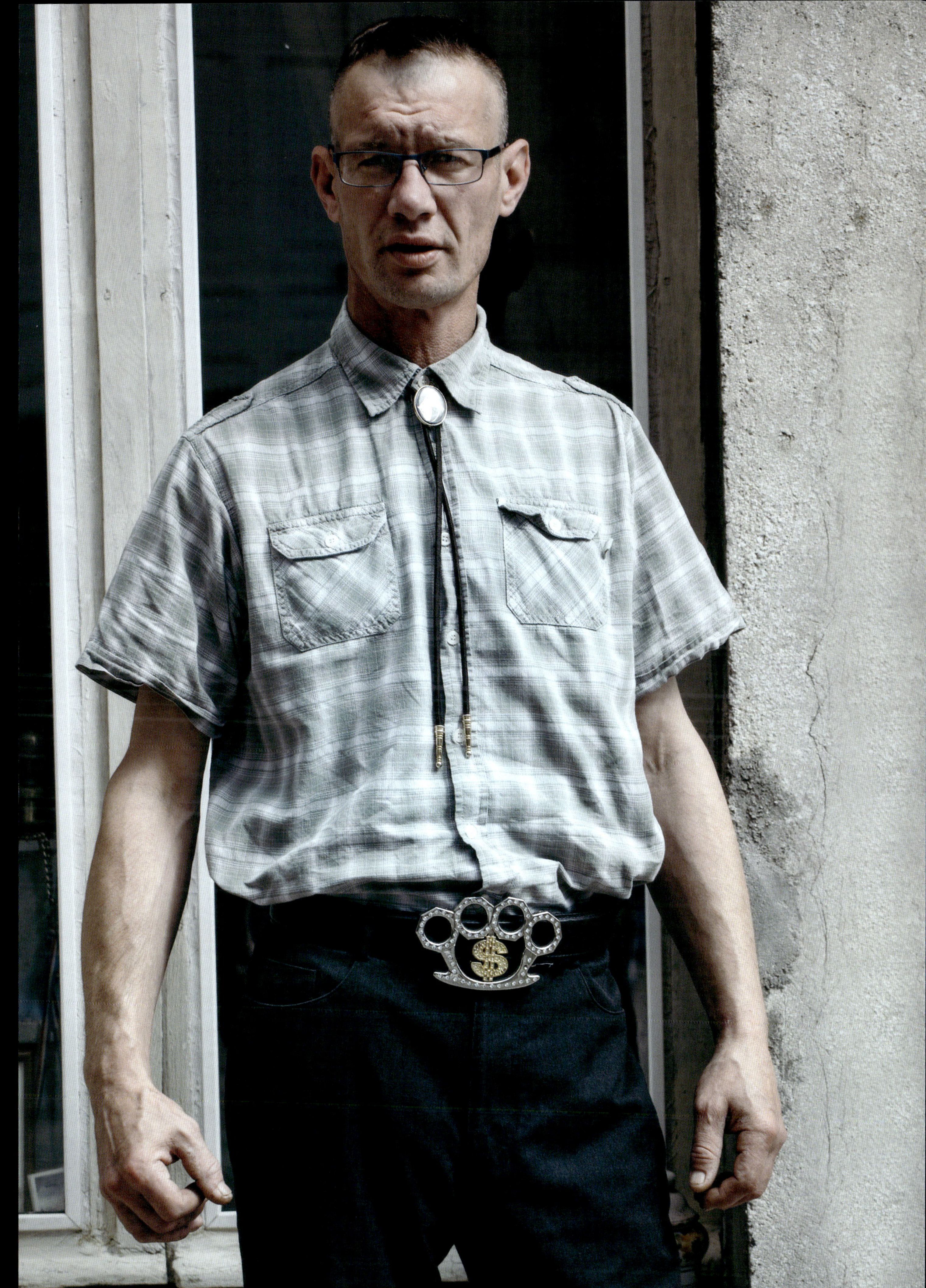

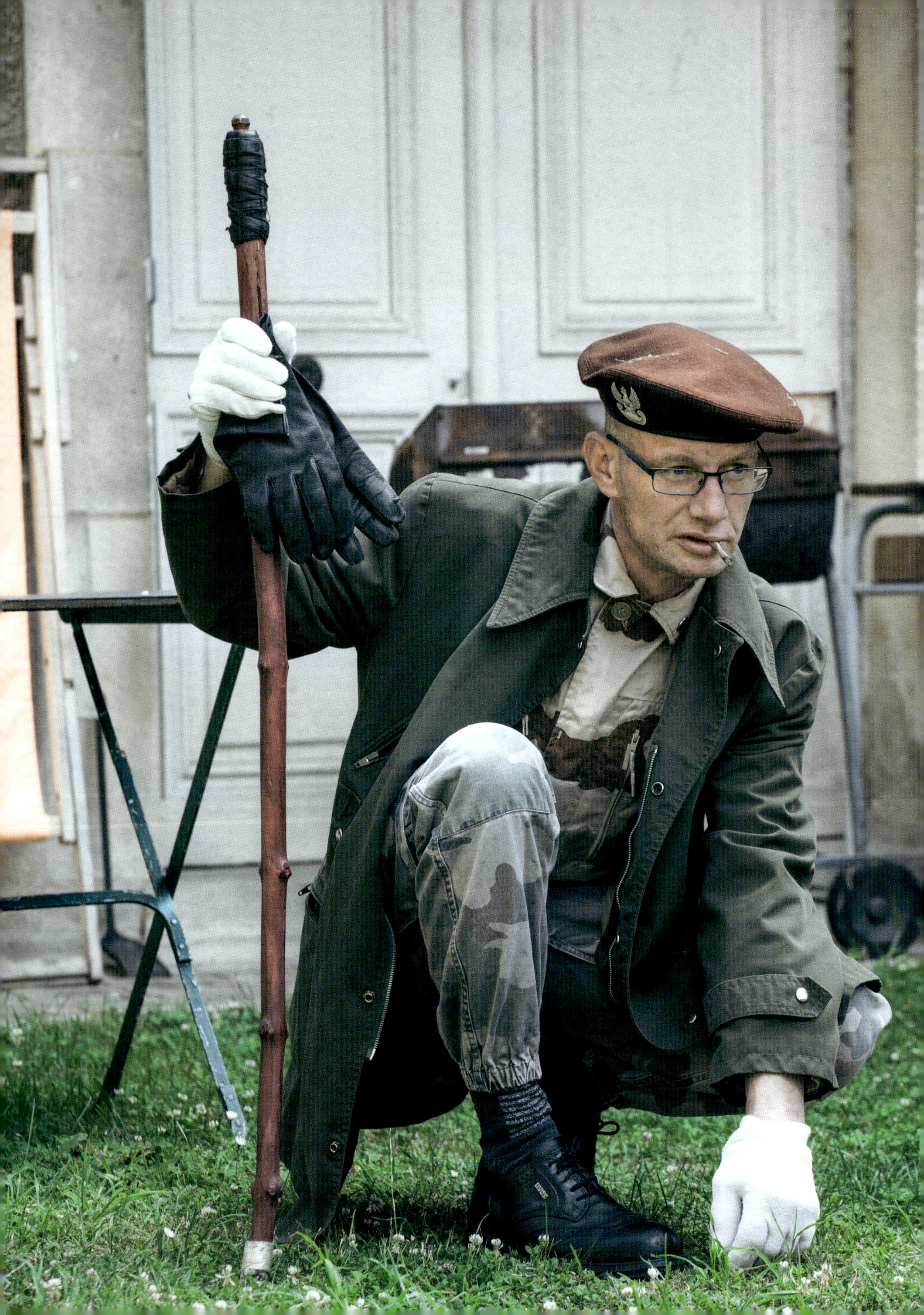

For several years now, I've been offering my artistic services to the fashion industry. This was an evolution from my previous practice, as an artist in service of the art market. After art school, my work environment had prompted me to redefine *artistic practice*. Rather than stay confined to the art world's insularity, it seemed more gratifying to apply my skills *interdisciplinarily*. With distance and a new routine, I believed I would better understand what making art—in its essence—really meant.

To be precise, though, my current work as a stylist is closer to that of a curator than that of an artist. I look at designers' collections—presented on bodies and assembled to form looks—a multitude of individual parts that collectively make up a statement. Each look stands for itself, while all the looks together compose a collection's overall image. In my work, I consider (or ignore) collections, cherry-pick individual items, and collage them with items from other designers into new looks; like a curator, a stylist submits items to be recontextualized in her vision. At least that's the idea in theory. In practice, there are also *gatekeepers*: press agencies, among others, who hold sway in place of the designers, and restrict access to material.

WHEN IT COMES TO ARTISTIC VISIONS, FASHION IS A PRETTY RELUCTANT MATERIAL.

When it comes to artistic visions, fashion is a pretty reluctant material. More unwieldy, in fact, than any material I've ever worked with as an artist. In its earliest stages, fashion is already fraught with commercial interests. Moreover, resources are limited and often shared competitively between many stylists—I can only get my hands on material for a small timeframe, *if* it is made available to me. There must always be an occasion and clarity regarding your intent of use: where and when will your work be shown? In other words, which magazine do you work for? While ideally, the photographed fashion editorial is independent in its vision, it is first and foremost a framework for product placement. This is evident most explicitly in the fashion credits, where a given photo's list of brand names, or a page's few lines of fine print, convey the editorial's conditions for production—that is, sponsors who loan or grant access to the material must be acknowledged, and thereby promoted.

In my experience, the artistic act itself is brief, and only pops up when I'm immersed in my own intentions, surrounded by stacks of fashion samples, having divested their original claims. It's an act of mild stoicism to ignore everything and everybody for a brief moment, toward visualizing an idea, which too will join the discourse. In light of the industry's strict regulations, this moment of conceptualization brings delightful freedom, a win for the artist in the service of fashion: this is the critical moment in which I have autonomy. For a moment, I can use my skills on my own terms to manifest my personal agenda. Beyond this momentary refuge of artistic freedom, however, lies the jungle of commercial interests that endlessly vie for product placement, image making, and positioning.

The fashion scene is a hub and transmitter of myriad genres and social classes. It illustrates an image, observing a certain lifestyle. Take, for instance, the "Russian Suburbia" look—worn on the streets of Russia, before its elevation to high fashion by designer Gosha Rubchinskiy. Adapted for and cannibalized by the industry, "Russian Suburbia" was quickly converted to a platform for product placement—the style was reproduced with recognizable, hence marketable, fashion items. Consider the image making successful if the same look later pops up on the body of, say, a wealthy London gallerist—once the fashion industry has worked its wonders, and has made it socially acceptable and available for purchase. Our growing awareness of self-marketing, boosted by social media, has added a new dynamic too. It is easier than it has ever been for people to socially proclaim their identity with a scene or lifestyle, in the fields of music, art, and fashion. Lifestyle, in turn, informs the aesthetics of each professional field. Although there is thus a semblance of interdisciplinary transgression, each field inevitably yields to a commercial framework that sets priorities different from those of the milieu it first drew inspiration from.

I believe a subconscious practice is the only practice that can escape being determined by market, lifestyle, and positioning strategies. A subconscious practice arrives at self-determination by following an inner logic; it also possesses a displaced sense of environment that doesn't foreground self-awareness and strategy. Within any socially determined group—from teenage skaters in suburban Russia to elderly tourists at a resort in the Dolomites—aesthetic conventions and idioms develop for many reasons: practicality, conformism, marginality, availability (or lack thereof), money (or lack thereof), or sheer coincidence. Their aesthetic statements, consequently, do not emerge as by-products of an external strategic intention but follow a sense of internal necessity.

This spontaneously emerging aesthetic logic deeply fascinates and inspires the fashion industry. An untrained or inattentive eye might register no more than a visually cohering group identity. But the skill and work of the stylist, as I see it, is to identify the nuances and specificities within these participatory codes—isolating and extracting their essence, as a biologist might do with a pipette. Ultimately, my job as a stylist is to capture the look of a certain scene on the street, or elsewhere in everyday life. Thus appropriated, this look is staged by stylists and photographers in editorials, presented on the runways of the world's fashion capitals, and positioned as luxury products for sale in fashion boutiques. While I may sympathize with the symbolic, cultural, or economic origins of a certain aesthetic, my work nonetheless relies on the *derived* looks and finished products of the fashion industry—if only for the credits.

In my fashion editorial for PROVENCE, I have dispensed with credits. In a way, this possibility is afforded to me by my double position as an artist: styling here is a form of expression, freed from its industry constraints. I have decided against using these spreads for product placement of any sort—neither as points for a stylist, nor as publicity for a label. This editorial was conceived together with Éric Remba, who works as a gardener at an artist residency in the French provinces. During my stay, I was struck by how he would change his outfit several times a day. In the morning, Éric would be in the kitchen wearing a Rotterdam gabber outfit; two hours later, I'd spot him dressed in a black suit, white shirt, and white gloves, digging weeds up in the garden. In the evening, he might turn up in a Western outfit to prepare dinner. I observed him like this for two weeks: new looks every day. There seemed to be a unique need behind his choices. I was very fascinated, since there was no change of scenery that could have somehow motivated his wardrobe changes. He must have had his very own logic. Working on this editorial—shot by Nadine Fraczkowski—shed light on his logic. Éric presented his wardrobe with ideas for every single piece in his closet. "This shirt can only be worn with these pants; these shoes and this hat are for this occasion... And this outfit is for cutting the lawn, this one for grocery-shopping, and this one for making coffee ..." He also constructs outfits to correspond to objects, for instance, he created a special look befitting his white e-bike.

THIS SHIRT CAN ONLY BE WORN WITH THESE PANTS; THESE SHOES AND THIS HAT ARE FOR THIS OCCASION ... AND THIS OUTFIT IS FOR CUTTING THE LAWN, THIS ONE FOR GROCERY-SHOPPING, AND THIS ONE FOR MAKING COFFEE ...

Éric approaches fashion as an independent form of self-expression. At its best, fashion gives voice to one's whims, idiosyncrasies, and strivings. The everyday work of styling often opposes creative self-expression, producing images primarily aimed at positioning a label or a stylist within a commercially determined hierarchy. My role as an artist, as opposed to a stylist, has afforded me a unique freedom here.

On the following pages, you can see some of Éric's everyday outfits, all styled and chosen by him.

Nina Hollensteiner works as a fashion stylist, creative director, and artist at the intersection of art, fashion, performance, and installation. She studied Fine Art Practice at University of Fine Arts in Hamburg and at Goldsmiths University of London.

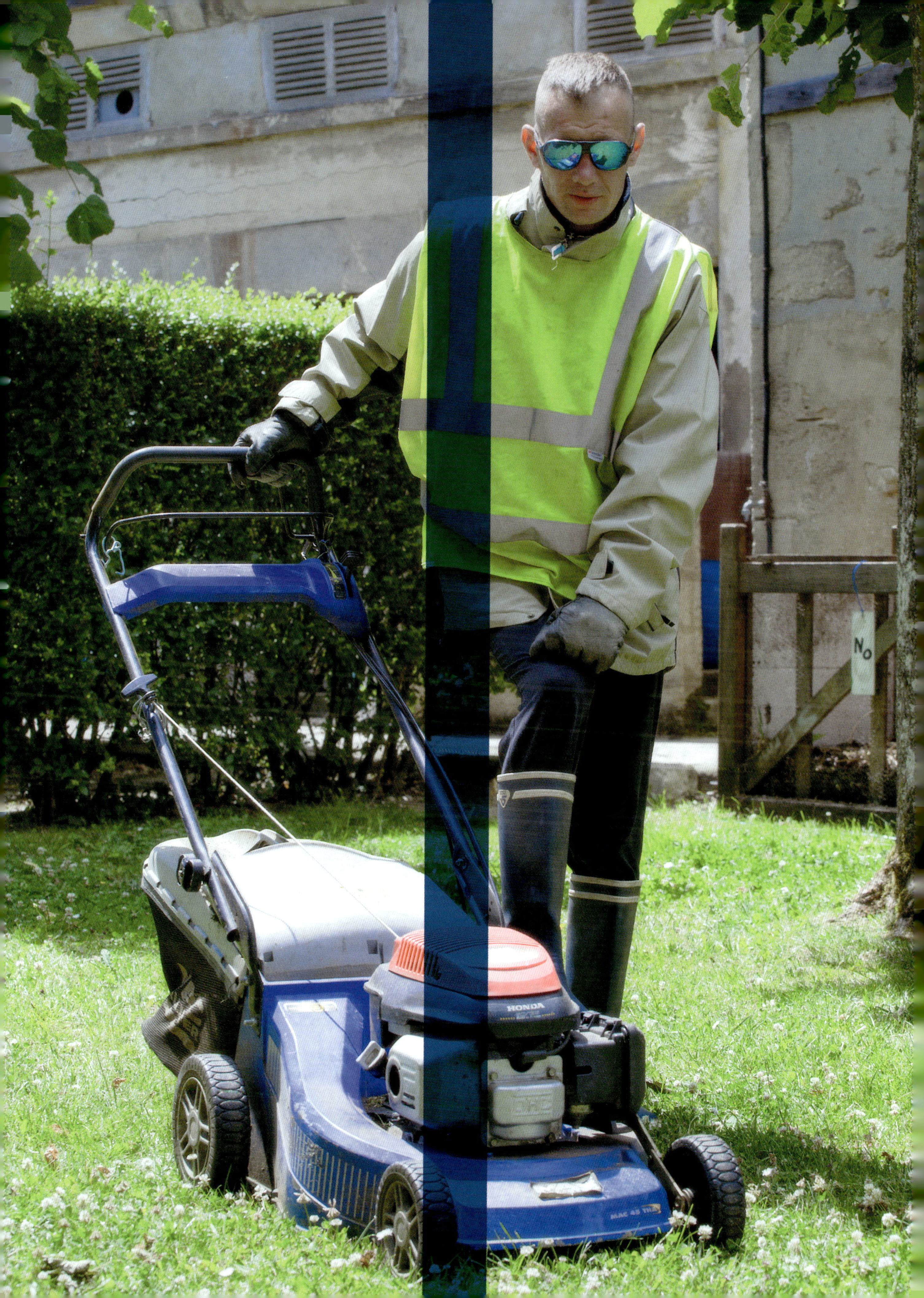
No
HONDA

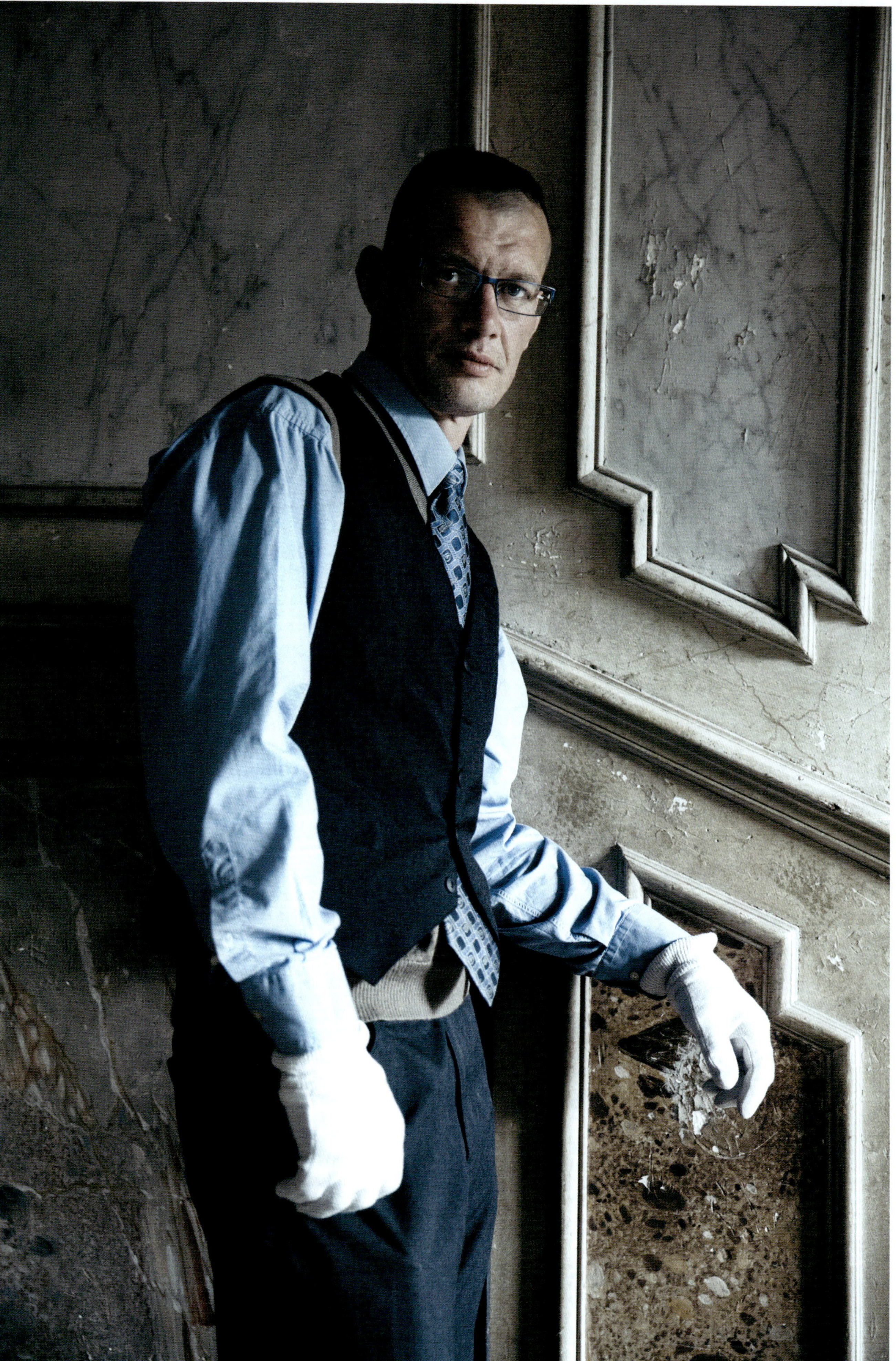

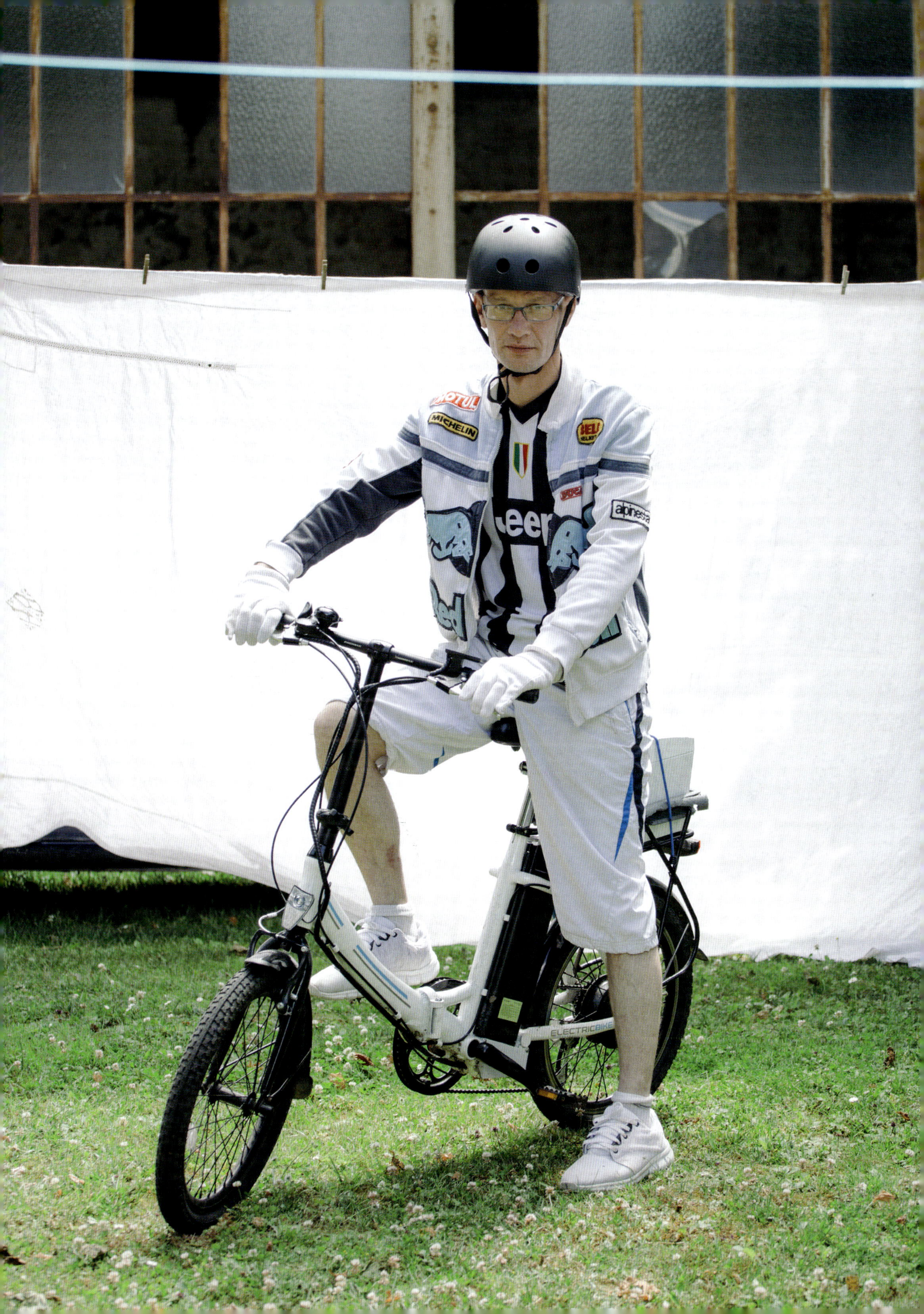
MICHELIN
ELECTRICBIKE

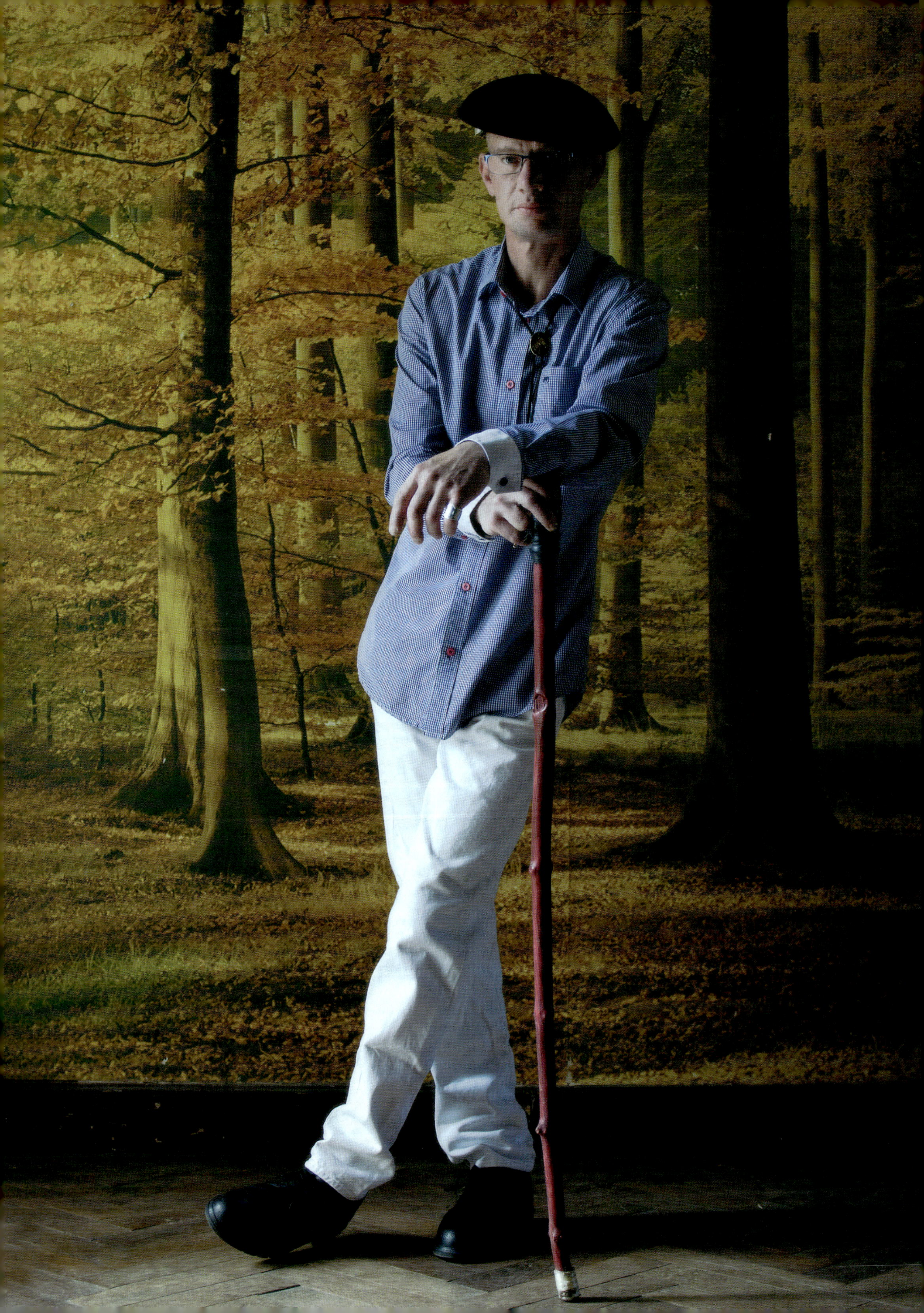

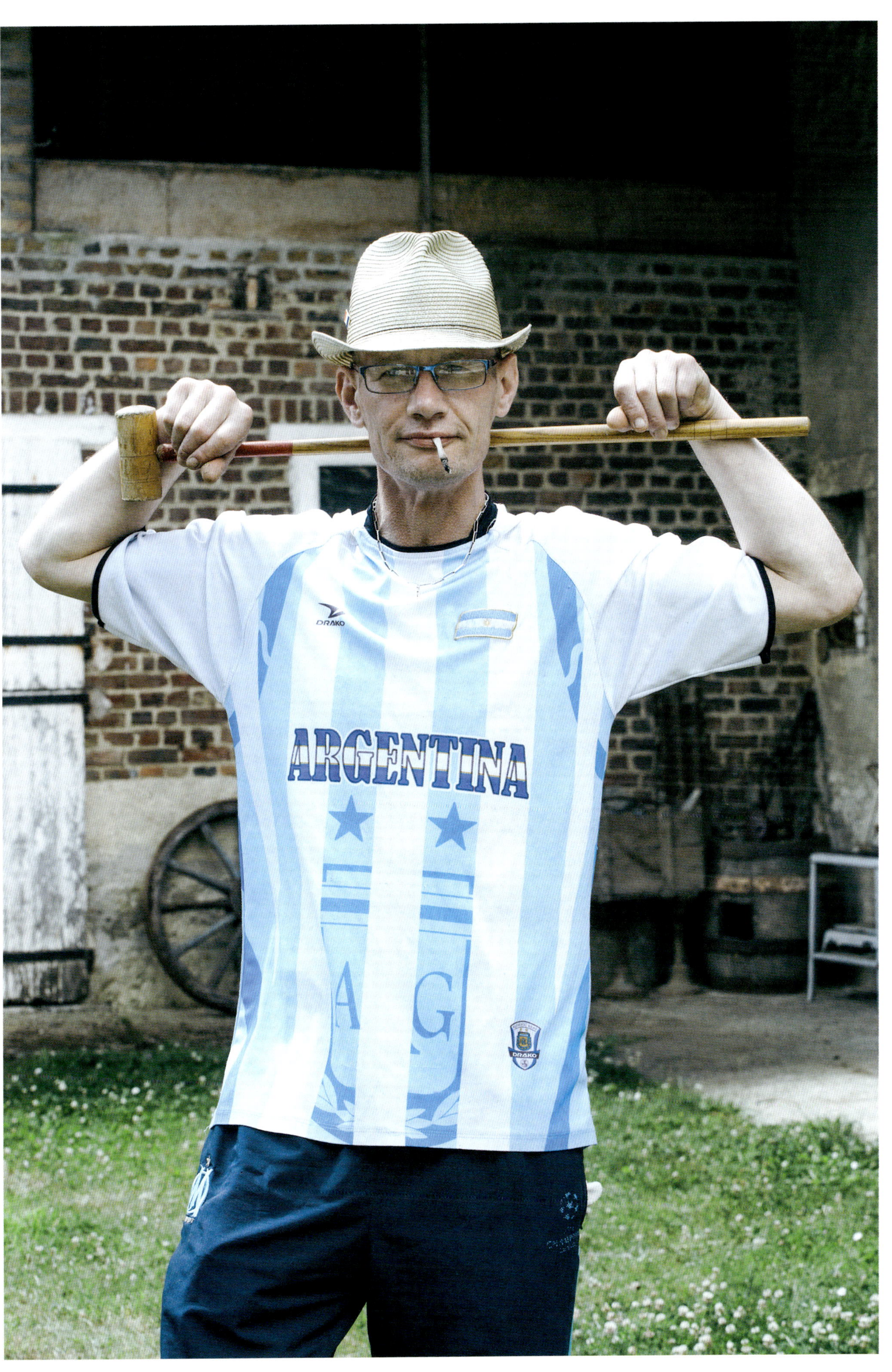
DRAKO
ARGENTINA
A G
DRAKO

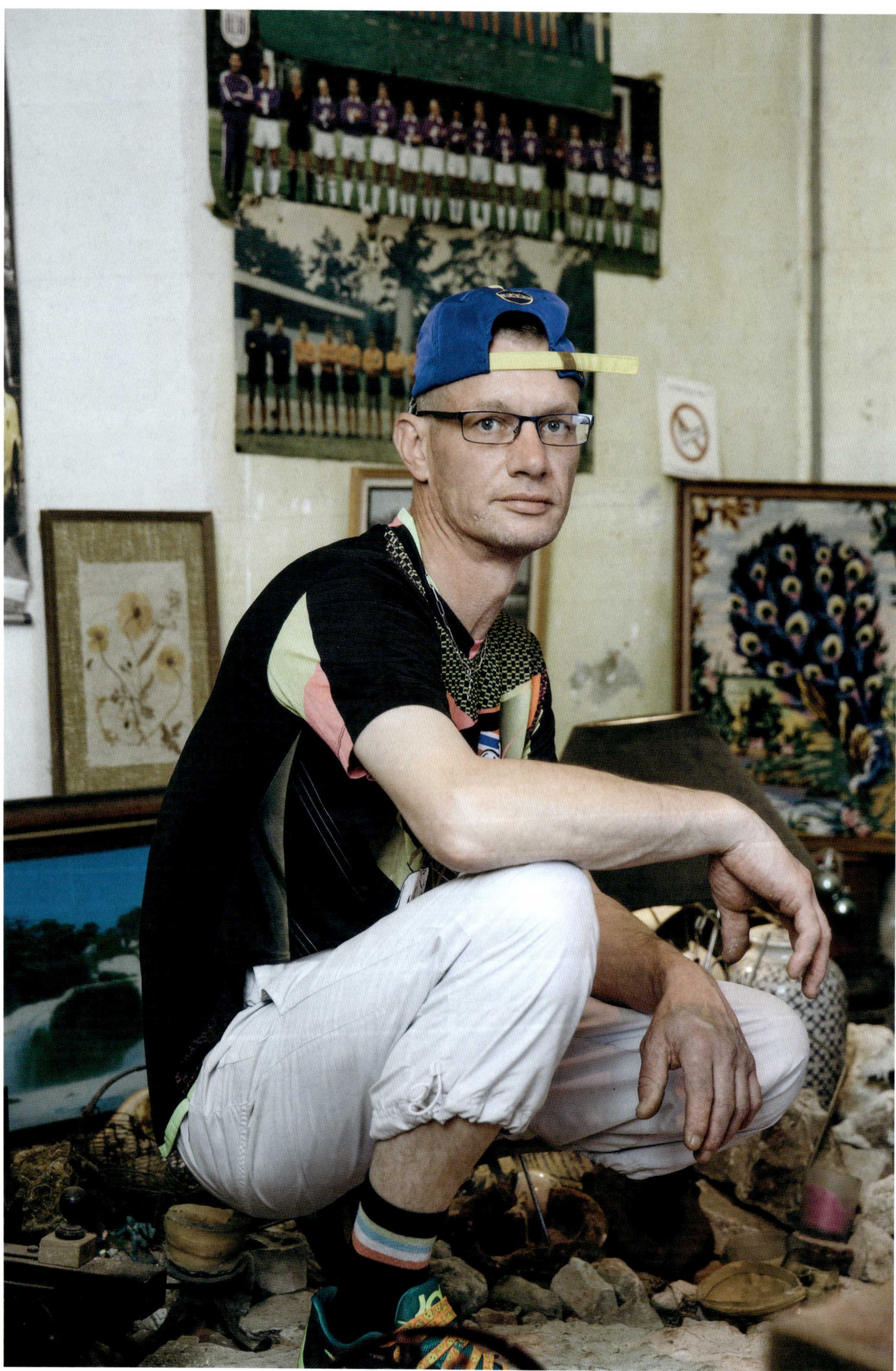

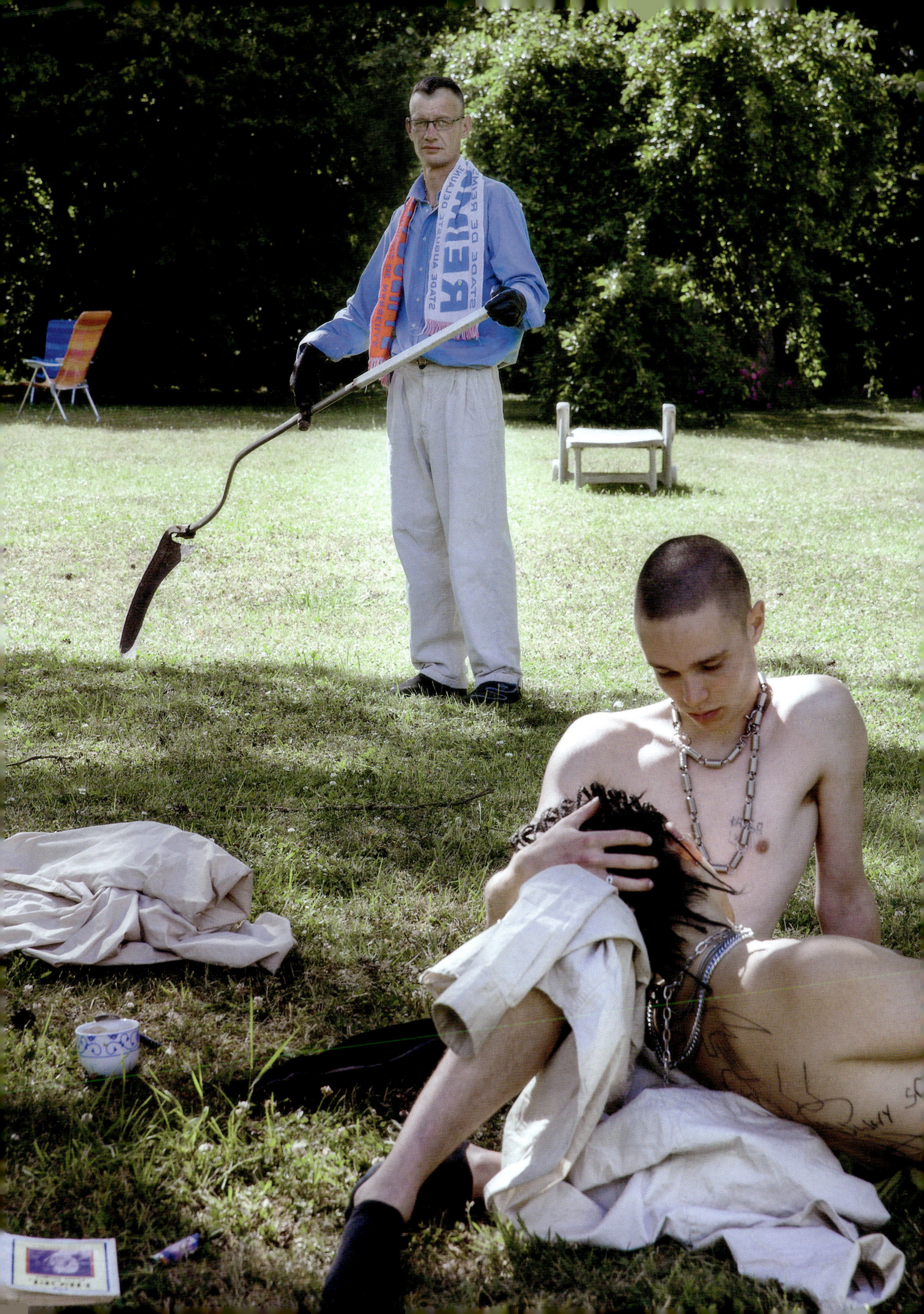

POSING AND WAITING: ON VANESSA BEECROFT

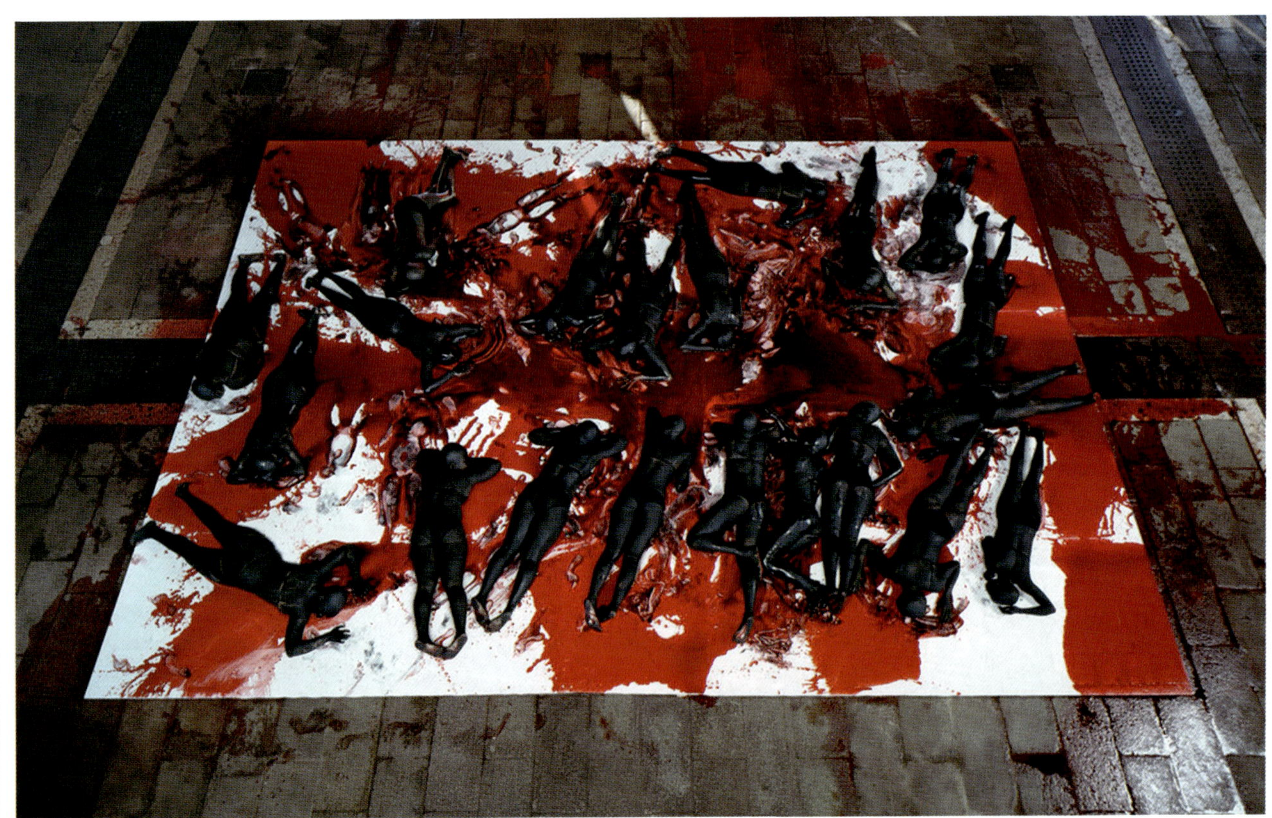

VB61.399.NT, 2007
Courtesy of the artist and Galleria Lia Rumma, Milan / Naples

Text Raphael Gygax

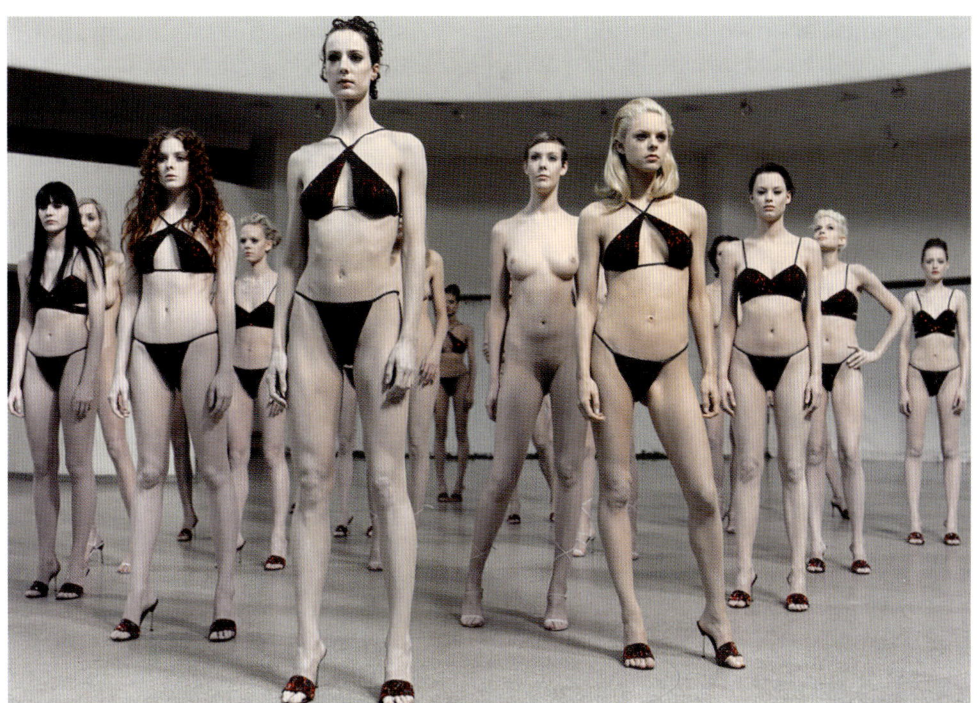

VB35: SHOW, 1998
Courtesy of the artist and Galleria Lia Rumma, Milan / Naples

Venice, 2007: Thirty dark-skinned women lie motionless on a white platform measuring roughly 270 square feet. The scene recalls pictures of massacres of the sort that appear on the news channels with some frequency. An atmospheric acoustic environment composed of the sounds of bells frames the overt allusion to some kind of humanitarian disaster. A light-skinned woman enters carrying a bucket. She cautiously steps around the prone bodies and then starts dousing them with a blood-colored liquid. The platform's white surface gradually disappears beneath the mass of red paint. The audience assembled on all sides observes the ritualistic proceedings, as do numerous representatives of the media; several cameras record the event.

The scene is a performance, by the artist Vanessa Beecroft, and its title is *VB61: Still Death! Darfur Still Death?* (2007). In the late 1990s, theatrical presentations of surfaces in actions that often involved numerous performers made Beecroft one of the best-known women artists of her generation.[1] Her performances usually consist of young women whom she instructs to stand as still as possible for hours in meticulously composed formations: frozen collective bodies that ultimately begin to crumble as the participants near the point of exhaustion. Many of the young women Beecroft recruits for her performances are professional fashion models, whom she has always referred to as her "girls" and the "material" for her work.[2] Playing a key part in her pieces, they are nonetheless effectively extras. Although the artist's work has been fairly widely discussed, the function it assigns to women, and to fashion models in particular, has drawn strikingly little critical scrutiny. The references in Beecroft's art to the world of fashion and its mechanisms would seem evident, but her employment of the model's body as a mute extra has not yet been subjected to systematic analysis.

If the "material" of Beecroft's work—the model—is drawn from the domain of fashion, so are central aspects of her practice and more specifically the way she prepares the performances, which she produces in collaboration with renowned fashion labels. The women are selected in time-consuming castings held with assistance from modeling agencies. In rare instances—as for *VB55* (2005) at the Neue Nationalgalerie, Berlin, her largest piece to date, with a hundred performers—Beecroft has also staged open casting calls.[3]

The artist's performances are consecutively numbered, a titling scheme she instituted when she started her career; some also have subtitles. The appearance of her initials in the titles combines this strictly linear cataloguing routine with a personal element.[4] The work of art is inscribed with her name, as it were, and so explicitly associated with her as an individual and personality. Like the products of the major fashion labels, Beecroft's performances are "branded." The media—especially the lifestyle and fashion press—have shown considerable interest in the correlation between life and work this practice suggests.[5] Her biographical background figured prominently in the discussion of her very first piece, *VB01* (1993), and to this day, most articles on her work make some reference to it. Thanks to Beecroft's deft self marketing, the "physicality" of her performances, and perhaps most importantly, her cooperation with Gucci, Louis Vuitton, and other luxury labels, the "Beecroft brand" is inseparably associated with "fashion," "beauty," and "glamour."[6] Like the Swiss artist Sylvie Fleury, Beecroft is a prominent representative of the coalition between contemporary art and the fashion and beauty industries, with cooperative ventures generating new works of art.[7] The presentation of these luxury brands produces lucrative synergies. The fashion industry occasionally hires the artists to create commissioned works that add luster to its brands. Still, I think it would be simplistic to conclude that Beecroft's interest in using models in her work does not extend beyond the glamour effect that comes with association with the world of fashion. As I will argue in the following, by transplanting the icons of the media and popular culture of the 1990s into the art system, she articulates a critique of the dogmas of the fashion and luxury industries as well as the art system as such, which increasingly mirrors these values. *VB35: Show* (1998), probably one of Beecroft's best-known works, is a perfect example in which to scrutinize the role of the 'girls' in this perspective.

HER EVENTS ARE REGARDED AS OBLIGATORY OCCASIONS FOR NEW YORK'S UPPER CRUST AND USUALLY ATTRACT CONSIDERABLE MEDIA INTEREST.

In many ways, *VB35: Show* presents the signature elements of Beecroft's oeuvre in condensed form, allowing for a nuanced critical reading of her artistic strategy. The performance was staged at the Guggenheim Museum, New York, on April 28, 1998; attendance was by invitation only. For the duration of the two-and-a-half-hour event, twenty models stood in characteristically Beecroftian formation, some in bikinis, some naked save for their high heels, their gazes rigid in the face of the audience. As the art critic Roberta Smith put it:

> "It was a circuit-jamming combination of fashion, theater and art; a two-and-a-half-hour spectacle of languorous immobility and reciprocal staring, appropriately titled 'Show.'"[8]

Given the venue's prominent place in the history of architecture and its social and cultural significance, the use of Gucci apparel, and the nudity of several models, the performance stands as a key work in Beecroft's oeuvre to date. *VB35: Show* was mounted by the curator and patron Yvonne Force Villareal, whose nonprofit organization Art Production Fund has underwritten the realization of lavish performance and installation art projects since the 1990s.[9] Her events are regarded as obligatory occasions for New York's upper crust and usually attract considerable media interest.[10] Looking back on the performance in an interview for a catalogue of her work in 2003, Beecroft describes the piece as follows:

> "This work, commissioned by an independent curator, Yvonne Force Inc., was originally conceived as a collaboration with a fashion designer. Unable to think of a wardrobe however, I came up with a nude piece specifically for the Guggenheim building. The nudity I wanted to show was an urban nudity, not naturalistic or anthropological. It was another type of outfit, a statement, a uniform. I wanted to use high heels, like pedestals, to stick the girls to the ground and make them assume non-natural poses. At the end I had to submit to the independent curator's plan and I was allowed five naked women [...] The fact that some women were naked and some were not created a hierarchy and sense of injustice. As we stare at the girls, their appearance makes us feel out of place, improper, inadequate. We face our desire and our fear at the same time—a girl is unknown, hidden inside an opaque world, unapproachable, separated from us, foreign, lonely."[11]

In retrospect, the artist characterizes the performance as a commissioned piece in which her creative freedom was constrained. As she recalls, she originally wanted all models to be naked save for the high heels. Instead, fifteen models in red rhinestone-studded bikinis and matching shoes by Gucci surrounded five nudes.[12] Under its creative director Tom Ford, Gucci was then a zealously coveted luxury brand.[13] The same bikini also featured in the advertising campaign for Gucci's spring/summer 1998 collection.[14] I have been unable to ascertain whether the fashion company supplied the apparel for the event for free, but the circumstances suggest as much—comping material for this sort of event was and is standard practice in the fashion industry.[15] The label is listed in the performance credits.[16] This kind of honorable mention, which allows the company to infiltrate its name into the art system, exemplifies a marketing strategy called "uptrading" based on the notion of a hierarchy of the arts in which fashion ranks below visual art. Beecroft's chumminess with the fashion industry has prompted controversial debates in the critical literature.[17] Remarkably, the possibility that her exploitation of her "girls" is a deliberate artistic strategy and conceptual aspect of her art has never been explored at length.

REMARKABLY, THE POSSIBILITY THAT HER EXPLOITATION OF HER 'GIRLS' IS A DELIBERATE ARTISTIC STRATEGY AND CONCEPTUAL ASPECT OF HER ART HAS NEVER BEEN EXPLORED AT LENGTH.

I believe it would be a mistake to portray Beecroft's close association with the fashion industry as a purely affirmative collusion with its system. The sometimes trenchant subtitles she chooses for her works, I argue, open up another dimension and support the hypothesis of a critical employment of the "other

VB82.018.NT, 2017/18
Courtesy of the artist and Galleria Lia Rumma, Milan / Naples

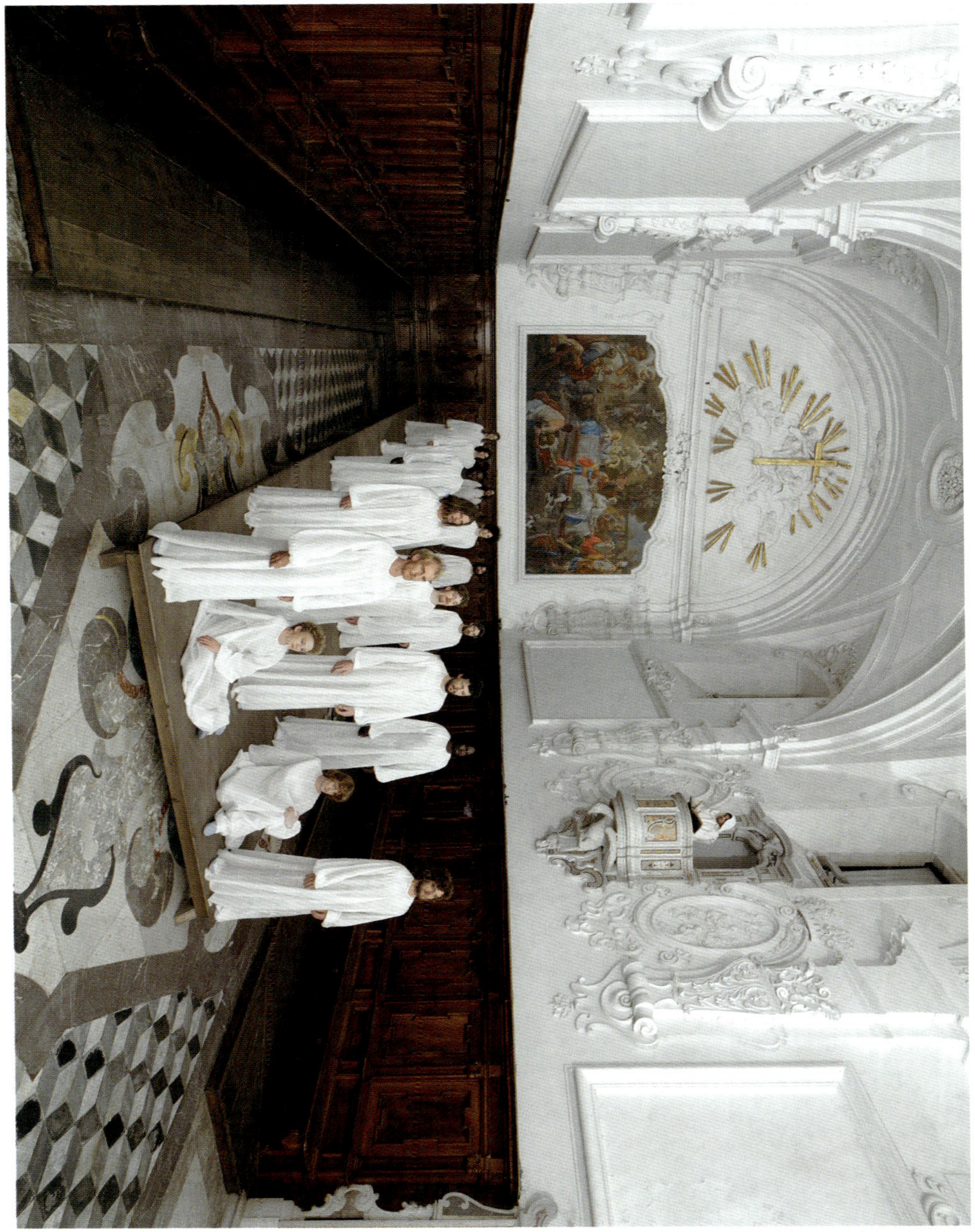

VBSS.002.MP, 2006
Courtesy of the artist and Galleria Lia Rumma, Milan / Naples

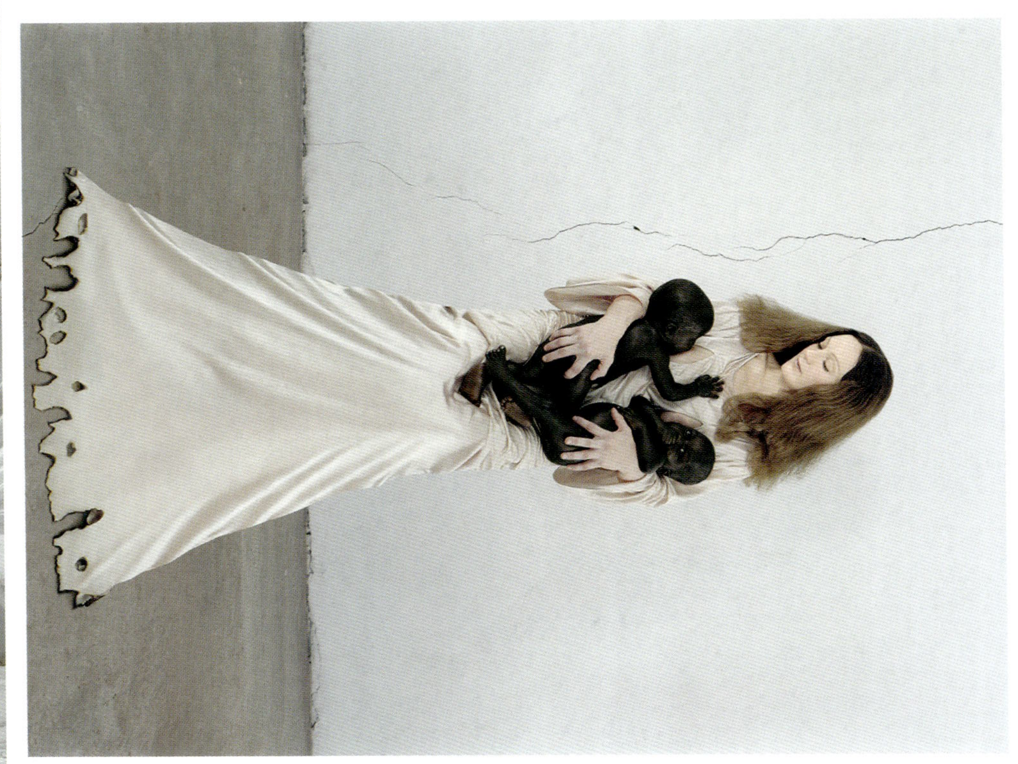

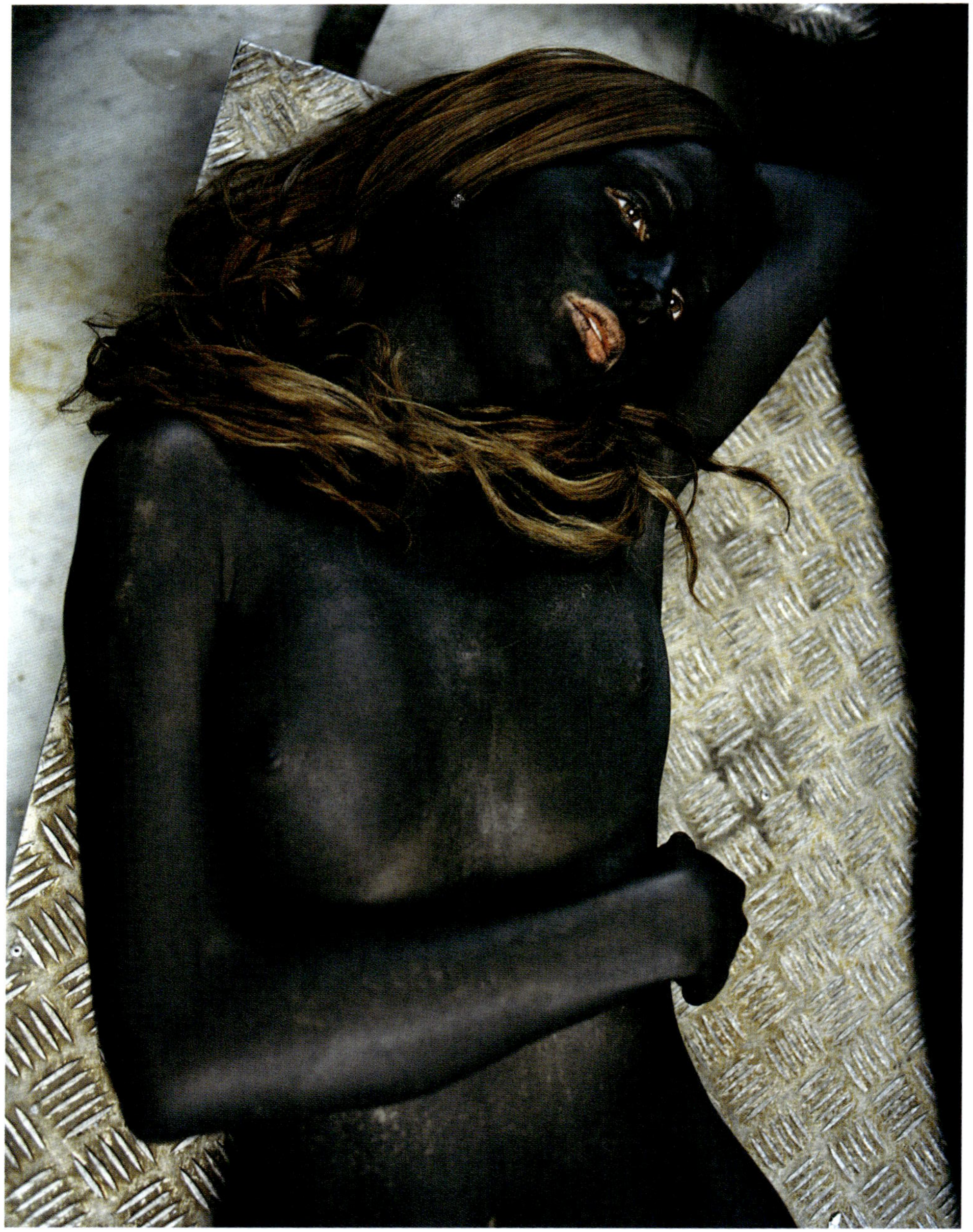

VB66.140.VB, 2010/11
Courtesy of the artist and Galleria Lia Rumma, Milan / Naples

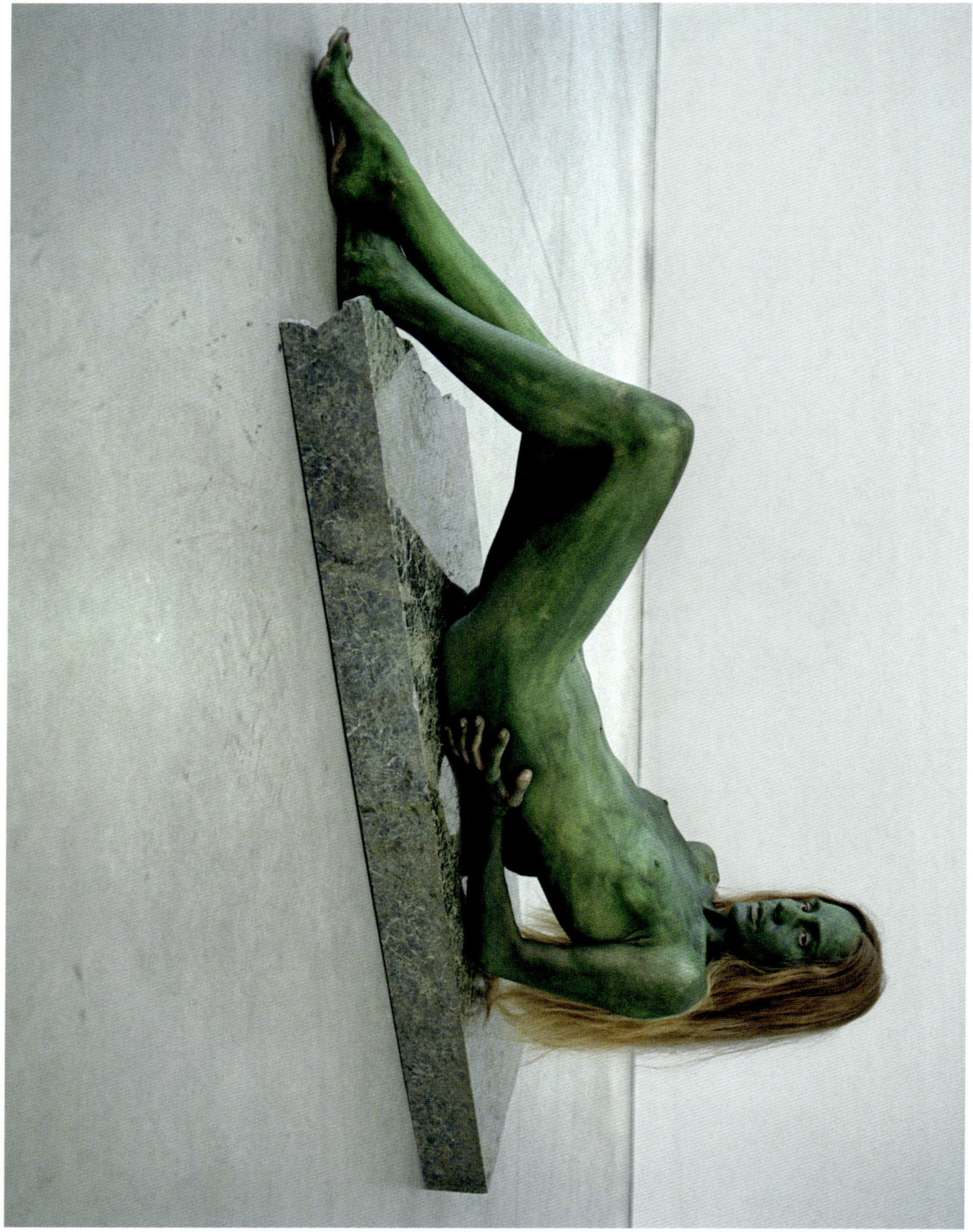

VB70.105.05.VB, 2010/11
Courtesy of the artist and Galleria Lia Rumma, Milan / Naples

body." The subtitle of *VB35: Show* highlights the act of presenting, exhibiting—exposing—the models. Such exposure is heightened when the women are scantily clad, as in many of Beecroft's pieces, or altogether naked. Then there are the extraordinarily strict instructions she gives the performers on how to act, or more properly, not to act, through which she controls the situation down to the smallest detail. Before any one of her performances, the artist presents her "girls" with a catalogue of rules they are to comply with to the best of their ability during the piece:

> "Do not talk, do not interact with the others, do not whisper, do not laugh, do not move too theatrically, do not move too quickly, do not move too slowly, be simple, be natural, be detached, be classic, be unapproachable, be tall, be strong, do not be sexy, do not be rigid, do not be casual, assume the state of mind you prefer (calm, strong, neutral, indifferent, proud, polite, superior), behave as if you were dressed, behave as if no one were in the room, you are like an image, do not establish contact with the outside, maintain your position as much as you can, remember the position that you have been assigned, do not sit down all the time, do not make the same movements at the same time, alternate resting and attentive positions, if you are tired, sit, if you have to leave, do so in silence, hold out until the end of the performance, interpret the rules naturally, do not break the rules, you are the essential element of the composition, your actions reflect on the group, towards the end you can lie down, just before the end stand straight up."[18]

Beecroft's briefings are designed to establish a focused situation of a kind that art critics have variously characterized as "vacuous," "chilly," or "eerily rigid."[19] Yet the artist's 'girls' are not the only ones on whom she dictatorially imposes rules of behavior; the same can be said of the audience. Before the performance *VB55*, for instance, the spectators were given a handout that prohibited speaking loudly or touching the models and noted that they might appear in the photographic documentation of the event.[20] This strict protocol lets Beecroft install the necessary frame of reference in which to initiate an intra-theatrical communication between spectator, artist, and model. The rules she sets down for her "girls"—which are in some ways self-contradictory—effectively require non-acting as defined by Kirby. More specifically, Beecroft's conception of the role her "girls" play matches the third stage of the continuum, what Michael Kirby labels "received acting."[21]

The artist compiles comprehensive descriptions of her works including detailed fact sheets with the names of everyone involved, down to the camera operator and the casting assistant.[22] Only the models remain uncredited, presumably a deliberate decision on the artist's part meant to underscore their status as anonymous extras. The point is for them to muster and take up position as a nameless "collective body." The aspect of "emergence"—although what emerges is not altogether unexpected—manifests itself in the models' incipient exhaustion, the moment when they start sitting down, breaking up the original composition.

THE ARTIST COMPILES COMPREHENSIVE DESCRIPTIONS OF HER WORKS INCLUDING DETAILED FACT SHEETS WITH THE NAMES OF EVERYONE INVOLVED, DOWN TO THE CAMERA OPERATOR AND THE CASTING ASSISTANT.

Being a model in a Beecroft performance is not just psychologically demanding but also physically arduous. In many pieces, the women must stand stock-still on high heels for hours. Susann Schweizer, one of the models in *VB43*, later recalled how taxing she found her role in the piece:

> "It was exhausting. There were two different kinds of high-heeled shoes. I had the bad luck of being given the higher ones. And since I'd spent the entire day before standing in those shoes, wearing them the afternoon of the performance over time became very painful."[23]

In subjecting her models to a test of stamina, Beecroft also reenacts a part of their everyday professional experience: posing and waiting. She uses them the way the fashion industry does—they are dolls without individuality, blank screens on which to project ideals and fantasies. And she draws on a very specific system—the world of the "rich and beautiful"—transplanting its stereotypical values and norms, in which looks and luxury occupy a central place, into the art setting. In the above mentioned review of the Guggenheim performance, Roberta Smith pointed out the affinity between the two systems:

> "The women stared into space, aloof and indifferent. Occasionally they stretched, crouched or walked slowly around. The invited audience of about 500, also standing, did much the same, and was often just as stylishly, if more thoroughly, attired."[24]

This overlap supports the hypothesis that Beecroft's work articulates a critique of the art system. The "other body"—in this instance, the body of the fashion model as a representation of status and success, a mass-cultural object of longing—is turned to account for the message the artist's work conveys: she avails herself of the fashion world's icons while "catering to" its aficionados. Beecroft avails herself of the mechanisms of luxury fashion and makes them a mirror she holds up to the art world.

In Beecroft's later performances, the extra body takes on a far more explicitly political cast. The above-mentioned performance *VB61: Still Death! Darfur Still Death?* makes reference to a country in crisis in its very title; the audience was likely to associate the name with civil wars and the ensuing humanitarian disasters.[25] Beecroft used thirty models to illustrate her chosen theme, the genocide in South Sudan, which she had previously addressed in another work. One photograph in the series *VB South Sudan* (2006) shows a woman with long reddish hair wearing pale makeup. She sits on a chair, her upper body erect, two naked dark-skinned infants in her arms. The setting is austere, with a whitewashed wall with visible cracks serving as backdrop. The woman is clad in a white silk dress; circular openings with singed edges reveal her breasts. As she nurses one of them, the other gazes into the camera. The woman's head is turned to one side, her eyes downcast. The posture of protective embrace establishes a visual symmetry that recalls the motif of the Madonna and Child.

WITH INEVITABLE SIMPLIFICATION, ONE MIGHT SAY THAT GUCCI EMBODIES THE "NEW SPIRIT OF CAPITALISM," WHEREAS MAISON MARTIN MARGIELA DRESSES THE ANONYMOUS ANTI-CAPITALIST REBEL.

The photographs were taken in South Sudan;[26] the performance was staged during the opening days of the 2007 Venice Biennale.[27] The New Zealand filmmaker Pietra Brettkelly, who shadowed Beecroft during this period, turned the footage into the documentary film *The Art Star and the Sudanese Twins* (2008), which was released the following year.[28] Beecroft had met the director during her first trip to Sudan; shocked by a harrowing report in the press about the situation there, she had decided to see for herself. The experience politicized her, prompting her to create the two works. She also sought to adopt the twins. The film offers an extensive portrayal of her work on her art and especially the genesis of the Sudan cycle as well as her efforts to adopt.[29]

The only element in the ensemble *VB South Sudan* reminiscent of the complicity of art and fashion that formerly characterized Beecroft's work is the deconstructivist silk dress, a creation of the Belgian fashion house Maison Martin Margiela.[30] The fashion world remains part of the referential system, but it is now negotiated by way of the label itself rather than the body of the model: the artist communicates her political concern—her attempt to draw attention to the distressing humanitarian conditions in South Sudan by means of her art—through the prism of Margiela's brand philosophy. In the 1990s, Beecroft's preferred partner for her performances was Gucci, a brand whose image connoted unapologetic hedonism, but since the turn of the millennium, she has been more interested in Martin Margiela, whose deconstructivist approach suggests a critical perspective on the world attuned to the politically woke spirit of the time.[31] With inevitable simplification, one might say that Gucci embodies the "new spirit of capitalism," whereas Maison Martin Margiela dresses the anonymous anti-capitalist rebel.[32]

Yet Beecroft does not simply exploit the public images of the fashion labels for her purposes; in the Sudan series, she also puts her own body on the line. Its appearance in the photographs has remained an exception in her work. Brettkelly's documentary film insinuates that it is the project's political urgency and the artist's personal investment in the issue that, in this instance, compelled her to put her body on the stage. In formal terms, *VB61: Still Death! Darfur Still Death?* stands out among Beecroft's performances for the manifest reference to Yves Klein (*Anthropométries*, 1960), whose work has clearly been long a key source of inspiration for her. In the art-critical literature, Beecroft's art has been read either as reviving the *tableau vivant* or "living sculpture" genres or as a kind of portraiture—the latter interpretation has been proffered in particular for her work in photography.[33] In this reading, her work is formally aligned with the long tradition in art history of mise-en-scène and posing. In painting and sculpture, but also in early photography, having the model hold a pose for extended periods of time was not so much an artistic choice as a technical necessity. In its inquiry into the modalities of the (group) portrait with its constructed poses, attitudes, gestures, and backdrops, Beecroft's art may also be compared to the work of the artist duo Clegg & Guttmann (Michael Clegg and Martin Guttmann.)[34] Individual, double, and group portraits form a central strand in Clegg & Guttmann's oeuvre, extending an art-historical and iconographic lineage that goes back to Titian, Caravaggio, Frans Hals, and Rembrandt. In Beecroft's work, too, the aesthetic conventions underpinning individual and group portraiture in the sixteenth and seventeenth centuries serve as a point of departure and reference.[35] Yet Clegg & Guttmann's highly artificial and minutely staged portraits are more explicit in harnessing that historic form of representation to scrutinize social structures and hierarchies of power. They often feature named individuals who disclose their cultural background and economic and social standing. For the monumental photograph *The Art Consultants* (1986/2015), for instance, they lined up a number of curators before a mirror-inverted copy of Hugo Vogel's painting *Entrance of the Senate into the New City Hall on October 26, 1897* (1904).[36] The sitters were selected for their work: they all advise corporate art collections—among them are the buyers for AT&T's and Citibank's collections.[37] Clegg & Guttmann's "family portrait," that is to say, unites people who, by virtue of the financial prowess they represent, wield considerable clout in the evolving art field, and embeds them in a historically informed reflection on the politics of representation.[38] In interviews, Clegg & Guttmann have repeatedly said that their works are also intended as a critique of this representational culture.

Beecroft's art, by comparison, is decidedly more ambiguous, a quality reinforced by her insistence in interviews that her work is a meditation on compositional traditions in the history of art, more specifically of painting.[39] Such equivocation is apt to obscure the political potential of *VB: Still Death! Darfur Still Death?*.

The different modes and formats of the interrelated works that result from any one of Beecroft's projects have sometimes given rise to critical misunderstandings. As with *VB South Sudan*, one title generally stands for a performance and its documentation as well as photographs and footage that do not show the performance itself. The latter materials are usually created the day before the event and offered for sale as standalone works. For these pictures—which art magazines often print as accurately representative of the performances—the artist positions the models in a variety of formations and then takes detail, portrait, and composition shots that suggest her keen awareness of the precepts of photography and visual art; they would be impossible to take as such during the performance proper. A project thus spawns two different visual records that Philip Auslander has labeled "documentary" and "theatrical": one is generated during the realization of the performance, whereas the other renders an enactment of the performance situation intended solely for the camera.[40] Auslander has also used the term "performed photography" for the latter, tracing its ancestry to Marcel Duchamp's photographic self-portraits in the role of the fictional Rrose Sélavy from the early 1920s and Yves Klein's leap into the void (1960).[41]

IN THE "THEATRICAL PHOTOGRAPHS," INDIVIDUAL MODELS STAND OUT; IN BEECROFT'S PERFORMANCES, BY CONTRAST, THEY BECOME PART OF A 'COLLECTIVE BODY.'

In the "theatrical photographs," individual models stand out; in Beecroft's performances, by contrast, they become part of a 'collective body.'[42] To avoid legal disputes, she has the models sign a waiver with which they relinquish any rights in the photographs and films as well as the performance and its documentation. The models usually receive compensation in the form of a monetary fee and, in most instances, a special limited-edition photographic print Beecroft calls the models' edition.[43]

By the end of the new century's first decade, the Beecroft system seemed to have run out of steam. The artist increasingly retreated from the limelight and focused on her new preoccupation with classical sculpture. In 2010, she presented a series of marble sculptures; although these works still grapple with questions of the female body's beauty and fragility, they also cater to a conservative idea of sculptural art. Since her exhibition at Galleria Lia Rumma in 2011, Beecroft's use of live performers has been limited to the occasional model placed amid an ensemble of marble sculptures. Positioned next to a statue and wearing makeup in tones matching the marble, the model effectively becomes the sculpture's double.[44] The same principle underlay the artist's presentation at the 2015 Venice Biennale, where she packed a room with life-size marble sculptures. It would seem, then, that her more recent work has little bearing on an art discourse around the phenomenon of the "other body." Read in light of her performances from the 1990s and their skeptical scrutiny of the fashion and luxury industries' capitalist and exploitative system, however, such virtual identification of living models with marble sculptures may be seen as a more trenchant version of her critique of the powers that control the female body.

1 She is regularly mentioned in overviews of the contemporary arts scene and especially in discussions of "performance" or "feminism" and art. See, for instance, *Art at the Turn of the Millennium*, ed. Burkhard Riemschneider and Uta Grosenick (Cologne: Taschen, 1999) or *Art and Feminism*, ed. Peggy Phelan and Helena Reckitt (London: Phaidon, 2001).

2 See Massimiliano Gioni and Helena Kontova, "Vanessa Beecroft," *Flash Art International*, no. 228 (2003): 109sqq.

3 This performance was documented in a film by Marina Zenovich. See Marina Zenovich, dir., *Vanessa Beecroft in Berlin* (USA, 2006).

4 In some exceptional cases, performances have remained unnumbered. On the artist's homepage, they are listed as "special projects." Most of them are collaborations with fashion labels.

5 For example, in 1998 alone, the fashion and lifestyle magazines *Harper's Bazaar, Vogue Italia, The Face, Interview Magazine, I-D Magazine*, and *Purple Magazine* ran features on Beecroft. See the artist's homepage at www.vanessabeecroft.com (accessed November 30, 2017).

6 See, e.g., *VB: Alphabet Concept* (2005), an advertising campaign Beecroft developed for the fashion house Louis Vuitton. The artist posed several of her models so that their bodies formed the initials LV, the label's logo. This project is exemplary of Beecroft's mutually beneficial cooperation with several fashion labels.

7 *It's Clinique Bonus Time* (1991), likely Fleury's best-known series, consists of assemblages of branded shopping bags stuffed with the products of various luxury fashion and cosmetics labels, which she places in the exhibition space without any alteration. See *Sylvie Fleury*, ed. Éric Troncy (Dijon: Les presses du réel, 2001).

8 Roberta Smith, "Critic's Notebook: Standing and Staring, Yet Aiming for Empowerment," *The New York Times*, May 6, 1998, www.nytimes.com/1998/05/06/arts/critic-s-notebook-standing-and-staring-yet-aiming-for-empowerment.html (accessed November 30, 2017).

9 Formerly Yvonne Force, Inc.; the organization was renamed in 2000.

10 Note Force Villareal's frequent appearances in *Artforum*'s "diary" section, which largely consists of portrait sketches of the VIPs attending the opening receptions of biennials, art fairs, and major exhibitions. See www.artforum.com/diary (accessed November 30, 2017).

11 Vanessa Beecroft, "Conversation Piece—Interview with Vanessa Beecroft," by Marcella Beccaria, in *Vanessa Beecroft: Performances 1993–2003*, exh. cat., Castello di Rivoli Museo d'Arte Contemporanea, ed. Marcella Beccaria (Milan: Skira, 2003), 213.

12 The bikini was a centerpiece of the spring/summer 1998 collection and the first outfit to appear on the runway in the fashion show. See /www.youtube.com/watch?v=_PhwDmoJ3wY&has_ verified=1 (accessed November 30, 2017).

13 For the history of Gucci and its comeback under Tom Ford in the 1990s, see Sarah Mower, *Gucci by Gucci* (Munich: Rolf Heyne Collection, 2006).

14 The spring/summer 1998 campaign was photographed by Luis Sanchis.

15 To the best of my knowledge, this aspect has never been addressed in the critical literature.

16 Beecroft, "Conversation Piece," 213.

17 See, for instance, the piece for which a journalist asked selected curators and critics to rate Beecroft's work: Beate Depping, "Kontroverse: Vanessa Beecroft," *Kunstzeitung* (August 2008): 14–15.

18 This extensive catalogue of rules appears in Beecroft's interview with Marcella Beccaria; see "Conversation Piece," 218. Cf. Helena Kontova, "Modern Nomads: Vanessa Beecroft, Shirin Neshat, Marina Abramović," *Flash Art*, no. 225 (July–August 2007): 107.

19 Riemschneider and Grosenick, eds., *Art at the Turn of the Millennium*, 42.

20 See Zenovich, dir., *Vanessa Beecroft in Berlin*.

21 Michael Kirby, *A Formalist Theatre* (Philadelphia: University of Philadelphia Press, 1987).

22 See, e.g., the comprehensive catalogue published in conjunction with the exhibition at the Castello di Rivoli: *Vanessa Beecroft: Performances 1993–2003*, ed. by Beccarin in 2003.

23 The interview is published in Raphael Gygax, *Extra Bodies*. Über den Einsatz des 'anderen Körpers' in der zeitgenössischen Kunst (JRP|Ringier: Zurich, 2017), 97–100.

24 Smith, "Critic's Notebook: Standing and Staring."

25 See Paolo Bianchi, "Weiße Madonna: Das Projekt 'VB South Sudan' von Vanessa Beecroft," *Kunstforum International*, no. 195 (2009): 128–31.

26 Beecroft's productions always involve a sizable team including a photographer, stylists, and several assistants. In addition to the photograph described above, there are others that show the artist working with the extras. See Dirk van Versendaal, "Meine Werke beschämen mich: Interview mit Vanessa Beecroft," *Stern*, no. 42/2006, www.27stern.de/lifestyle/mode/573816.html (accessed November 30, 2017).

27 The performance, which ran for several hours, was held on the Pescheria di Rialto, the fish market near the Rialto Bridge, on June 8, 2007. The event was open to the public. An outline of the work may be found on the artist's website, where several works are also represented by short video clips; see http://www. vanessabeecroft.com (accessed November 30, 2017). More video footage is available on YouTube, including a clip from *VB 61: Still Death! Darfur Still Death?*; see www.youtube.com/ watch?v=Vom9-Nxa4vA&feature=related (accessed November 30, 2017).

28 Pietra Brettkelly, dir., *The Art Star and the Sudanese Twins*, USA, 2008. The film is available on DVD. For more information on the film and its making, see www.theartstarandthesudanesetwinsfilm.com (accessed November 30, 2017).

29 In the artist's telling, the entire ensemble of works started with a newspaper report on the enormous humanitarian crisis in Sudan. The reading left her so shattered that she resolved to travel to the country and learn more. During her first trip to Sudan in 2005, as she visited an orphanage, she was asked to breastfeed the newborn twins Madit and Mongor (her own son was an infant at the time); see Bianchi, "Weiße Madonna," 128. The encounter instilled the wish in her to adopt the two children. During the same trip, she met the New Zealand film director Pietra Brettkelly, who decided to make a documentary film about the adoption process and the various legal obstacles. Brettkelly was unaware at the time of the "Beecroft brand" and what it represented in the art world, and so did not recognize the close parallels with superstars such as the singer Madonna and the actress Angelina Jolie, who started a trend when they adopted children from African countries. Beecroft subsequently sought to prevent the release of the film and took legal action to block it.

30 See van Versendaal, "Meine Werke beschämen mich"; and Bianchi, "Weiße Madonna," 128.

31 Founded by Martin Margiela in 1989, Maison Martin Margiela is distinguished by its philosophy, which emphasizes the collectivity of the label's output and the anonymity of its chief designer. Margiela avoids being photographed. The apparel is set apart by the predominance of white and the designers' deconstructivist approach. Maison Martin Margiela rose to renown with garments made out of recycled clothes. See *Maison Martin Margiela: 20: The Exhibition*, ed. Bob Verhelst (Antwerp: MoMu Fashion Museum, 2008); and see www.maisonmartinmargiela.com (accessed November 30, 2017).

32 See Chris Dercon, "Das unbekannte Gesicht," *Das Magazin*, no. 39 (2008): 12–22.

33 This critical consensus is most evident in coffee-table surveys of contemporary art for popular audiences that put the focus on visual representation. See, for example, Raimar Stange, "Warten für die Schönheit: Vanessa Beecroft," in *Women Artists—34 Künstlerinnen im 20. und 21. Jahrhundert*, ed. Uta Grosenick (Cologne: Taschen, 2001), 48–53.

34 Michael Clegg and Martin Guttmann (both b. 1957) have been collaborators for more than thirty years. Their work is strongly informed by a conception of art as a "social-communicative process." See *Michael Clegg, Martin Guttmann: Monument for Historical Change and Other Social Sculptures, Community Portraits and Spontaneous Operas*, ed. Verein zur Förderung von Kunst und Kultur am Rosa-Luxemburg-Platz e.V. (Vienna: Schlebrügge Editor, 2005); also see *Clegg & Guttmann*, exh. cat., Württembergischer Kunstverein Stuttgart, ed. Tilman Osterwold (Milan: Giancarlo Politi Editore, 1988).

35 *Vanessa Beecroft: Performances 1993–2003*, ed. Marcella Beccaria, 19.

36 The painting was commissioned to commemorate the inauguration of the new Hamburg City Hall.

37 Included in the photograph are, back row, left to right: Judy Solomon (Metropolitan Life), Laura Miner-van Leeuwen (Citibank), Carla Caccamise Ash (Seagram), Pari Stave Choate (Equitable), Larry Levine (Chemical Bank); front row, left to right: Jack Boulton (Chase Manhattan), Natalie Jones (AT&T), Frances Chaves (Reader's Digest), Merrie Good (Chase Manhattan).

38 Clegg & Guttmann's pictorial politics is further complicated by the fact that they also create commissioned portraits for corporate clients. In the past, such projects have repeatedly entangled them in legal disputes. However, the artists control many aspects of the creative process by means of contractual stipulations. For instance, they reserve the right to reproduce works in monographs on their art and present them in exhibitions even when the client rejects them, and to sell such works to third parties. The art historian Wolfgang Ullrich has discussed the implications in the example of commissioned portraits of three Deutsche Bank managers that were rejected by the client. See Wolfgang Ullrich, "Takeovers und Deutungsmonopole? Wenn Unternehmen Kunst konsumieren," in *Kunst & Karriere: Ein Kaleidoskop des Kunstbetriebs*, ed. Oskar Bätschmann, *outlines*, vol. 9 (Zurich: SIK-ISEA, 2015), 155–66; see also Wolfgang Ullrich, *Siegerkunst: Neuer Adel, teure Lust* (Berlin: Wagenbach, 2016), 114–29.

39 See Thomas Kellein, "The Never-Ending Film: After Raphael," in *Vanessa Beecroft: Performances 1993–2003*, ed. Marcella Beccaria, 29–30; and see *Vanessa Beecroft Performances*, ed. Dave Hickey, 5–8.

40 Philip Auslander, "The Performativity of Performance Art," *Performing Arts Journal*, no. 84 (2006): 1.

41 Ibid., 2.

42 This observation is borne out by my own experience: in *VB61: Still Death! Darfur Still Death?* it was impossible to identify and recognize individual models; they blended into a *collective body*.

43 Prints from these special limited editions occasionally surface in the auction market; see, e.g., the records of Christie's and Sotheby's.

44 See http://www.liarumma.it/artists/vanessa-beecroft/ (accessed November 30, 2017).

VB84.044.NT, 2017/18
Courtesy of the artist and Galleria Lia Rumma, Milan / Naples

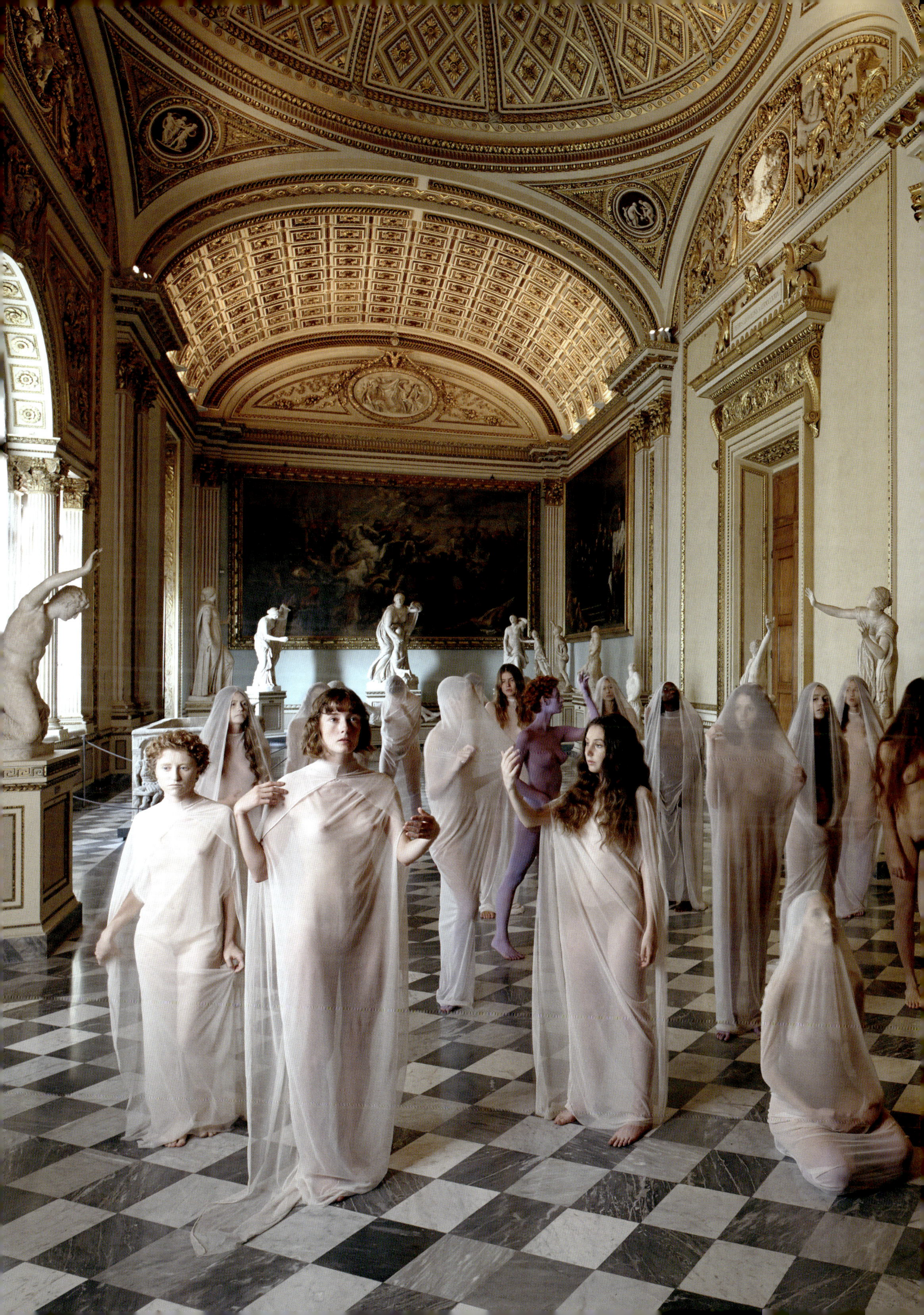

TRAYS OF SALMON MINI BAGELS

"It all starts with desires. Nothing unusual, they live paycheck to paycheck just like most honest hard-working civil servants. They drink on the sidewalks. This is what I thought before arriving at the bar."

Italian artist Emanuele Marcuccio on his experience as an assistant for various jobs during different fashion shoots in Milan.

Text / Images

Emanuele Marcuccio

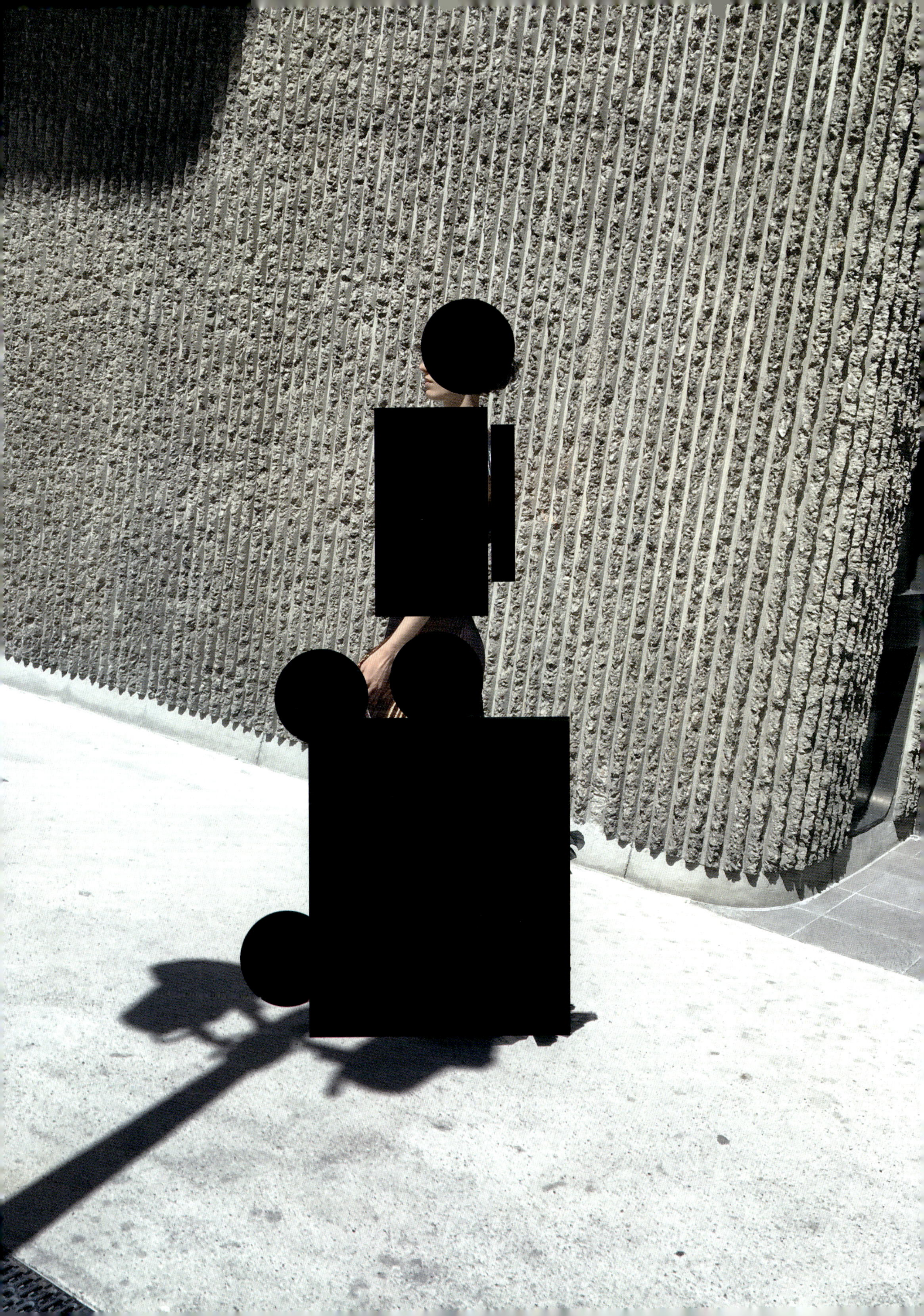

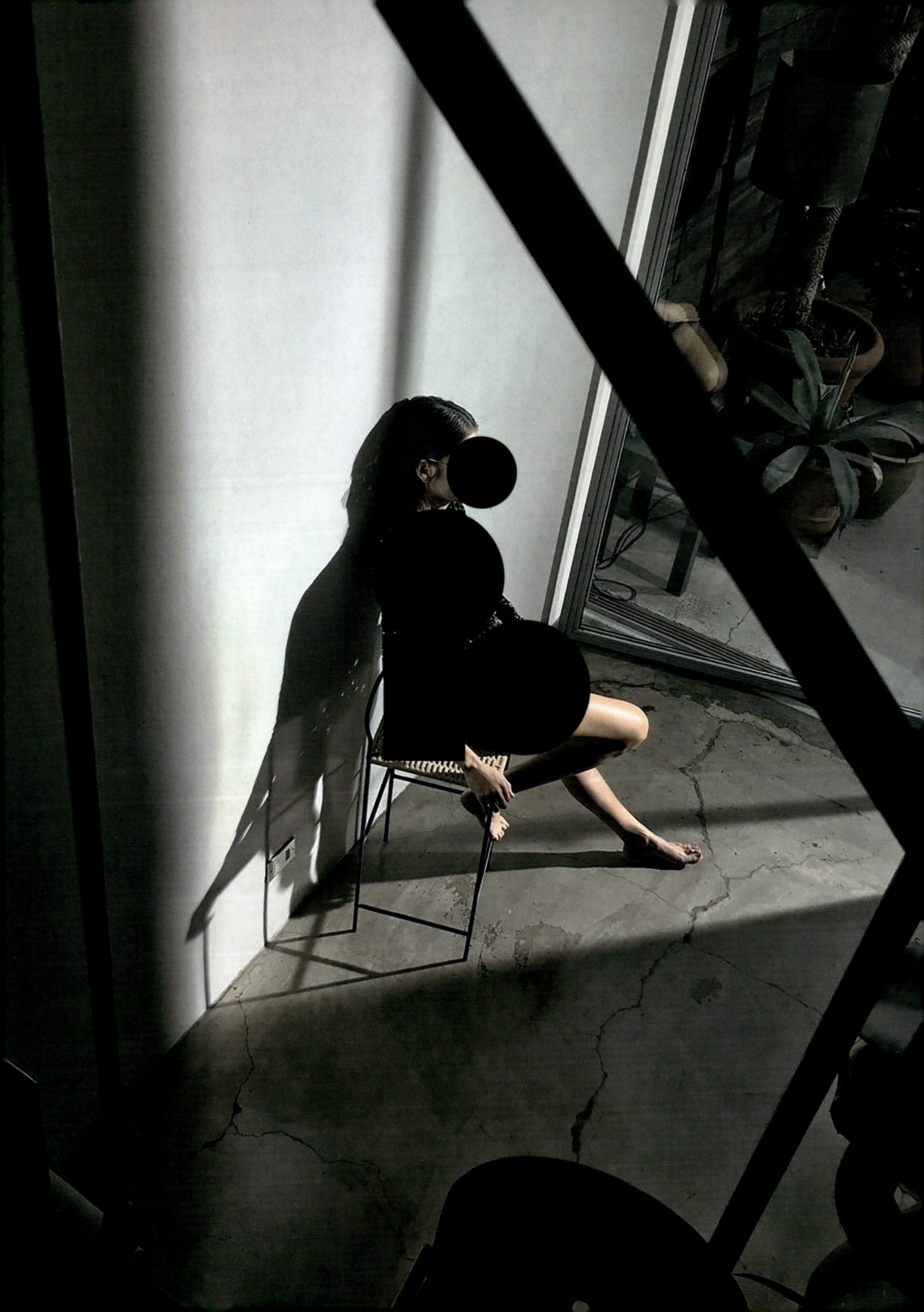

THE PHOTO ASSISTANT

At the bar, we're in a circle.

A couple of art directors, a fashion photographer fascinated with contemporary art, a stylist and few producers. (We all met in 2009, because of a party called Bruttoposse, a party in a regular bar where creative kids were introduced to alcohol.) We all discuss my money issues again. The photographer asks me to help him with a photo shoot for a famous fashion brand.

I order a beer.

"I need a second assistant. I need someone who can help my assistant to set up lights and cameras, no worries it's easy, 150 euros cash right after."

I say yes. He's a generous friend.

I wake up before my alarm clock at 7am. Positive that I would oversleep again, I realize my alarm won't go off for another fifteen minutes. Good.

I know the location, I've been there before for a private sale, I bought nothing I remember. It was just about being at the private sale.

There's a woman smoking cigarettes at the balcony waiting for us, I can hear her from the street arguing with someone inside. Her voice sounds deep like a trombone, evidence of many years of smoke. She's the client, I think. She throws the cigarette down and it falls on the ground, a meter away from me.

The first assistant is here, he's a well-born Milanese, the haircut doesn't lie. He's younger than me.

Ciao, how are you? Nice to meet you.

We start to set up the lights. He's extremely excited about the equipment. You can tell because he keeps repeating the full technical name of anything he touches.

The role of the second assistant today is about cables. I just need to follow the movements of the photographer and make sure that each cable draws straight lines on the ground. Everything must seem clean and safe.

THE PRODUCTION ASSISTANT

I receive a call from a friend, he wants to offer me a job. He's the creative director of a worldwide famous magazine for alternative kids. Over the past years the magazine has turned more and more into a creative agency. Video contents, events, and brand strategies. Profitable business.

We need an assistant producer/runner next week. 4 days. 1.000 euros.

I say yes.

Production means organization. The producer is essentially in charge of making things happen. The job title "runner" has not been chosen at random. You run. Typically, you'll be expected to perform a wide variety of tasks, some more menial than others. For instance, you may be required to deliver messages, run errands, carry equipment.

The pick up is at 7am in front of my place. It sounds nice. A black Mercedes Class V is waiting. I meet the producer.

She is older than me. She wears a pair of Vans, not a cool one though. She's not living in the city center. Elbows up. Both hands on her iPhone close to her face. It seems the weight of what she writes on WhatsApp is balanced by a heavy Oakley backpack she wears on her back. The backpack is definitely too low.

I run.

THE VIDEO ASSISTANT

I have no idea how video making works. My friend thought I could help on the set just because of my past experience as an assistant photographer. He likes my art and he keeps repeating to me that he prefers to work with a friend.

You are my creative consultant Emanuele!

I would be happy to be introduced as a creative consultant rather than whatever assistant.

We're in Paris. The shooting is big. At least 50 people are working here.

At this point, considering my past experience as a production assistant, I pay more attention to the way this big shoot is organized. There are two different production teams. The first is in charge of the logistic. The second deals with primary needs like food and beverage.

The catering is everywhere.

Trays of salmon mini bagels.

First day is over.

Black Mercedes Class V.

I check the price of my room at the hotel. It costs more than what I am being paid.

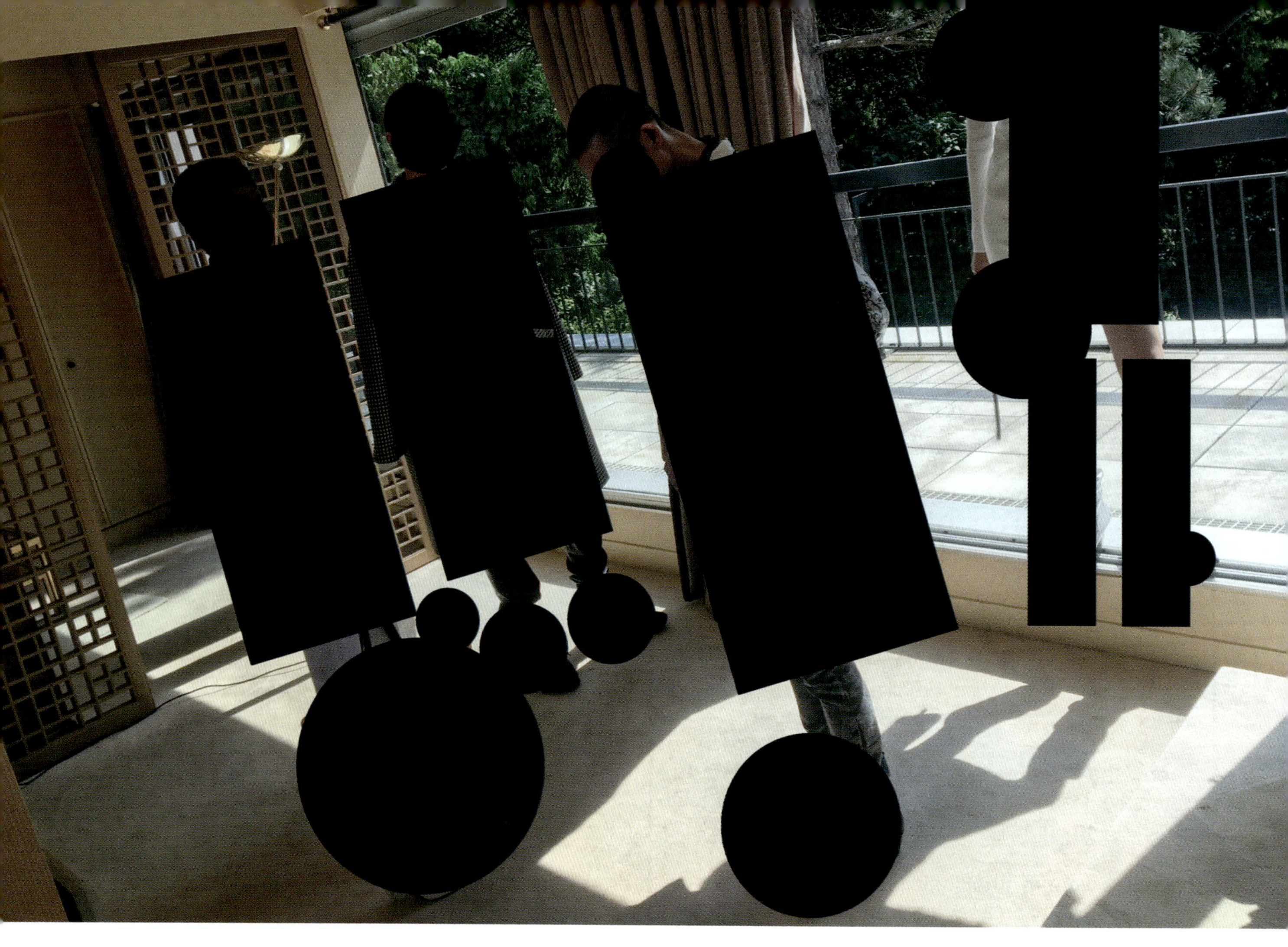

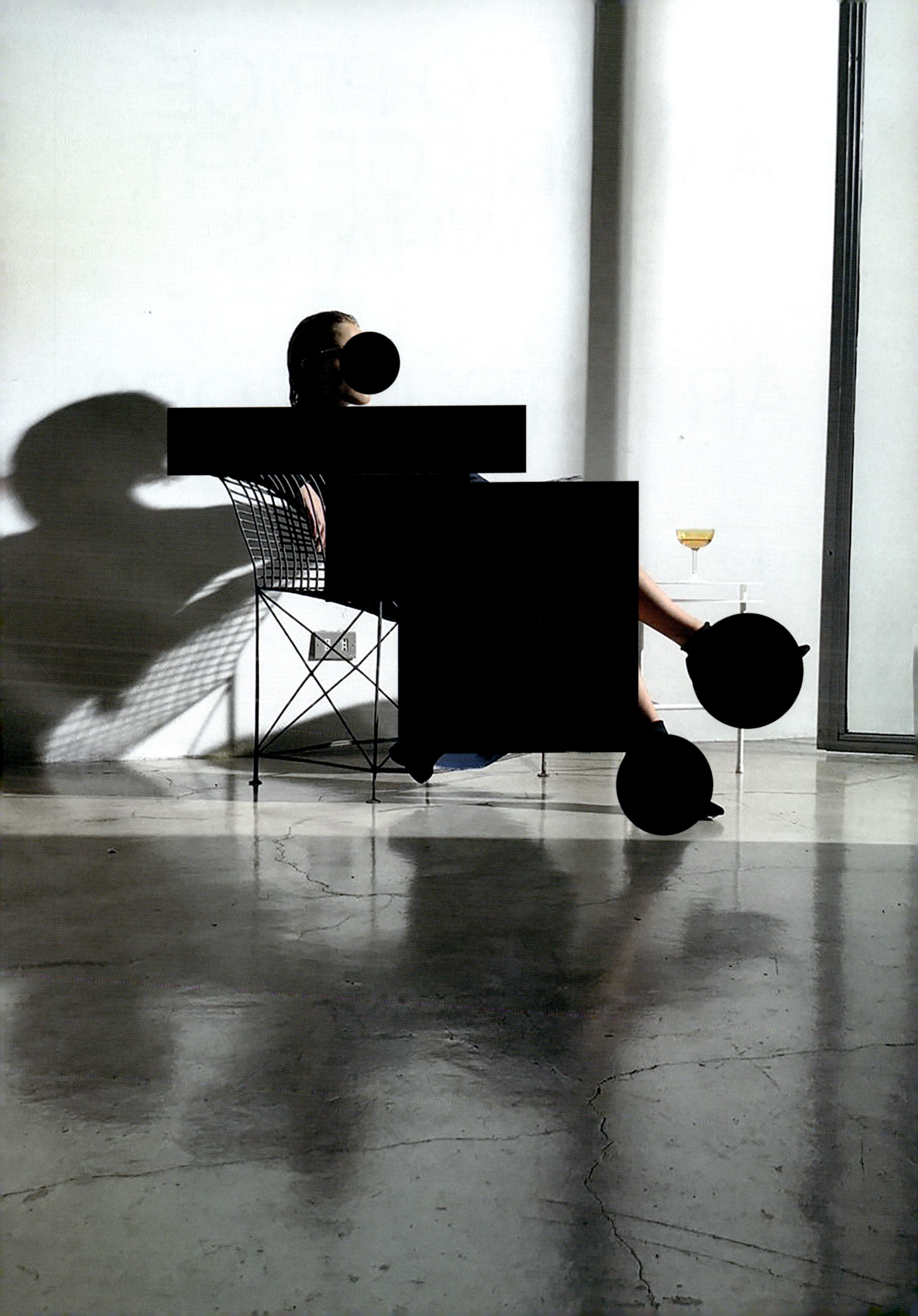

HOW TO PRICE A WORK OF ART, OR: WHAT'S THE VALUE OF ARTISTS' LABOR?

Text

Silvia Simoncelli

"How *should* prices of works of art be determined? Before trying to answer that, we need some sort of answer to how prices are currently determined. Clearly, a price can only be fixed to a particular market structure."[1] The first lines of Ian Burn's contribution to the inaugural issue of *The Fox*, a short-lived publication edited by the New York group of artists affiliated with the British conceptual art group Art & Language, hit with precision one of the topics which attracted the attention of many artists in the early 1970s, who—beyond individual artistic discourses—were trying to deal with and resist the unprecedented pressure of the art market on artists' lives and production, while making a living out of their work. In line with a recurring observation that "the fine arts have been integrated into the commodity market in ways not conceivable for other works of art,"[2] Burn stigmatizes the extent to which the exchange market for art—the secondary market where works circulate totally disjoined form the authors' control—had come to determine also the logic of the production market, the one within which living artists operate and get remuneration from[3], so that "we are no longer able to talk about our art production independent of market coercion— the fusion is complete."[4]

The emergence of a substantial market for contemporary art in the US during the 1960s was a novelty to which the prosperity of the decade had provided a fertile ground: contemporary art with its innovative language perfectly matched the needs of an up-and-coming class of "young, mobile, affluent, highly trained technocrats" who were looking for tools of representation in the public sphere and were equally "eager to enjoy the comforts of their class."[5] Analyzing the changing situation in an article in *Artforum* tellingly titled "Notes on Patronage: the 1960s," Francis V. O'Connor noted that art appealing to such audience depended both on the fact that "it was prestigious to own and conspicuous to display, and vied with the stock market in investment potential." Financial vocabulary had infiltrated art-related literature already in the 1950s, when the market for impressionist pictures had enjoyed a very positive trend. In the following decade such discourse moved from modern to contemporary art, as the latter reached "a larger audience in new ways, by improved marketing techniques and by mass media."[6] Widely distributed magazines such as *Time* and *Life* regularly featured articles presenting artists as celebrities and artworks as "blue-chips," as well as interviews with influential private collectors, as in the case of Robert Scull and Leon Kraushar, who would enthusiastically compare their pop art pictures to, respectively, their AT&T and IBM stocks.[7]

"We've all noticed how the art market behaves and reacts like a stock market—how prices paid for a 'promising' new artist rise virtually on the ground of some well placed rumors," Burn pointed out commenting on the situation.[8] While some artists enjoyed the new circumstances, a wider number—including names who had benefited from greater exposure in the expanding market[9]—started to develop critical views on the new conditions under which they were operating. At the end of the 1960s, when the climate was permeated by the ethos of the civil rights movements and the anti-war protests, artists felt it was the time to openly question the economics of the art system and discuss their role as cultural producers in society. The Art Workers' Coalition (AWC) started in 1969 as a spontaneous reaction to the exhibition policies at the Museum of Modern art, New York (MoMA), and gathered in a very short time a large number of artists, mostly active in New York, who expressed through a series of meetings, documents, and demonstrations their shared desire for a reform of the institutions of the art world and the art market.[10] In the "Statement of Demands" presented to MoMA's director Bates Lowry on January 28, 1969, the founding group put forward thirteen requests, stigmatizing the institution's elitism and advocating for artists' rights, including those pertaining to the economic relations between artists and their work. Reading through the minutes of the open hearings organized by the AWC on April 10, 1969 at the School of Visual Arts in New York, where more than sixty artists took to the stage to put forward requests and proposals to ameliorate the relations between artists and museums, galleries, and wider society, it is evident that economic preoccupations were widespread and artists felt the pressure to address them with great precision.[11] While some would be ready for negotiation, there would also be extremely critical voices who would call for the art world in its entirety to be "repudiated, abandoned, crushed like a cigarette" as the money-driven system governing it had become, in the worlds of Carl Andre, "the curse and corruption of the life of art in America."[12]

WHILE SOME WOULD BE READY FOR NEGOTIATION, THERE WOULD ALSO BE EXTREMELY CRITICAL VOICES WHO WOULD CALL FOR THE ART WORLD IN ITS ENTIRETY TO BE "REPUDIATED, ABANDONED, CRUSHED LIKE A CIGARETTE."

One of the most enduring legacies of the discussions developed within the AWC regarding which practical actions should have been taken by artists in order to gain some control over their work and economic situation outside the turmoils of the art market, was "The Artist's Reserved Right Transfer and Sale Agreement." Drafted by conceptual art dealer and curator Seth Siegelaub and lawyer Robert Projansky in 1971, the agreement aimed, as stated in its preface, at remedying "artists' lack of control over their work and participation in its economics after they no longer own it."[13] According to the portion of the Agreement focusing on the economic relations between artist and collector, artists had to be entitled to receive 15% on the increase of value for every sale following the direct acquisition of the work from their studio (the so-called artist's resale right), shares on any loan-related fees received by the owner of the work in case of temporary exhibitions and full payment of all reproduction rights on the work—all requests originally discussed during the AWC Open Hearings.[14]

The AWC officially continued its activities until 1971.[15] The artists participating were not separating their artistic activity from that of the AWC, trying to build a network to sustain its life as to make its proposals heard in the art system. Curator Lucy Lippard organized, for example, "Number 7," an exhibition at Paula Cooper Gallery, which functioned as a benefit for AWC in 1969.[16] Among the artists participating, there was also a young Adrian Piper, who would join the AWC one year later.[17] Even if not part of the original AWC group of artists, Piper was already experimenting with her artistic practice in order to find alternative formats of exhibition and distribution of her work. Her closeness to some of the protagonists of that period including Sol Lewitt, Hans Haacke, and Seth Siegelaub, for whom she worked as an assistant for the show "January 5–31 1969,"[18] might be seen as fertile ground on which her views on the economic position of the artist in society would develop.

In 1975 with her text "A Proposal for Pricing Works of Art," Adrian Piper publicly entered the debate revamped by Ian Burn, following his timely reflection in *The Fox* on the issue of the remuneration of artists' labor and the value of art as a commodity.[19] As many other artist-led magazines, *The Fox* functioned as a space of dialog where artists could exchange their thoughts in threads and, to a greater extent, provided a platform where ephemeral conceptual art practices could find a space of circulation.[20] Not intended as a direct reaction to Burn's positions, Piper's contribution was rather a sedimentation of her reflections on the same issues, already presented and tested in some art projects in the previous years.

Like many other artists at the time, Piper had abandoned an object-based art practice in favor of projects based on maps, instructions, and statements. Soon after, she turned to performance, acting directly in the street as an unexpected presence and dealing with "questions of identity, as well as inter-personal relations" among the impersonality of the crowd.[21] After the *Catalysis* series (1970), which consisted of actions "based on direct and immediate confrontation"[22] with the viewers, where the artist would make her body public by turning herself "into an object"[23], she started working on the Mythic Being series, where she introduced the topic of race, which would be an enduring one in her work. Mythic Being started in 1972 as an experiment in which Piper turned herself into a fictional male character, dressing up in her apartment. The private performances were then disseminated via pictures published monthly in advertisement spaces in the gallery listing pages of the *Village Voice*. Later, Piper took the Mythic Being out in the streets of New York and Cambridge, Massachusetts, where she moved in 1974, after starting a PhD in philosophy at Harvard University. In her text "Notes on the Mythic Being I–III" (1974–76), Piper elaborated on her decision to take the performance into the streets, explaining that the choice not to rely on a discrete, spatially unique space for the presentation of her work, and especially to avoid galleries, was a result of her will to resist the cooptation of the art system.[24]

In 1975 Piper was invited to present the Mythic Being in "Lives," a show organized by Jeffrey Deitch at The Fine Arts Building in New York. She decided to exhibit a series of posters with images similar to those published earlier in the *Village Voice* ads, and to include in the catalog a text which detailed the conditions of production of the exhibited work. According to it, artworks had to be materially inexpensive, context independent, duplicable, simple and inexpensive to reproduce, easy to distribute and, finally, their exchange value had to be equal to their production value.[25] A very similar text appeared in the same year with the title "Seven Conditions on Art production" on the reverse of the posters announcing her solo show at Montclair College. Here she added one more condition: the work had to maintain a stable market value, a result which could have been obtained by inscribing its exchange value directly in the work, as she did.[26]

ARTWORKS HAD TO BE MATERIALLY INEXPENSIVE, CONTEXT INDEPENDENT, DUPLICABLE, SIMPLE AND INEXPENSIVE TO REPRODUCE, EASY TO DISTRIBUTE AND, FINALLY, THEIR EXCHANGE VALUE HAD TO BE EQUAL TO THEIR PRODUCTION VALUE.

When she wrote her contribution for *The Fox*, Piper's view on the value of artists' labor and her ideas for an alternative price setting mechanism for artworks had already been developed and put to the test in recent projects. In the text, Piper analyses the role of the artist as worker, addresses the topic of the value of artists' labor, and proposes an original price-setting strategy. "A Proposal for Pricing works of Art" is divided into three main sections, which present the main thesis, detail how to implement it in practical terms and provide possible future scenarios that might be generated by a large scale adoption of the proposal. An in-depth reading of the text could pro-

Adrian Piper, *Mythic Being: Look But Don't Touch* (posters from Montclair State College), 1975. Poster, 11×17″, (27.9×43.1cm). Detail: recto. Collection of the Adrian Piper Research Archive Foundation Berlin.

ADRIAN PIPER

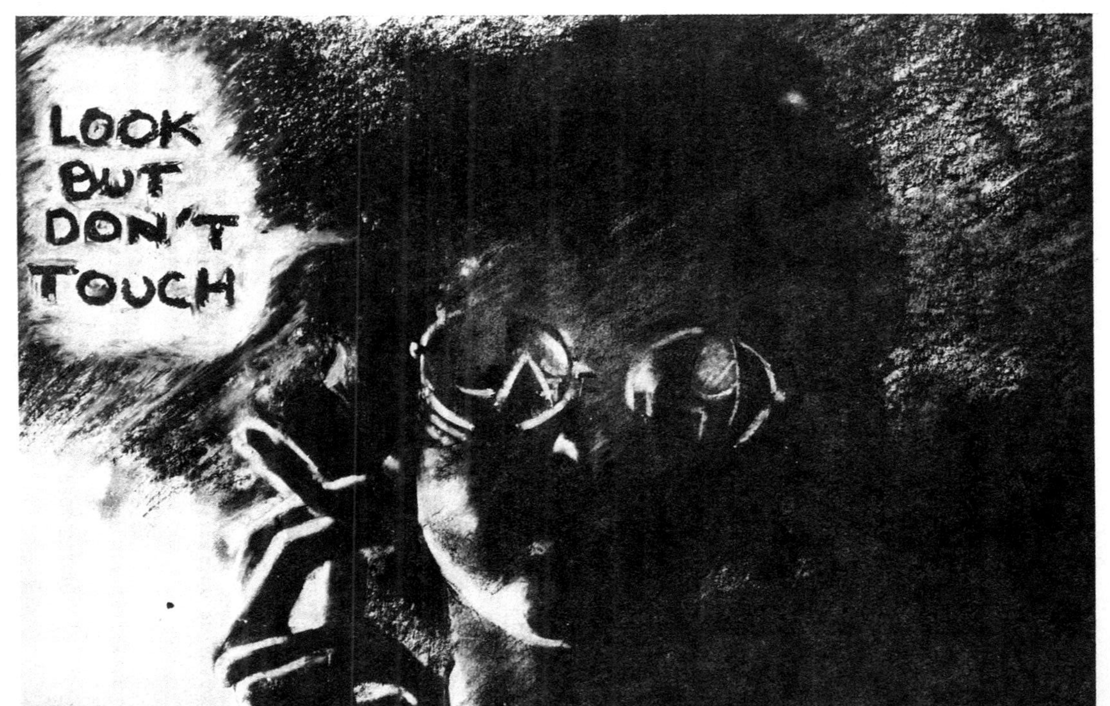

POSTERS

Photography: James Guttmann

GALLERY ONE Montclair State College, Upper Montclair, N.J. 07043 (201) 893-5112

February 23-March 19

The exchange value of this work is $21.00

SEVEN CONDITIONS ON ART PRODUCTION

My work in this show was executed under the following voluntarily-adopted prescriptive constraints:

1. Materially inexpensive.

   The works do not depend for their realization on scarce, expensive, or relatively inaccessible natural or human resources.

2. Context-Independent.

   The works do not require a particular type of context in order to be displayed to best advantage. Any natural or artificial environment is equally acceptable.

3. Duplicability.

   The works are conceived as multiples, or multipliable tokens of a type. Their aesthetic value depends on (among other things) the uniqueness of the type and not on the relative scarcity of the tokens, which exist in unlimited editions.

4. Simple and inexpensive reproduction.

   The reproduction of the works does not require highly complex or expensive labor and technology.

5. Accessibility of distribution.

   In addition to 2. and 3. above, the works are realized in such a way as to be accessible, in theory, to a general public on the same basis as other goods and services, i.e. through the usual commercial channels.

6. Exchange Value = Production Value.

   The price of the works is computed in such a way as to compensate me for labor (at the average blue-collar wage rate of $7.50 per hour) and materials, rather than estimated according to a price scale purporting to correlate market value with aesthetic value.

7. Stable market value.

   The following measures are taken to prevent fluctuations in the market value of the works: a. the exchange value is permanently inscribed on the works; b. the exchange value of all works sold will be publicly advertised in a national or international periodical at unspecified future times; c. see 3., above.

I choose to impose these conditions on my work because they are -- unlike most other social determinants of my attitudes and my work -- within my conscious ability to control; and because, of <u>all</u> the social forces that shape my work, they seem to me most pressingly in need of conscious control.

12/75

Adrian M.S. Piper

75002.2.1

Adrian Piper, Mythic Being: Look But Don't Touch (posters from Montclair State College), 1975. Poster, 11×17", (27.9×43.1cm). Detail: verso. Collection of the Adrian Piper Research Archive Foundation Berlin.

vide an interesting insight to the relation between some economic terminology used by Piper and other artists at the time within the framework of a conceptual artistic practice, while at the same time testifying the urgency of the debate on possible responses to the art market logic which was strongly influencing the art system of the time.

In the first section, Piper proposes the exchange value of an artwork to be identical to its production value, intended as the sum of retail cost of materials used and labor cost. "Labor is a function of actual work-hours, that is, time engaged in thinking about, planning and/or physically producing the work. This can be computed either on an hourly or a weekly basis [...]. In either case, this amount should not exceed the wage or salary scale of an average blue- or white-collar civil service worker."[27] Embracing the idea that the artist's remuneration can be calculated on an hourly basis—as for any other worker—Piper goes on defining the value of the artist's time as equal to that of an average worker, or better: to that of a civil service worker, a specification that is not only practical, but includes a clear indication about the role of the artist in society.

EMBRACING THE IDEA THAT THE ARTIST'S REMUNERATION CAN BE CALCULATED ON AN HOURLY BASIS—AS FOR ANY OTHER WORKER—PIPER GOES ON DEFINING THE VALUE OF THE ARTIST'S TIME AS EQUAL TO THAT OF AN AVERAGE WORKER, OR BETTER: TO THAT OF A CIVIL SERVICE WORKER.

The term "worker" was at the time an extremely loaded one, in the context of both conceptual art and artists' political activism. It was Sol Lewitt who famously stated that "the idea or concept is the most important aspect of the work" and that in conceptual art "all of the planning and decisions are made beforehand" and who described the conceptual artist as a "clerk cataloging the results of his premise;"[28] while curator Lucy Lippard, who transformed the format of the exhibition by the use of artists' documentation, was to define her role "as that of a compiler."[29] As a consequence of the shifting of artistic production towards plans, projects, and instructions, the artist's work in conceptual art started to appear as being close to that of an intellectual worker. This vision was reinforced by the fact that conceptual and minimal artists started selling their work in the form of certificates, which sometimes included even their signature as a proof of authorship, together with all the needed instructions to fabricate the work—as in the case of Donald Judd—thus leaving all the connected practicalities and expenses to the owner.[30] Correspondingly, in Piper's text, the term "work-hours" includes the "time engaged in thinking about, [and] planning" and only as a third option the time engaged in "physically producing the work."

In the context of the AWC the term "worker" became further politically loaded. The idea that artists were contributing with their work to the ongoing cultural and political debate, called for a recognition of the relevance of their role outside the enclosed space of the art system. This would include also practical sides: in a later version of the *Statement of Demands*—documented by Lucy Lippard—the proposal of a trust fund, to be financed with tax levied on the sale of the work of dead artists, to provide stipends, health insurance, and other social benefits to artists, was added.[31] In her proposal, Piper also advocates that artists should be entitled to social benefits, where she maintains that further to work-hours, artist's labor cost should also cover secondary labor costs. These include all the "needed long-term materials, working space, tools, equipment, and so on. Ideally these should be provided by government or community agencies, just as work space and adequate equipment are provided for other civil service workers."[32] As previously noted, this paralleling of artists and civil service workers reinforces the idea of the relevance of the artists' role in society. Piper returns with more clarity on this topic in "Cheap Art Utopia" (1976), a text published in the following year in *Art Rite.* Here she maintains that if art was more affordable it could reach a larger portion of the population, meaning that "the social responsibility of artists would increase proportionally."[33]

A side effect of the implementation of Piper's proposal, based on the equation of production value and exchange value, would be cheaper prices for art and, by consequence, its affordability for a larger public. But for art prices to remain low in the long run and to resist the speculation on the market, a specific strategy had to be developed, as Piper explains in the second part of her text.

> "This suggests the possibility of incorporating the computed production value of the work into the work itself, for example, by inscribing it somewhere in the work. It might, for example appear as part of the work, or be added to the artist's signature, date of completion, or title of the work. Provided that this (I.) is adopted, this inscription [...] could be recognized as binding on the buyer as a condition of sale of the work [...]. This would prevent any fluctuation in the market value of the work, because the exchange value of the work (= production value) would then be constant."[34]

On the front of the poster realized by Piper for the exhibition at Montclair College, a tiny inscription reads: "The exchange value of this work is $21.00." On the back side of the poster, Piper clarifies that such value was calculated considering a wage rate of $7.5 per hour. Piper refers to the price inscribed as "binding on the buyer as a condition of sale of the work."[35] This inscription recalls yet another attempt at including information about the artwork's economics—that could otherwise be extremely volatile—directly in the work of art. In the paperwork constituting "The artist's reserved right transfer and sale agreement," Siegelaub included a detachable notice which had to be filled out after the purchase and affixed directly onto the work as a necessary condition of the agreement's validity. Both Siegelaub and Piper tried to administrate the economics of the work of art by adopting measures which could prevent speculation—a fixed price for Piper, the 15% clause for Siegelaub[36]—at the cost of turning more clearly the art object into a recognizable object of trade.

In the third and final part of the proposal, Piper presents two possible future scenarios that could develop following the implementation of her program. In the first case "it might happen that because under this program neither the artist nor the dealer nor the buyer stands to make a substantial profit on works of art, interest in producing and acquiring art might die out. Art, as well as art-as-speculation and art-as-investment security, might disappear."[37] This first option appears extremely dark. If it were to come true, it would prove, according to Piper, that the production of art "depends on a capitalist economy after all."[38] Piper coldly faces the possibility that her idea might cause the extinction of art production at large. To better understand Piper's paradoxical position, it is necessary to consider the context of general discontent with the compromises and contradictions of the art system, which brought several artists to the point of considering stopping work in the arts so as to remain true to their own values. Lucy Lippard, facing the difficultly of resisting being co-opted by the art system, once said "I can never figure out if I should keep on plugging for the work and the values I care about and provide at least a whisper of dissent from the art world mainstream, or quit entirely in protest."[39] She was not alone in this dilemma, as *General Strike Piece* by Lee Lozano proves. In January 1969, the artist formulated a statement detailing the conditions of her temporary withdrawal from all "official or public uptown functions or gatherings related to the art world in order to pursue investigation of total personal and public revolution."[40] Lee Lozano presented this idea at the AWC Open Hearings, and put it in practice between February and the Summer of 1969, turning down invitations to participate in exhibitions, ceasing visiting galleries, museums, concerts, film screenings, and denied to attend parties and events, as a critique of art and artists as commoditized entities.

In the second case—according to Piper—the new price setting strategy might happen to facilitate "producing art as a modest means of self-support for more artists by making it more economically accessible to more people."[41] If art was cheaper more people could afford to buy it: as a result a larger number of artists would be able to sustain themselves with their work. If positively undertaken, this program would also "bring out more clearly the de facto viability of conceiving artists as workers rather then as constituting a privileged class."[42] On the one hand it would put an end to the winner-takes-all model which dominates the art market and allow a more equal distribution of wealth among artists while—at the same time—it would "make possible a greater solidarity with other workers."[43]

Piper's Proposal was received very coldly if not negatively by Ian Burn, who in his contribution on the pages of *The Fox* had already provided criticism for the positions of those members of the AWC advocating the introduction of a wage system remuneration for artists as a means to overcome income disparities and allow a greater number of artists to live on their work.[44] For Burn, the idea that "the way out of the current market debasement of art is to set per-hourly rates on artists' time" was nothing but an "out-of-the-frying-pan-and-into-the-fire" situation that would possibly bring to bear an even more exploitative economic system for artists.[45] He would rather advocate for a "ruling out of the system of private property in the fine arts" so that there would "no longer [be] any issue of price,"[46] which sounds like an equally unrealistic perspective. Piper later provided some self criticism on her proposal too.[47] But the fact that she integrated her reasoning on the issue of artists' remuneration directly into the process of art production makes the Proposal and the related artworks still inspiring for the present age—in a time, when the vast majority of artists are still struggling to make a living out of their work and keep discussing what viable solution could be undertaken to make the art system more fair and less exposed to the influx of the market. Or, whether in fact, they should leave the art world behind.

At the beginning of the new millennium, the AWC has inspired a number of artists' initiatives around the world, from Carrot Workers in the UK, to Lavoratori dell'Arte in Italy, to W.A.G.E. in the US to name just a few.[48] The question that lies at the core of many of these endeavors is again the development of a system of remuneration for artists and the definition of applicable parameters to define what artists' labor is worth—not disjointed by a reflection on the social function of the artists' work and on its impact on culture, beyond the enclosed spaces of the gallery and the museum.

31 the village VOICE, April 25, 1974

Continued from preceding page

closed, graphite on the hands, and estimating a lapsed time of three minutes, both hands attempt to descend the page with identical touching motions in an effort to keep to an even vertical column of touches."

"Voice" entails four large speakers and various texts read on tape, mostly simultaneously. It looked right but it didn't sound very interesting to me. Morris's most interesting work this time around is the poster for the exhibition. It shows the muscular artist stripped to the waist, in shades and helmet, with chains and a spiked "dog collar." I'm not sure what it means. I'm not sure I want to know. But at least it's a memorable image.

SOMETIMES I WONDER about things. Is it merely a coincidence that we are now treated to the terrific paintings of Gerald Murphy at the Museum of Modern Art when the expensive "The Great Gatsby" has recently opened? In the foreword to the dry but informative catalog to this splendid show, Murphy's friend, the poet Archibald MacLeish, writes, "It is often asserted that Murphy was the model for Fitzgerald's Dick Diver in 'Tender Is the Night,' if not for Fitzgerald himself."

Even if the timing is not a coincidence, perhaps we need more "coincidences" like this, if a great show can result. Murphy was rich, an expatriate, and a friend of almost every important Paris art figure of the '20s. He didn't begin to paint until he was 33 and he stopped, apparently because of personal tragedies, only seven years later, leaving behind an extremely small body of work, but one I think extremely significant, as late Cubism (related to Precisionist painting), as American painting, and as just damn good art.

Here we are able to see just about all there is of his work: "Razor," "Watch," "Doves," "Wasp and Pear," "Cocktail," and "Library," which has never been exhibited before. This list is expanded by some photographs of lost or destroyed works. Needless to say, this is a very small output, but the clarity and the beauty of what remains speak for themselves.

Murphy's backdrop for a ballet with music by Cole Porter, called "Within the Quota," is a knockout. It is a fake front page, a composite of sensational headlines, led by "Unknown Banker Buys Atlantic." I wonder what the music was like? Does anybody know?

Galleries

PHYLLIS LUCAS GALLERY
"TRIBUTE TO DALI"
LARGEST COLLECTION OF OLD PRINTS AND FINE GRAPHICS
EXCLUSIVE PUBLISHERS DALI LITHOGRAPHS
981 2nd Ave., N.Y., N.Y. 10022 (52nd St.)
Illustrated Color DALI catalog $1-Foreign $2.00

JOHN FISCHER thru May 11
LERNER-HELLER
789 MADISON AVE., N.Y.

ED OATES
April 16-May 4
IOLAS GALLERY. 15 E. 55, N.Y.

Robert HENRY
GreeN Mountain
135 GREENE STREET

REBA ROTTENBERG
Motor Vans
April 23—May 11
GALLERY 84
1046 Madison Ave. (80 St.) NYC
Tues-Sat 12:00-5:00 P.M.

Peter HOMITZKY
Paintings
Thru May 25
ROKO
90 E. 10th Street

WILLIAM BECKMAN
BARTON BENES
alan stone
48 E 86

PERFORMANCE EXHIBIT BY DOUGLAS DUNN ON VIEW
101
TUES–SAT, 2–6 PM THRU 18 MAY 508 BROADWAY (NEAR SPRING) 3RD FLOOR $1

HOUSTOUN
Second Story Spring Street Society
APRIL 13 - MAY 3
167 Spring Street

pat MAINARDI
GreeN Mountain
135 GREENE STREET

THOMAS GEORGE thru May 11
BETTY PARSONS
GALLERY 24 W. 57, N.

JULIAN LEVI
PAINTINGS
thru May 18
Frank Rehn Gallery
655 Madison Ave.

Sandi Gross
"Ambiguity of Subconscious Vision"
solo show of textural paintings & collages at Central Hall Gallery, 402 Main St., Port Washington, LI, NY. 12-5PM Wed-Sun thru May 12 / 516-767-9550

MAY STEVENS
APR 20-MAY 15
SOHO 20 99 SPRING

14 SCULPTORS GALLERY
GROUP SHOW
Opening Sat. April 20
Until May 8th
Tues-Sat. 12-6 p.m.
75 Thompson St.

SARIANO
AT THE
ROSENHOUSE GALLERY
33 GREENWICH AVE 675 2107
12 to 9 WEEKDAYS AND SAT.

PETER CARELLA
Paintings
April 26 - May 15
THE FIRST STREET GALLERY
118 Prince St.

Paul Sharits
Thru May 2
Bykert Downtown
484 Broome

'sh te-,fän 'in(t)s
3'ner-se(r)
'krō-bär an(d)
'pūl-ē sa(a)l

ALICE AYCOCK
112 Greene Street
April 20 - May 2

MARGE HELENCHILD
APR 20-MAY 15
SOHO 20 99 SPRING

Visit America's Largest Art Gallery
CIRCLE GALLERY, LTD.
Weekdays 10 to 10/Sun. 12 to 8
1081 THIRD AVE. & 64TH ST.
(212) 752-2577

TOM BOUTIS
RUTH ANN FREDENTHAL
EMILY MASON
GABRIELE ROOS
April 27-May 16
LANDMARK GALLERY
469 Broome St. NY 10013

Thru May 25th
WESSELMANN
Sidney Janis 6 W. 57

ALVIN LOVING
FISCHBACH
489 BROOME

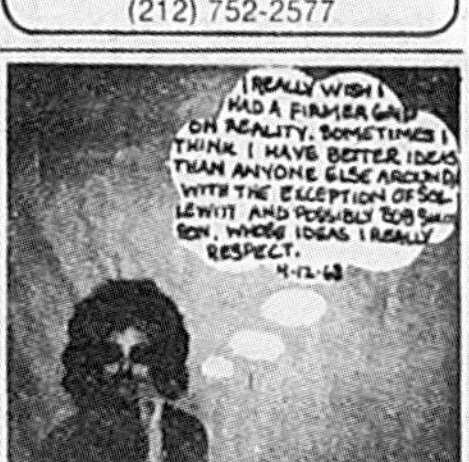

PAINTINGS BY MYLO QUAM
NOW THRU MAY 12
WAVERLY GALLERY
103 WAVERLY PLACE 477-6710
Open daily 1-9PM Closed Mon.

BENEFIT SALE
MAY 1-10
nader
OF HAITI LIMITED
ART GALLERY
Baruch College
155 E 24
673 MADISON AVENUE, NEW YORK 10021
TELEPHONE (212) 751-3337
Entrance 25 East 61 Street

PHOTOGRAPHS
BEATON NADAR HORST HOYNINGEN-HUENE
SONNABEND GALLERY 924 MADISON

CHINA HOUSE GALLERY
presents
TANTRIC BUDDHIST ART
CHINA INSTITUTE IN AMERICA
Guest Curator, Eleanor Olson
Fully illustrated catalog available
$5.75 plus 30 cents postage
125 East 65th Street, New York 10021

10 Downtown
1974 April 20-21, 27-28, May 4-5, 1-6 p.m.
The Seventh Annual show of artists' work in their lofts
▪richard samuelson 133 west 24 st.
▪roz seelig 48 west 22 st.
▪david james 121 west 17 st.
▪diane levin 812 broadway
▪meredith johnson 379 west broadway
▪sally ehrlich 482 broome st.
▪james zver 16 greene st.
▪isabella corwin 140 baxter st.
▪carol engelson 164 bowery
▪anne sharp 45 east broadway

Lloyd Glasson
Bronzes, Ceramics, Drawings
April 16th—May 4th
DORSKY GALLERIES
111 Fourth Avenue, NYC
(between 11th and 12th Sts.)

to May 11
CARL HOLTY
MEMORIAL EXHIBITION
Fully illustrated color catalogue $5.00
ANDREW CRISPO GALLERY
41 EAST 57 STREET NEW YORK CITY 758-9190 2nd floor

This and the following page (detail): Adrian Piper, The Mythic Being, Cycle I: 4/12/68, 1974. Village Voice Newspaper Ad of April 25th 1974, #8 of 17 from the Mythic Being Village Voice Series, 14.88×11.5″ (37.7×29.2 cm). Collection of the Museum of Modern Art, New York. Purchased with funds provided by Donald L. Bryant, Jr., Agnes Gund, Marlene Hess and James D. Zirin, Marie-Josée and Henry R. Kravis, Donald B. Marron, The Edward John Noble Foundation, Jerry I. Speyer and Katherine Farley, and Committee on Drawings Funds in honor of Kathy Fuld. © Adrian Piper Research Archive Foundation Berlin.

1081 THIRD AVE. & 64TH ST.
(212) 752-2577

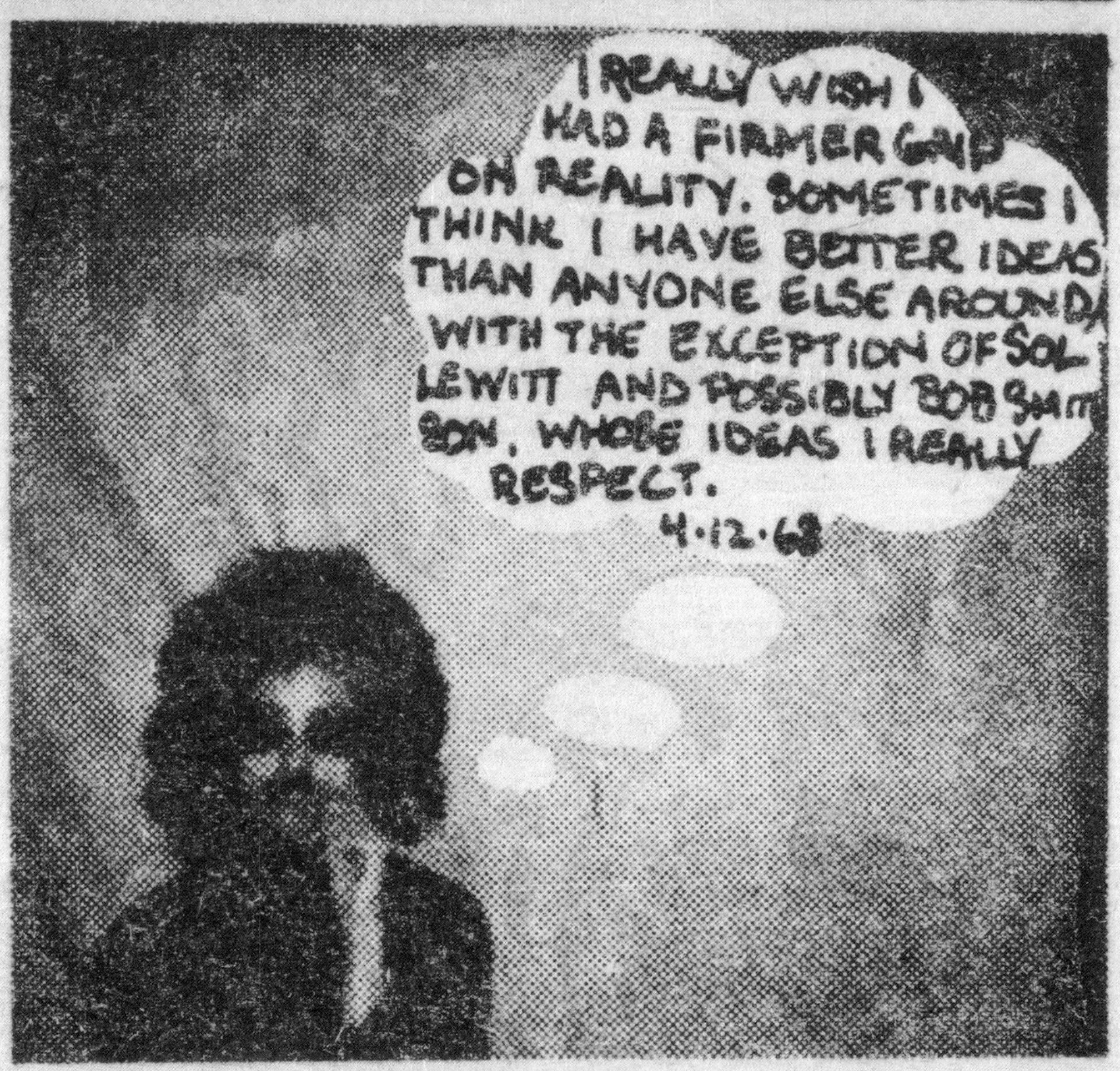

E GALLERY
nts

ODHIST ART

1 Ian Burn, "Pricing Works of Art," in *The Fox*, 1 (1975), 53. The same year Burn published an article in *Artforum* expanding on the negative influx of the art market on contemporary artistic production. Ian Burn, "The Art Market: Affluence and Degradation," *Artforum*, vol. 13, no. 8 (April 1975), 34–7.
2 Ibid., 54.
3 Ibid., 55.
4 Ibid., 54.
5 Francis V. O'Connor, "Notes on Patronage: the 1960s," *Artforum*, vol. 1, no. 1 (September 1972), 52. For a more articulated discussion on the circumstances which prompted the emergence of a market for contemporary art see also Alexander Alberro, *Conceptual Art and the Politics of Publicity* (Cambridge, Mass.: The MIT Press, 2003), 6–10.
6 Lawrence Alloway, "Network: The Art World Described as a System," *Artforum*, vol. 11, no. 1 (1972), 29.
7 Sophie Cras, "Art as an Investment and Artistic Shareholding Experiments in the 1960s," *American Art*, vol. 27, no. 1 (Spring 2013), 8.
8 Ian Burn, 55.
9 See for example Barnett Newman, Marc Di Suvero, Joseph Kosuth: all three were participating in the AWC Open Hearings (see note 11). Di Suvero exhibited with Green Gallery (first show 1960) and was one of the funders of Park Place Gallery. Joseph Kosuth was active as artist, critic (under the pseudonym of Arthur Rose), and gallerist, he had his first show at Leo Castelli in 1969. Although Barnett Newman didn't have a show in a commercial gallery until 1969 (M. Knoedler and Company) he mounted several museum shows in the 1960s. Harold Rosenberg's laudatory biographical essay "Barnett Newman, A Man of Controversy and Spiritual Grandeur," appeared in the February issue of *Vogue* in 1963.
10 For a detailed account on the history of the Art Workers' Coalition see Julia Bryan-Wilson, *Art Workers. Radical Practice in the Vietnam War Era* (Berkeley: University of California Press, 2009).
11 *Art Workers' Coalition, Open Hearing*, http://www.primaryinformation.org/product/art-workers-coalition-open-hearing/, accessed 11.7.2018. Among the speakers: Carl Andre, Gregory Battcock, Robert Barry, Rosemarie Castoro, Mark di Suvero, Dan Graham, Hans Haacke, Joseph Kosuth, Sol Lewitt, Lucy Lippard, Lee Lozano, Barnett Newman, and Seth Siegelaub.
12 Carl Andre in *Art Workers' Coalition, Open Hearing*, 34.
13 "The Artist's Reserved Right Transfer and Sale Agreement" written by Seth Siegelaub with the help of lawyer Robert Projansky was first published in *Studio International* in 1971. For a more detailed account on the elaboration of the Agreement see Alberro, *Conceptual Art and the Politics of Publicity*, chap. 7.
14 See for example the proposals by Rosemarie Castoro, David Lee, and Sol Lewitt in *Art Workers' Coalition, Open Hearing*, 15, 42, 54.
15 Julie Ault, *Alternative Art New York: 1965–1985* (Minneapolis: University of Minnesota Press, 2002), 5.
16 Sabeth Buchmann, "Introduction: From Conceptualism to Feminism," in *From Conceptualism to Feminism: Lucy Lippard's Numbers Shows 1969–74*, ed. by Cornelia Butler (London: Afterall Books, 2012), 14.
17 Adrian Piper, "Chronology," in *Adrian Piper: Reflections 1967–1987*, ed. by Jane Farver (New York: The Alternative Museum, 1987), 47.
18 The show was held at the Mc Lendon Building, New York. See Maria Eichhorn, "Interview with Adrian Piper," in Maria Eichhorn, *The Artist's Contract*, ed. by Gerti Fietzek (Cologne: Walther König Verlag, 2009), 200.
19 Adrian Piper, "A proposal for Pricing Works of Art," in *The Fox*, 2 (1975), n.p., reprinted in Adrian Piper, *Out of Order, Out of Sight, Selected Writings in Meta-Art 1968–1992*, II, (Cambridge, Mass.: MIT Press, 1996), 31–2.
20 The editorial board was formed by Sarah Charlesworth, Michael Corris, Joseph Kosuth, Andrew Menard, Mel Ramsden, Preston Heller, and Ian Burn. Chris Gilbert, "Art & Language and the Institutional Form," in *Collectivism after Modernism. The Art of Social Imagination after 1945*, ed. by Blake Stimson and Gregory Sholette (Minneapolis: University of Minnesota Press, 2007), 105. For a brief account of the development of the magazine over the three issues published between 1975 and 1976 see Blake Stimson, "The Promise of Conceptual Art," in *Conceptual Art: a Critical Anthology*, ed. by Alexander Alberro and Blake Stimson (Cambridge, Mass.: The MIT Press, 1999), xliv-xlv. On the role and typology of artists' magazines in the 1960's and 1970's see: Gwen Allen, *Artists Magazines. An Alternative Space for Art* (Cambridge, Mass.: MIT Press, 2011. Here on *The Fox* see pp. 41, 141–2, 261–2. On the same topic, see , *Numbers: Serial Publications by Artists Since 1955*, ed. by Philip E. Aaron and Andrew Roth (Zurich: JRP Ringier, 2009). Here on *The Fox* pp. 72–4.
21 Clive Phillpot, "Adrian Piper talking to us," in *Adrian Piper: Reflections 1967–1987*, 7.
22 Adrian Piper, "Talking to myself: The ongoing autobiography of an art object," in Adrian Piper, *Out of Order, Out of Sight. Selected Writings in Meta-Art 1968–1992*, I, (Cambridge, Mass.: MIT Press, 1996), 34.
23 Lucy Lippard and Adrian Piper, "Catalysis: An Interview with Adrian Piper," in *The Drama Review*, vol. 16, no. 1 (March 1972), 78. In the introduction to the interview each performance of the series is briefly described through Piper's own words. Among these: "Catalysis I, 'in which I saturated a set of clothing in a mixture of vinegar, eggs, milk and cod liver oil for a week, then wore them on the D train during evening rush hour, then while browsing in the Marboro bookstore on Saturday night'; [...] Catalysis VI, 'in which I attached helium-filled Mickey Mouse balloons from each of my ears, under my nose, to my two front teeth, and from thin strands of my hair, then walked through Central Park, the lobby of the Plaza Hotel, and rode the subway during morning rush hours'; Catalysis III, 'in which I painted some cloth-ing with sticky white paint with a sign attached saying 'WET PAINT,' then went shopping at Macy's for some gloves and sunglasses.'" Ibid, 76.
24 Adrian Piper, "Notes on the Mythic Being I–III," in Adrian Piper, *Out of Order, Out of Sight*, I, 117–40.
25 Adrian Piper, "Six Conditions on Art Production," in *Lives*, ed. by Jeffrey Deitch, exhibition catalog, Fine Art Building, New York, November 29–December 20, 1975, n.p.
26 Adrian Piper, "Seven Conditions on Art production," reprint in Piper, *Out of Order, Out of Sight*, I, 159–60.
27 Adrian Piper, "A proposal for Pricing Works of Art," reprinted in Piper, *Out of Order, Out of Sight*, II, 31.
28 Sol Lewitt, *Serial Project #1*, 1966, in *Aspen*, 1/ 5 + 6 (1967), n.p.
29 Lucy R. Lippard, "Curating by Numbers," in *Tate Papers*, 12 (2009), http://www.tate.org.uk/research/publications/tate-papers/12/curating-by-numbers, accessed March 10, 2018.
30 For a discussion on the use of artists' documents for the sale of artworks and on the theoretical and practical issues connected to such practice, see Martha Buskirk, *The Contingent Object of Contemporary Art* (Cambridge, Mass.: MIT Press, 2003), 1–6, 25–53.
31 Lucy R. Lippard, "Art Workers' Coalition: Not a History," in *Studio International*, 180/972 (November 1970), 171–4. The initial requests included also the payment of rental fees to artists lending their work for temporary exhibitions and for the enforcement of the *Droit de Suite* legislation in the US.
32 Adrian Piper, "A proposal for Pricing Works of Art," reprinted in Piper, *Out of Order, Out of Sight*, II, 31.
33 Adrian Piper, "Cheap Art Utopia," in *Out of Order, Out of Sight*, II, 34.
34 Adrian Piper, "A proposal for Pricing Works of Art," 32.
35 Ibidem.
36 This refers to the obligation to each new owner to pay the artist a percentage of 15% on the increase of the artwork's price in order for the artist to get a share of each subsequent sale of an artwork.
37 Adrian Piper, "A proposal for Pricing Works of Art," reprinted in Piper, *Out of Order, Out of Sight*, II, 32.
38 Ibidem.
39 Lucy Lippard, "Freelancing the Dragon," in Lucy Lippard, *From the center: feminist essays on women's art* (New York: E. P. Dutton, 1976), 23.
40 Lee Lozano, *General Strike Piece*, 1969, reprinted in Helen Molesworth, "Tune in, Turn on, Drop out: The Rejection of Lee Lozano," *Art Journal*, 61/4 (Winter 2002), 64.
41 Adrian Piper, "A proposal for Pricing Works of Art," reprinted in Piper, *Out of Order, Out of Sight*, II, 32.
42 Ibidem.
43 Ibidem.
44 Adrian Piper, "Ian Burn's conceptualism," *Art in America*, 85/12 (December 1997), 72–9.
45 Ian Burn, "Pricing Works of Art," 56.
46 Ibid., 58.
47 See Maria Eichhorn, "Interview with Adrian Piper," 203.
48 To these a number of academic studies and essay collections should be added: *Art Work. A National Conversation About Art, Labor, and Economics*, ed. by Temporary Service, http://www.artandwork.us/i/art_work_web.pdf, accessed July 12, 2018; *Art Workers. Material Conditions and Labour Struggles in Contemporary Art Practice*, ed. by Minna Henriksson et al. (Berlin/Helsinki/Stockholm/Tallinn: Nordic-Baltic Art Workers' Network for Fair Pay, 2015), http://www.art-workers.org/download/ArtWorkers.pdf, accessed July 12, 2018.

SERVICE IN EXCHANGE

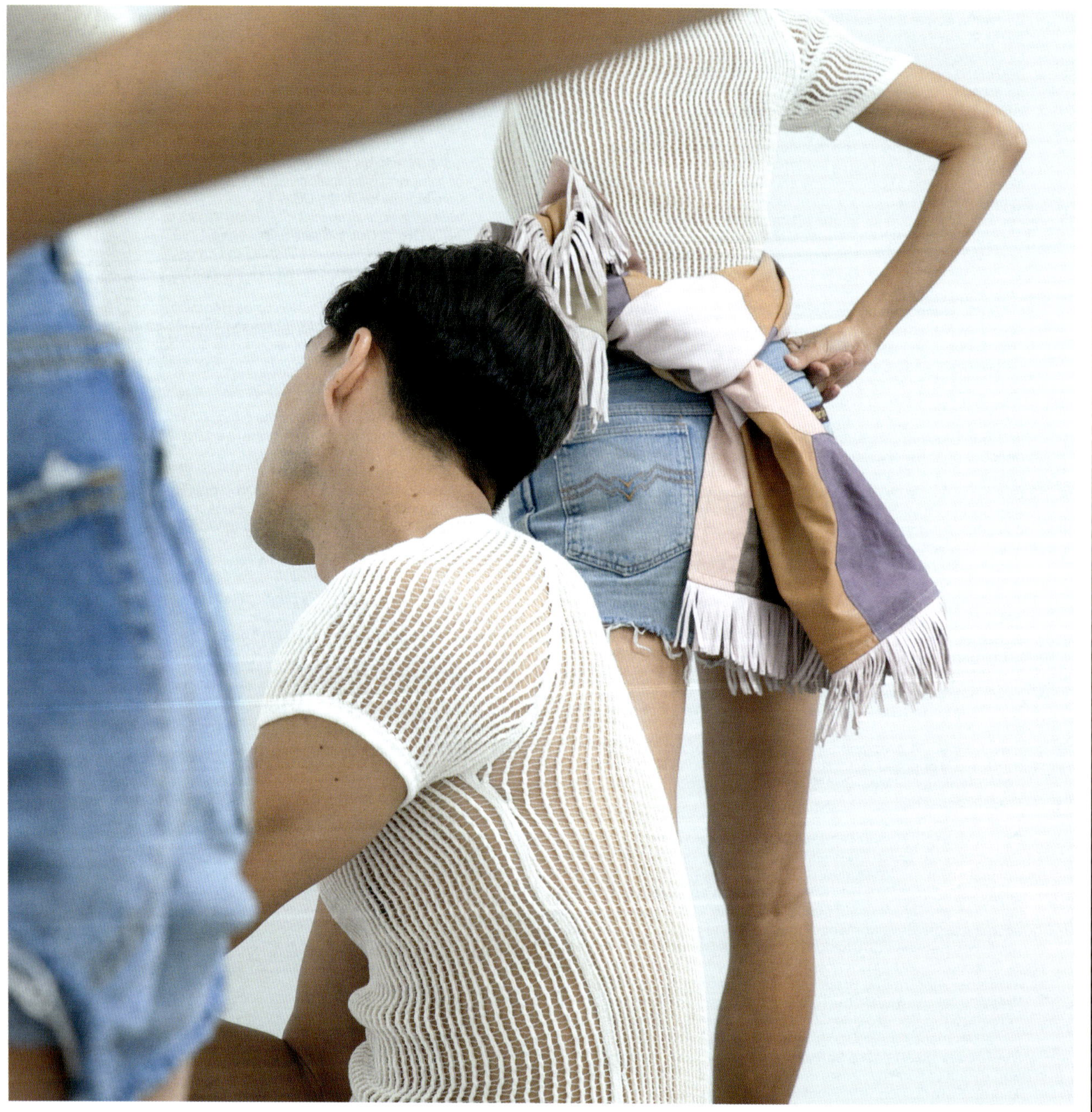

Adam Linder, *Footnote Service: Some Trade*, 2018. 3 dancers and a saxophonist. Courtesy of Adam Linder and Hannah Hoffman, Los Angeles.

Interview

Adam Linder
Hannes Loichinger

Adam Linder is a choreographer and dancer based in Los Angeles and Berlin. Through offering services that can be bought on an hourly basis, Linder conceives formats for dance outside the theatre, exposing his and his co-performers' "labor" to contracts and systems of exchange. For *Some Cleaning* (2013), one of his earliest works in the field of contemporary fine arts, a performer had been hired by the inviting institution to metaphorically clean the space through systematic movements, thus drawing attention to the relation of work and labor in the symbolic economy. Linder's reflection on his environments—whether that be a private gallery, an art institution, or a production center for contemporary performing arts—presents itself to be read in a tradition ranging from Yvonne Rainer's early dance pieces to Mierle Laderman Ukeles *Maintenance Works*. Recently he developed the project *Footnote Service: Some Trade* (2018) with Hannah Hoffman Gallery in Los Angeles. Instead of exchanging cash for services, the signatories enter into barter relations for the hiring of the "choreographic service," performed by three dancers and a saxophonist.

Hannes Loichinger: You recently had a show at Hannah Hoffman Gallery in Los Angeles. The announcement for *Footnote Service: Some Trade* included a quote from a lecture turned book by Diedrich Diederichsen: "The tendency, associated with the commodity, for exchange value to dominate in capitalist societies results in the fact that certain methods of transferring, aggregating, and storing time are better than others in terms of how practical they are in an exchange value context." The book is about systems of recording and reading out time and value. How does this relate to your work?

Adam Linder: In *Footnote* the performers hustle the walls. They track back and forth with their faces against the walls, loitering on the corners, angling for a prospect. I thought about this particular choreographic intention as a suspended come-on that embodies the passing of time whilst the subject waits for or attempts to solicit an exchange. It is all played out in a very detailed, low-key seductive, choreographic fiction that the performers materialize in real-time. Hearing Diedrich Diederichsen lecture on this topic made me think of *Some Trade* as having a very particular reading out of time in relation to exchange value. Importantly, the work is exchanged with a non-monetary trade so whoever wants to show / hire the work must offer a good or service for trade. It could be thought about as dance hustling the typical walls of art, or the performer hustling the expectation of delivering a performance, or a non-monetary relation hustling the place where monetary exchange is the status-quo of relations.

HL: Your practice also inspires others, referentially. Many texts base their arguments by pointing to your practice. At the same time, these references position your work within a lineage of institutional critique and "services" provided by artists or the cultural field at large. Do these writings influence your practice?

AL: Indeed my use of the service format or the form of the contract as an instrument of exchange has often led people to write about my work within these existing movements or discourses from art. Of course I have digested these i.e. aesthetics of administration or institutional critique or "performance" as a post-Fordist labor definition, but to be honest I do not think the writing has ever really hit directly on what is at stake in my work. Which is the fact that each service is proposed with a highly nuanced choreographic physicality that is integral to that individual service and what happens to that physicality over the course of a single hiring or over many hirings and many years. Writers have not talked about the fulfilment of these very skilled actions as being the crux of my service provision, because what my indispensable performers—Justin, Stephen, Brooke etc.—are doing is really detailed and virtuosic and this is why it is offered as a commodity on the market, not just because I call it a service. Much like how we would discuss exactly what a good physiotherapist had to do to fix an ankle problem, we would not waste too much time discussing how she or he structures or publicizes their fees or why they define themselves as a physiotherapist.

HL: Still, do you see yourself in a tradition of critical conceptual practices?

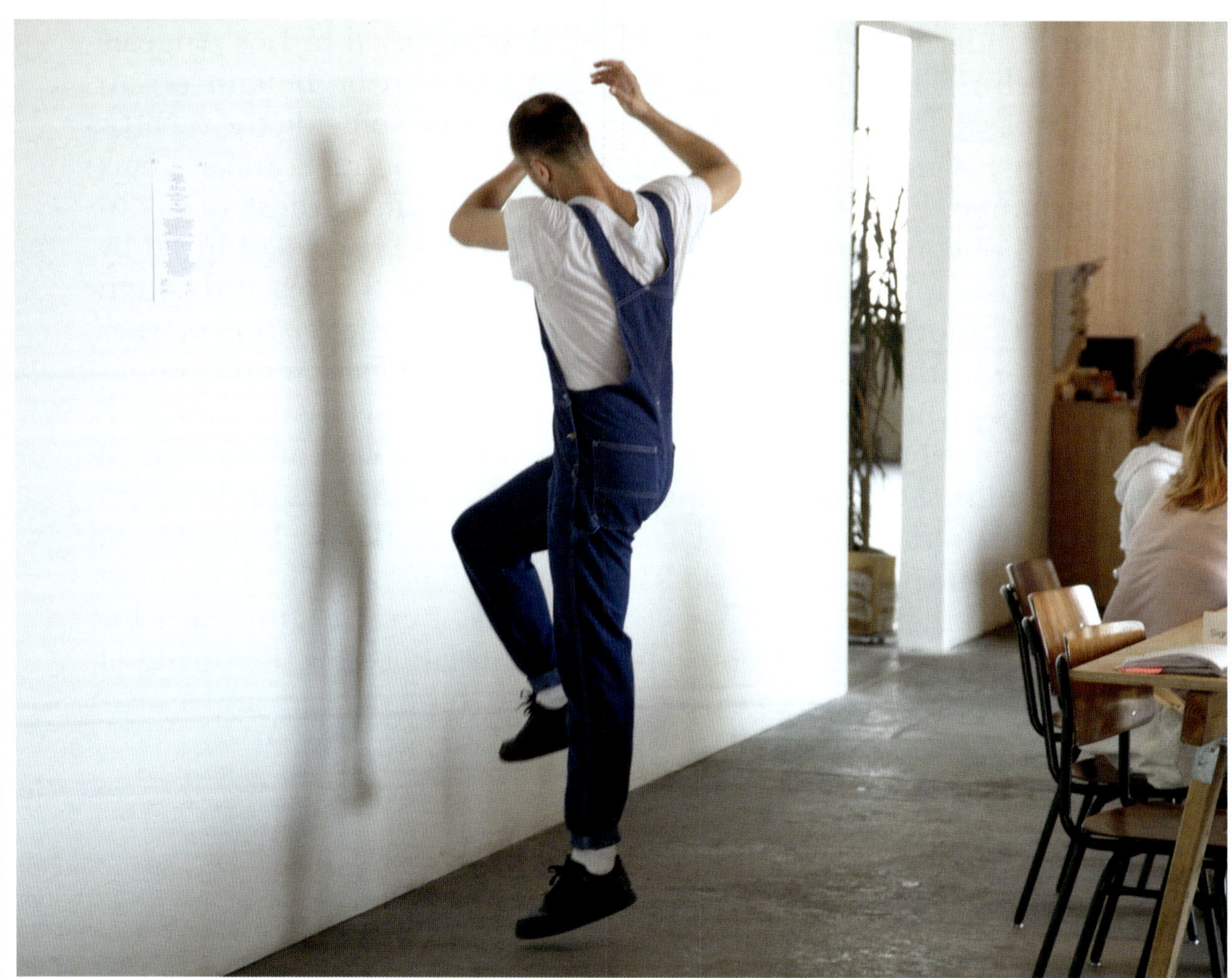

Adam Linder, *Choreographic Service #1: Some Cleaning*, 2013. Duration variable, 1 dancer. Pictured: Adam Linder at 356 Mission Rd., 2015.

AL: Perhaps. I guess that this is not necessarily for me to judge. My interest in criticality comes from its contrast with expressivity —to be both inside and outside—a productive friction. I do not believe I have witnessed many positions thinking conceptually about critical formats in dance whilst remaining indebted to technical virtuosity, seductive theatricality and color.

HL: Last year, Benjamin Buchloh penned a harsh critique of Anne Imhof's "Faust" at the Venice Biennial, reading it as the epitome of the cultural industry. Sabeth Buchmann recently wrote a more nuanced review of Imhof, pointing to the "refusal to communicate" and the performance as "a counter-model to the dominant logic of the feedback." However, Buchmann draws a possible connection between the "(self-)disciplining of performative bodies" and the "logic of (self-)evaluation" at the conjunction of "cultural, economic, and technological performance." She also describes the "double nature" of a performative praxis critical of institutions as "both symptomatic and capable of reflection." The question then arises: does the "double nature" of performance "(un)consciously cater[ ] to the modus operandi of the contemporary evaluation society?" How do you position yourself in relation to these discussions?

AL: If we are discussing a "double nature" of performance practices that have a critical reflexivity, then we would be inclined to discuss both of those natures. In this article that you refer to, Buchmann characterizes my work *Some Cleaning* as hinging upon the breaks taken from the physical labor to discuss the nature of the work and its contractual conditions with a viewer. But what is this physicality? What does it look like? Where does it go in the room? How is it sequenced? What is the nature of the choreographic vocabulary? Is it referring to something? How can we characterize the focus or intention of the performer within the act? How long does the act go for? If the work is reflexive, what are the aspects within which this reflexivity is nested—both in terms of content and context. In *Some Cleaning* I use this conversational mode not as the crux of the work, but as choreographic punctuation, one that breaks-up the highly representational, wryly devotional relation to mimesis, which is a very particular form, one that is at odds with the "performed authenticity" that most visual art performance has been imbued with—I mean dusting a wall with a faggy-ass wrist!

The articles mentioned are Benjamin H.D. Buchloh's "Rock Paper Scissors" in *Artforum* (September 2017), p. 278–91 and Sabeth Buchmann, "Feed Back: Performance in the Evaluation Society" in *Texte zur Kunst* (June 2018), p. 34–53.

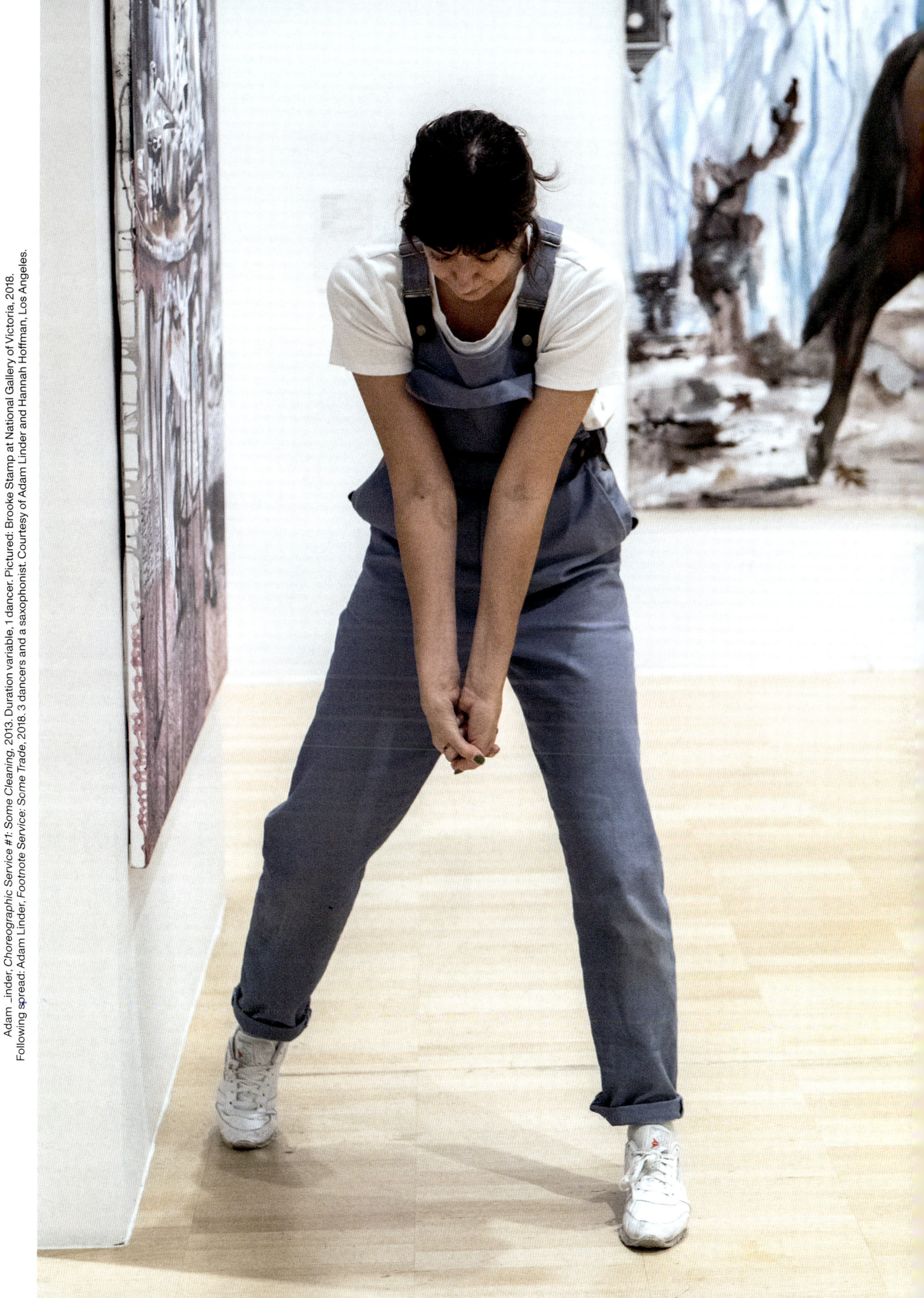

Adam Linder, *Choreographic Service #1: Some Cleaning*, 2013. Duration variable, 1 dancer. Pictured: Brooke Stamp at National Gallery of Victoria, 2018.
Following spread: Adam Linder, *Footnote Service: Some Trade*, 2018. 3 dancers and a saxophonist. Courtesy of Adam Linder and Hannah Hoffman, Los Angeles.

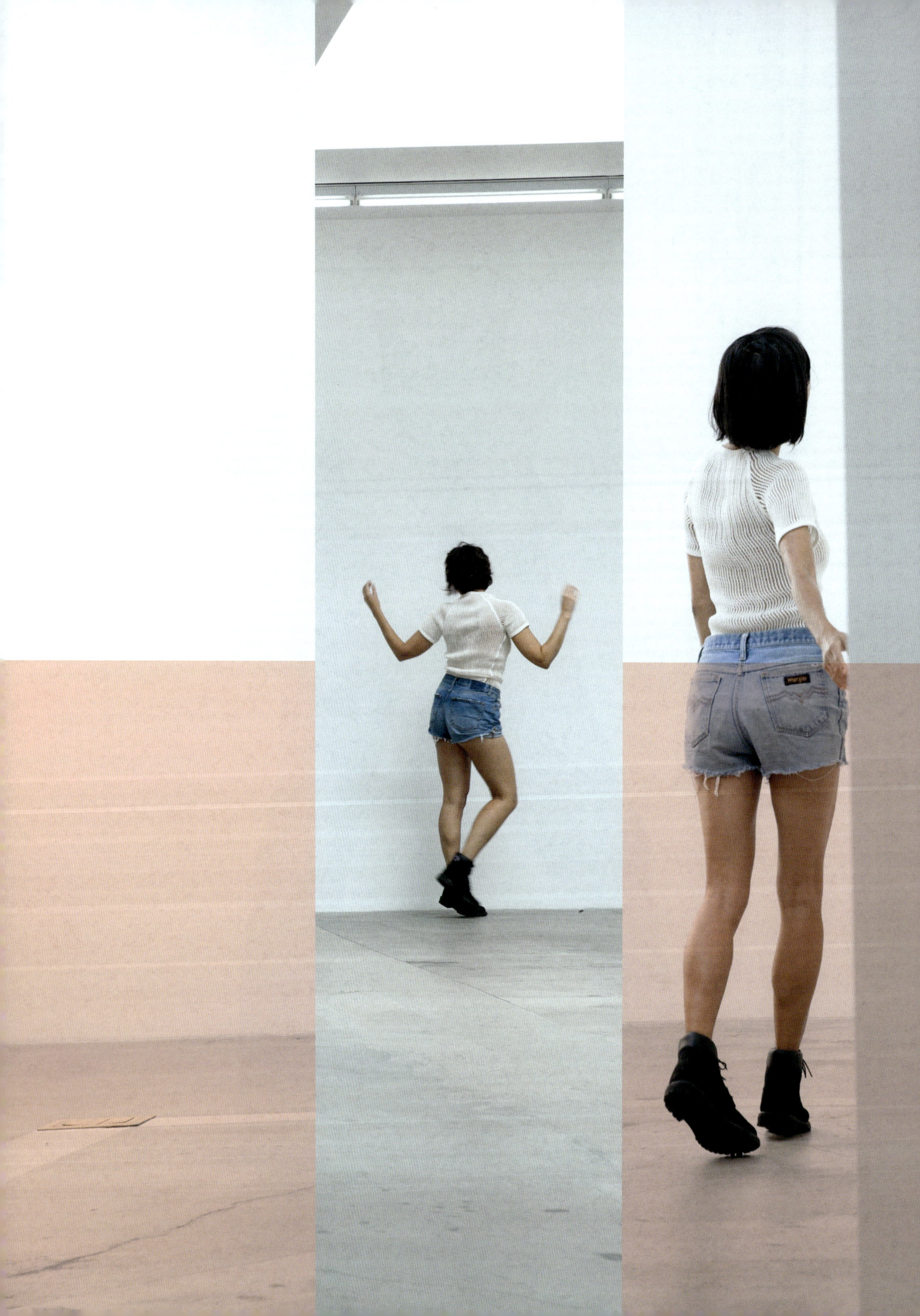

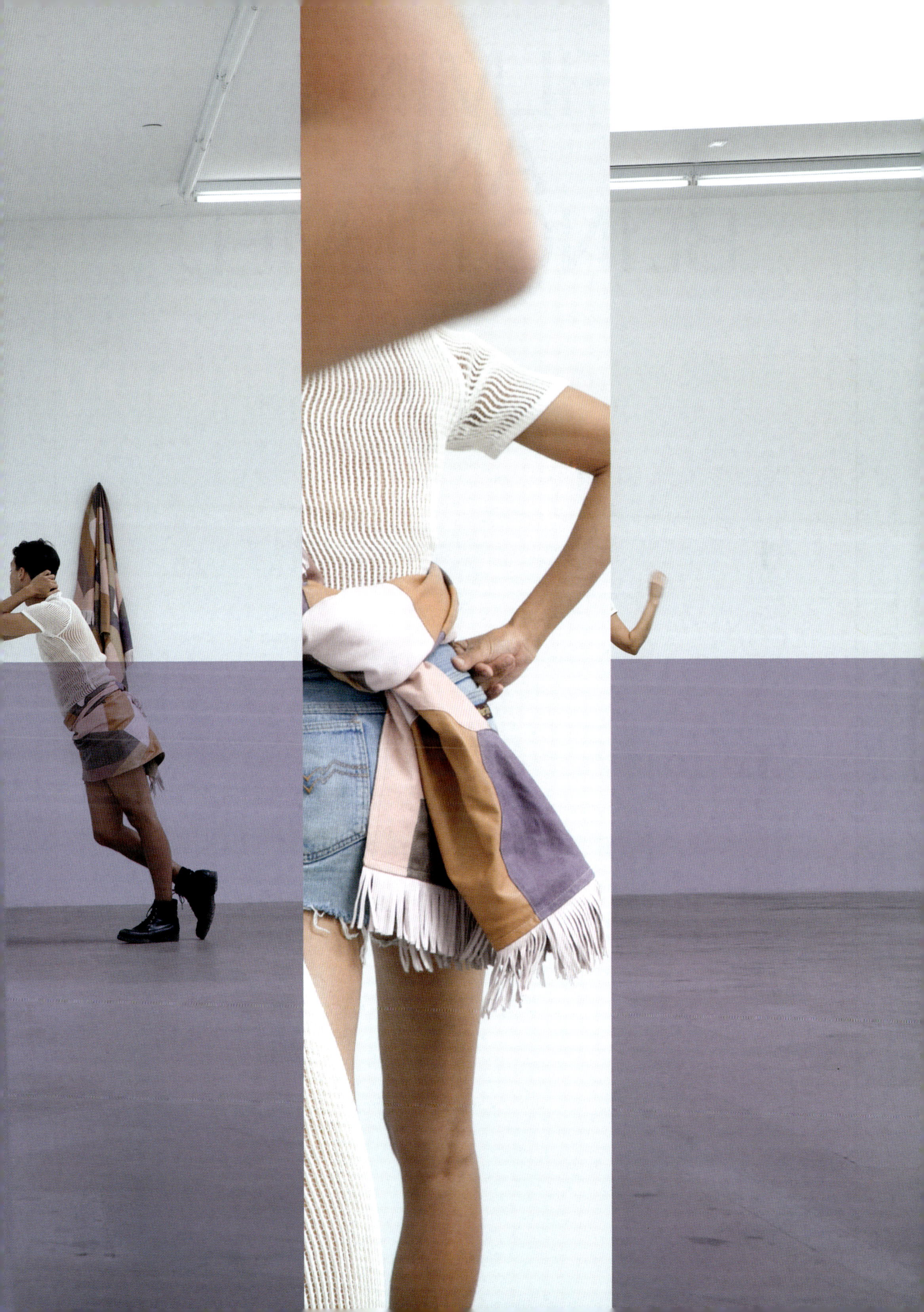

FILMING AND BEING FILMED

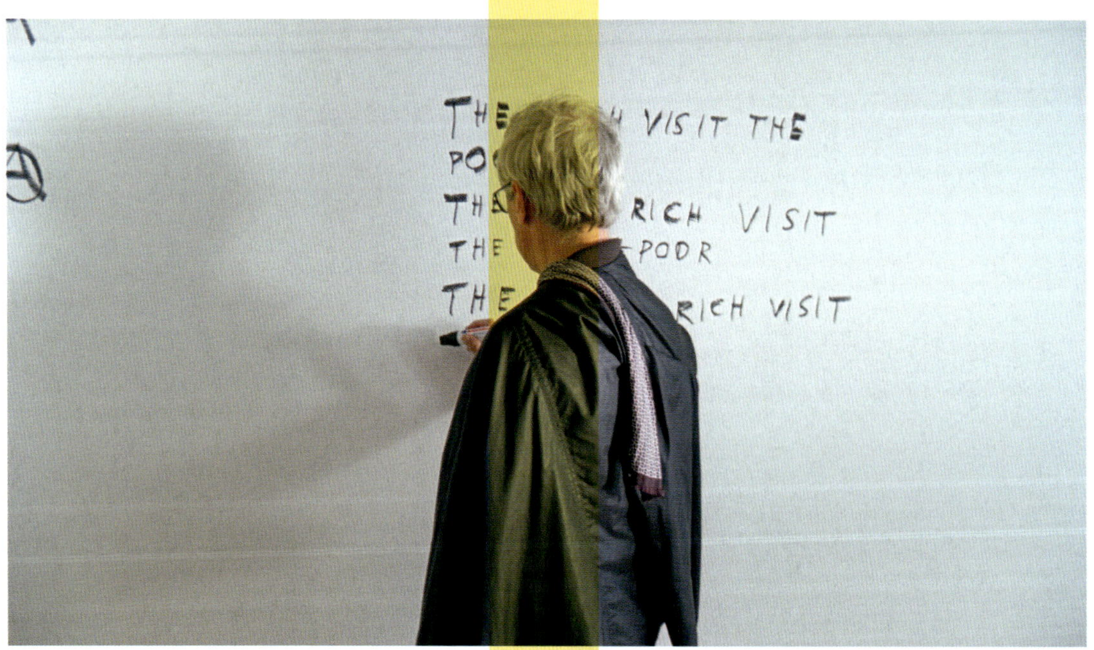

Karl's Perfect Day, 2017, 94 min., directed by Rirkrit Tiravanija

Conversation

Karl Holmqvist
Tobias Kaspar
Inka Meißner
Rirkrit Tiravanija

Earlier this year in spring, Karl Holmqvist, Tobias Kaspar, Inka Meißner, and Rirkrit Tiravanija met up in Rirkrit's Berlin apartment to discuss his new film, *Karl's Perfect Day* (2017), being friends in the art world, and working together in general.

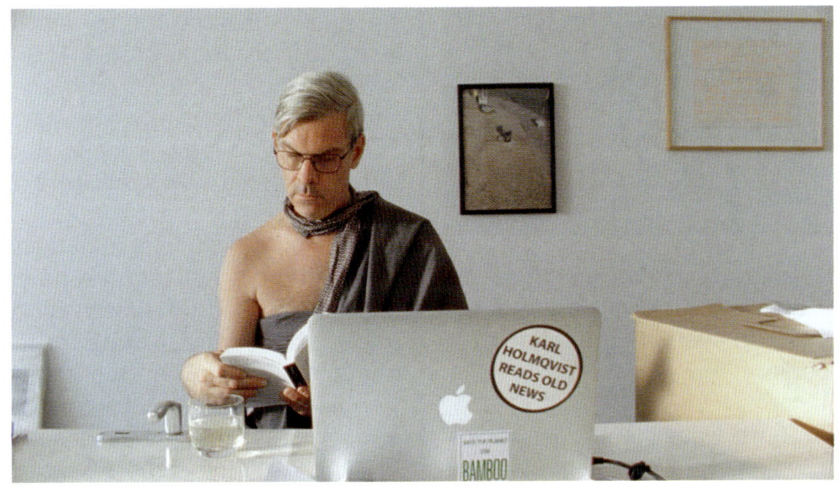

Karl's Perfect Day, 2017, 94 min., directed by Rirkrit Tiravanija

Rirkrit: You want to make coffee? You guys want coffee?

Tobias: With pleasure.

Karl: What kind of coffee?

R: Keto. I'm on this fat diet. I only eat fat. So…

Inka: There's this coffee made with butter.

R: Yes, that's Keto Coffee. It's made with ghee and basically coconut oil.

I: Yeah. It actually works. Lars did it with the blender…

R: Well, maybe we should do the Keto Coffee. You can have a taste. It will keep you warm. Maybe you need to be used to it. But anyway, you basically change from sugar power to fat power. And then there's all these health concerns that comes along with it. It's good for diabetics and actually also good for the metabolism.

T: Rirkrit, you recently finished the film *Karl's Perfect Day*. Where and when did the film premiere?

R: July 2017. I didn't really make it for the art-system, in the sense that I wasn't making it to put it in a museum or a gallery. I tried to put it in the film industry, which is not so easy if you don't have a real connection.

T: Do you have a professional film distributor on your side?

R: No, the person I work with in Mexico, my kind of partner / producer, he's the one who has been selling it to different people. Partly already when we were fundraising, you know. We sent it to different possible funders in the film system, so some of them knew about it already. But no. And I'm not pushing it. It's more like somebody saw it and they say something to somebody and then they ask for it.

T: When did you, Rirkrit and Karl, start thinking about this film?

R: My approach for this film was based on my first film, which was also kind of a documentary portrait of a particular person.

T: The film about the Chiang Mai rice farmer?

I DIDN'T REALLY MAKE IT FOR THE ART-SYSTEM, IN THE SENSE THAT I WASN'T MAKING IT TO PUT IT IN A MUSEUM OR A GALLERY.

R: Yes. That film was a very small production, kind of like a fairytale. The filming was done in eight days, in two different seasons: four days and four days. We just followed the rice farmer around and everything that happened in the film was just happening in front of us. The film made itself in that way. The initial first four days of shooting were supposed to be a test run, but when we went back and looked at it there was great stuff in it. Afterwards we went back and shot in the rainy season

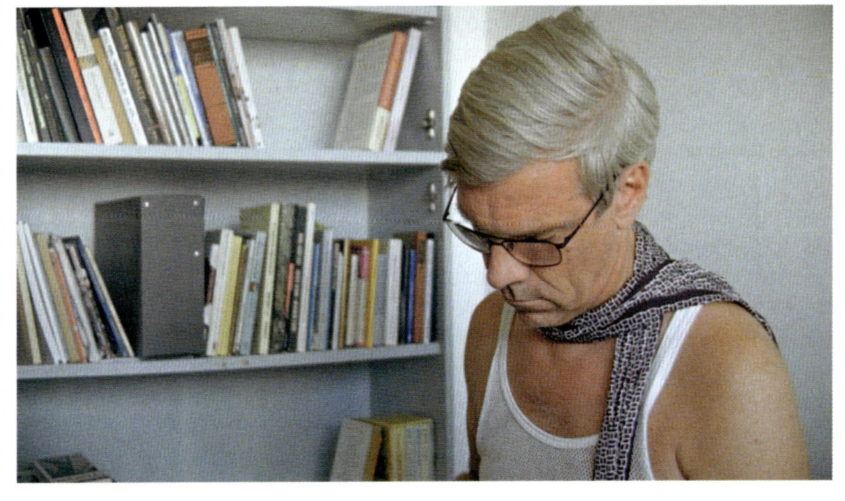

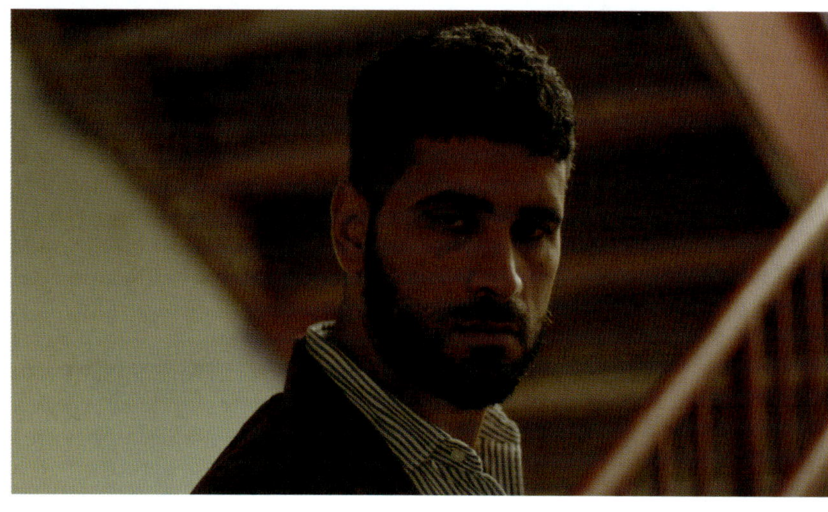

again and got more great stuff, but when we put it together, I decided to switch the seasons. So it starts off with the rainy season, partly because I had some structure in mind that follows a certain logic, and that logic only really started on the second shoot, because the first one was a test. I really didn't plan anything.

THE IDEA WAS TO MAKE A FILM ABOUT KARL'S PERFECT DAY—FROM WHEN HE WAKES UP TO WHEN HE GOES TO SLEEP.

The idea was to make a film about Karl's perfect day—from when he wakes up to when he goes to sleep. I didn't know what he would think, but I've known Karl for a long time. On the other hand I had no idea what Karl's perfect day would be. We shot some scenes in New York. He went for a jog through Central Park. He did some things I never knew he did like jogging and exercises. It was kind of a shock to me. Then Karl wrote a whole kind of script. Like a scenario. He wrote down what he would want his day to be like.

When I said to Karl, "perfect day," I really thought he would wake up in Berlin and have coffee in Paris and he would jog in central park, because in a way the perfect day could be the perfect place. It could be anywhere. Also it's supposed to be kind of fictional anyway, but Karl is too modest a guy so everything happened in Berlin.

K: There were these possibilities of doing extravagant things, but I was thinking that this is also going to somehow define my person to others and it's quite personal. And I know that if I do this kind of crazy thing, then the rest of my life is going to seem so boring. Everyday is a perfect day in a way. So I'm going to my favorite restaurant, I'm going to my favorite bar, I'm jogging in my favorite jogging pants and whatever. So that was perfect.

R: There were moments like going to Hannah Höch's house, which was something you wanted to do but never did until in the film. Or meeting Arto Lindsay—the musician having a cameo in the film. So in a way there were things Karl wanted to do but hadn't done. Every perfect day is staged eventually, even if it's all the usual things simply compressed into one day.

T: How much time passed between the initial idea and the final result?

R: My things take a long time just because I have no money and I don't go to get money really. Then at some point, you've got some money and that's how we start. But yeah, it's a long process. But when we shot it, it was really like a week.

I studied film in school; people don't know that. I actually have shots in my head, so I pretty much know what I want. I don't try to shoot more than one take. I let people rehearse but I wouldn't shoot more takes. In that sense, it doesn't take much time, it's more just organizing people and things together.

T: You mentioned this behind the camera moment as being a very social moment and that it is important for you how you choreograph the team that works with you on the film. It's almost like your cooking sessions which are social gatherings although filming is more controlled. Do you have a personal relationship with everyone on set?

R: Yes and no. For the first portrait film there were three people shooting. But my vision of Karl's perfect day was a bit more cinematic, so we needed more people. My producer actually didn't pull it together. It was quite difficult. The film didn't have enough

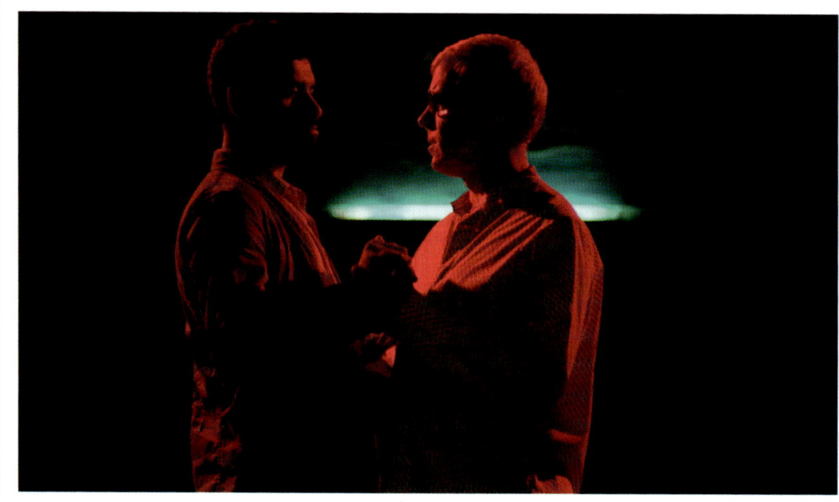

Rirkrit Tiravanija, *skip the bruising of the eskimos to the exquisite words vs. if I give you a penny you can give me a pair of scissors*, 2017, 94 min., directed by Rirkrit Tiravanija

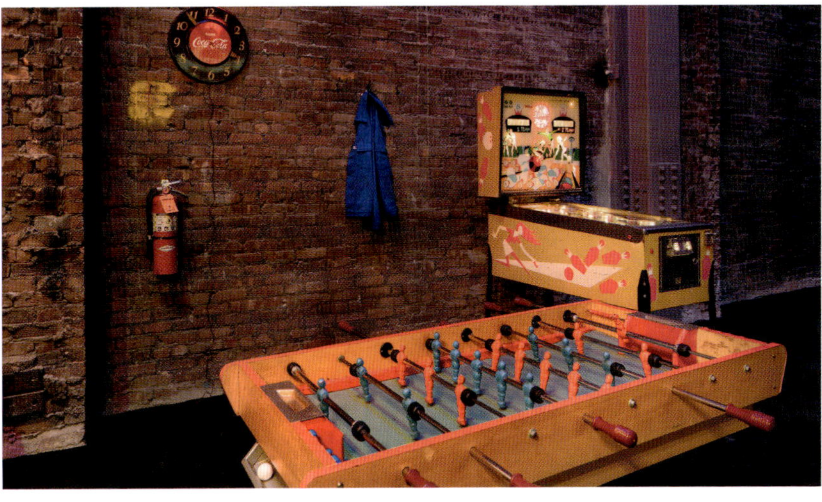

money and he was arranging it as if it would play out like my first film. Then, of course, I knew certain things wouldn't work and they didn't. So we had to reshoot some scenes at the end.

I: What was the difference between shooting with someone you didn't know and shooting with someone who's very familiar?

R: Well, it's not like I give Karl a lot of direction. He's already directing himself because it's his story in a way. So he choses the places and the way he wants to do it. In that sense, he was kind of self-directing and we were just on the other side. From my experience everything was quite easy except dealing with the producer, who was this friend of mine who I felt

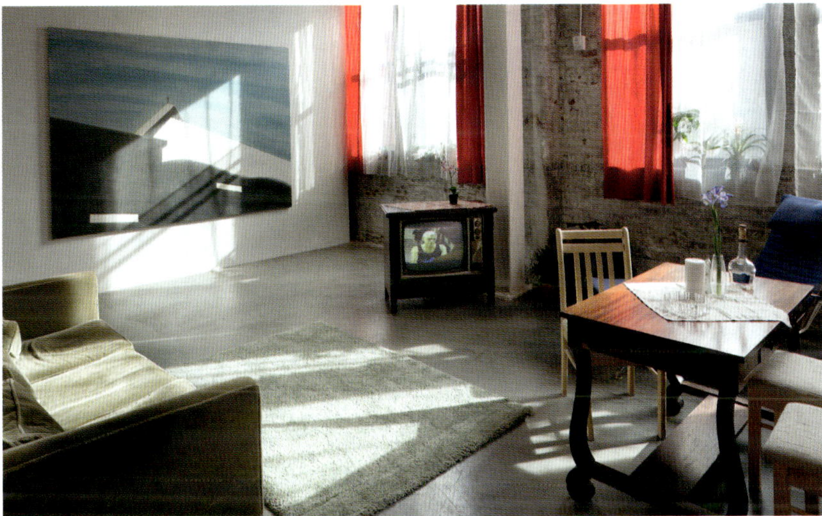

wasn't really understanding my vision. But we also got through it.

I also see this movie as part of a trilogy. There's one more film that I'm planning to make and the approach is about focusing on a particular person at a particular moment. In *Karl's Perfect Day* we have a lot of other characters involved.

T: Friends?

R: Yeah. Most of them were friends so that was fine. The only odd person out was the boyfriend who he meets in the bar.

T: That wasn't planned?

R: No, that was planned but it wasn't somebody that we knew. Originally Karl wanted Radcliffe… What's his name?

K: Daniel.

R: … Daniel Radcliffe as the boy he meets in the bar. That's the actor I would try to reach but we couldn't get him. Then Karl came up with another person he didn't really know, but thought would be good. And now they're like Spencer Tracy and Katharine Hepburn because they appear in other films together.

THE PICKUP SCENE ITSELF WAS LIKE TWO MINUTES [LAUGHING]. IT WAS JUST LIKE, "HEY, WANNA COME?"

K: The pick-up scene was very good. There was a traveling camera. It was shot in Berlin's bar Möbel Olfe, so they had to change the whole floor so that the camera could travel on a rail and they worked on the lighting for hours. The pickup scene itself was like two minutes [Laughing]. It was just like, "Hey, wanna come?" But I think it works in the film.

R: Do you want some tea?

I: Thanks, yes. Where did you meet the first time?

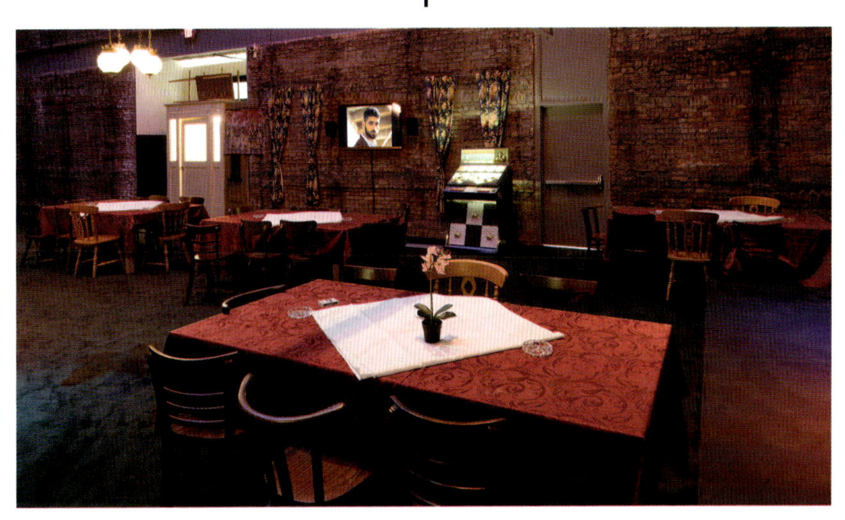

Rirkrit Tiravanija, *skip the bruising of the eskimos to the exquisite words vs. if I give you a penny you can give me a pair of scissors*, September 24–October 28, 2017, Gavin Brown's Enterprise, Harlem, NYC

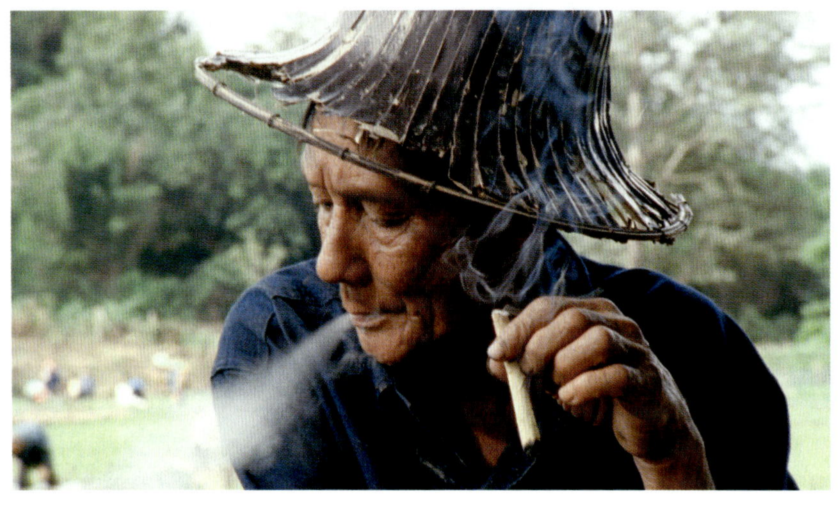

K: 1990, I think.

R: Yes, in New York. I always thought back then that Karl was more of a writer and poet kind of thing, you know.

AS AN ARTIST YOU SPEND A LOT OF TIME ALONE AND THAT'S ACTUALLY QUITE SATISFYING, BUT MAYBE NOT SO INTERESTING FOR PEOPLE TO WATCH.

T: Before this film, have there been other ways of working together or using each other's work, besides having an on-going conversation?

R: No, not from my point of view. We have this on-going project or something that doesn't end but it's a kind of constant conversation. And things take their own path. Like after meeting Arto Lindsay in the film, you went to Brazil, right, Karl?

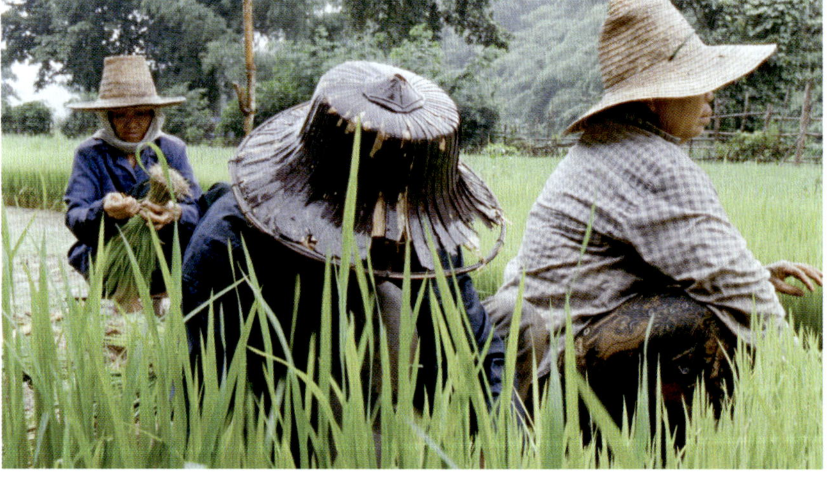

K: Yes.

R: And you made a recording together, so it starts to expand a bit.

T: And Arto was someone that you worked with before?

R: Yeah, he's somehow a friend and we've collaborated on other things, and I also like doing that because Arto doesn't really consider himself as an artist though he is, even if he's not perceived that way. I don't think Karl was perceived that way for a long time either, but they're there and they're doing things in a way that is interesting to me. Right?

K: Yes. I was just thinking about Arto, what he does, which is great. I was always very impressed by Arto's parade so we could have squeezed that in. But enough was enough. As an artist you spend a lot of time alone and that's actually quite satisfying, but maybe not so interesting for people to watch. So there are moments between loneliness and social life—too much social life stresses me. I need to have my own time.

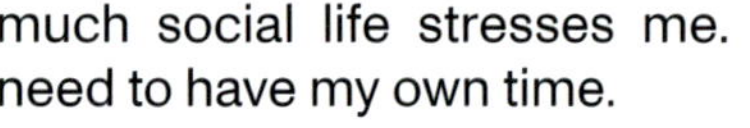

T: You also mentioned this notion of Kreuzberg and maybe that's also why you decided not to have breakfast in Rio and dinner in New York, but stay in the very small daily places that you visit every day when you're in Berlin?

K: Kotti is the most dangerous place in Berlin, there's a lot of drugs and petite crimes and stuff going on. I was a big fan of *Lung Neaw Visits His Neighbors* (2011), Rirkrit's first film, and after the kind of time travel or time expansion that happens with the farmer and his friends in the jungle I kind of felt it should be possible to have something like that. This time not in the rice fields in Chiang Mai but

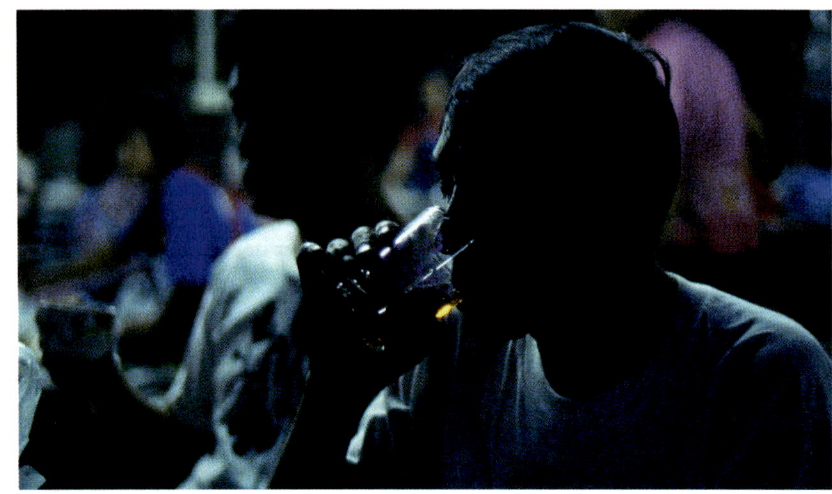

Lung Neaw Visits His Neighbors, 2012, 154 min., directed by Rirkrit Tiravanija

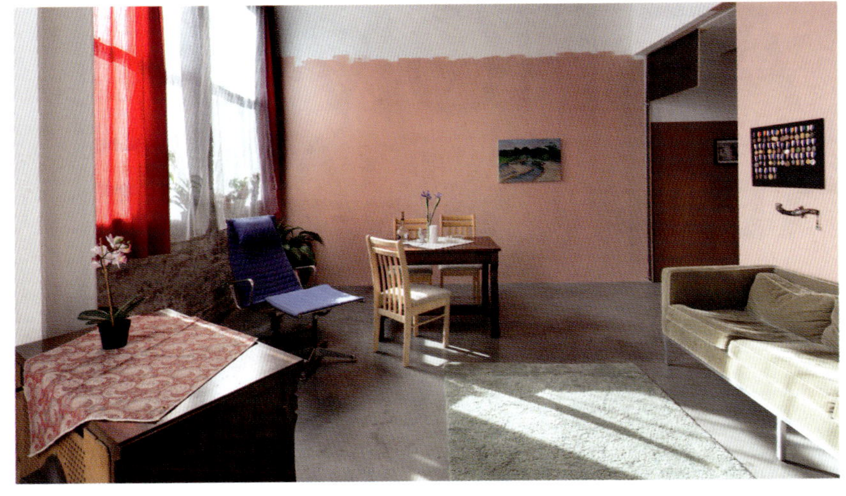

Rirkrit Tiravanija, *skip the bruising of the eskimos to the exquisite words vs. if I give you a penny you can give me a pair of scissors*, September 24–October 28, 2017, Gavin Brown's Enterprise, Harlem, NYC

in the middle of Kreuzberg, so that was somehow part of it and just kind of walking around discovering something that leads to something else. There is this idea of stretching and expanding time etc.

T: Rirkrit, you worked with the film *Angst essen Seele auf* (1974) before, right?

R: Yeah, the first time I worked with that film was probably in the bar in Cologne in '95 with Esther Shipper. I made this bar—where was that?

K: At Friesenwall?

R: At the time Esther had a storefront and she wanted artists to do the window, but it was like a shop. I didn't really understand so I made a bar which was based on this Fassbinder film. It was a time with a lot racial tension and violence going on, just like now.

I: In re-enacting the Fassbinder film, did you also consider the behind the scenes hierarchies between the artists?

R: What do you mean with hierarchy?

I: I think looking back to the days Fassbinder made his films this became a topic; the implicit and explicit tensions and relations between the director and the actors; even more so because they were this group of artists and friends.

R: I'm more concerned about the actors than directing them. To me it's kind of like curating, I take care of the artist because I feel like that's more important. The artist feels good, the show will look good. So I was more interested in making sure that everyone was happy with what they were doing. I usually work with people locally but it was quite tough since we only had a limited time because we literally finished shooting two days before the show opened.

K: The day after we finished shooting in NY I left to fly to Münster to look at the Skulptur Projekte. I was super tired and the next morning when I woke up in the hotel bed I was like, "Where is the camera?!" I'd been doing it for so many days.

R: It's like when you've been on a ship and you still feel like you're on the ship, even though you put a foot on land. You're still moving with the thing.

T: Unemployed actor; "I'm in between roles."

I: But would it be a preferred state of being? I mean the possibility to slip in and out of this situation of being in front of the camera again and again.

THE ARTIST FEELS GOOD, THE SHOW WILL LOOK GOOD. SO I WAS MORE INTERESTED IN MAKING SURE THAT EVERYONE WAS HAPPY WITH WHAT THEY WERE DOING.

K: I don't know. It's always very embarrassing. It's exciting and it's embarrassing and it's exciting. I think we're privileged as artists to get to do a lot of different things and hopefully get some interest in it.

R: We've answered all questions?

T: Yes. Only this one: What happened at Paris Bar?

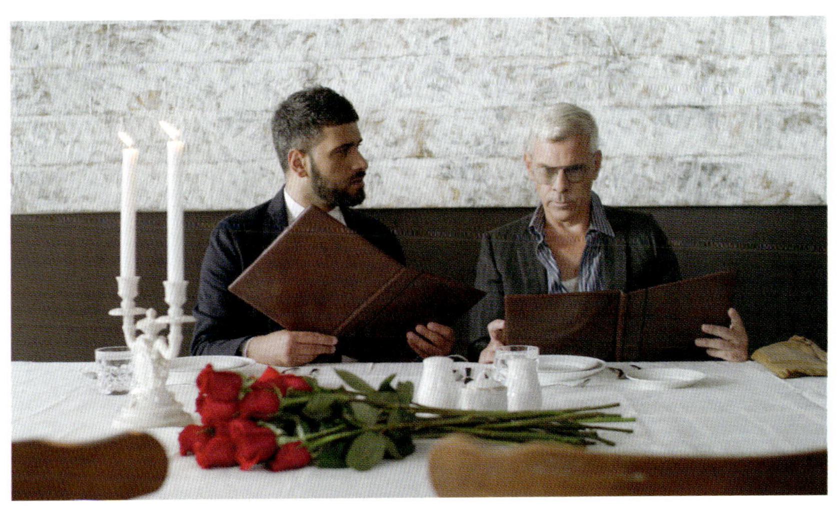

ART AT HOME: MILDRED'S LANE

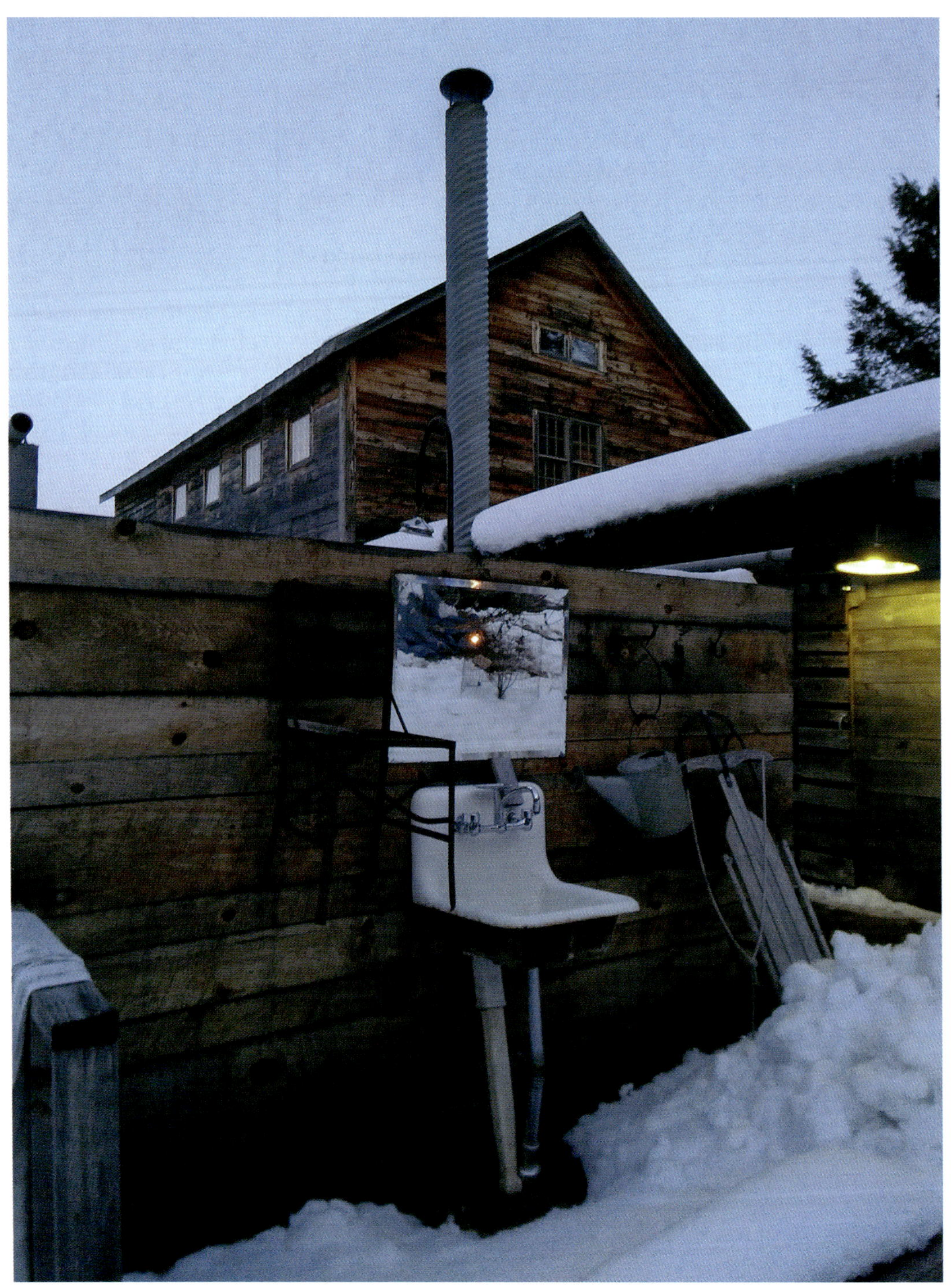

Mildred's Lane, Beach Lake (Pennsylvania); Photo: Tue Greenfort, 2018

Text

Julia Moritz

Young Mildred could not have known other. The woods, the critters, the kin. She was born in that house. That was at the very beginning of this story, at the very beginning of the twentieth century. The house is older. It has seen most of the previous century rushing by. Or has it? Tucked deep in the upper Delaware River Valley, it oversees a steep 96 acres lot of land. It's quiet there. In the winter, you can hear a snowflake drop. This is northeastern Pennsylvania. Close, very close, on the other side of the river begins New York. First come more woods and rural land, and more land, like Walden or Woodstock. Then come the affluent small towns, the aggrieved suburbs, the outer boroughs, the big city. Old Mildred never saw it. Destined to farm until she died aged 86. The house was left empty. Winds whirling through the windows.

FIRST COME MORE WOODS AND RURAL LAND, AND MORE LAND, LIKE WALDEN OR WOODSTOCK.

Leaves falling in Central Park. Mark goes there often. Drawn to things living, then falling, then—what? He sets out to become an artist. Morgan feels the same. Or Mark feels like Morgan? Not quite perhaps, she has a thing for fashion too, and people dig it, quite a bit. In her few hours off, she too strolls through the park. Looking for colors? Looking for life. Not for Mark. But there he is. Here they are. Lights on in the big city. He starts school at the Whitney, not the museum just off the park, but the artists program downtown, where everybody hangs out, Nils and Renee too. They drink, debate, display, design, detour, do well. Music on in the high life. And yet, the friends are united by yet another craving: the walks, the park, the leaves. They find peace even further. In country houses upstate, or even a bit further. They find space. The house is empty.

It's the end. Not of our story, but of the century, of Mildred's century. It's 1998 when Mark Dion, Renee Green, Nils Norman and J. Morgan Puett get hold of the house. They call it "Mildred's Lane," in memory of the woman in the woods. At the end of that century, the idea of the household proper seems exhausted however. At least for our funky friends. It's an opportunity for them to merge lives and works in a more inspiring, more sustainable manner—more challenging manner, that is, for sure. Snow falling, years passing, the lives walk different ways, the challenge remains. Morgan is up for it. She has not known other. And yet she has seen enough, enough not to return but to retreat from most private practice. She makes the house hers, but not hers alone. The others are always there. The woods, the critters, the child. And the friends, some old and some new, and newer and newer.

A home is a site of harm. A home is a city of harmony. Between those poles operates "the Lane" (as they say). A "lane" being some sort of way, meandering somewhere between private and public space already. An extended domesticity. As is Mildred's. Because what's different about it is that it operates from within the sphere of domesticity. It was, is, and remains a home, first and foremost. A home, though, that takes the very nature of home as a site of opportunity to revisit and rearrange the problems of home: namely the deep-rooted division of labor; the capitalist devaluation of the domestic type of labor, that is, the reproduction of workforce—the family; the gendering of the different types of labor; and the structural inequalities that arise from such division, devaluation, and allocation. Cultural concepts of harmony—from the supposedly purely aesthetic to political propaganda—form the social glue at home. Full house at Mildred's.

Broad brushstrokes for a universe of oppression, sublimation, and subtraction; for the harm done at home, done by householding, as we know it—the economy, stupid. A sensitive subject still. Sensitive to site, the answers must be. Here comes the service, and its peculiar pitfalls at home. Remember this: "immaterial labor" is a fantasy. Tertiarization, the rise of the so-called service sector, is obliterating the binary code on which capitalism stands; through which capitalism looks out; with which capitalism hears, manufactures, breathes. It is organ/ized: private (0) – public (1). Remember also: suppression must micromanage, the helical threads weave a tight tissue; wounds bandaged, windows curtained. You may want, or having been made to want, to think yourself a "prosumer" of whatever. However, such simultaneity implied within the labor of service makes you a producer and consumer even more, not less: a heightened state of privatization, with no capacity for the formation of a critical public subject, let alone a public sphere.

REMEMBER THIS: "IMMATERIAL LABOR" IS A FANTASY.

But what, if domesticity itself must be serviced, in order to exist? Assume the harmony of sedentary existence as having been installed to leverage the harms of nomadic life. Two souls, alas, are housed within this: the breast and breath of art. The New York State soul of Mildred's settler heritage and Morgan's artful mobility. The transitory New York City soul of Morgan's émigré desire and Mildred Lane's cultural homestead. The relationship of Art and Home (the two institutionalized nouns proper, and their interstice) is more complex still. Complicated by modernity's main objection to all things useful in art, their favorite domain of functional disinterest. And then again, if you think art and home, you think pretty pictures on the walls, or small sculpture on the shelves, or film on the screens. Simple as that, and true enough for the remaining 99% of art; or even for the 1% who may own the original, who mandate the public collection houses to drag the rest into public light and enlightened discourse; or to commission straight from the private (economy) artist studio (home); or even to drag the whole artist/ic subject/ivity into (nomadic) residence, perhaps the most crucial of late (we wish) cultural capitalist paradox. Here, like elsewhere, it is domesticity itself that is serviced by art, in fact, and in the many faces of both of the terms and their terms. Culture produces the cave to be painted.

Take, for example, the renewed mission statement of Mildred's Lane for their twentieth anniversary (2018), at the beginning of the twenty-first century, and the related collaborative projects:

> "At Mildred's Lane, we nurture, enhance and collaborate with this landscape. At the intersections of the organized historical periods and disciplines living side-by-side are the emergent and boundless poetics of playful 'houseness;' a transhistorical vessel. Mildred's Lane as a think tank, residency program, and makin/doing workshops explore archaeological methodologies with tools to understand more deeply the physical site. Artist and other cultural producers with a core concern for history, contemporary art, archaeology, and the natural sciences are brought to bear in this curiosity landscape of vernacular structures, wildlife and events."[1]

Two semi-conclusions can be drawn from this:

I. The notion of value must be taken into our art-home-equation. According to the project's policy, "service" clearly denominates the force field between use and value. The neologism "houseness" is being introduced: not simply the state of being"at home," but, in a larger than life situation, "at house." A situationism of practice springs forth from such grounding, to nurture and to enhance. It is a situationism of the site and geography, rather than of time and history. The landscape becomes valuable as a collaborator, a potential co-laborer in the production of value.

The underlying mantra of site specificity, however, reveals the historical situatedness of the project, and furthermore, that of value as such. No physical site and its apparent productivity without a discursive site (and vice versa). Young Mildred, the Lane, must have known, quite evidently, the 1990s: the heyday of neo-pop relational aesthetics and neo-conceptual artistic research taking place in New York. In a sort of self-fulfilling prophecy, amidst the racket of speculation on value—be it "intrinsic" or critical artistic value, or cultural capital already transferred to other means of investment—"producers" here still make "workshops," their two souls sweating in Mildred's shop-window displays (in neighboring Narrowsburg).

II. The notion of critique enters the arena. Introduced by the historically sited jargon of "project" practice, the founders, participants, and public of Mildred's Lane—as an example for contemporary artistic work around the notion of domesticity—more or less openly adhere to the type of institution-critical practice emerging from New York's Whitney Independent Studies Program and its alumni canonization. For the institution of Institutional Critique, "service" is a household name, at the latest since Andrea Fraser and Helmut Draxler's 1994 project of the same title, which drew in many of the then cutting-edge critical thinkers, and revolved around processes of de-/valorization.[2]

PRACTICE IN THE GREEK IS "PRAKTIKOS," MEANING "FIT FOR BUSINESS."

The questioning of the value of a work of art leads to the questioning of private property: the artwork as an object—or service, for that matter—to be owned, on the one hand; the private pleasures at stake in their use, on the other. The pitfalls of ephemeral practice were the lessons to be learned, like Land Art's grand gestures of escape, their imminent privacy, and their almost instant recuperation by media—mainly printed matter, and video. And it was artists like Mark Dion and Nils Norman who spearheaded the '90s' resurgence of combatting property with Nature—knowing, however, (as indicated) of the institutionalization of the woods within and outside the city. In a pre-modernist move, the use side of things had to be strengthened, to weaken certain traces of capitalist value in art.

And here we are back at the house.

Some signposts for a journey into the etymological unconscious:

A. ECONOMY

That *"eco"* as *"oikos"* means household is no news to many.
That *"nomos"* means law is good to know too.
The rules of the game of domesticity we have seen.
And yet the *"oikos"*-household of "Mildred's" aims at unsettling more than eco/nomy.

B. ECOLOGY

That *"eco"* as *"oikos"* means household we have seen.
That *"logos"* means word is good to know too.
The nature of discourse is no news to many.
And still the *"oikos"*-household of "the Lane" aims at unearthing more than eco/logy.

C. PRACTICE

Ultimately, the concept of private property, complicated by the project's notion of service as a forcefield between use and value, also affects the meaning of practice: that Mildred's Lane is an artistic project does NOT mean that the house is not the property of Mark Dion and Morgan Puett. It does NOT mean that the artistic practice pursued by Puett does not service anything or anybody else. The creative uses of the house by its founders and friends DO create symbolic and, ultimately, economic value. The project lives off participatory practice. Practice in the Greek is *"praktikos,"* meaning "fit for business." And yet the house is no business as usual, no nightmare of participation.[3] It nurtures a domestic sphere that services the many. And this includes (quite in synch with the latest shift in today's participatory paradigm) all non-human agency at the lot.

The law of this household (its economy) rests on the discourse, not about, but WITH nature, and encompasses the delicate meaning of this, too.

D. DOMESTICITY

Remains this problem with re/cognition. However much a practice or project may wish to merge with it's eco-social environment, we need those margins in order to look, and enter. It is the "domus," the house, which provides the frame all art needs. As in normative domesticity too, the frame functions as a manager of relations. It is the nature of "Mildred's" relations—towards the outside, a rather clearly definable outside (of the lot), as well as within, those very walls—that differs from domesticity as usual. And it does so precisely by giving the word to the woods. And so Mark branched off, Morgan took root, I temporarily nest, others flock seasonally. In sum, Mildred's Lane seems a site of affection, a habitat for conceptualizing the variations of being.

Too pretty a picture?

Stones cracking in Central Park. Bob, too, goes there often. That's how his wife, Nancy, used to call him. His real name is Robert. But you already knew that. Because you've seen him take that picture[4], for some other magazine. He already has had quite a career. Nancy and Bob have been roaming the deserts and swamps, salt lakes and dump sites. And still keep coming back to the park. It's those off-hours for others that are so productive for their kind of art. Struggling for an outside to the inside, half-heartedly though, you might say. Lights off in the big city. Bob starts to write.

> "Now the Ramble has grown up into an urban jungle, and lurking in its thickets are "hoods, hobos, hustlers, and homosexuals," and other estranged creatures of the city [...]. Walking east, I passed graffiti on boulders. [...] On the base of the Obelisk along with the hieroglyphs there are also graffiti. [...] In the spillway that pours out of the Wollman Memorial Ice Rink, I noticed a metal grocery cart and a trash basket half-submerged in the water. Further down, the spillway becomes a brook choked with mud and tin cans. The mud then spews under the Gapstow Bridge to become a muddy slough that inundates a good part of The Pond, leaving the rest of The Pond aswirl with oil slicks, sludge, and dixie cups."[5]

Not a walk through the park, that essay, *Frederick Law Olmsted and the Dialectical Landscape* from 1973, for which he took the photo above; another convergence of law and word, which sheds light on Mildred's Lane too. The notion of the picturesque is what Land Art icon, Robert Smithson, was after, when he looked at Central Park's present condition, and its creator's,—Olmsted's—aesthetic. The relationships at stake here, according to Smithson, are of dialectic nature: a static idea of the park in contrast with the dynamic inside-out of New York City. In the service of whom? we shall ask; for "the picturesque" clearly is a concept, foundational of capitalist bourgeois times, namely our nineteenth century. What use for it today, other than to hold it against the potential pastoral, the harm of harmony upstate at "the Lane?"

It is the value of disruption, I think, that we may wrestle from those variations of landscaping, of land in the service of man, that might well be man servicing the land too (like centuries without grooming—why would a tree even want that!?). A layer cake to have, and to eat too, I believe. In the wider sense of discursive digestion and metabolistic meaning. The urban jungle is us, wherever we are. Cruising the bushes and spray painting the caves, I hope. Like Smithson, Mildred is immersed in the dynamics of evolution, that is, of multi-species co-evolution. Yet while he still thinks this work as "scar," she thinks "trace," like scripture, by hand, the word amending the wound, the law.

From this bird's eye perspective—the perspective of Nancy Holt, perhaps—the contradictions of frame versus field reveal a dialectics of devouring, of difference and inhabitation. The music fades. The Young and old Mildreds, the ones of the then and there, and the ones of the here and now, melt into memory. Ink blends into paper. Bark sinks into soil. All they form the community. The community of difference. The community that knows other. The kids.

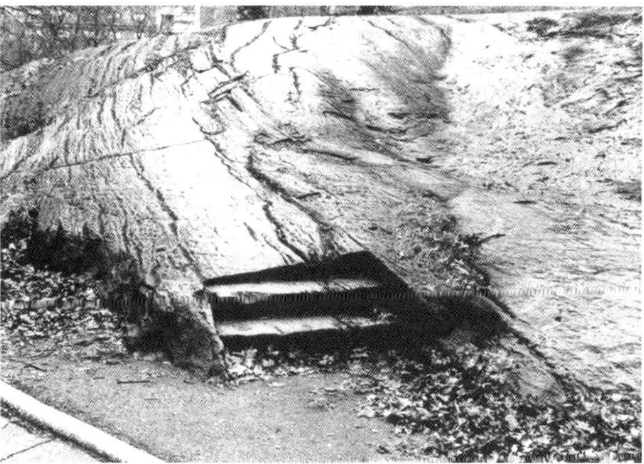

Rock Stairs, 1972, © Robert Smithson, *The Collected Writings*, 1996, p. 166.

1 J. Morgan Puett on the webpage of Mildred's Lane, accessed July 1, 2018, http://www.mildredslane.com/sessions-2018.
2 See Helmut Draxler and Andrea Fraser, "Services–A Proposal For an Exhibition and a Topic of Discussion," (1996), accessed July 3, 2018, http://kunstraum.leuphana.de/texte/edraxlerfraser.html.
3 Markus Miessen, *The Nightmare of Participation* (Berlin: Sternberg Press, 2010).
4 Robert Smithson, *The Collected Writings*, ed. Jack Flam (Berkeley: University of California Press, 1996), 166.
5 Ibid., 169–170.

C

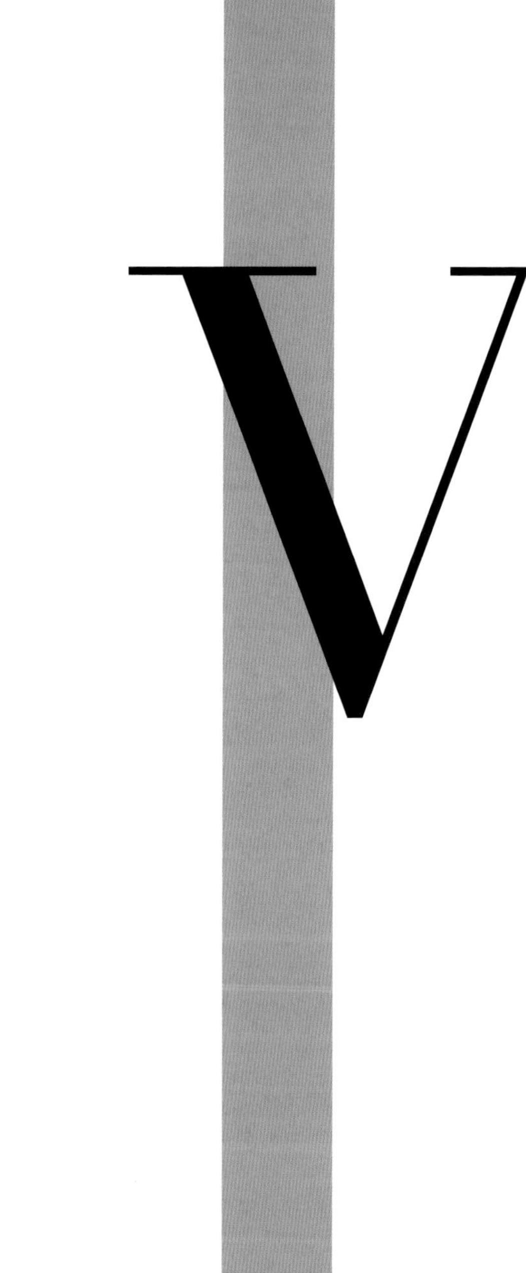

S

T

N

R

N

FLYING THE READY-MADE

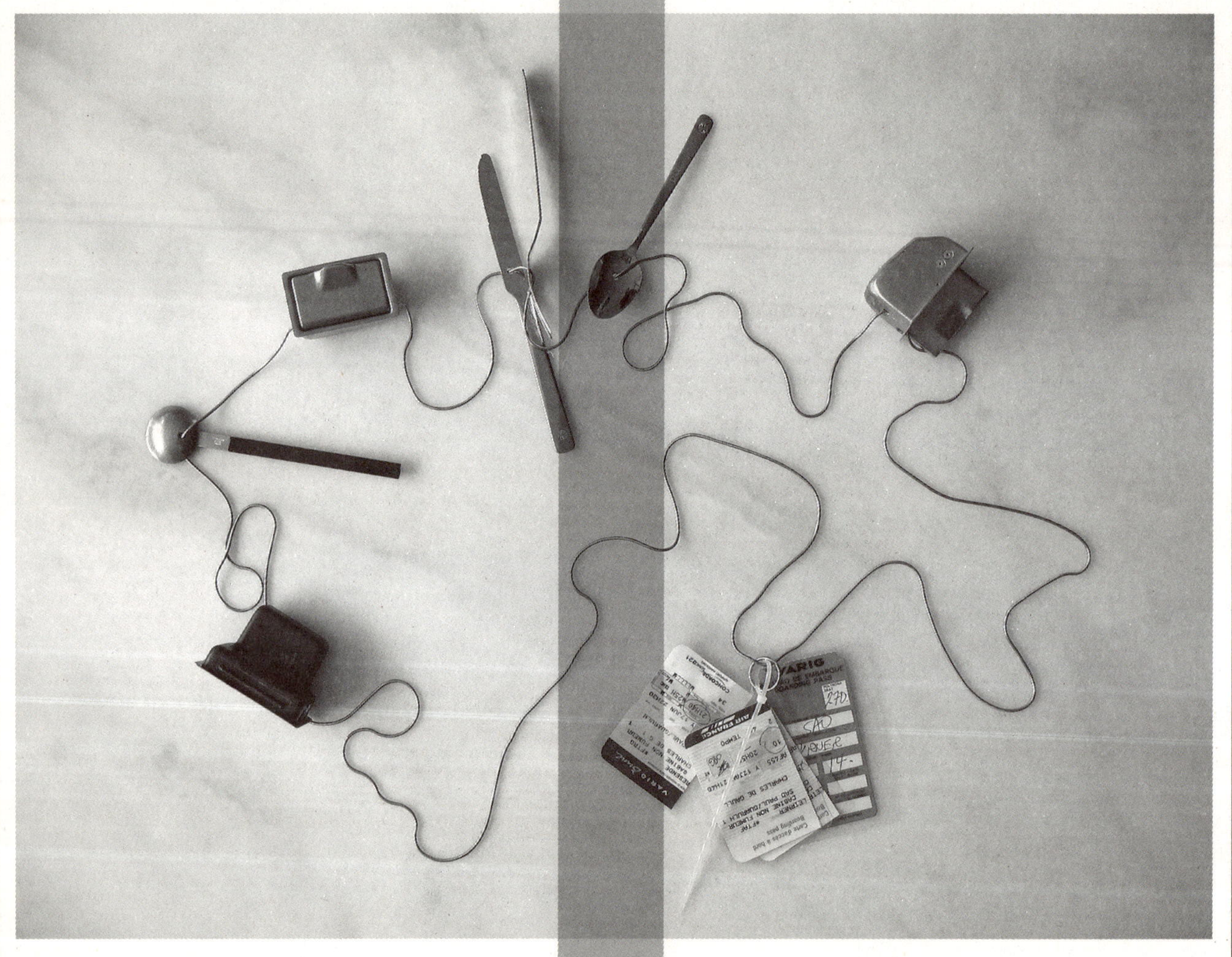

Jac Leirner, *Corpus Delicti*, 1992–2006. Boarding passes, cutlery, ashtrays sealing wax and chain, variable dimensions. Photo: Eduardo Ortega; Courtesy Fortes D'Aloia & Gabriel, São Paulo and Rio de Janeiro.

Conversation

Tobi Maier
Jac Leirner

Jac Leirner is one of the most influential artists working in Brazil today. Since the early 1990s, she has collected airline cutlery, blankets, trays, air sickness bags, stickers, ticket stubs etc., and produced a series of sculptural works that appropriate the stolen ready-made in a poetic fusion with support materials such as bubble wrap or a Rimowa suitcase. Inevitably, her works tell a story of airline corporate identity design. However, Leirner's foremost interest is to fix our fascination on the non-place: the hours we are cushioned in a (dis-)comfort zone of the airplane seat, at a loss, taken away from everyday obligations, and unable to make choices. In this regard, the *Corpus Delicti* series discussed in this interview runs parallel and in dialogue with much of Leirner's work related to voluntary drug intoxication.

After a studio visit in Rua Helvétia, I sat down with Jac Leirner at her home in the Pacaembu neighborhood of São Paulo, to speak about her work employing memorabilia and design utensils taken from aboard aircrafts.

Tobi Maier: Jac, you were born in 1961 in São Paulo, where you still live today. Actually, now you live again in your childhood home. Did you ever consider moving abroad?

Jac Leirner: Yes, I grew up in this house. I arrived aged 1 and left at age 11 and came back when I was 27 years old. As for living abroad, I lived in Oxford for six months and in New Haven at Yale for three months. At Oxford University, I gave tutorials, was a fellow at the University College, and had a residency at The Modern Art Museum, where afterwards I had a show in 1991. All this was related to the British Council. After that I had some sort of residency in Minneapolis, related to the Walker Art Center, but I decided to go three times over shorter periods rather than attend once for a longer period of time.

TM: You have been travelling a lot since early childhood...

JL: On my first international trip, I was 7 years old—we went to Argentina. The first time I went to Europe, an intercontinental trip, I was already 14 years old. Since then, I've been travelling almost every year. Now I have family in Switzerland and I go back there to see my nieces and my sister. The work also takes me everywhere. My first international gallery was in Geneva, and my first international fairs were in Frankfurt and in Basel. This was in 1989/90 and these were the only international art fairs that I ever attended, not counting the one in New York recently. But in 1991 and 1992 I had several solo shows in important institutions, mainly in the US. My first big European solo show was in 1992 in Geneva at the Centre d'Art Contemporain.

TM: You were 31 years old in 1992. That must have been a special moment, to have a solo exhibition there at such a young age.

JL: It was. I was travelling a lot, the work was taking me all over, and I was taking it all over too. In my hand luggage!

TM: For the purpose of this interview, I am particularly interested in your work that deals with aviation. When did you start collecting items from airlines?

JL: I had *Corpus Delicti* in mind since 1985, before all these working trips. I was at a friend's house in the suburbs of São Paulo during a rehearsal of a hard-core band, *Ratos de Porão*. At the house, there was an ashtray, outside of a place where it should be—it was a car ashtray. As soon as I saw it, it became the spirit of the work. It was not yet a real project, just the spirit of one. Since then, ashtrays from airlines became an obsession. I was a heavy smoker, and we used to smoke on flights back then.

I WAS TRAVELLING A LOT, THE WORK WAS TAKING ME ALL OVER, AND I WAS TAKING IT ALL OVER TOO. IN MY HAND LUGGAGE!

TM: The first work of yours that I came across, many years ago, was also from the series *Corpus Delicti* (1993). The piece I saw consists of green felt, flatware, glass, and headphones. It is in the Chateaubriand Collection in Rio de Janeiro. How did you conceive of the assemblage aesthetically? Why did you choose the green felt reminiscent of gambling or billiard tables?

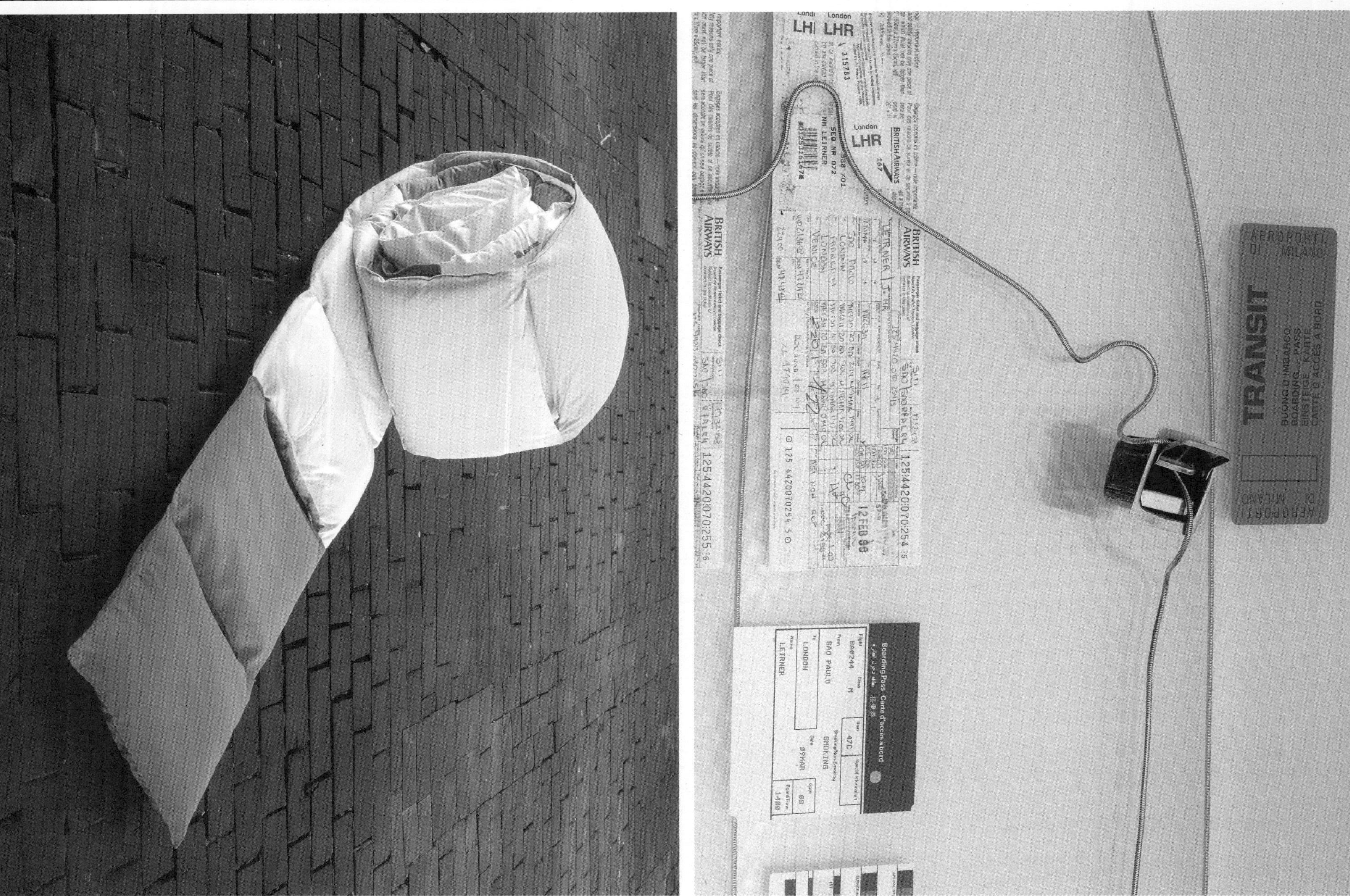

Jac Leirner, *Corpus Delicti*, 1993. Pillows, variable dimensions. Photo: Georg Rehsteiner.

Jac Leirner, *Corpus Delicti*, 1992 (detail). Ashtrays, boarding passes, flight tickets, chain, glass and bubble wrap, 20×70×300 cm each. Photo: Dirk Bleicker.

JL: My first projects from the series were the ashtrays with the boarding passes, which in terms of material, meant paper and metal. Soon after, other airline materials became part of the idea. For years, I kept thinking about what to do with all that: napkins, pillows, blankets, and cutlery. I kept thinking and taking, collecting, experimenting, and trying to find the best solutions for each material. It was hard. It is a very complicated project and I made lots of drawings trying to find solutions. Finally, for *Necessaire Corpus Di Licti* and *Corpus Delicti (Forks, Knifes, Spoons)* and *Corpus Delicti (Porcelain)* (all 1993), I used felt to build boxes with holes. Yes, the green one had to do with those games. Otherwise, I would have used another color. I used grey and white felt for other pieces.

TM: They seem to be welcoming materials; they are sort of comforting. They cushion the works. I have been thinking about how these elements that exist in a non-place—on the plane—are transformed by you, imbued with a sense of belonging and permanence, then at last, sited in a place.

JL: The idea of a home and a place is inherent—by putting these elements together, I give them a place. They finally have a body. *Corpus Delicti* means "the evidence of the crime." At the same time, it relates to the body. So I thought it makes a lot of sense to give this name to this group of works. You spoke about the felt and how I accommodated the work. With the ashtrays, I had the bubble wrap that, in a huge quantity, became a pedestal produced mainly out of air. I had this pile of bubble wrap first, before I placed the chain and the glasses with boarding passes between them. At the top came the chain with the ashtrays. But in spite of that and these materials—felt, glass, chain, and plastic bubble wrap—I tried to use a minimum of material, to build the work with airline elements. These other materials are used to connect the airline pieces. I try to select and use found material with as little material intervention as possible. I want to maintain them in their original form and to connect them with their equals. Blanket with blanket, boarding pass with boarding pass, business card with business card, Marlboro pack with Marlboro pack.

I WANT TO MAINTAIN THEM IN THEIR ORIGINAL FORM AND TO CONNECT THEM WITH THEIR EQUALS. BLANKET WITH BLANKET, BOARDING PASS WITH BOARDING PASS, BUSINESS CARD WITH BUSINESS CARD, MARLBORO PACK WITH MARLBORO PACK.

TM: You just mentioned the work exhibited at Documenta 9 in 1992, *Corpus Delicti* (1992), which consists of ticket stubs, boarding passes, and ash trays laid out on bubble wrap and covered with blue glass. This work seemed to relay a postmodern design aura. Can you say more about your choice for the design and the double presentation in two adjacent rooms?

JL: The bubble wrap, the chain, and the glass came to life because I kept thinking—for years—how to combine ashtrays and boarding passes. The nature of these two materials is completely different. One is simply paper, and the other is a totally designed piece of steel. How could I combine these two distinct objects to create a sculpture? I discarded a hundred ideas to solve this equation. And the winner of this competition was the bubble wrap with the glass top. The ashtrays are part of a chain that is fixed by the glass; the glass created a display situation for dozens of ashtrays.

TM: This also relates to your obsession with smoking that transpires in other series of works. The cigarette packs, scans of your lungs...

JL: Yes. The cigarette papers, the exhibition "Junkie"[1] with all the packages of cigarette papers, as well as the sequences of images of little sculptures made from cocaine stones.

TM: I have just visited an exhibition by Dan Reisinger at the Israel Museum in Jerusalem. He created the corporate identity of El Al. Also, Lufthansa and other airlines are continually redesigned. You are creating this patchwork of national identities and design identities by juxtaposing pieces that come from different geographical backgrounds. How do you feel about the history of airline design when you first contemplate these items removed from the aircraft? How do you think about these design legacies that come into the work?

JL: I don't think the design is a part of these works. One of the most elegant sculptures from the series is called *Cloud* (2017) and it is produced out of the junk of the junk: the luggage tags, the priority stickers, and the ones that feature a barcode with our names. At first they would cross the rooms on a single wire. After some experimenting, I arrived at a new situation for these tags, which is a *mobile* with a brass structure. It's a very colorful and elegant, light piece, featuring all the rotten paper from the luggage tags.

TM: So could one then say that the more precious design objects are brought to the floor, while the more trashy objects get to fly? Like the airsickness bags, which also float across the galleries.

JL: Well, you see, there is nothing else, only airsickness bags or napkins connected by steel wire.

TM: I remember in your exhibition at Pinacoteca do Estado in São Paulo in 2011, you had a line spun through the entire central gallery with *Airsickness Bags* (1993) attached to it. There was also *Small Circles* (1992), consisting of airline ashtrays lifted from seats. These were connected by a chain. Given that these were exhibited next to one of your business card series, I am inclined to agree with Carlos Basualdo who—in the January 1994 issue of *Artforum* magazine—wrote about your work as parodying strategies of late capitalism. Would you approve?

JL: I don't think about parodying capitalism; it is the thing in itself. I never believed the work was about any other subject. No globalization, no economy, no politics. Of course, all these big topics are part of the work, but I never meant to make works about anything but art. It's not about crime. It is crime. It's not about the economy—it is the economy.

IT'S NOT ABOUT CRIME. IT IS CRIME. IT'S NOT ABOUT THE ECONOMY—IT IS THE ECONOMY.

TM: Let's stay with the Pinacoteca, where you also exhibited *Adhesive Zero* (2000) and *Adhesive 44* (2004), which together feature a lot of air travel memorabilia: essentially, stickers like "Please wake me up for meal service" or "Occupied" and "Fragile", as well as stickers by Embraer, the Brazilian airplane manufacturer. Although *Adhesive 44* (2004) is a later work of yours, it feels more reminiscent of a kid's bedroom assemblage. It's much more wild.

JL: Yes, totally. *Adhesive 44* (2004) is the last piece I did with the stickers. All others are much more formal and beautiful, in terms of color, because I used colorful acrylic glass plates—but this piece features all the adhesives that I had left at that moment. I really had in mind the teenage windows that we see all over the world. The smaller pieces have bank or band stickers, artist stickers or art fair stickers; each one with a different subject. There is one piece that features mainly "bad taste" stickers. *Adhesive 44* (2004) is about quantity. The material for this piece, I gathered over decades. When you see the work, you see also different styles and different times all together in the same place. When I walk through it, I sense an intense presence of time because all these stickers refer to different subjects and trades. From Rock music to car manufacturing...

TM: During our studio visit today, we looked at a lot of airline memorabilia, like socks, sleeping masks and earplugs, blankets and *necessaires*. Were they all stolen or did you also receive donations from defunct Brazilian airlines, such as VASP or VARIG, for example?

JL: Yes, many times. As these are often long flights, I visit the flight attendants in the kitchen and tell them that I am ashamed of taking things from the plane, such as a tray, for example. Then I show them the works I have done, through pictures on my phone, the flying luggage tags for example, and they can't believe that these items could be sculptures, jewels really. I show them the works in museum collections, and they understand all about it and give me stuff. It's an enchanting situation.

TM: Now that air travel has become so ubiquitous, do you feel your work has changed? After all, in the early nineties, when you produced the first pieces, air travel was still more exclusive ...

JL: Well I think my work has changed in the sense that there are other items and designs available now, but if the public views it differently now, I cannot say...

TM: If you were invited to produce a work for an airport or an airplane, what would you do? Would you be interested?

JL: I would not think of my own work in the first instance. I would visit the place and see how it could inspire me. I would think of art and other artists. Not my own work. Yes, I might be interested. The same way art inspires me—I mean the art from all times, or the art being unfolded by my pals—places also inspire me. They may remind me of situations I have lived through, or movies I have seen, or books I have read. They have their own spirit, which is already a lot to start with. My work is inspired by so many moments in history, be it Pop, Arte Povera, Constructivism, DADA... so in an airport, Renata Lucas' work might come to my mind and the magic she does with space.

TM: So you would act more as a curator than an artist. Would you agree that the airport is an ideal site for you to curate an exhibition?

JL: Makes sense. That would be great!

1 "Junkie" was the title of Leirner's exhibition at White Cube, London in 2016.

Jac Leirner, *Corpus Delicti (Iberia Jay)*, 1985–2018. Steel and nylon, 150×18×5,5 cm. Photo: Edouard Fraipont; Courtesy Fortes D'Aloia & Gabriel, São Paulo and Rio de Janeiro.

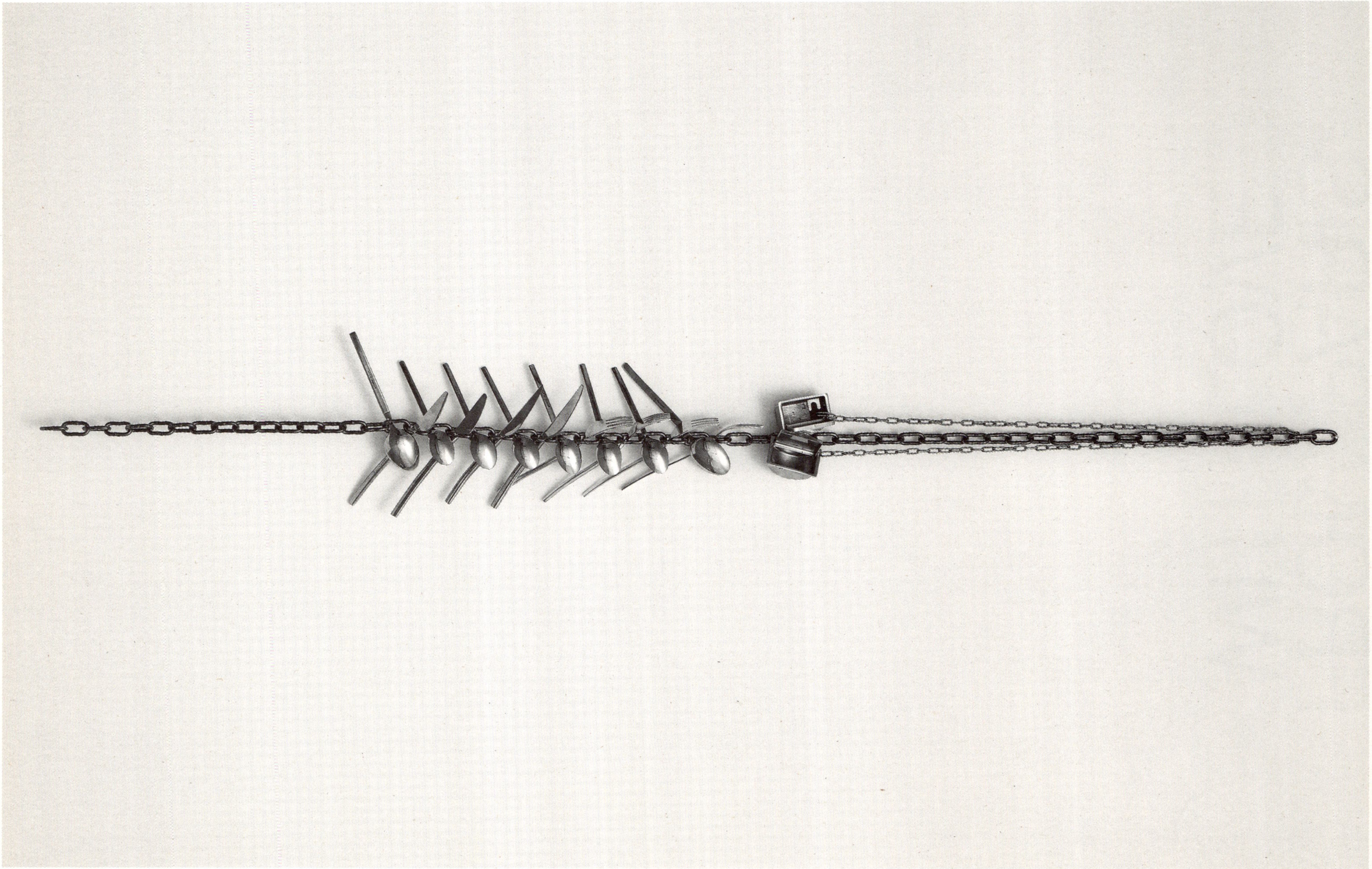

FROM PARIS WITH LOVE

Conversation

Shahryar Nashat
Anne Dressen

Paris, June 2018. Fashion week is over. Art Basel is over. Everything is over. Virgil Abloh arrives at Vuitton. Is it over before it started? Artist Shahryar Nashat sits down in Paris with Musée d'art Moderne curator Anne Dressen to talk about Virgil Abloh's debut as LV's Men's Artistic Director.

Shahryar Nashat: I want to talk about the Louis Vuitton Men's Spring-Summer 2019 collection designed by Virgil Abloh that was staged on June 21st in the gardens of the Palais Royal in Paris. My interest in fashion is only sporadic and somewhat distant, but this is a particular occasion I would like to discuss with you.

Anne Dressen: Yes, he *made* it. And this is great, and exciting! For many reasons. The first African American designer in the luxury industry. Hard to believe, but true.

SN: What is also striking is that he brings a streetwear vernacular into the luxury vocabulary. Kim Jones had these elements but he works in street wear from a referential perspective whereas Abloh's relation to streetwear feels more personal, because of Off-White and his beginnings in graphic design and a proximity to hip hop music.

AD: Yet, I do not want to be *trouble fete* or kill joy, like French people usually are, but one could also wonder *why* he was invited in the first place? And even more interestingly, since he accepted the job: let's talk about *what* he really made and created?

SN: LV will have a lot to gain by hiring the hip founder of the success that Off-White was and there is clout from this hire.

AD: It makes sense business-dream-plan-wise. Everyone was talking about it. But let's admit it right away: neither of us two saw the actual fashion show. I always go to only one fashion show each season, which is the one of Rick Owens that happened just before Abloh's, and I think they share some similarities and many differences.

SN: I saw neither of them in real time, only the videos. I was not even in Paris!

AD: Maybe that explains the distance we have to it? But, from this distance—that I also have to the fashion industry in general—, I have to say that I was disappointed after I looked at the LV official video shot by a drone camera. It was rather strange, like a computer generated video game ...

> IT FELT LIKE THE SHOW WAS PRODUCED EQUALLY FOR ITS LIVE AUDIENCE AND FOR ITS BROADCASTING...

SN: The drone view that was way above the trees of the Palais Royal was, I thought, quite fascinating. It felt like the show was produced equally for its live audience and for its broadcasting... But what were you going to say?

AD: First thing, I can not help thinking of two other Americans' recent and highly mediatized buzzes, that happened in Paris: Marian Goodman's birthday celebrated at the Château de Versailles last month, which is perhaps anecdotal—yet a bit problematic on the symbolic level? But also Beyonce and Jay-Z's new music video shot at the Louvre for their *Apeshit* song, pointing out some specific works. Amongst others the *Nike of Samothrace*, the *Venus de Milo*, Egyptian sculptures or the less famous yet beautiful *Portrait of a Black Woman* by Marie Guillemine Benoist. "I can not believe we made it," is what the Carters' couple is singing. While Abloh wrote on his Instagram account: "you too can do it," somehow reinterpreting Nike's "do it" formula.

SN: Their video and the choreography are disappointing. The one good thing though is that they pretty forcefully impose their bodies onto the bodies that are in the paintings and totally call out the marginalization of black bodies in Western art. And art is only used as a backdrop: except for the Mona Lisa at the end, they never acknowledge the works by looking at them... It's quite bold I think. Measure their star status to the dead lady in the painting.

What sucks is that now the Louvre is offering guided tours of the works that were in the video but they don't explain what the politics behind the video are... but let's go back to Abloh.

AD: With Abloh's show I thought it was going in too many directions, there was a bit of everything: from tie-dye, streetwear, fur, and way too many boring and conservative monochromatic suits... they all looked rather flat and plain to me. Except maybe the flowers' sweat-shirts... Was there an undercover statement about fluidity of gender?

SN: I liked the flowers... I also liked the way he retrofits classic designs of the *maroquinerie*.

AD: A friend and fashion connoisseur confirmed that the very reason of this collection was actually the accessory, meaning a pretext to sell the new LV bags. As I could understand from the video, most of the bags were in plastic, with chains, but is this really interesting or provoking? Using plastic today sucks, no? Isn't it ridiculous? I do not sense any irony there...

"OFF-WHITE" IS APPARENTLY ALSO USED TO DESCRIBE "A COOL ASS, NOT PATRONIZING, WHITE BOY; A WHITE DUDE THAT DOES NOT SUFFER FROM THE WHITE SAVIOR COMPLEX."

SN: ...these tiny high contrast details—that he likes to call the 3%, which is "the exact ratio needed to twist a normative object into something special." I generally liked the plastic color details. These accessories worked well with the spray painted catwalk that the drone view camera turned into that one long strip of rainbow. He talks about how looking through the prism of the Vuitton world gave him the desire to work with a wide range of colors.

AD: To me it was a bit too obvious gay-friendly symbol. All inclusive, too literally optimistic...

SN: No. I don't think that was the first reference. I see it more as what he describes being a progression from off-white to polychromatic.

AD: I actually realized by looking recently on the internet (on the Urban Dictionary actually), that "off-white" not only means "*blanc cassé*" as I thought. It is apparently also used to describe "a cool ass, not patronizing, white boy; a white dude that does not suffer from the white savior complex." This is very interesting I thought!

SN: He works these questions into many layers of the show. Like the diversity of the models, and the hanging of a map showing that they were from all over the world (except Antarctica!).

AD: Yes, but he could have gone a bit further. If we think of today's migration and the way it is dealt with in Europe and the US. In any case, I was a bit shocked to read Abloh saying that his idea was to point out the "travel DNA of the brand" instead of any other statement. First of all, I hate this term of "DNA" for a brand, and this phrase was really too soft for me at every level and really not very political in the end—or?

SN: And besides, the DNA of a brand does not change with one collection. And although LV invented branding with their monogram, the (over-)consciousness of branding nowadays is where fashion seems to be going most of the time. It seems to me that branding and creating desire for individual items, or just for the label in general, is the priority. A visionary language for the craft of designing clothes might not be needed for luxury fashion anymore.

AD: I just would like to mention here Rick Owens' *BABEL* show that he did on the steps between the Palais de Tokyo and the Musée d'Art Moderne de la Ville de Paris, in this Art Deco and also fascist architecture. So different yet so colorful, too. But the color he created was not on the clothes, or the catwalk. It was in the air. He diffused colored smoke. It was also monochromatic, but way more dystopian! Some of the models were wearing masks like warriors in postapocalyptic dark outfits.

I also do not know if I am right or over interpreting, but I thought some of the pieces—vinyl constructivist ponchos—were resembling homeless migrants' tents that we see disseminated all over Paris and regularly dismantled by the police...

SN: You also see those tents in downtown Los Angeles.

AD: Yes, my reading is maybe too literal. I do not want to say Owens is literal, it has nothing to do with the shitty new Benetton ad that was released a few days earlier and created a scandal: a press photo appropriated by Oliviero Toscani and published in Italian newspapers showing African boatpeople waiting in line, with the green stamp of the brand Benetton at the bottom! So even if they might refer to the same topic, the approach is completely different.

SN: That is so lame. I hated the Benetton 1990s vision that used the real world to advertise their brand.

AD: I agree. But to keep going on with Rick—the smoking was super intense, physically effecting, not only visually I mean.

SN: When I saw the images of Owens' show, I thought of lachrymal gases that the police use against demonstrators?

AD: Funny you say that, myself, I thought more immediately about pollution and climate change. Actually it was extremely heavy as a smell and black face masks were distributed to the guests so they could breathe.

WHAT SUCKS IS THAT NOW THE LOUVRE IS OFFERING GUIDED TOURS OF THE WORKS THAT WERE IN THE VIDEO BUT THEY DON'T EXPLAIN WHAT THE POLITICS BEHIND THE VIDEO ARE.

SN: Abloh also had something distributed, different color coded T-shirts, but only to some of the guests. He opened the show to fashion students and non-professionals.

AD: Yes, and to LV staff. It was a very inclusive and seductive gesture, revolutionary for fashion, but actually a bit like how we call in French the *poulailler* in the theater.

SN: In English they call it "paradise."

AD: I quite liked that these extra guests, not usually there, were at the end standing in the shade, while the other VIPs were grilling under a heavy sun in the front row. The *poulailler* was for once the best spot?

I also thought that it was the best part of the whole show, pretty straight forward and pragmatic: he invited other types of guests but also used them—they had to wear a LV logo! And they look *good* (meaning fake!) on the video.

SN: Keep the hierarchy. Like in the movie industry. The VIPs are the protagonists and the employees and fashion students are the extras.

AD: Yes. In Rick's show, everyone attending was wearing the face masks, it also made us part of the whole show—a very dark picture. But again, the smell was super strong. I almost cried... it was windy... really disturbing. And I wonder if it was a deliberate or unconscious choice...

SN: About cries... I almost cried at the end of Abloh's show, when he comes out to greet the audience but walked straight into Kanye's arms and burst into tears.

AD: Yes, it was almost too moving, no? Come on! Crocodile tears, at least for Kanye. Kanye needed this after all the bullshit he uttered in the past months. I also was not so impressed by the music. A jazz fusion reinterpretation of Kanye West's songs in Abloh's show vs. a super strong Tommy Cash soundtrack in Owens'... way stronger and much more ambiguous! Owens steals the show for me, and does so, since the 1990s. He stated back then that he "would lay a black glittering turd on the white landscape of conformity." He definitely succeeded.

SN: Well, he is for sure part of a different breed of designers who don't compromise.

I QUITE LIKED THAT THESE EXTRA GUESTS WERE AT THE END STANDING IN THE SHADE, WHILE THE VIPS WERE GRILLING UNDER A HEAVY SUN.

AD: And Michèle Lamy is way more than just Rick's muse. She is simply the best.

SN: The one thing both shows for sure had in common was A$AP Rocky in attendance.

INSOMNIA

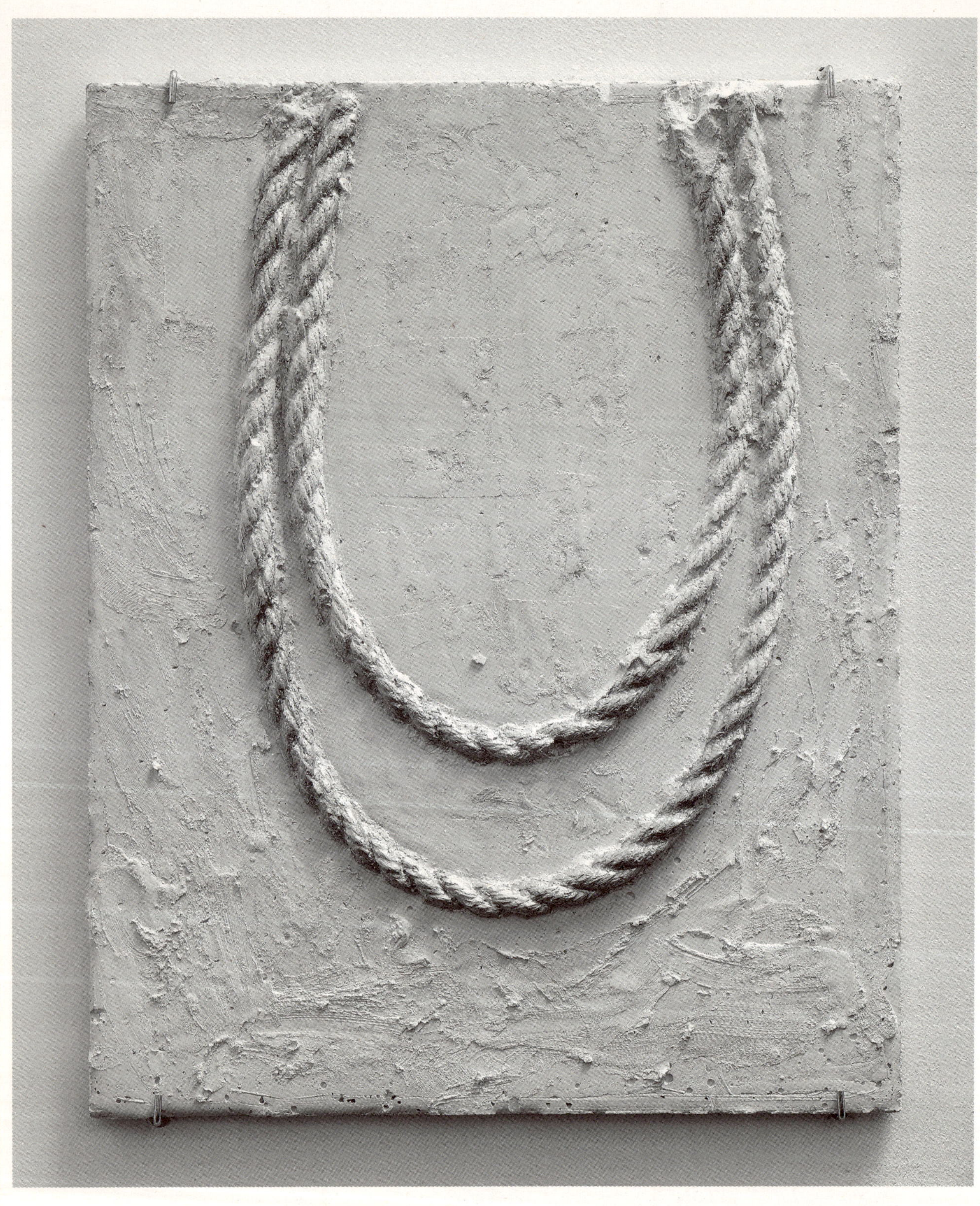

Conversation

LaKela Brown
Inka Meißner

The response to Childish Gambino's song and music video "This Is America" opened heated discussions about the alleged contradiction between the "particularity" of one's individual social position and "objective" reflections on media images, strategies of social staging, and possible appropriations in both artistic work and aesthetic reception. In their conversation, Inka Meißner and LaKela Brown touch upon the "insomnia mindset" and ask whether the identities reviewed in identity politics actually match the ones of those addressed and what comes first: subjectivity or discourse.

Inka Meißner: I wanted to talk about insomnia. What do you see at night when you can't sleep?

LaKela Brown: Unfortunately, my mind tends to dwell on things that are on the dark side, so when I cannot sleep that is what I see. What could've, would've, and should've been said or done. Mostly I see my mother, and wonder what her life and mine would be like if she had recovered and lived. Sometimes, when I'm excited about a project, I visualize how to make it, and how it will look.

IM: In your work, there are categories like relief and sunken relief. Does the latter have a special connotation for you? Is it purely technical or does the sunken evoke something else?

LB: My use of the sunken relief originally came from the molds that were left over from the creation of new casts. I realized that I had invested a lot of time and material into the molds and that they had the exact composition of the castings (in reverse) and many of them had equal or greater quality. So I decided to start experimenting with them to see if they could be incorporated into my work.

I spent some time afterwards looking at the use of sunken relief through history and noticed the way it was sometimes used to save space or maybe even materials. I also like the way that sunken relief can utilize a kind of optical illusion, and also simply the idea of the *image being below the surface* and how that might be an opportunity for future exploration.

IM: Ropes appear both in the relief work and also in the sculptures you make. They gently hang in loops and one does not really see where they come together or how they are fixed at the ends. Are those ropes tear or to be in tow (or none of that)?

LB: I don't totally understand the second part of the question. But the ropes are meant to reference gold rope chains worn from the late 1980s until now in black American culture. They are a continuation of the visual aesthetic of the grillz and door knocker earring imagery I use in my work. The ropes also have secondary and tertiary references—because of the iconic nature of this kind of rope in America in particular (lynching, swings, cowboys), which adds meaning as well, hopefully. I have kind of avoided

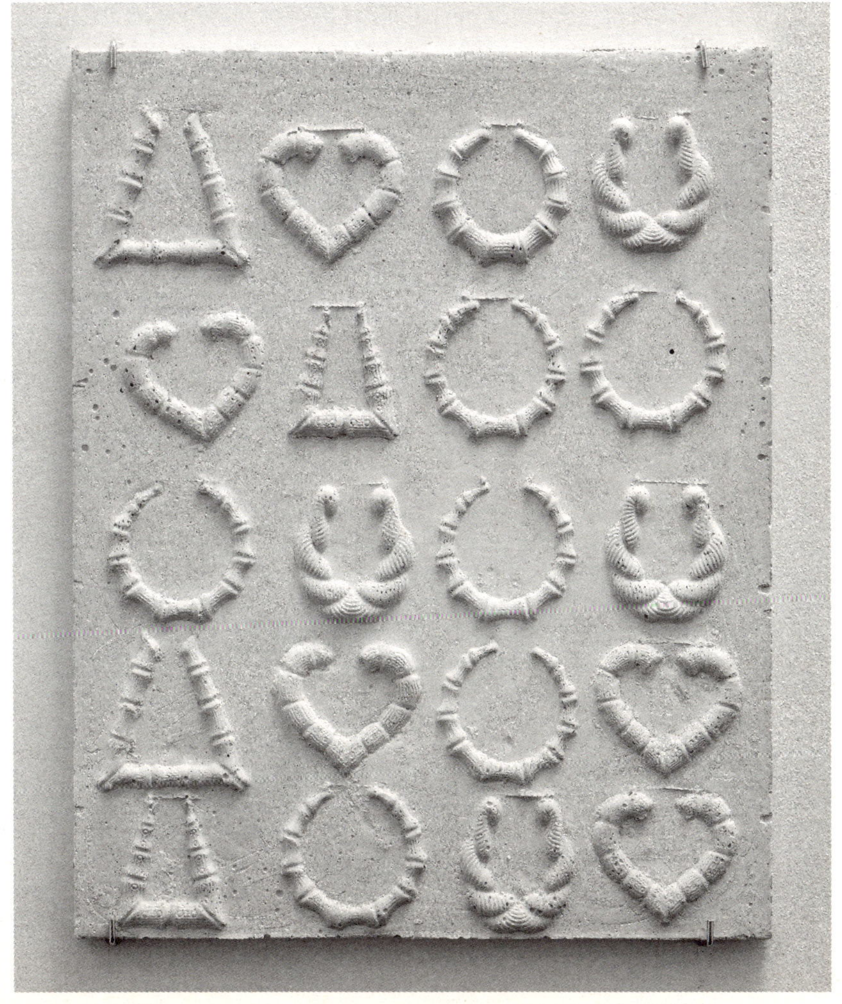

showing the ends of the rope because I am still not sure if it is broken. But I'm also hoping that not showing the ends gives the rope a continuous movement.

IM: With tear or to be in tow, I mean a sense of active or passive feeling towards the ropes. But that may correspond to the continuous movement, which keeps the question open.

Do you listen to Jay-Z, for example? I was wondering… his latest album, if I got it right, is also a kind of educational work on relationships: how might one overcome a moment when the endless repetition of the same patterns leads to the same outcome? In this case, infidelity, which leads to, I assume, very unstable surroundings to bring up kids, etc. It's a moment of generalizing personal affects as socially embedded statements. Do you relate to this in your work? Do you think this kind of collective education has an effect, does it have one on you?

LB: I do listen to Jay-Z. I feel like his latest work comes from a combination of origins. His work is explaining the need for, and act of, personal introspection after being confronted about his behavior. He is recognizing societal, familial, and personal patterns, and trying to cause change in a meaningful way. He is thinking critically about the sources of these pathologies too, and trying to understand his own role in perpetuating them. However, I feel that if things are really to change for him as an individual or in our society, the problem goes beyond acknowledging the wrong of the act of infidelity, to the relinquishing of the power and privileges that enable cis heterosexual men to behave in ways that prioritize their indulgence over the safety and stability of the people closest to them.

Also, it must be said that Jay-Z is a successful business man who understood that he needed to respond to the work that was publicly addressed to him by the biggest pop star in the world. I do relate to recognizing cultural, familial, and personal patterns, trying to make sense of them, and sorting out my honest feelings about my position.

UNFORTUNATELY THOUGH, DISCRIMINATION IS A PART OF OUR SOCIETY, AND AS A PERSON WHO HAS INTERSECTING AND INSEPARABLE IDENTITIES (SEEN AND UNSEEN), THERE IS NO WAY TO KNOW WHICH PART OF MY IDENTITY SOMEONE IS REACTING TO.

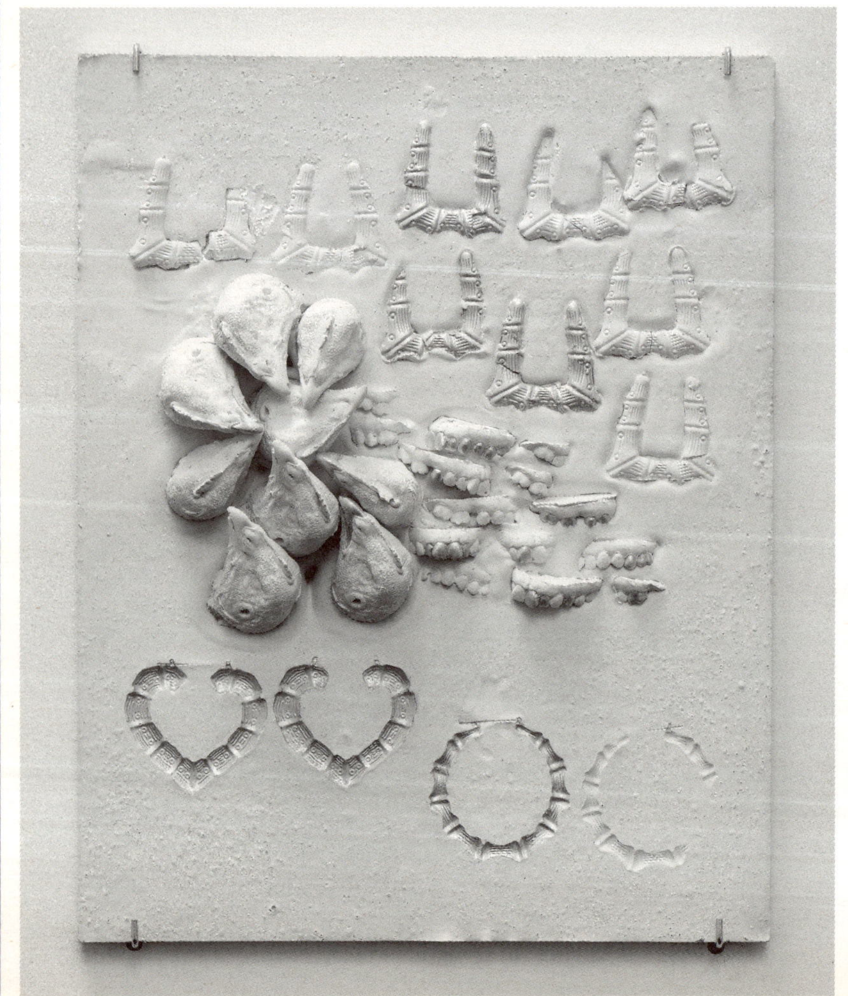

IM: If your sculptures or works were songs, would they address a pattern? If yes, what kind of songs would they be? Also, have you seen the Childish Gambino video? It's all over the news here.

LB: If my work were songs, they would be in the sub-sub-subgenre that I'm going to call retro-future-acid-conscious-Afro-Americancentric-womanist-intersectional-trap. I have seen the new Childish Gambino video. My Instagram feed was full of clips that people were posting here in the U.S. I'm exhausted from seeing images of black people being killed, real or artistic. I'm not saying he shouldn't have made his work the way that he did, I'm just saying that I am tired. But I understand the messages: gun-violence, violence against black people, apathy, distraction, senselessness, desensitization, fear, et al.

IM: In regard to intersectionality in your song genre, do questions of discrimination / identification impact your work and your life as an artist?

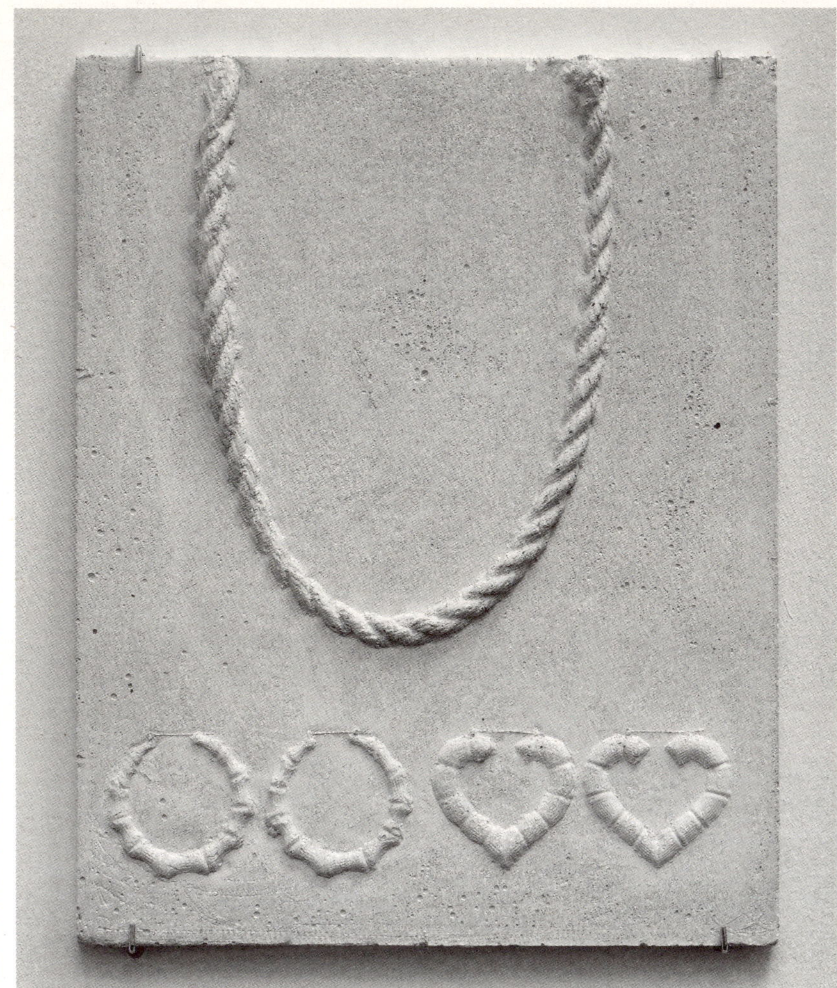

LB: The genre that I just created and, specifically, the use of the word "intersectional" was meant to include as many of the larger forms of discriminations that we see in society as possible, and even ones that have not reached the awareness of the society at large, and future issues that we haven't even begun to understand. I wanted to use the word intersectional because I wanted to acknowledge the people who are fighting issues that do not personally affect my life. It's hard to say which issues have impacted my career the most, as you often never know why an opportunity doesn't work out. It may have had nothing to do with prejudice at all, but with compatibility. Unfortunately though, discrimination is a part of our society, and as a person who has intersecting and inseparable identities (seen and unseen), there is no way to know which part of my identity someone is reacting to. I wouldn't know how it feels to only wonder if people have a problem with my femaleness, or blackness, often it feels like the combination is the problem. Race and gender resolutions often fail to consider the impact of one on the other in people who deal with multiple intersecting identities.

IM: Between your personal reality and your productive output as an artist, what do you think is more powerful: an attempt to analyze or an acceptance of one's inability to know?

LB: I think that the only way to be an artist and really maintain a practice is to use your subjectivity. That is the only thing that you know from the inside. Even if it's ill-informed or immature, it is a unique position that only you can truly and fully be in. It may also be, and is often the case, that other people share similar point-of-views, or relate to your communications. In the best-case scenario, the work of an artist could provide a much needed perspective for change.

IM: Is the insomnia mindset about the twilight zone between sociological measurability and life's more chaotic, uncontrollable elements, in terms of open questions and possible answers? And maybe from here, what does that do to the artistic work itself?

I THINK THAT THE ONLY WAY TO BE AN ARTIST AND REALLY MAINTAIN A PRACTICE IS TO USE YOUR SUBJECTIVITY.

LB: I feel like the answer to this question would vary by age and location. That being said, it is impossible for me to fully answer this question, I have to acknowledge the prevalence of social media and the reality of living in New York City. I think that many creative people with the means to do so, have often kept non-traditional lifestyles, including irregular sleep schedules. However, social media has widened our exposure, and given us more place to spend time. New York City has long been known as "The city that doesn't sleep." It is still perhaps most important that artists speak from their own experience, whatever that is, while also maintaining an awareness that their perspective is subjective, and that there may not exist such a thing as one truth, or ultimate reality.

All photos have been taken by Timo Ohler in LaKela Brown's first solo show at Lars Friedrich gallery in Berlin, January 11–February 17, 2018. As the press release suggests, the exhibition played with several forms of the "reality of the abstract," from casting real objects in plaster to making coins, from the modernist grid to the forms in which (social) history is mediated.

LYNNE TILLMAN'S CRITICAL FICTIONS

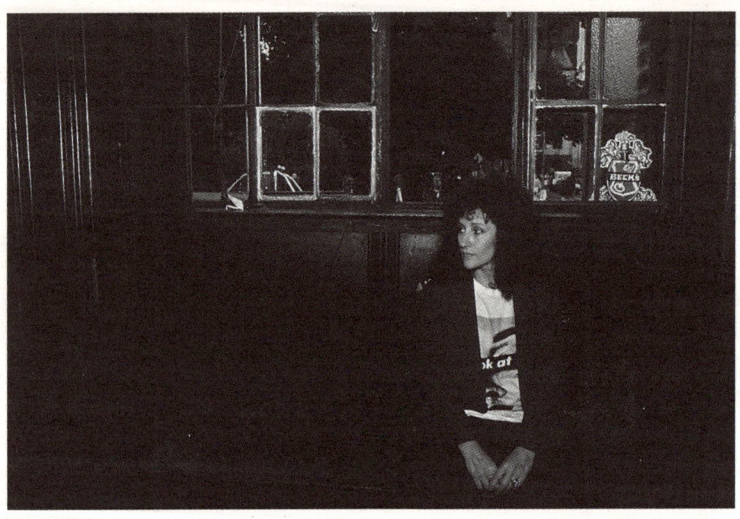

Lynne Tillman photographed by Nan Goldin, 1986

Fragments of an encounter between

Isabel Mehl
Lynne Tillman

Saturday, September 21, 2013

My sister's birthday. It is summer in New York and I'm waiting for a reading of Chris Kraus' *Aliens & Anorexia* to start on the occasion of its re-launch at the bookstore McNally Jackson. I am on my own when I encounter a small Semiotext(e) edition titled "The Madame Realism Complex" by Lynne Tillman. Shortly after I dive into the stories to slip out of a sense of social awkwardness the event begins. Masha Tupitsyn, Kate Zambreno, Ariana Reines, and others read from Kraus' book. About a month later I order my own copy of "The Madame Realism Complex." A year later I'm back in New York for reasons unclear to me now. On the night I arrived I found myself on some rooftop party close to Kosciuszko Street. While feeling like a stand in for someone else's life it dawned on me that the transatlantic desire that made me return was a projection that only functioned through digital devices. I wish I would have known Tillman's novella "Weird Fucks"[1] at that stage—short stories of drifting female desire (mis)leading its protagonist through different cities, states of mind, and body: "In the morning Scott tells me he's into being macho. "How do you mean?" I ask. "Well," he says, "it's sort of feminism for men." I tell Scott I have an appointment, which seems like a lie but isn't."[2]

IN THE MORNING SCOTT TELLS ME HE'S INTO BEING MACHO. "HOW DO YOU MEAN?" I ASK. "WELL," HE SAYS, "IT'S SORT OF FEMINISM FOR MEN." I TELL SCOTT I HAVE AN APPOINTMENT, WHICH SEEMS LIKE A LIE BUT ISN'T.

Somehow, through my amorous disillusion, I won time. When returning home from work at Printed Matter, Inc. I often sat on the couch staring at the immense book shelves in the flat where I was staying. It was hot and I was in search of distraction. And there she was again. "Madame Realism"—text by Lynne Tillman, drawings by Kiki Smith, 1984. The story goes that when Tillman was asked to contribute to a magazine on Surrealism she said no, but kept on thinking about male dominance in Surrealism and the role of women as passive muse. A topic she had discussed ten years earlier in an interview with Surrealist, Meret Oppenheim.[3] The first of two days of conversations between them ended by Oppenheim stating: "Yes, there are problems for women, [...] but we must work and not cry."[4] In a way, following this line, Madame Realism appeared ten years later. Tillman wrote a text titled "Madame Realism," revisiting the female in Surrealism and deconstructing the idea of male genius. Afterwards Kiki Smith did drawings alongside the story. It is the birth story of the character, Madame Realism. "It's when Kiki drew sperm for the first time," Lynne Tillman said in an interview.[5] The outcome of their collaboration was published as a chapbook in 1984. What I found that afternoon was a signed original copy, thirty-years after its publication.

"Madame Realism" looks into a mirror. She wonders whether the mirror is cracked or her identity fragmented when she projects into it.

> "The mirror is not cracked. And stories do not occur outside thought. Stories, in fact, are contained within thought. It's only a story really should read, it's a way to think. She turned over and stroked her cat, who refused to be held longer than thirty seconds. That was a record. She turned over and slept on her face. She wondered what it would do to her face but she slept that way anyway, just as she let her body go and didn't exercise, knowing what she was doing was not in her interest. She wasn't interested. It had come to that. She turned off the television."[6]

The table I was sitting at was flooded by sun, yet unstable.

* * *

In 1992, eight Madame Realism stories, along with other stories, were published as "The Madame Realism Complex" in Chris Kraus' "Native Agents Series." Kraus started the imprint for Semiotext(e) in the 1980s to publish feminist, unconventional first-person fiction. In 1986, two years after Madame Realism's birth, Lynne Tillman was invited by Craig Owens, a senior editor at Art in America at the time, to write about a major exhibition of French painter Pierre-Auguste Renoir in Boston. It turned out to be the first job for the fictional art critic Madame Realism, who eventually lost her voice in 2007.

IT WAS A VERY POPULAR EXHIBITION. I DECIDED TO WRITE THROUGH A FICTIONAL CHARACTER. I COULD HAVE HER SAYING THINGS OR THINKING ABOUT THINGS AND MUSING.

At first Tillman was reluctant to take that job because of not being a trained art historian as other contributors such as Linda Nochlin, Benjamin Buchloh or Rosalind Krauss were.[7] Nevertheless, art had been an important reference for her thinking for a long time, not only was she involved with the experimental film scene but she also studied studio painting with Ron Gorchov and Doug Ohlson at Hunter

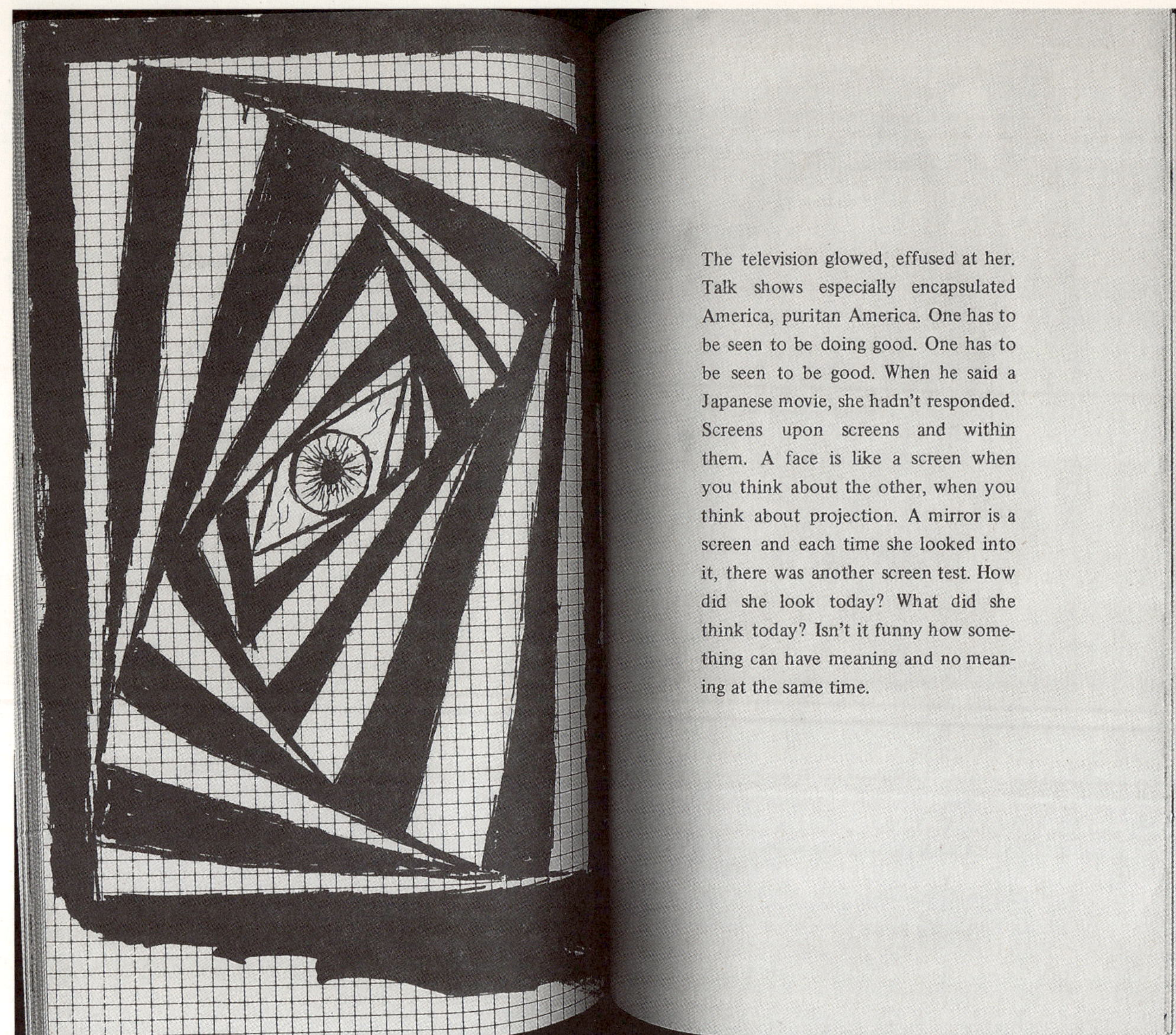

Lynne Tillman's *Madame Realism* with drawings by Kiki Smith, 1984

College. Unswayed by Tillman's doubt, Craig Owens reacted by saying that she was invited as a fiction writer. "So because of that I brought my character Madame Realism back. I took her with me to Boston and used her as a vehicle through whom to write about Renoir—whose paintings I mostly don't like. It was a very popular exhibition. I decided to write through a fictional character. I could have her saying things or thinking about things and musing. And it was a way for me not to prove something about Renoir, or disprove it. I didn't want to make claims and substantiate them, which is what historians of any kind have to do. I didn't want to have to do that."[8]

The "Madame Realism Complex" spans 16 texts in total. Madame Realism is a fictional art critic who takes artworks and exhibitions as a starting point for her in-depth reflections on the pre-conditions of our perception of the art/world. Madame Realism questions institutional frameworks and its instruments, e.g. audio guides or catalog texts, and points to the disputable entanglements between art institutions, politics, and power. Not only is Madame Realism a cipher, she is also a means to formulate critique with and through. She lives in downtown New York together with her cat, has a preference for cheese and beer while watching TV—a set up that brings class consciousness into her reflections. She's a loner drifting through the city, the periphery, and museums. She takes notes on what she encounters, what she hears others say in front of artworks. She documents her own as well as other people's associations and problematizes the notion of identity, situatedness, "the other," the construction of "femaleness" and language itself. Madame Realism is not bound to a certain appearance; she can morph into a catalog text or become part of an artwork herself. In the story "Madame Realism Lies Here" she becomes a Jeff Koons sculpture, and an artist.

Madame Realism occupies a position of critique that is not primarily based on (academic) knowledge or authority but takes place in a staged thinking process. The seductive qualities of Madame Realism invite readers to identify a space for the ambivalence of critical thinking. The constant drift of Madame Realism makes readers orient themselves by establishing a critical position for themselves. Madame Realism drifts in the spaces between—between fiction and non-fiction, criticism and literature. She is cipher and dissolution. Whatever may happen, Madame Realism does not give up her search for (the possibility of) truth. The only permanent characteristic of hers is a political stance of doubt, a questioning of what we think, see and encounter, and why. It has always been fundamental to literature to say something about the world that cannot be said otherwise. Madame Realism does not settle on a single poetic argument, nor on an art critical one, but she examines how starting off from the subjectivity of a fictional critic something like "truth" can be constructed at all, and read. Hybrid forms of criticism are very much en vogue today under an umbrella of a long list of rather undefined buzzwords like "art writing," "autofiction," "critico-fiction," and "fictocriticism." After a reading, held on June 21, 2018 in Lueneburg, Tillman stated: "I have a character, called Madame Realism, who came into being in 1983 and through whom I wrote many different essays, stories—also combining the two. There are many names for it, I just call it fiction." While literary practices in the art critical field have arrived in the mainstream, I asked Lynne Tillman about where she positions her own practice in relation to these more recent developments when I met her in New York on Friday, April 13, 2018 at the Fales Library where I was researching in her archive. It was one of the first sunny days in spring. She arrived 30 minutes late by cab: "traffic."

* * *

Lynne Tillman: In the 1980s I started writing so-called "critical fiction" or just stories in response to art. By the mid to late 1990s some well-known novelists were being asked to write for artists' catalogs; some wrote stories, others essays about the art. They weren't doing what I was doing. I was using a character for one, and because I had made films and studied painting, I approached art differently. I felt I had a handle on some of the thinking and processes that go into making visual art, I think this distinguished my practice. There can be so much conceptual work done in making a painting or a photograph, even if in the end it's not a conceptual piece. As I said, I had made films and did studio painting, and I was trying to think about the various mediums from the inside out, from an artist's point of view, all mediated through writing. So, I was making different choices, moves. Being aware of the formal qualities of an artwork is central. If you're not, then you're making a nice story. Supplying interesting words to accompany art. You might be explaining it, as you see it, interpreting it, in narrative terms. Describing the thinking in art is more interesting to me. The thought process of the process. It's hard to talk about. Now, I also write critical essays that don't use characters. Because I want to play with forms, and norms. I recently wrote one on Andy Warhol and one on Raymond Pettibon. I still take liberties. I don't write conventional essays I suppose. I continue to write stories, which I did for Justine Kurland and Liz Deschenes. Sometimes I combine them, I wrote a mix recently for work by Anne Collier. Not all artwork gives you that window, that opportunity. Different work is doing different things. Artists are engaged in various problems, or issues, or projects, and for me it's about finding a specific way in the writing, in form, in voice, and in address, that I can approach its issues. Not everybody is interested in the same problems, or issues, or projects, and for me that's okay. I'm quite catholic in my tastes.

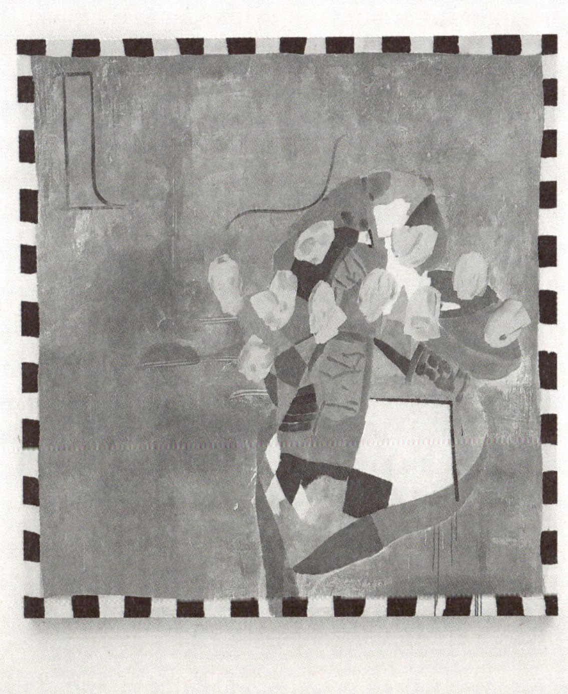

Charline von Heyl, Deichtorhallen Hamburg, 2018. Photo: Lynne Tillman

I WAS TRYING TO THINK ABOUT THE VARIOUS MEDIUMS FROM THE INSIDE OUT, FROM AN ARTIST'S POINT OF VIEW, ALL MEDIATED THROUGH WRITING. SO, I WAS MAKING DIFFERENT CHOICES, MOVES. BEING AWARE OF THE FORMAL QUALITIES OF AN ARTWORK IS CENTRAL. IF YOU'RE NOT, THEN YOU'RE MAKING A NICE STORY.

Isabel Mehl: In a conversation with artist Isa Genzken in 2005 photographer Wolfgang Tillmans said: "I truly believe that artworks can translate thinking and psychology beyond words, and an interesting take on the world will yield an interesting result in a form that doesn't necessarily follow speech or writing patterns." Where is the difference in thinking in art or in writing for you?

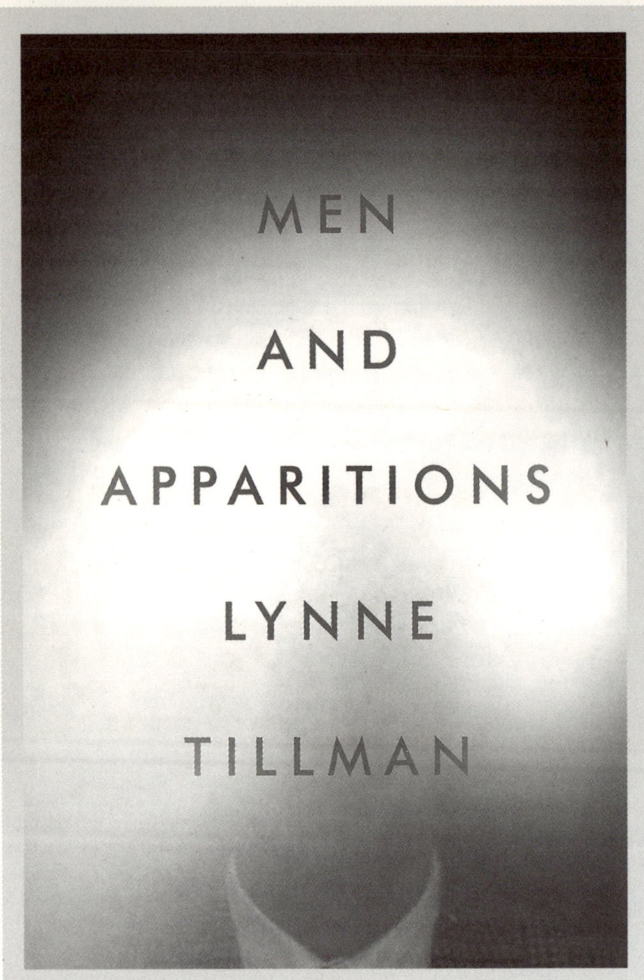

"There is a glut of information on every page of *Men and Apparitions*, but always the sense—ethnographer, heal yourself—that something is missing, is wrong, has vanished—and that we wait for it to reappear, aware it may never have existed."

Emily Labarge for *The White Review*

Men and Apparitions by Lynne Tillman, 2018. Image courtesy Soft Skull Press

Lynne: This is also hard to articulate. Using language, words—though oral language is different from written language—seems close to how we live. I mean, it's available to everyone. Making visual art seems a more abstract form of representation. Maybe not, if it's mimetic. But it seems to me that artists think differently from writers, it's a different medium, they think about negative and positive space, say. They're thinking spatially, in abstract terms, and about color, form, composition. The space before and around work. The way a person approaches it. And you could say it is like writing in a way, by making a composition. But Tillmans is right, it won't follow procedures in writing or speech. Also, art is abstracted from the world, and a part of it. We use words to describe it or explain it. But it's not the same thing. While writing about writing is using words. Words on words. It's the same language, but not necessarily accurate. It's another irony.

It's very hard to understand someone else's desires. Human beings want to find reasons for what they do in life. We had an ant invasion in our apartment. Because part of the apartment faces the back of our building, where there's a garden, ants can come up the wall. One night I returned home, turned on the light in the kitchen and there were hundreds of ants, blackening the wall. First I was horrified, terrified that they would go further into the apartment. But they stayed in one place because it was near where the hole was, the fastest route to the queen. One group went up the wall, one group went down. Up and down. Whenever they passed each other, they touched, providing genetic information. They don't wonder, I don't think, about what they are doing. They just do it. We humans, we can imagine that we're doing things because we've chosen to do them. But so much goes into that that is unconscious. And, of course, you have to eat, have a roof over your head, and we construct lives in order to survive. We give our lives meaning by thinking that what we're doing has an objective value. People are wrapped up in ideas, made of beliefs, that become part of their identity.

* * *

I introduce myself to Lynne in person for the first time on April 2, 2018 at a reading of hers. I wear a shimmering blue autumn coat and a fake fur west that Lynne notices when I leave. When introducing myself with "Isabel" she corrects me, stating "Your name is Isa," information she must have gotten from Corrine. It was her "Madame Realism" book that I found in the apartment of her sister in 2014.

* * *

Isabel: Your latest book, a novel, "Men and Apparitions" is split in two parts. The first deals with the protagonist, thirty-eight-year old ethnographer Ezekiel (Zeke) Hooper Stark, and his different crises. Before the second part of the novel, there is a gallery of photographs showing men in different ages. This section separates the "narrative part" from his research-like project "Men in Quotes." He conducted it to explore the "new man," men born under the sign of feminism. After we get to know the protagonist, we learn about his research and hence we cannot read it without having in mind what we have already learned about him. This split resonates for me, and calls into question what role desire plays, often unconscious, in what we are interested in. By its—the novels—structure, you challenge the idea of objective research.

Lynne: I don't think of the novel in two parts, because "Men in Quotes" is an outgrowth of Zeke's thinking and work. But I did want to challenge the idea of objectivity, for sure. That was definitely in my mind. Not to defame it. Not to say that research shouldn't be done. But is there ever complete objectivity? The notion that doing it can be divorced from an individual's psychology, perceptions, wishes, or that your choices are purely theoretical... no. We're drawn to interests from a very early age. And they may mutate into objects that might, later, seem entirely different and odd. But I would bet that if you'd talk to anyone about why they did molecular biology—there would be a story early in their lives.

READERS OFTEN WANT THE PERSON WHO'S WRITING IT AND THE NARRATOR TO BE THE SAME. AND THAT DRIVES ME CRAZY. I WANTED TO CONTINUE TO PROTEST A CERTAIN VERSION OF IDENTITY POLITICS THAT SAYS YOU CAN'T WRITE FROM ANOTHER POINT OF VIEW.

Isabel: You chose to write from the perspective of a man. This meant also to slip around the understanding of the book as autobiographical.

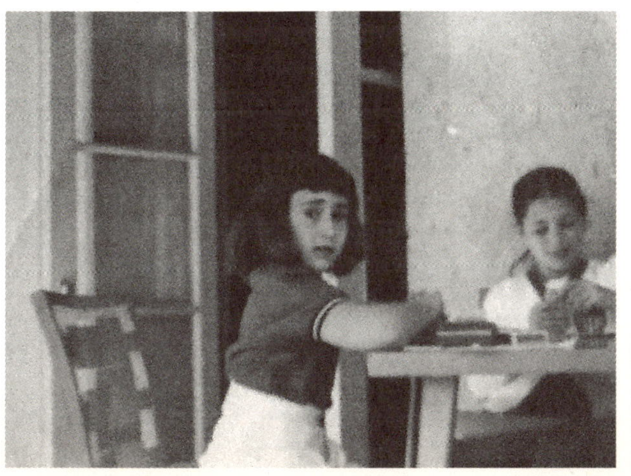

Lynne Tillman at the age of 8 playing cards in Miami Beach

Lynne: Women writers are especially damned by that idea. Readers often want the person who's writing it and the narrator to be the same. And that drives me crazy. I wanted to continue to protest a certain version of identity politics that says you can't write from another point of view. The imagination might be gendered but maybe it's not. Who knows? I felt very comfortable writing in that voice. I wasn't writing men, I was writing a specific male character, Zeke. Younger men, men in their twenties and thirties, are telling me how much they identify with him. The way men in their thirties talk about their relationship to women is different to the way men in their sixties do. And that has a lot to do with images. The protagonist Zeke represents some of the confusion happening in this contemporary situation. He's of a certain generation, but still he represents a specific character, a man not "men." We women, whatever kind of women we are—class, race, sexuality, how we identify etc.—from the moment we start reading, we have read from the point of view of male writers. We've been reading male writers who write female characters, male characters. We've always been doing this. I think we're all quite capable of writing from very many different points of view. Credibly. Not all women are going read this book in the same way. Or men.

There is a lot of foolishness in the world. I feel I can only do what I can do which is not to fall prey to what I think is seriously misguided and constricting. And that really doesn't allow for understanding. I mean, the notion that no one can understand the other sex, sexes, and therefore couldn't create a character different from oneself—we have as much difficulty understanding ourselves as anyone else, so what's the difference.

***

In Lueneburg Tillman gives more insight into why she chose to write from the perspective of a man. She said that there simply is no feminism without men. She referred to the problem that the majority seems to attribute the need for change as coming from the minority, and that this view frees them of their responsibility. "For anything to change, it's the majority that has to change. In my country, with its racism, the problem is that white people want black people to change, and not to make demands—that's speaking in very black and white terms. But they don't need to do the changing, it's white people who need to change."

***

Isabel: Ezekiel has difficulties in situating himself in the world in relationship to others. He turns to the mediated reality of the photographs he's studying to pause and focus. At first glance that's surprising as we're flooded with images that come at a much too high speed.

Lynne: Photographs are the object he's studying. He's an ethnographer who has a special interest in family photographs. When he's looking at photographs he's able to focus. As many people who do theoretical or scholarly work, or when I'm writing a story or an essay—whatever is going on around me or in my life, when I'm writing, whether it's a story or an essay, whatever hell is going on around me—I can focus. When Zeke looks at the pictures, he can focus. He has a job to do. And I suppose for me, in my own life, one of the pleasures of writing is that that happens, that that focus happens and the world can disappear. I don't see it, I don't hear anything else. Everything else is background.

ONE OF THE PLEASURES OF WRITING IS THAT THAT HAPPENS, THAT THAT FOCUS HAPPENS AND THE WORLD CAN DISAPPEAR. I DON'T SEE IT, I DON'T HEAR ANYTHING ELSE. EVERYTHING ELSE IS BACKGROUND.

Isabel: In the book the text is interrupted by photographs. To use images in books is in no way new. One prominent example that comes up is W.G. Sebald's "The Emigrants" from 1992.

Lynne: Using illustrations is part of the history of the book. I've read "The Emigrants." The photographs are used so differently; they are not analyzed. They remain images. Sebald uses them as a kind of mood, or a distant sense of so-called "reality" being remembered. For "Men and Apparitions" I knew I'd use pictures, because that's what he's dealing with in his job. I couldn't have this novel exist without them. They have a very specific role, play a part, showing how Zeke does his work.

I'm very aware of the fact that we keep photographs, and don't look at them. Now we have so many, we delete them constantly. I became interested in the differences between the digital and the analog, and how people in 1950 would pose differently for a picture, because it would be more important—the picture would be more important. Pictures are, in a sense, not as important anymore and they don't mean or signify what they once meant. They certainly don't document anything. You have had them supposedly as proof of something, a form of positivism at photography's birth, but then there was its other. Almost immediately there was spirit photography. So you can never trust any particular discipline or idea not to incorporate its other. And I was interested in that.

Isabel: Where are the photographs from?

Lynne: I found two bags of photographs in Hudson, New York, and mostly selected from them. I also had a small collection of old photographs, and borrowed some from friends. I was stunned by the number of pet photographs, especially children with their pets, and the depiction of celebrations of different kinds.

That's the job of an ethnographer, to see repetitions, cultural habits, rites, patterns. I felt this worked in the novel, looking at patterns. The pictures were also fun to write about. I was reminded of photographs by French painter Pierre Bonnard, he used them as studies for paintings. I'd seen them in Paris. I was struck by how he used the camera, so I wanted Zeke being struck by that too.

* * *

The photographs are also a way to propel the narration. Zeke says "I take a photograph, I don't take an image."[9] But we humans constantly want to transform photographs into images that correspond with our ideas of ourselves and the world around us as we perceive it. Another quote by Lynne Tillman comes to mind: "From images or words, meanings run rampant; human beings are like interpreting machines. Whether one wants to be against interpretation or for it, meanings occur, haphazard, benign or malignant, often unconsciously: only consciousness of one's responses affords any freedom from them."[10]

* * *

Isabel: If our access to reality is increasingly image-based, the realities we construct become more and more dependent on our projections triggered by this visual material that is always already narrated.

Lynne: I remember Craig Owens once gave a lecture in which he said the history of art is the history of slides of art. In that sense we're further and further from some actual event, the actual painting. What could be considered the "real" is always mediated, at a distance. We don't have access to it. Perhaps pictures seem to show what was once a reality. And now, because of all the innovations in photography, the Internet, Photoshop, all of this, the notion that any picture could be a reliable narrator has been undone. Zeke talks about this, when he says, "A photograph doesn't speak. If it did it would be just another unreliable narrator." So we don't really know reality through pictures. We know representations of realities. I always love this quote from Timothy Leary: "Reality is an opinion." I think Leary's statement is true, and it's not "a value judgement," rather an explanation of why we can think so differently of the same event.

Isabel: One reoccurring and important reference in your writing, especially in the Madame Realism texts, is psychoanalyst Sigmund Freud. The main instrument of psychoanalysis, the "talking cure," brings forward the idea that even within ourselves we are

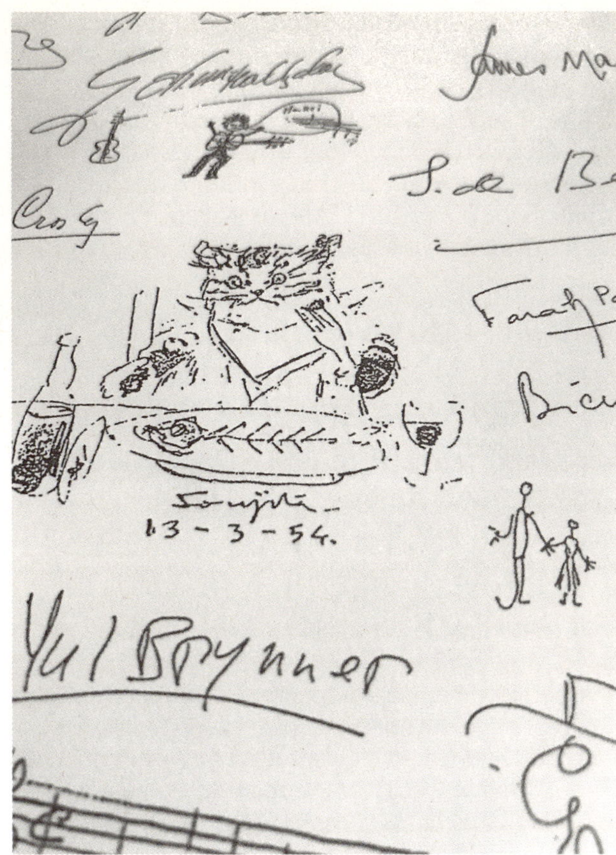

Dinner at Café Paris, Hamburg, 2018. Photo: Lynne Tillman

confronted with different realities, the unconscious, our dreams... We only, if at all, have access to one version of reality which doesn't match the other person's reality.

Lynne: That's why siblings can be hell. [Laughter] That a Marxist, say, Habermas, looks for the totality is bizarre to me. Though the desire, psychoanalytically, for wholeness, a desire for non-separateness, a sense of oneself and the world's intactness, persists potently. The totality is an illusion. I don't know what it would be in fact. A basic idea would be that people would not feel alienated from their labor. I suppose if everything you do is to feed yourself, you might feel less alienated. I don't know—does one feel alienated when one has a horse pulling a wagon, and it's no longer you yourself carrying everything? All of these things are kind of separations that could be alienating. I feel myself divided, fragmented, discontinuous, and sometimes I feel content. That's as whole as I get. [Laughter]

Isabel: Do you feel alienated from your work?

Lynne: From writing? No, I don't think I do. I can feel very alienated from the contexts in which my writing appears. So for instance having something published, like this book that I worked on for many years, even when I wasn't working on it I was thinking about it, even when I wasn't writing, or couldn't write—I was teaching, doing other things—I was thinking about it, it was always in my mind. And once it's published, it's not yours—mine—anymore. The book is quite alien to me in some sense now. It's separate from me while it once was part of me, my daily life. And I've been saying this for years, it's incommensurable, your labor on a book, your writing of something, bringing together many ideas and feelings that one has thought about for so many years to find a way to put it into a novel... There is no way that anything that happens to the book afterwards, when it becomes a book, can equal or can be near that experience. The experience of writing the book is what writing is to me. The absorption in it. The experience of it.

Isabel: This can be linked to what we discussed earlier that writing is a moment of focus, where everything else becomes background. Joan Didion once said, "I write entirely to find out what I'm thinking, what I'm looking at, what I see and what it means. What I want and what I fear." For me the process of writing opens up a space that doesn't exist otherwise. In the moment I send the text to my second reader, it's impossible for me to rework the basic idea because distance has seeped in. I'm not alone with it anymore. And I guess for longer pieces this might have a much bigger effect.

Lynne: There is a difference between something being only yours as you are working on it: you're creating it, constructing it, it's in your mind. And then it's no longer only in your mind.

I had to figure out Zeke's relationship to photographer Clover Hooper Adams and how to work that into the story. It was a while before I realized how I could do it. But the pleasure that I had in figuring that out... Whatever anyone else says about the novel, however wonderful, say, will never be commensurate with my feelings about making it work.

In this novel I wanted to deal with an immense life crisis. I've never done that before. I really wanted to try it. I thought I had the ability to do it. You don't always have the craft to pull off certain things you want to do but I felt I could. I wanted him to have a crisis, and more than one, ultimately. People in their twenties and thirties—the twenties are a really difficult time, and I wanted that to be there. I had great fun writing the crisis. It was exciting to write it, and then I wrote him wandering around in a fugue state. Zeke tries to be a different man with different women and pretends to be someone else, and he "tries on" different fictions. He's living his own fictional life, fictional world, using different guises, trying to be something other than he is. Zeke continues on his way, and you see that he's still in crisis. And then later on Little Sister commits suicide.

Isabel: I was shocked that the other characters in the story did not seem to have anticipated it beforehand. Her selective mutism made it obvious that there was something going on. Still, while reading it came out of nowhere.

Lynne: Zeke has to acknowledge to himself that he never saw it. That's the thing about suicide. I had such an experience. A friend whom I hadn't seen for about a year committed suicide. And no one saw it coming. No one. And she was a good friend but we didn't see each other that often. I had known her for years, twenty years, but people who had been seeing her more frequently, in her last six months of life, said she kept on breaking dates with them, they didn't think that there was something very serious going on because usually we don't. Somebody breaks a date with you, they say they've got so much work to do... In our world of writing and scholarship, there is so much work to do; but still she hadn't ever done that before. But you don't think this is coming. Suicide is terribly shocking. Which I wanted Zeke to go through. Writing that was hard. That was very upsetting and it was also hard technically. In craft. How do you do this without making it overly sentimental.

Isabel: Thinking about your choice of words, the language you use—you often refer to the concept of heteroglossia by Russian literary critic Mikhail Bakhtin and the idea that all language, all words, are already dialogical.

Lynne: Yes that's right. And that fiction, and especially the novel, he said, is heterogeneous. When I read Bakhtin, it was very important to me. Because of the notion of language being social and carrying, in a novel, not just one voice, but many voices; it's not unitary. I try to embed that in my writing, I think, in different ways. Even when I'm not consciously thinking "Bakhtin, Bakhtin," for me using characters and having different points of view or conflict even within one character's mind represents that sense of the heterogeneity of language users. I've heard some poets, to my great shock, talking about a private language, or secret language. There is no such thing as a private language, language is developed socially.

Isabel: I kept thinking how it is or might be different for you to write under your own name, as you do for your Frieze column "In These Intemperate Times" in contrast to writing as Madame Realism, Paige Turner or the Translation Artist?

I'VE HEARD SOME POETS, TO MY GREAT SHOCK, TALKING ABOUT A PRIVATE LANGUAGE, OR SECRET LANGUAGE. THERE IS NO SUCH THING AS A PRIVATE LANGUAGE, LANGUAGE IS DEVELOPED SOCIALLY.

Lynne: Not using characters to write through... About six years ago the editor of Frieze, Jennifer Higgie, got in touch and asked if I wanted to do a column. I had never done that so I was interested because I want to do things that I haven't done. But I was scared to do it. Because I would write under my own name about movies, art and theater. I think it's still fiction because basically any form of writing is, you have to put something down on the page, and use certain creative means. Whether it's non-fiction or fiction, you're working with words. There are different ways to say it, that's fiction. Virginia Woolf wrote that words move in all different ways, mean differently to different

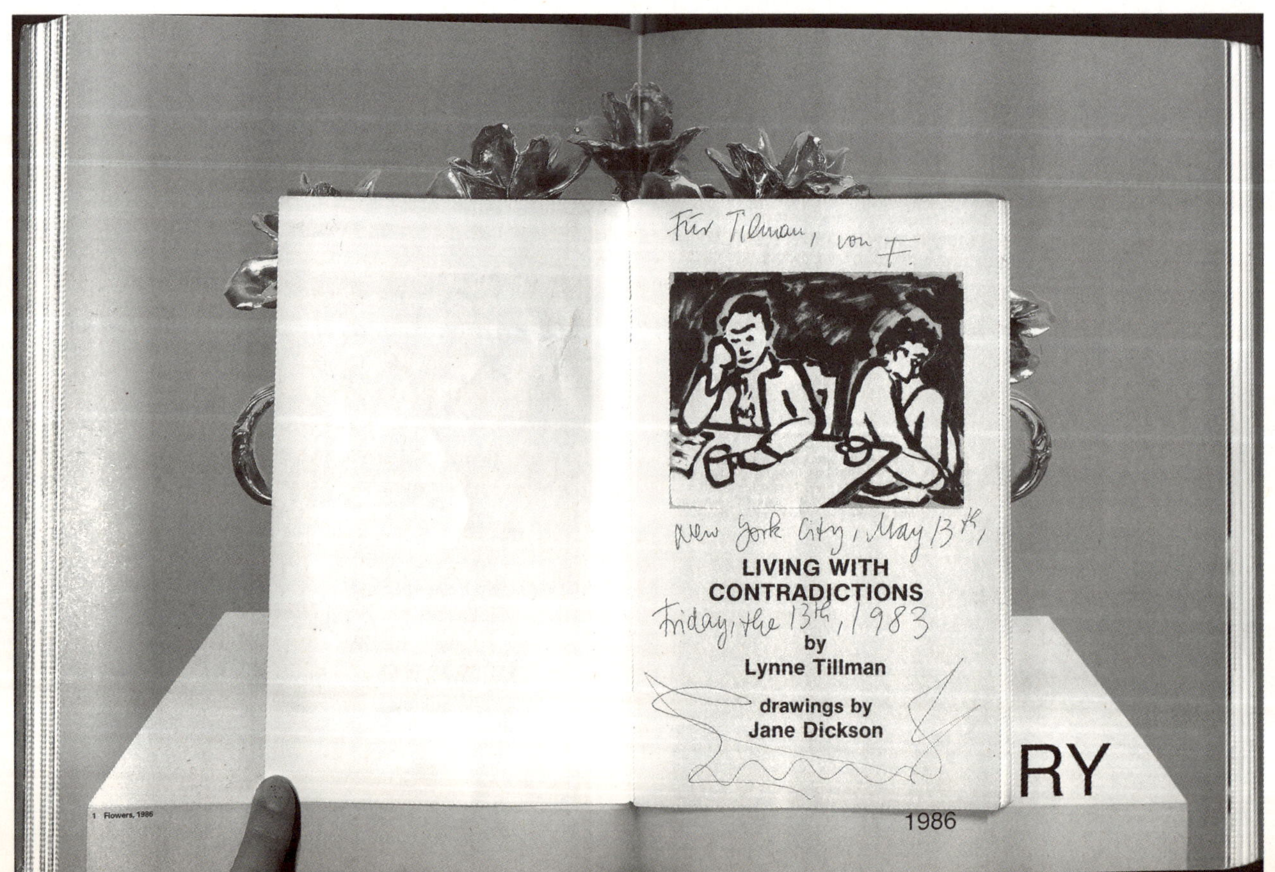

Living With Contradictions by Lynne Tillman with drawings by Jane Dickson, 1982

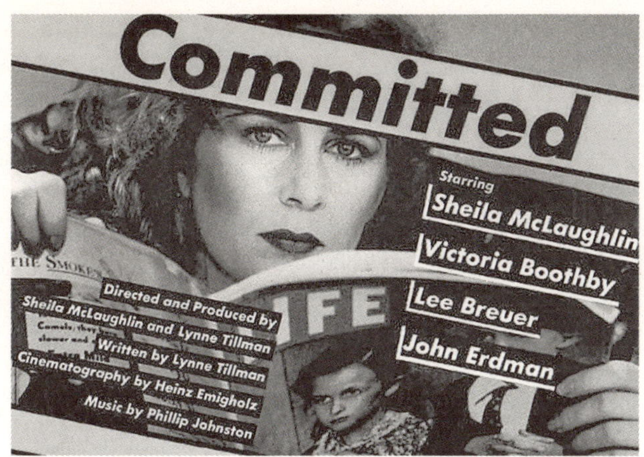

Poster *Committed* by Barbara Kruger, 1984

people. How do you make them sit on the page in the way you want? I'm creating myself as somebody who's saying things. There is such a distinction between how I feel about myself and how I feel about what I've written, or this is better: how I feel as I write. It is such a difference between the two for me. I'm not interested in myself when I'm writing at all. And unfortunately, I am interested in myself when I'm not writing and that's where it gets very depressing. [Laughter]

Isabel: What role does context play for perceiving a text, a work of art as critical?

Lynne: Context is important, in all senses. We say here, location, location, location. In writing who publishes it, who's your agent, who's your editor? In art and writing, who sees it, what gallery shows it, who writes about it, where does that commentary get published? What school did you go to, who are your parents? It's huge, context—we are in fact born into contexts. Race, sex, class... How we write, what we write about, and I guess for whom... these are contextual issues. I didn't think of myself as a commercial writer, nonetheless, any writing that is published enters into the market, the system, and it is judged, and hierarchies exist. Context is also a kind of frame. One of the artists who frames her work, is entirely aware of contexts, is Barbara Kruger. When asked or commissioned to make a work, and often she does site-specific work, she will interrogate the location, the city, she'll address the architecture of the space, the political moment, all will be the context for her art. Who sees it, in what place, and in what language? Hers is very bold and strong work.

Isabel: Did you think about your audience when you started to write?

Lynne: I was a naive young writer, having wanted to be a writer from the age of eight. I never considered, until my first novel was published, that anything but the merit of the writing counted. I should have known, I'd read so many literary and cultural histories, biographies, etc. But dreams and wishes are far different from realities, the market, the social system... I didn't think about "audience." I didn't write for an audience. There was none for my books when I began. Why should there be? I did think about readers. But I had few for a long time, and as Harry Mathews said the writer is her own first reader. Satisfy yourself, first.

Isabel: What role does criticality play in your writing?
Lynne: In my writing, criticality is a process, and exists in the writing. It's not outside it, it's embedded in it. First I am self-critical, which is a huge leap from self-hating. I can't write when I am depressed. I don't write about myself, I use experiences, which I mediate through writing, so that whoever reads it can move into the space of the narrator or protagonist. The questions I ask myself, about what I want to write next—say, "Men and Apparitions"—they're part of my criticality. I wanted to answer a question: what does it mean to live in a glut of images? That question, trying to answer it as a narrative, through a character who lives that, was very hard. I did a lot of work in order to write it, through research, for one, a lot of reading in his field, cultural anthropology and photography. I researched Clover Hooper Adams, I read about her, and I read Henry Adams, including his two novels published under a pseudonym. Finding Zeke's voice—that was a very critical process: how could he talk about his family, and ethnography, and photography, and have the voice always there, in whatever he thought.

* * *

Lynne puts down her glasses that have an intense, green frame. She is a little tired. The night before she came back late from teaching in Albany, a three-hour train ride away. She is a Professor and Writer in Residence in the English Department at the University of Albany. Once, she answered the question if one can teach writing, and was a little bored by the question: why should it be possible to teach all forms of art apart from writing? Sure, you can teach the craft. Can you teach talent? No.

* * *

Recently I ordered another chapbook by Tillman with drawings by Jane Dickson, "Living with Contradictions" (1982). It is signed "13th May 1983, New York" with a signature that's hard to identify as real.

1 First appeared in *Bikini Girl Magazine* in 1980.
2 Lynne Tillman, "Weird Fucks, Chapter 12: Going to Parties" in , *Absence makes the Heart* (London: Serpent's Tail, 1990), 37.
3 "Don't Cry: Work—Lynne Tillman interviews Meret Oppenheim," *art and artists*, 91 (October 1973).
4 "Don't Cry: Work—Lynne Tillman interviews Meret Oppenheim," *art and artists*, 91 (October 1973), 22.
5 Lynne Tillman with Jarrett Earnest, *The Brooklyn Rail*, November 1, 2016, www.brooklynrail.org/2016/11/art/lynne-tillman-with-jarrett-earnest?platform=hootsuite.
6 Lynne Tillman, *The Madame Realism Complex* (New York: Semiotext(e), 1992), 43.
7 However, of the named only Linda Nochlin ended up contributing for that "written seminar."
8 Lynne Tillman, "Untitled," lecture given at *Critical Stances Conference*, Leuphana University Lueneburg, June 21, 2018.
9 Lynne Tillman, *Men and Apparitions* (New York: Soft Skull Press, 2018), 7.
10 Lynne Tillman, "Stories Tell Stories;" in *The Complete Madame Realism* (New York: Semiotext(e), 2016), 277.

KP A CAPELLA

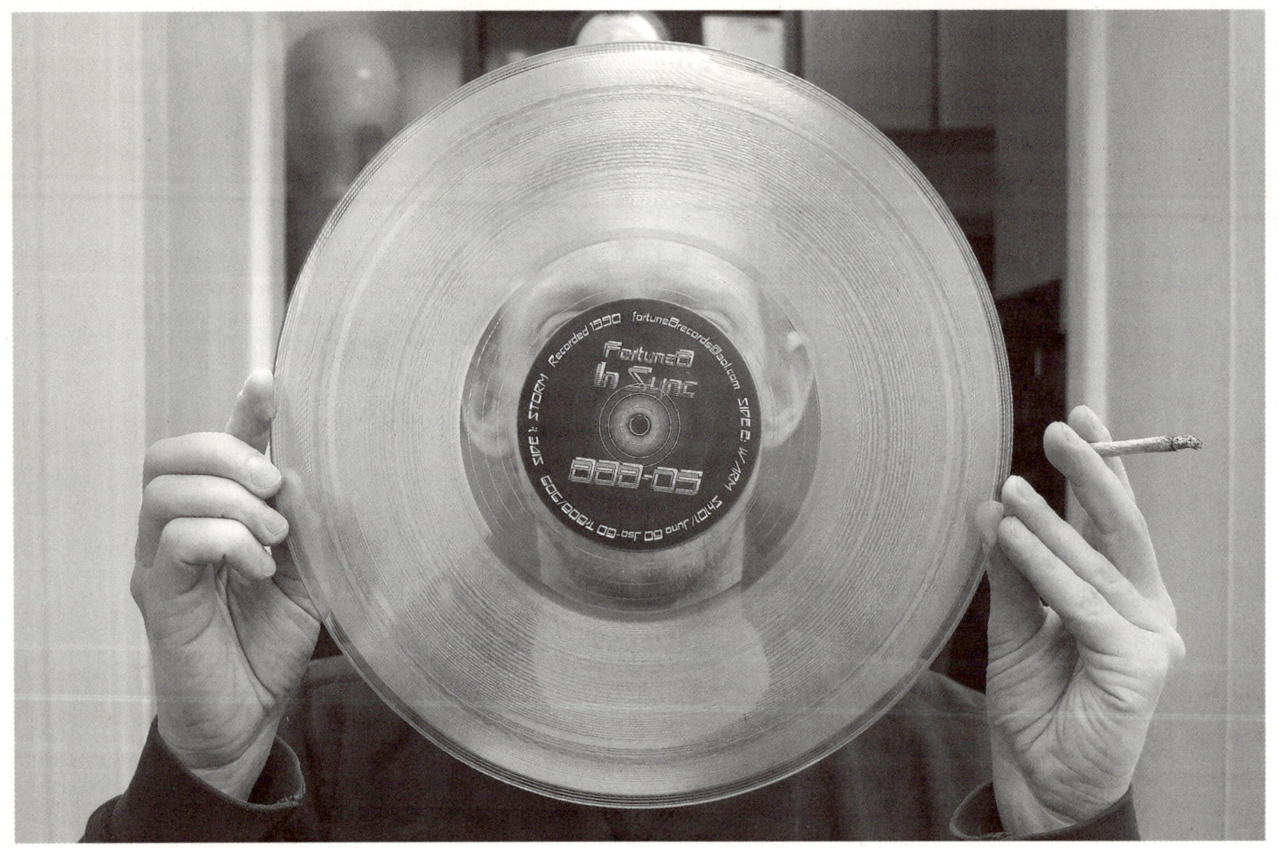

In Sync, *Storm* (Fortune8, UK 1990)

A note on the history of our friendship: Jacob Helverskov, under the name Karsten Pflum, and I used to live in the same city—Aarhus—in Denmark, 10 years ago. At that time, Aarhus was a city with a vibrant experimental scene for electronic music. Regular events included international concerts at small underground events, and festivals reared by the diverse community of artists and musicians of which we were both part.

Conversation

Cecilie Norgaard
Karsten Pflum

I have come to meet Jacob at Reichenberger Straße in Berlin in his combined off-space and studio TAMAGO, which he runs with a friend, the artist Anton Peitersen. Accessed by the street, one enters a very slim and bright piece of room; stops for coffee and a chat in the small square kitchen that glues the rooms together; afterward, one passes into a dark behind-the-scenes type of room with high walls culminating in a bed. It feels like a control tower of sorts—a narrow, tall room, alive with equipment.

Cecilie Norgaard: I've seen one other studio of yours—years ago at Flughafenstraße in Berlin—which was very reduced, compared to this.

Jacob Helverskov: That was a low point in my life, where—funnily—the machines somehow reflected that, and all broke at the same time. This turned out to be when I seriously started to make simpler, like more ambient and drone-type music, which I've been making now and again since. With this current setup, where I have to stand while working, I find it hard to make ambient, and that's a problem actually.

CN: That pretty much defines your approach, though, that what you make reflects your general conditions—which then become your working conditions?

JH: Right. In the end, the most important thing is that the scenario shifts.

CN: Do you have a favorite piece of gear? Not necessarily in terms of always using it, but...

JH: This kind of love relationship? I have a basic core in my setup that I've had for many years: a sampler. Instead of keys, it has pads that I can play and program differently... typically, I'll make drums with it of different sounds I find, or make otherwise. It's like an all-round work station. It's versatile, you can make a lot of different stuff with it. It's far from the most advanced piece of gear I have. It generates fundament. It's an MPC, an old-school hip-hop sampler.

CN: Would you say something about the relation between sampling and hip-hop? As far as I know, the most explicit sampling took place in hip-hop, not in terms of recording a sound and its manipulation, but of "stealing" and collaging pieces.

JH: Back then, they were sampling vinyls. Take unlike elements from different records, sample them into the MPC, and shape them together. Later this was picked up by different genres born out of hip-hop, like jungle music, techno, electro, etc., where the feel of the music, the beat, and the tempo changed—but it was a similar approach, of sampling different sources and mixing them together as a collage into something new. Some would argue that electronic music has a much older history, with people doing electro-acoustic and avant-garde music way before hip-hop, but the more beat-oriented, popular music basically came out of the hip-hop tradition. An example of a legendary sample that moves between genres is the vocal line, "bow wow wow yippy yo yippy yay" from the track "Atomic Dog" by George Clinton (1982). That's been sampled by Herbie Hancock, Ice Cube, Snoop Dogg and Dr. Dre, and 2Pac, and has gained more fame than the song itself. Another example is Kraftwerk's "Numbers," probably most famously sampled by Afrika Bambaataa, DJ Shadow, Luke Vibert and Underground Resistance.

CN: It's interesting to think of all these new club genres being products of collage... and also that, in the end, perhaps it isn't even the singular pieces—samples—that hold the references, but the whole participation within a tradition that holds it. A technique or an attitude.

JH: Right, and this has got to do with convenience too. I do think that a sound that's been used for decades in various types of music matures in a way. Not the sound itself, but people's perception of it. Imagination adds something to a sound when it is continually repeated.

CN: Right, this is what makes a piece of gear legendary too. A synthesizer is famous for the way in which it filters the sound.

JH: I was just playing with this new synth, Roland D-05, which is a re-issue of an old digital synthesizer, Roland D-50, and I could hear sounds from early Michael Jackson tracks! One of my students had it so we were playing with it.

CN: Where do you teach?

JH: I teach at the music conservatory in Esbjerg, Denmark. It's a quite small school, adjacent to the Danish Institute of Electronic Music (DIEM), which was the first education for electronic music established under the Danish music conservatory. I enjoy teaching in Esbjerg because there's nothing pretentious, it's not a hip place at all, and in that sense, not a hip school either. It means more freedom, less pressure and more content. Studying there, you acquire a conservatory degree, meaning a university degree of a

Bachelor's and a Master's. Five years.

CN: Were you educated at DIEM?

JH: Yes, I went there from 2005–08 or '09 and never graduated. I made a decision to move from Aarhus to Berlin when I was close to finishing the Bachelor's, but commuting didn't really work out. Also, I was fed up with studying, and I was quite busy with the music. There was a lot happening in Berlin—it was a much more interesting place to be. Making music and playing concerts instead of studying...

CN: I'm curious about DIEM. How many people are admitted on a yearly basis? And are there any women?

JH: Four or five students are admitted every year. My class had two women, Heidi Mortenson and Ane Østergaard [Band Ane].

CN: What does a Bachelor's there entail? I've come to understand the education as academic, in the sense that the music is just one part of a greater technical research or verbal investigation. I'm thinking in particular of our common friend, René Middelhede [Maulex], and the projects he makes: conceptual setups of different components producing what one hears. And he was an A+ student there.

JH: The perfect student. Yes, but at the same time, it is an artistic education in an expressive sense as well. If you read the curriculum, it focuses on aesthetics and creativity. The main subject is composition, which could mean a lot of things. It has to do with the student's creative output. But, saying that, the majority of the subjects are technical—be it learning about acoustics, computers, how sound behaves and reacts, all the physics. Music history is quite a big part of it, which, of course, deals a lot with aesthetics. I think, for the people who study there, and who study there the whole time, the technical aspects are most rewarding, because that's what's really hard to acquire outside of the school. By technical aspects, I mean learning some common ground about the logic of the machines and software: what the consequences of certain actions would be, and so on. People were being stimulated to go in quite experimental directions. From the teachers' and professors' sides, they appreciated when people like René, whom you mention, directly built upon the theory they were taught—but I think it was more between the lines than the students being directly encouraged to develop in specific ways.

CN: Who was teaching when you were a student?

JH: A professor called Wayne Segal. He's of the old electroacoustic school, I think one could say. Wayne likes generative music, and very conceptual music. The last thing he was doing that I'd read about was using information from a weather satellite as data for a program he'd written, so this data would be translated into music. He was the founder of DIEM, and opened up to younger teachers from different backgrounds; I quickly started studying under Kristian Vester [Goodiepal] who deals with "radical computer music," as he calls it. He works with the relationship and gap between artificial and human intelligence, and immerses his whole character in it. He didn't study himself, but had a name and a radical reputation, so the school had interest in having him as a teacher. He'd always be talking very fast and very unclear, but his energy and charm carried him through. And he was smart. He bridged the gap between an old story about electronic music and a contemporary self-taught point-of-view that some of us had. He tried to join these two approaches. He helped me release an album through some of the contacts he had for vinyl manufacturing, etc. He was very hands-on, a very dedicated teacher. Unfortunately, it became too much for the conservatory in the end. Not so much for DIEM, as for the classical and rhythmical departments—the people in the faculties there just didn't understand what he was teaching.

Despite the minimal size of the studio and its better fit for standing, we decide to find pillows for the floor to sit on, and to stay here and continue the talk.

JH: I think this studio embodies my angle on what electronic music is. Instead of having a big desk with a mixing console, fancy monitors, reference monitors, and everything lined up in a nice rack and stuff, I prefer this more clustered, messy situation. If everything was fixed in a rack, it would annoy me a lot as I wouldn't be able to connect things in different ways, it would be more tedious. I like it when cables are hanging through the room.

WHEN I WAS YOUNGER, I PUT A LOT OF ACTIVE THOUGHT INTO THE PROCESSES OF CREATING AND PRODUCING, WHEREAS NOW, I THINK ALL THE THOUGHT HAPPENS WHEN I'M NOT IN THE STUDIO.

CN: You're lucky that the room is so small that you can actually connect machines with just a cable hanging through. It makes a certain setup less important, when everything is enmeshed with itself. I'm really impressed with how much you have, I have to say. And earlier, I was impressed with how little you had, compared to others.

JH: Yeah, some friends here in Berlin even had two of every machine [laughs]—that's fanatic, but that's really a thing, I also share that partly, this gear fetish. Nowadays, you find people who have studios consisting of a huge touch pad, or something like this, and optical cables, or no cables at all because everything is communicated by Bluetooth. But I like this more tactile universe with rusty buttons, more like an old spaceship.

CN: Here you have a hands-on practical praxis related to the process—here you can touch your ideas, although the finished product is extremely intangible. Hardware music is more like playing... with software editing as the abstract part following. Composing the things after they've been recorded. Much like writing this interview.

JH: Yeah, the editing is more tedious, and really not the creative part. That's the engineering part, it's a completely different hat to wear. Some people might say differently, of course, and prefer the computer as instrument.

CN: How are your editing processes? You like this very hands-on part of the making, but then, how does it work—just a general example?

JH: It's changed a lot through the years; I used to edit much more with the computer. For many years, I found the computer a super potent tool, through which one can so effortlessly do amazing things. But I think it has to do with age too. Being younger, you want to prove you're skilled and able. There's some degree of showing off—not necessarily in a bad way—but when you're twenty-two or twenty-three, you have this crazy energy, you want to show everybody how amazing you are. Now it's a bit more relaxed for me. I don't care so much for being the best or some genius. I'm more into the soulfulness of it, and I think the soulfulness is easier to achieve using the hardware machines, and playing them like you would play regular instruments. It is less thought and more intuition; more feeling and less technical hassle. At the moment, I make things quite quickly with the machines and then try to do a minimum of editing with the computer afterwards. Maybe this approach is more old-fashioned—actually, this resembles the way people made music in the early 1990s or late 1980s.

WELL, WE ALL USED TO LISTEN TO BOGDAN RACZINSKY BACK THEN, AND I THINK HE'S A GOOD EXAMPLE OF AN ARTIST WHERE THE TECHNICAL PART OF THE MUSIC-MAKING IS SECONDARY.

CN: Would you say there's a greater distance between you and what you produce, through the process of computer editing?

JH: This is what I see happening now: there's a greater distance created through the insertion of thought, compared to going without the computer, and trying to channel my musicality through hands and ears. When I was younger, I put a lot of active thought into the processes of creating and producing, whereas now, I think all the thought happens when I'm not in the studio. Being reflective and thinking about the terms of music—about what I make, what I like, and how to achieve it—that happens more on a subconscious level now, I think. Maybe because I'm more trained, I find it easier now.

CN: I guess, over the years, what you really want and what you do move closer together. What were you informed or inspired by earlier? And is there any idolization happening still?

JH: I'm equally inspired now, as I was back then, by other people's work. For example, I'm listening to a lot of weird, quirky techno and house music now from the early 1990s. It's not really an active choice. The fact is this kind of music really speaks to me, and it falls in the range of the type of music I'm doing myself, in terms of an attitude. This more soulful approach. Earlier on, the really complex, difficult stuff appealed to me.

CN: When you listen to music, do you try to figure out how it's been made?

JH: Sure!

CN: And isn't it much easier to read in the type of music you're listening to nowadays?

JH: Yes, on a technical level. But on an aesthetic—or even spiritual—level, I'm still very occupied by how they get in this mood, or how they channel emotions and feelings into this technically very primitive music.

CN: Who are these artists?

JH: An example is a record label called Irdial Discs. Cameroon Massif! It's basically techno and house music from the UK, from about late 1980s to mid 1990s. It's a kind of mix between electro and more acid-like stuff, trance-like, house music, deep house. But this is really subtle, it's in all the fine details and gestures. The guys of this label had different slogans, one of them was "we suffer to bring you beautiful music." They were idealistic. This wasn't mainstream music then—it was their take on techno and house, but in much quirkier, humorous ways. Perhaps it also had filmic qualities. There was a strong atmosphere to the music that belonged with what these people did, a unique thing. By using fine nuances and subtle language, they made it theirs. It is political, in the sense that it was a commentary on the more consumerist music of their time.

CN: In my acquaintance with you and some of the friends we share—Nikolaj Gerstenfeldt, Badun, Sofus Forsberg, Senko, to name a few—this common interest in music of less technical skill contrasts the technical brilliancy you all used to praise.

JH: Well, we all used to listen to Bogdan Raczinsky back then, and I think he's a good example of an artist where the technical part of the music-making is secondary. It's in his ideas, his character, his mythology that everything happens.

WHEN I FINISHED HIGH SCHOOL, I MOVED TO COPENHAGEN, GOT A PART-TIME JOB IN A SUPERMARKET, AND WHEN I WASN'T WORKING, I'D JUST BE IN MY BEDROOM MAKING MUSIC. THIS WAS IN 1999, I THINK.

CN: He was very admired, as there was this whole shared interest that I want to call "a nerdy gear competition," a constant talk about how the music has been made. And then you had this guy who would burn a shopping cart and run, and name his tracks "That First Time I Met Her And She Hugged Me (And Then Laughed At Me Heartlessly When I Said I Wanted To Know What It Meant To Love Her)."

JH: That's the thing. There were a few people trying to do what he was doing, but he was probably the most poetic one.

CN: Where is he released?

JH: He released on Rephlex back then.

CN: ...which is a record label founded by...

JH: [dramatizes] by "The Aphex Twin."

CN: [laughs]

JH: The grandfather of modern electronic... oh I hate these genre names, I really hate them. But then again, it's pretty handy to have specific names to use, so you know what's being talked about! So it's called "IDM"—Intelligent Dance Music. Aphex Twin is the grandfather of that. He's widely regarded as the "Mozart of IDM."

CN: Right, the "genius." There's been such intense talk about genius in relation to him, and of originality, which informs a general striving towards so-called "genius" among musicians. Aphex would somehow generate that.

JH: He encouraged it... But once you look into music history, you find loads of his contemporaries doing similar stuff that obviously inspired him. The 1990s were a decade of simultaneous happenings. Aphex was a provocative character, and if you look at bands like Nirvana, just to give an example, they had a bit of the same fuck-the-establishment attitude. He didn't care what was the "correct" way, and he didn't want to stand half-godlike on a stage, jerking off. He rarely showed up, and got this secretive myth going about him with years and years of no releases, etc. Interestingly, in 2015, he started uploading a lot of unreleased tracks on a Soundcloud account, something like 200 or 250 tracks. Some of them are really good, and some really not. It just proves that okay, this is also just a very hard-working person who's been making music on an almost manic level since the age of sixteen, seventeen.

Speaking about what artists had a big impact—inspired a lot of people and myself—one has to mention Aphex Twin, and the obvious ones like Bogdan, Autechre, Phoenecia, Squarepusher... It's always nice to move on in different directions. For me, living in Berlin, where there's a really vibrant (club) music scene, the city is still a source of discovery for new music and tendencies. I don't listen to Aphex Twin nowadays because I know it all. It's just like a fundament to stand on.

CN: I would like a very basic introduction to "what got you in the first place?" Where did the inspiration come from, what did you do?

JH: At a very early age, I had my first childhood revelation of music that really touched and stimulated me. It opened up my imagination and a whole new world—with colors and pictures inside my head. This was at the age of four or five, listening to Michael Jackson with my brother. My brother is, like, four, five years older than me, and he was always introducing me to new music throughout the 1980s and 1990s: Depeche Mode, KLF, etc. We had a quiet agreement that while I may have been more talented, he had the knowledge and the taste, you know. So whatever good stuff he fed me, I could sort of pick up and use it, bring it somewhere. I think he understood this too. So around the age of high school, I got really interested in electronic music because of the quality it had—it wasn't like one person standing on a stage showing off; it was about a world that I would picture when I closed my eyes and listened. A world that felt nostalgic though it was something new. It triggered cool emotions, I think. So I decided to find some music that I liked, which was really difficult as I was living in a small town in the countryside. This was before the internet so there was nowhere to really find music. Except for Björk, for example, and I slowly figured out that I liked some of her tracks better than others, particularly the ones reminiscent of strictly instrumental music. So, for instance, through Björk I became acquainted with a guy called Mark Bell [LFO] who did some productions and

Sleep concert at Himmelbjerget, Denmark 2017

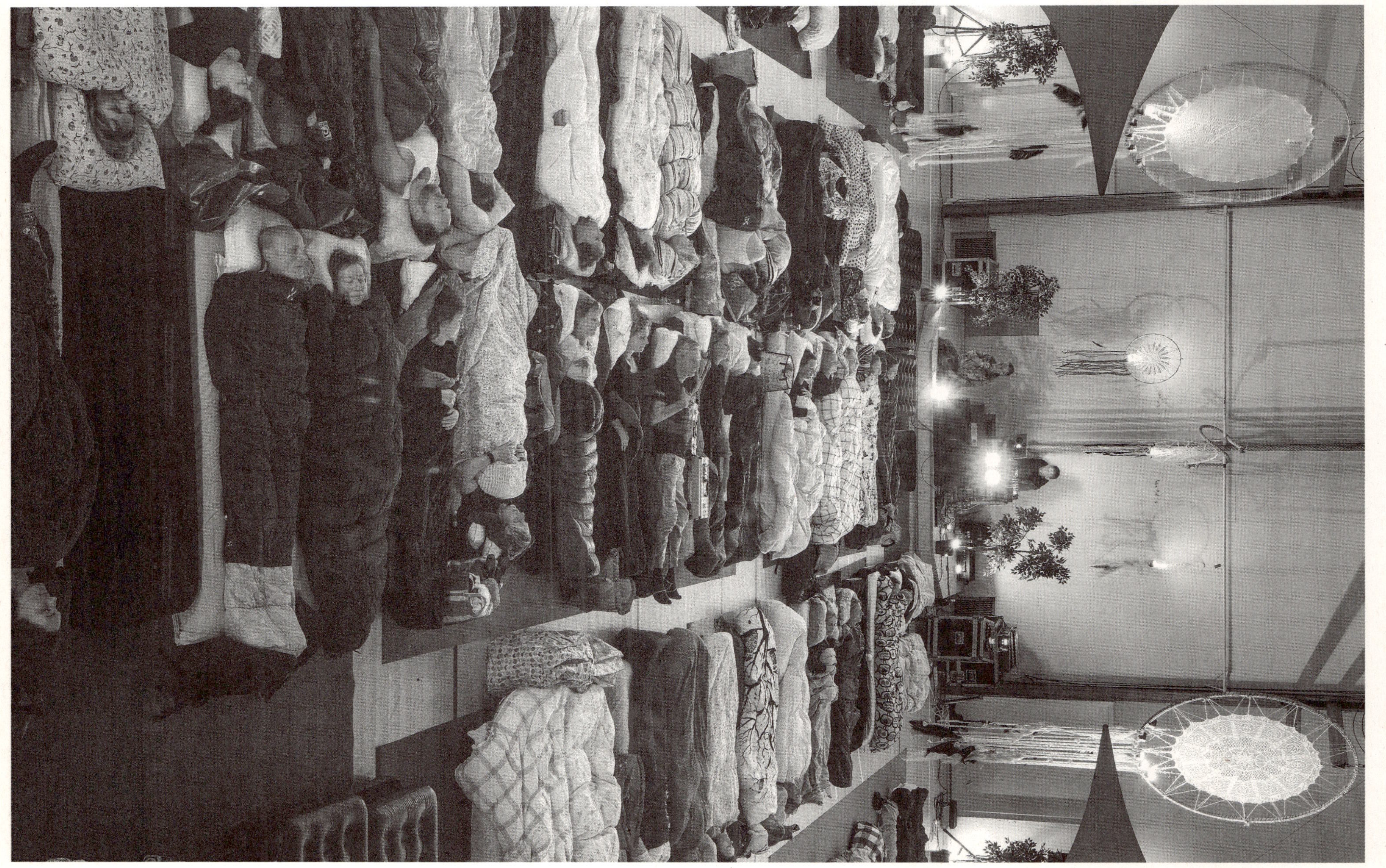

remixes for her. Now when I look back, all the Björk tracks that I preferred were ones he was involved in. Then, of course, I met some friends in high school who were also into electronic, techno, and house music, and they lived in a town that was a bit bigger than mine, so I would go there and hang out with them. They were also doing radio on a small local station every Sunday for a few hours, where high school kids were allowed to make their own radio program etc., so I became a part of that. This was Jonas Olesen, among others, and this was such a luxury. We could do whatever we wanted on this local radio. They also had a huge record collection of very mixed music, most of it was Danish schlager, but then you'd also find a Ryuichi Sakamoto record, David Byrne, or even Brian Eno, Depeche Mode, stuff like this. There was a huge room of vinyls. This was also where I met Bjørn Svin. I remember they made an ambient festival in the local cinema where Bjørn was playing, and Opiate was playing. It was really cool. At some point, my friend Jonas Olesen [Hector Rottweiler] got a bit of money, and then he bought a very basic home-studio: a sampler, a small mixer, and an effect-module. I saw this and thought, "wow this is so cool, you can do this relatively cheap and you can make your own music!" So I wrote a letter to my grandmother, who had set aside some savings for me for when I turned eighteen, and I asked if I could have that money, which she was cool with. So I went out and bought my first sampler and small sequencer and stuff, and from then it gradually grew. When I finished high school, I moved to Copenhagen, got a part-time job in a supermarket, and when I wasn't working, I'd just be in my bedroom making music. This was in 1999, I think. 2000. I was living with my brother in a flat, which was cool as he was still very interested in music. He'd have something to say about it. For about two years, I was just making tracks. A lot of tracks.

CN: Were you also thinking of sharing those tracks? Was it easy for you to finish tracks?

JH: Sure it was. I could only make one track at a time because my gear was very primitive. I probably made two or three tracks a week in the most productive times. And then—it was really a very lonely and monotonous thing, I was just making music and smoking a lot of weed in my room every night—I started thinking, I had to have other people hear it, I wanted that. It became a very clear idea that I wanted to release music, and I wanted to be a part of this whole music scene, and play concerts too. I needed to get it out somehow. So I sent a demo tape to Thomas Knak [Opiate, Future 3]. I didn't really know him, but I'd met him a few times and talked a little. I sent him a tape with a lot of tracks and he was very, very kind and helpful. He responded and gave it some critique, and recommended two labels where I might try to send it: Worm Interface and Toytronic. Worm Interface was a small label based in London. I didn't know it when I got the recommendation, but when I looked into it, I could see some cool people who had released there, like Squarepusher [Tom Jenkinson], before he got famous, and Freeform, and Gescom too. I sent out these two demos, and Worm Interface got back to me pretty quickly. I wrote Karsten Pflum on the demo tape. I was struggling to find a cool name.

CN: And you knew you had to have a name?

JH: You had to have a name! These were just the rules. If you were making music, you needed some cool alias. I don't even remember why I chose Karsten Pflum—I think it originated back in the radio-making times of calling each other silly things.

CN: I think there's been an interesting shift in how people are interested in their products or activities leading back to their actual personalities. For me, the shift came with something like Facebook. Before that with Myspace, for example, it wasn't customary to engage social media with your own identity—it was about coming up with random names and using pseudonyms. Then again, not even pseudonyms, because pseudonyms involve more conscious decisions. A pseudonym may even come across as more singular. If you have one, it's likely to be just this one other character. Anyway, you sent your demo tape to Worm Interface, and then?

THAT'S HOW SOME LABELS USED TO OPERATE. IF THEY PICKED UP AN ARTIST WHO BECAME POPULAR, THEN THEY WOULD OWN THE LICENSE TO THE TRACKS, WHICH MEANT THEY COULD THEN SELL THEM OFF TO BIGGER LABELS, AND MAKE MONEY THAT WAY.

JH: Then they called. On the phone. I was sleeping and my brother picked up the phone and they were like, "Umm, is Karsten there?" My brother didn't know about this name, so he was like, "No, he doesn't live here." I remember this morning. The phone kept ringing, and I could vaguely hear him speaking English, and it took a while for me to realize. Then I talked to this guy on the phone who just said, they liked the demo and that they'd like to release it. Very direct. They knew a guy who would master it, and they paid for it.

CN: So they were now covering your production costs?

JH: Yes, they sent me a record contract. That was in 2000. They had full control, selected the tracks, and picked the person to make the cover. I got help from an attorney connected to Danish Musician's Union, where they'd offer free counseling on record deals. I sent him the contract, and he advised me I shouldn't release there—I shouldn't have anything to do with these guys because it was, like, the worst conditions one could have. It basically meant that they would own the rights to the music I'd write for the following three years. That's how some labels used to operate. If they picked up an artist who became popular, then they would own the license to the tracks, which meant they could then sell them off to bigger labels, and make money that way. I'd get something like 30% after breaking even. I think they pressed 500 copies or so. And even though the attorney advised me not to do it, I was like, fuck it, you know. Something's got to happen. I was super excited. I was only twenty or something. It took them almost three years to release it though, and I was almost twenty-three when it came out. In the meantime, they put out a 7"—small single with two tracks—just to try it out, to use as a promo. The label was run by two English guys who were connected to a record shop in London called Ambient Soho, in Soho. They asked me to come to London and Barcelona to play a few times before the CD came out, which was big for me. Most of my idols were from the UK, adding to the people we've already mentioned comes Mu-ziq, Autechre, Boards of Canada, etc.

CN: Do you have something to say about the "English scene"? A lot of good electronic music is British. Why do you think the UK is such a hub for rave culture?

JH: Rave culture started in the United States. In cities like Detroit and Chicago, people from the underground techno and house community would throw massive parties in abandoned warehouses. Parties were all about the music: one big room, a huge sound system, and a strobe light. Some key Detroit musicians through the 1980s and 1990s were Juan Atkins, Derrick May, and Jeff Mills, and record labels like Metroplex, Underground Resistance, and +8. The UK adapted to this rave culture in the late 1980s and added something "specifically British" to it. The new drug was Ecstasy, and in the UK, something like a second hippie revolution was happening, all revolving around the techno parties. To cut it short, UK brought in breakbeats and melodies, and kind of merged the music into a thing of their own, which wasn't quite like Detroit techno but, say, had an ambient quality. Like, you know, Future Sound of London.

THE PERSONAL AND PROFESSIONAL ALL MIXED UP—THERE WAS NO DIVISION BETWEEN ONE AND THE OTHER. WE WERE ALL PERSONAL FRIENDS, AS WELL AS COLLEAGUES. EVERYBODY HAD NICKNAMES IN AARHUS. I JUST THINK IT WAS REALLY GOOD FUN.

CN: Right, melodic.

JH: Melodic, yes, exactly.

CN: Now I'd like to return to talking—perhaps in a more abstract sense—about what you think of your artist name. You are referred to as Karsten Pflum in public, and there is, in a sense, a distance between Jacob Helverskov and him. I'm interested in what you think about the distance—if that is something you've thought about—between you and your character.

JH: I think, in some cases, it still serves as kind of a shield. I feel it's quite practical that people who only know me for my music call me by my artist name. When someone writes an email to "Karsten," it's obviously a professional relation.

CN: But it's funny, because at the same time, your artist name is used as a nickname by the community we've both been part of. It turned into the opposite of a professional relation.

JH: [laughs] If any good friends from Aarhus would call me Jacob, it would be totally weird.

CN: It's also interesting how an alias can serve—even within a professional career—as a safe place for joking around. There might be desire for distance as well, between you and the particular role you play for a group of friends.

JH: I think that happened, and it's funny it happened at such a late point. I took an artist name that was already my nickname, which again became a nickname. It was so worn out that I grew really annoyed. People used it as a nickname, and so it became personal. At one point I considered changing my name to Karsten Pflum. The personal and professional all mixed up—there was no division between one and the other. We were all personal friends, as well as colleagues. Everybody had nicknames in Aarhus. I just think it was really good fun.

CN: Some artists really have many aliases; they name themselves differently with every project. Like using a pseudonym or a heteronym for literary works.

JH: Perhaps that dates back to, like, Detroit, where Underground Resistance would play anonymously. They'd always be called UR* and you wouldn't know who was playing as they were all wearing masks. Anonymity removes focus from the person, increases focus on the music, which can then, in turn, encompass so much more.

CN: Personally, I'm trying to figure out how I can build distance between myself and what I make. What I make will be considered in ways that I won't necessarily like to take personally. If I can divide what I make from myself, then perhaps what I make can more easily participate in a certain discourse, and I can go on existing more easily. One doesn't need to do it through pseudonyms, but it definitely makes it easier if one has this other identity to subscribe to. The work might be very personal; still, the personal becomes performed by the author. But performing what? Knowing you, I know you do perform, on several levels and in different ways, in private or public. Actually, I know you as more of a performer in private, whereas in public, your music sort of takes over and does the job for you, while you're somehow facilitating it by playing it. In relation to your mentioned mix-up of personal and professional, I think you're a good example of someone who continually deals with how and what one can be.

JH: I consider that type of performance stimulative, an option for freeing myself a bit from the conventions of being. This one person can actually be two people within the logic of the art itself; it's another logic that applies, as opposed to, say, the real world, where one person can only be one person. Within the art realm, one can easily be two people. But also, "we" are so many people, and one person consists of multiple facets, multiple personae. It's such a reductive thought-pattern to think of "being" as a singular size, as one thing only.

CN: Do you think we can build a link from how the situations in which your artistic product—your music, or Karsten Pflum—is being presented allows for shifts of identity? The concerts, the oft dark space, invites one to drift off, to erase the contours of things a bit.

WHEN ONE REALLY STARTS GIVING IT RATIONAL THOUGHT—LIKE: MY GOAL IS TO PLAY MUSIC IN A CLUB WHERE EVERYBODY IS DRUNK, ON DRUGS, AND PROBABLY WON'T REMEMBER THE DAY AFTER—IT IS GOING TO DEPRESS ME.

JH: The club or the party doesn't necessarily come with an answer, but it is stimulating that, right...

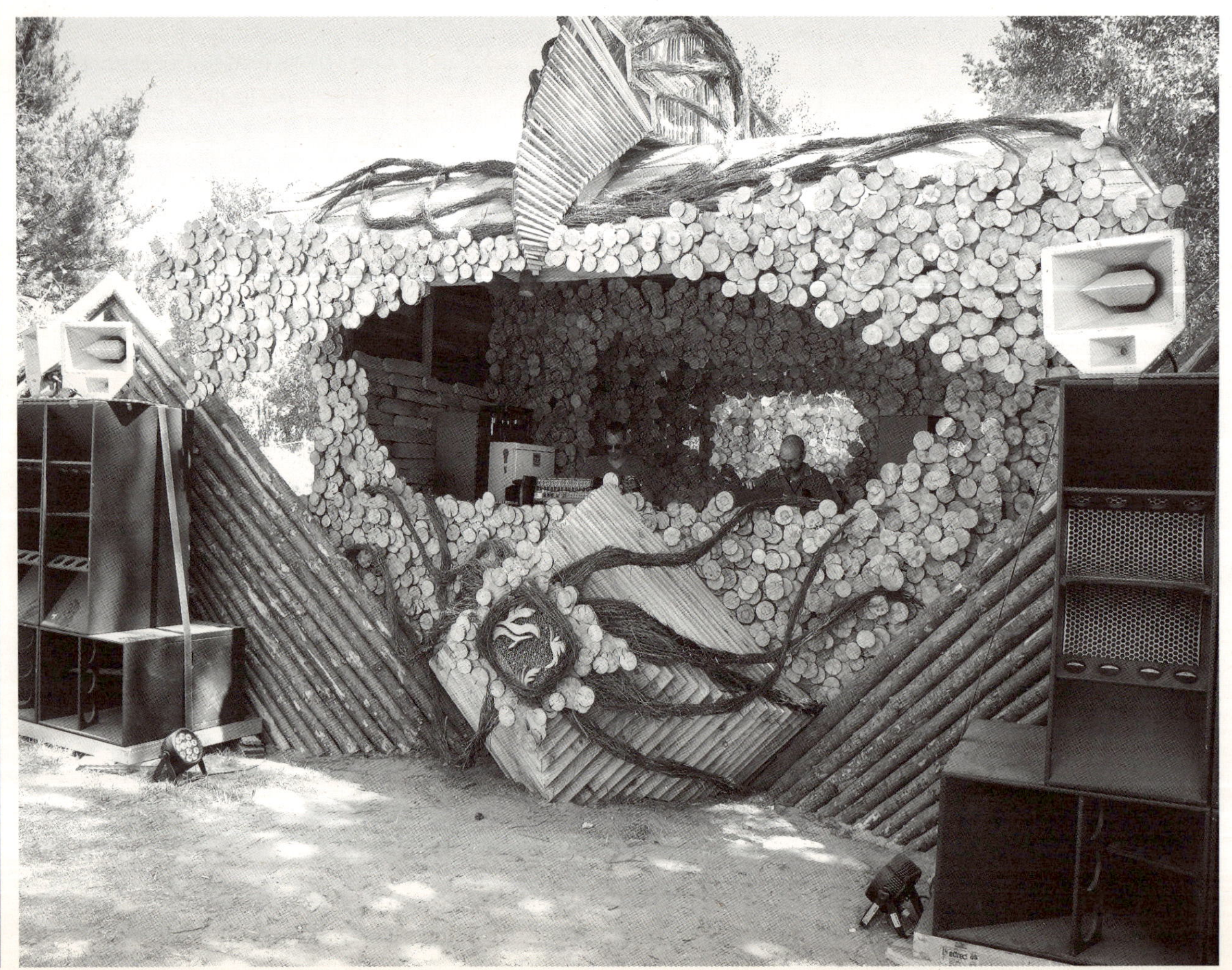

Karsten Plum playing at Freqs of Nature Festival, 2018. Photo: Cecilie Norgaard

I don't have one consistent opinion about "the party" as a main site for my music. When one really starts giving it rational thought—like: my goal is to play music in a club where everybody is drunk, on drugs, and probably won't remember the day after—it is going to depress me. It's like spending twenty-four hours traveling back and forth to a place, to only be able to play for two hours. It's a complete Sisyphus thing going on, it doesn't make sense on a rational level. Sometimes I think this kind of hedonistic setting is great, where everybody is practicing some escapism. Other times, it feels completely pointless. I think it shouldn't be taken too seriously. Sometimes I think partying is a waste of good people's energy, and other times the energy can just be amazing. It should be mentioned, though, that I am far away from only playing in clubs.

CN: Maybe we should try a gallery concert with Jacob Helverskov? I think you would be a brilliant performer in a bright space, where everyone is running around performing their own names. The immediate difference between a club and a gallery is the exposure.

JH: That sounds really nice, like being judged in a differently sober way. Because I do that so little, it would probably feel like I would actually be performing with an alias in a very weird environment.

CN: Let's speak about another environment you've been playing in.

JH: The sleep concert is a format I've been using. The concept is that the music is being perceived by the audience while they're sleeping, at best. These concerts will last anything from seven to twelve hours, which means that at one point, people stop obsessing about time, and surrender to the premise of a long stretch. The music I play at these concerts is relatively quiet with a reduced amount of information in it. It's facilitating a mental and physical condition rather than entertaining. It doesn't dictate what you're supposed to feel or think, and, ideally, leaves space for the listener—that's why I like the term "space-music." It enchants, lets say, the space from within, which one perceives. It appeals to more subtle parts of the consciousness. It stimulates empathy; the ability to enter this other realm exists there. One of the roots for this kind of music, or event, is gamelan music. Over sessions that would stretch over two, three days of continuous music, Balinese people would alternate between states of being awake, asleep, rested, etc. Gamelan music has a very repetitive, trance-like character. What happens is that the listener at some point lets go. The music becomes hypnotic; one gets a feeling of transcendence.

CN: This notion of being transported elsewhere—be it through nostalgia, or imagination—seems to inform your whole praxis.

I STILL APPRECIATE THE FORMAT, AND I KNOW IT HAS A LOT OF POTENTIAL, BUT I GUESS I LEARNED THAT A PARTICULAR ABSTRACT EXPERIENCE CAN'T BE TRANSLATED INTO MAINSTREAM CULTURE.

JH: Definitely. I think it's interesting to talk about the place one is transported to. I find this to be a very abstract place. Here, one is receptive in another way than in a conscious state, like dreaming. It's interesting to facilitate this through a concert, to create opportunities for abstract reception.

Interestingly—and frustratingly—this opting for creating abstract experience in, or with, people, turned the concerts into something I couldn't quite deal with. People with ideas of lifestyle or self-improvement started to come; it was less and less about the music. Having a preconception about the experience is the absolute opposite of what I meant to do with these concerts. The project was commercialized by Danish TV and newspapers, in ways I disagree with, which meant the aim of the concerts got flattened out, and thus attracted more people who came for other reasons. Because the concerts were commercialized, I obviously started earning significantly more money than with any other project, and I ended up playing them for much longer than I actually wanted. It totally messed with the notion of what "service" I was working in. I still appreciate the format, and I know it has a lot of potential, but I guess I learned something: A particular abstract experience can't be translated into mainstream culture. At least, not in Denmark. In any case, I prefer to stay small and true.

We pause to eat, and realize it has been five full hours of recording. After eating, we don't continue our conversation; instead, I crawl up to the ceiling bed of the studio and rest before catching my night bus. Downstairs, Jacob is playing records; one track after another, the soundtrack of my drifting. I don't get to ask him what he's playing there, but the music is groovy, it is fast, and warm. It is, indeed, soulful.

A list of soulful records: Insync vs Mysteron, *Exit 9* (Peacefrog Records, UK 1995), In Sync, Storm (Fortune8, UK 1990), 69, *Lite Music* (Planet E, Belgium 1994), Baruka, *The Lost Funk EP* (Night Vision, Netherlands 1994), CJ Bolland, *Neural Paradox* (R&S Records, Belgium 1995)...

RIBOCA

RIGA INTERNATIONAL BIENNIAL OF CONTEMPORARY ART

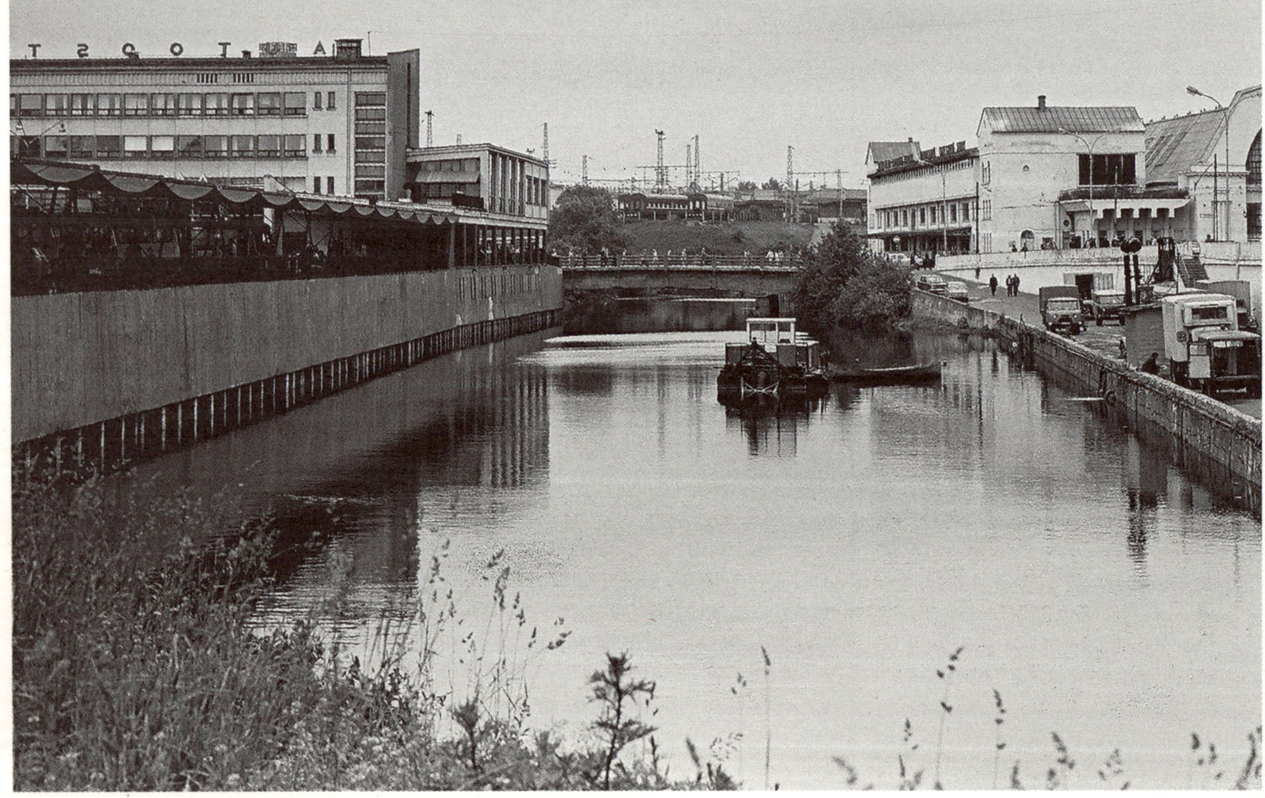

Canal between centrāltirgus (central market) and autoosta (central bus station), circa 1975. Photo: Māra Brašmane

Conversation

Inga Lāce
Katerina Gregos

With a jaunty-sounding acronym, the new private biannual art initiative RIBOCA, the Riga International Biennial of Contemporary Art, takes place in Riga for the first time from June to October this year. Founded by Agniya Mirgorodskaya, who is half-Russian, half-Lithuanian, a recent graduate of Sotheby's Institute of Art, and financed by her father, the owner of the North West Fishing Consortium, it is curated this year by Katerina Gregos, a curator with an impressive record in curating large-scale international exhibitions and biennials.

Since I put my questions to Gregos at the end of January, the biennial has already started to take a more concrete shape. A public programme with talks by participating artists has begun, along with the recent announcement of the list of artists, with almost a hundred names.

Nevertheless, the most interesting discussions so far have been outside official communication channels. I have had heated, passionate and challenging discussions with friends and colleagues from the art scene since the very first rumours about the biennial and its organisers, and its first awkward and later more polished statements. I have been called xenophobic by a friend after a careful expression of unwelcome feeling towards the new venture, because of where it originates from. I then thought again about my openness towards others on our art scene, when it is more than just the desire for a more international art environment, but an actual institution that has arrived. I have lunched, exchanged thoughts with and shared local insights with the people working at the new institution. I have also had several introductions by Russian friends to the entanglement of art and money in Russia since the 1990s, when the biennial was still associated with Emelyan Zakharov, the founder of the Triumph Gallery, as one of its initiators.

But beyond personal acceptance or refusal, the presence of the biennial is interesting in several other ways. Firstly, it shakes up the local art scene, at least by making it question the status quo that people who work here might have forgotten about. What is our relationship with the audience, and how can we reach out more? Why, how and on what terms do we collaborate with each other? What is and should be a fair artists' fee, and what about our own remuneration? And this kind of reflection can always be healthy, be it a simple sharing at the opening, or a bigger deal leading to our work environments, and perhaps instigating change.

And even though I am sure much more will come out once the biennial actually happens, especially over the years, I also think this is a very unique (and short) moment to think about its founding. In a recent conversation, trying very hard to understand the situation and my unease, another friend ended up by asking me a question: is it at all possible to organise a biennial in Riga in any way or form entirely funded by private Russian money which would not feel like a burden instead of a gift? Could any other structures be put in place, or communication used, to facilitate a different outcome? Part of the answer lies in the country's complex present and past, and the fact that there are invisible, but therefore even more effective, structures and mechanisms of colonialism which need to be actively addressed and countered, instead of just dressing them up in a discourse of generosity. However, and especially because the field we are working in is about imagining different and better futures, I think the answer can still be tried out, learnt, practised and instituted.

* * *

Inga Lāce: You are the curator and artistic director of the first Riga Biennial. There have been a lot of discussions about biennials and the necessity for them recently, in relation to their proliferation as a format for how art is produced and seen, and, of course, the relationship between the biennial format and the sustainability of art ecosystems when they often serve as marketing tools for a city or a private sponsor. Could you elaborate on your view of the necessity for a new biennial in Riga at the present time?

Katerina Gregos: With more than a hundred biennials in almost fifty countries worldwide, one might indeed ask, why another? The answer is: it depends *where*. It wouldn't make sense to start a biennial in London or Paris, but in Riga, and other countries of the so-called periphery, where contemporary art institutions and infrastructures are not as developed as in the metropolises, biennials can play an important role in nourishing the art scene, creating an interest in it, offering international visibility to (emerging) artists, and creating a significant platform for knowledge production and exchange, which is something we aim to do with both the exhibition and the public programme. Apart from promoting a city, a biennial can more importantly showcase and promote the country's and intellectual cultural power. The Riga Biennial is not a city marketing project, although Riga is definitely a gem to discover, and provides an extremely interesting context from which to work. It also makes sense to hold a biennial in the Baltic region, which is in the spotlight now, considering the geo-political shifts that are taking place there and which are followed with interest globally.

IL: Quite a few arguments have taken place in Riga regarding the private sponsorship of the Riga Biennial initiative. Since it hasn't been revealed, the fact itself has caused reactions, ranging from anger to suspicion, to the fear of possible political maneuvering executed through the platform of the biennial, to ignorance or cynicism, deeming it a clear money-laundering project or a process of gentrification. Most of these are, of course, well-known vices in the art world's relationship to money. What do you think of the situation, and perhaps the response to the suspicion and fear expressed in the local art community, and is it important to you where the funding for projects you engage in comes from?

KG: In general, large art exhibitions cannot be made without significant amounts of private and corporate sponsorship. The same applies to biennials (just think of Venice or Istanbul). At the same time, the art world is rightly getting more and more critical of the origin of its funding, which is a good thing, as it reflects the moral responsibility that art wishes to stand for. In this case, from the beginning, I also questioned the funding of the biennial, and it took me some time before I could decide, before which I asked a lot of questions. As soon as I found out that the money comes from a legitimate business (North West Fishing Consortium), and this is not a secret as you suggest, without any restrictions on my curatorial or artistic freedom, it was clear to me that there were no strings attached, no political agenda, or gentrification motives. The fact that I have received carte blanche to develop exactly the kind of project I wanted indicates that the biennial is in Riga in order to contribute, not to machinate. If there were any hidden agendas, they certainly would have shown by now (I have been working on the project for more than a year now). Rumours will always circulate, and they are difficult to refute. In this case, it should be clear that the onus is on the accusers to prove their allegations. If they cannot, they should refrain from spreading conspiracy theories.

IT ALSO MAKES SENSE TO HOLD A BIENNIAL IN THE BALTIC REGION, WHICH IS IN THE SPOTLIGHT NOW, CONSIDERING THE GEO-POLITICAL SHIFTS THAT ARE TAKING PLACE THERE AND WHICH ARE FOLLOWED WITH INTEREST GLOBALLY.

IL: Since this is the first Riga Biennial, your work as a curator is that of shaping it, giving you a lot of liberty, since no one has done it before, but also a responsibility for establishing something that is meaningful and worth continuing. Also, the founding body of the biennial is a managerial one, again giving you a lot of power for framing the actual event, as well as placing it here / there (in Riga, in the art world, in the local / international community) physically and discursively. What is your thinking, your strategy in relation to this situation? What decisions do you think you are taking differently to how you would work in an established biannual institution?

KG: It was important for me to address some of the problematic issues that biennials face: wrong priorities, unrealistic ambitions that collapse under their own weight, problematic financial structures that exploit cultural workers, too little time for artists to work / research properly; and to prioritise for the international rather than the local. In developing the mission of RIBOCA together with its founder, it became important to create a structure based on a best-practices model, and with sustainability in mind. First of all, taking good care of artists, investing time in them, making sure they have the proper conditions to develop and show their work, and ensuring financial remuneration for their work. At RIBOCA, all artists are paid a fee, whether they are making a new work or showing an existing one. If they are working on site, they get a *per diem*, and we offer research assistance in the form of (wo)manpower for all artists making new works. The exhibition itself will unfold as a sustainable experience for the viewer (unlike Documenta with its 46 [!] venues in Athens, which hardly anyone saw in total). Riga is the perfect place to decelerate perceptions, because of its human scale, and the proximity of the venues to each other. We are not another generic internationalist biennial. The local context is very important to us. That's why I actually started the curatorial process by first researching and meeting Latvian artists (and then artists from the Baltic region), and expanding outwards towards the international. Very often, biennials land in a certain location, disregarding the local context, except in a token way. We're very interested in contributing to the cultural landscape in Riga, and in Latvia; to this effect, the public programme we have instigated will have a wide variety of activities, addressed to different groups of citizens. And we're thinking how the biennial may have a life outside the scope of the exhibition format. I've been very fortunate in my professional life up till now to be able to play a role in shaping many of the biennial projects I've done, and so until now my core principles have not been compromised.

AT RIBOCA, ALL ARTISTS ARE PAID A FEE, WHETHER THEY ARE MAKING A NEW WORK OR SHOWING AN EXISTING ONE.

IL: In the curatorial concept, you take the notion of change as the guiding direction, describing the rapid changes currently under way in so many spheres, and touching on the history of Latvia and the Baltic region, naming the biennial after the book *Everything Was Forever, Until It Was No More* by Alexei Yurchak. He is one of the leading post-Soviet theoreticians, and thus almost a chrestomatic reference for the contemporary art field in relation to the post-socialist area. Could you elaborate on your choice of the title of his book? Do you perhaps plan to involve him in the programmes?

KG: Although I chose the title of Yurchak's book for the biennial, it would be a mistake to think that the biennial will focus only on the post-Soviet situation. In fact, I chose the title because I felt it worked very well as a metaphor for change, and not only change in the post-Soviet world. I also chose it because he describes aptly some of the problematics that arise out of systemic or violent change, and how people experience it. As I explained above, the biennial is about the current state of the world, and the rapid transformations it is undergoing, in terms of history, politics, society, technology and science. There will, of course, be a reference to the history of the region, because it would be amnesiac to forget previous chapters of Latvian history. The past and the present, after all, are not disconnected from each other, but form part of a continuum.

IL: A statement of the Riga Biennial describes the Baltic region as 'a territory which still remains relatively unexplored, despite its prolific artistic production'. This phrase reminds me of the discourse in the early 1990s, when the Soviet Union collapsed, and artists from the Baltic countries were suddenly invited to international exhibitions, and the post-Soviet condition was often highly exoticized by West European curators and their exhibition projects. Could you explain how you relate to this statement from the biennial, and what is meant by exploration? How, and by whom, has it not yet happened, and would it potentially happen during the biennial?

KG: Indeed there was a moment where there was a newfound interest in (post-socialist) art from eastern Europe but that moment was short lived; it was also a moment where there was more interest in art from Poland, Albania, former Yugoslavia etc., and less from the Baltic states if one looks at exhibition histories from the last 20 years or so. It is impossible to deny that the Baltic region is 'a territory which still remains relatively unexplored', as it is just a fact when one looks at the scant international interest in artists from this region. I don't think there is a Latvian artist, for example, whose name has risen to great international fame, meaning universal recognition in the field of art; and despite a certain success by a handful of artists abroad, the fact is that art from the Baltic region still remains to a large part a *terra incognita*. And this is not unusual in a small country, which was also occupied and isolated for a long time. It is the same in Greece, where I come from. I doubt that any of our colleagues can mention, off-hand, the names of more than one or two Greek (or Baltic for that matter) artists (who are not expats). So, an international biennial is a perfect platform to showcase work from a region or a place that is less well known. I fail to see the reason why the concept of 'exoticization' is smuggled into your question. The moment of exoticization has passed, because many of these countries that were considered exotic because they were coming out of the shadows are now part of Europe. Helping to put Latvia on the international art map by way of a biennial, in addition to the work done by colleagues in Latvia, in the past and nowadays, also increases the possibilities for Latvian artists to attain international recognition.

IL: You formed the core curatorial team from international curators (with the Danish associate curator Solvej Helweg Ovesen, and the assistant curator Ioli Tzanetaki from Greece). I emphasise this because the main management team is also almost entirely foreign to the Riga context. Considering your intention to embed the biennial in a local context as emphasised in the curatorial statement, could you tell us a bit more about this decision?

KG: Our team consists of thirty three people, and more than half of them are Latvian. The curatorial team is not only international, it is also Latvian. Our curators of the public programme, a very important position, are Latvian. My co-editor for the biennial Reader (one of the two publications we are issuing) is Latvian. The four members of our team who are responsible for research are also Latvian. So, we feel very privileged to work with a team that has inside knowledge of the city and the country, from different areas.

IL: I have recently observed several examples where public discussions and events were organised to create a new biennial (Oslo Pilot started two years before announcing the biennial, Bergen Assembly did research and held a symposium before embarking on a triennial format). Open discussions not only help to see the diversity of opinions in

Following spread: Centrāltirgus's (central market) flower square in Winter, 1969/70. Photo: Māra Brašmane

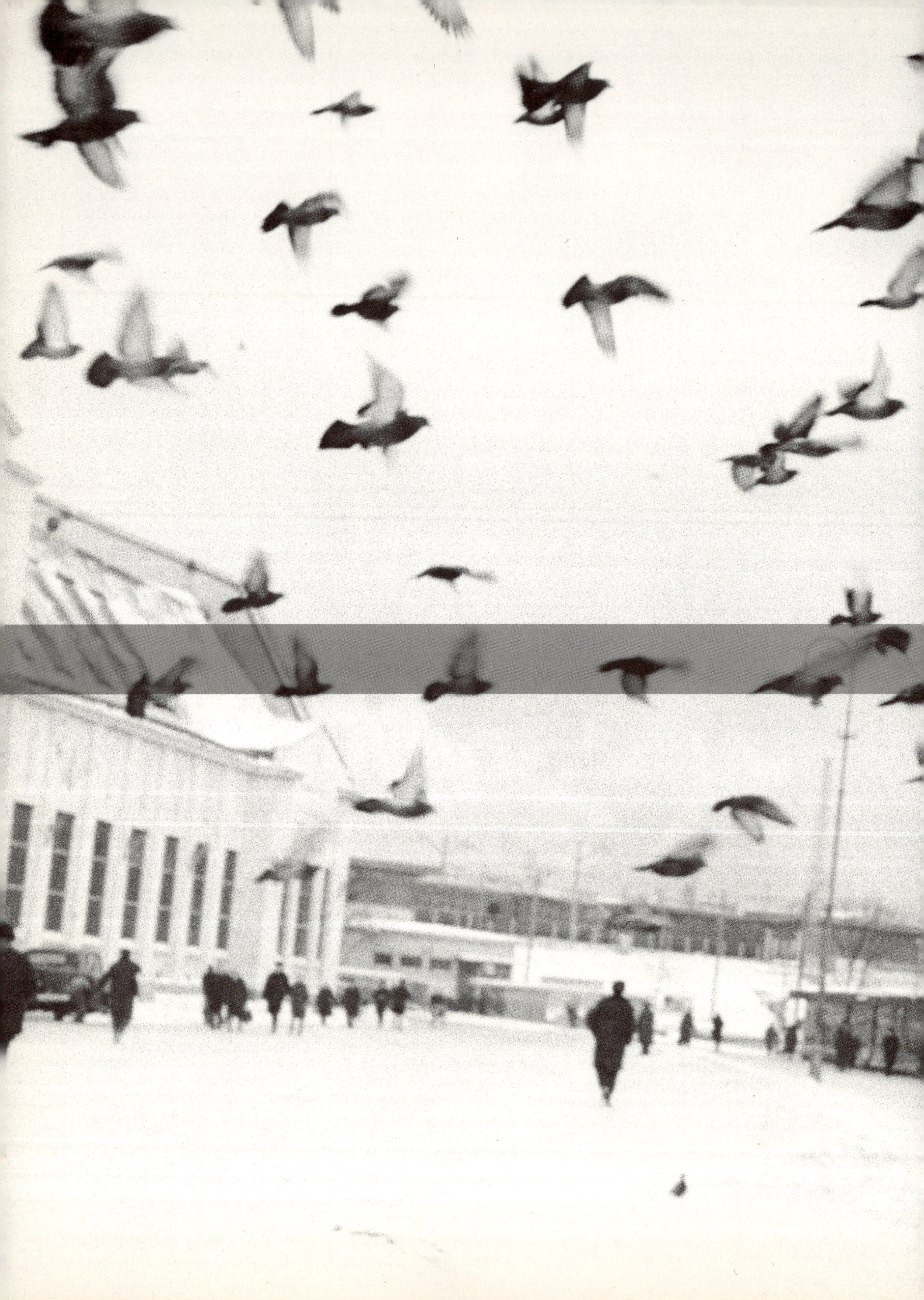

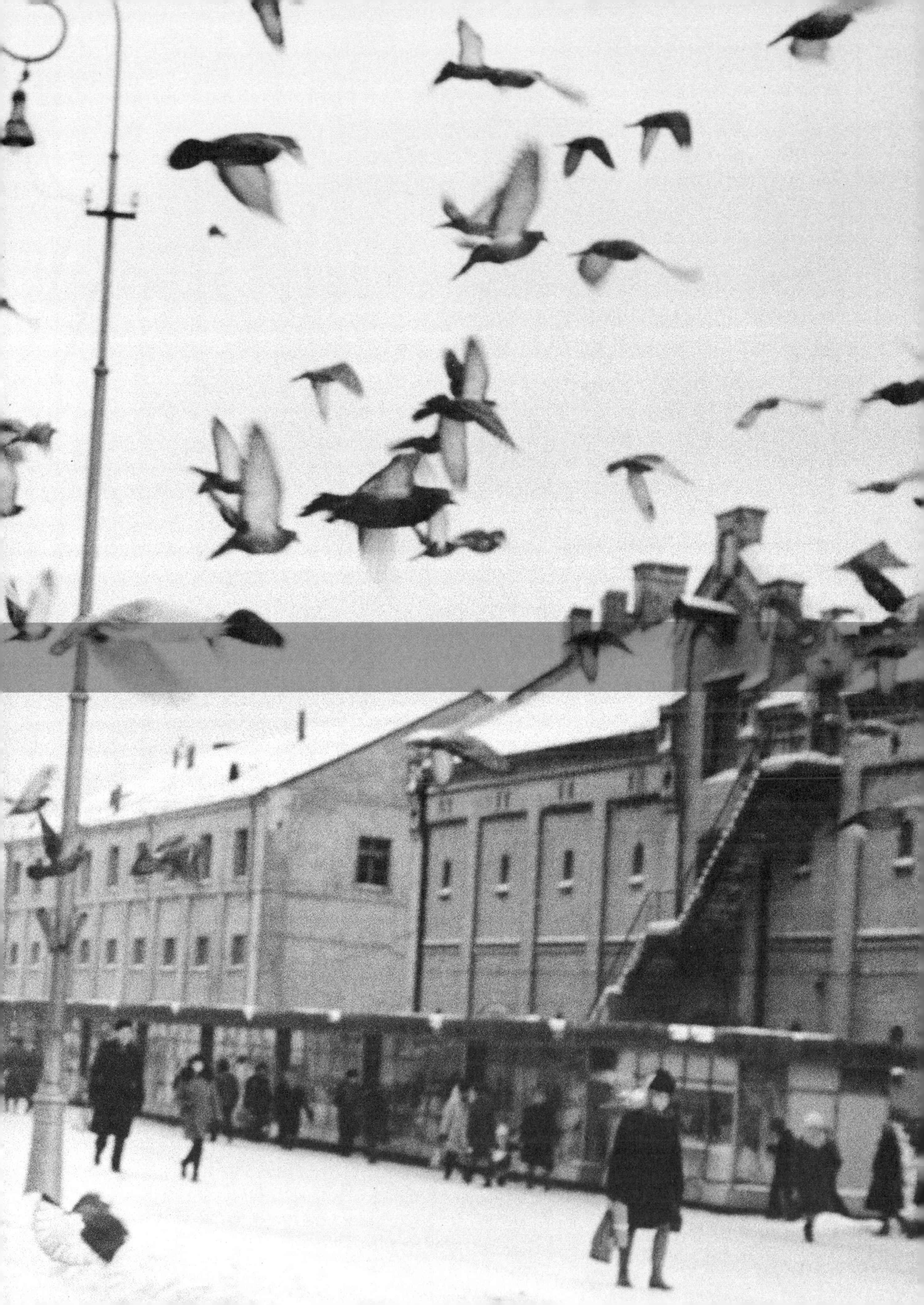

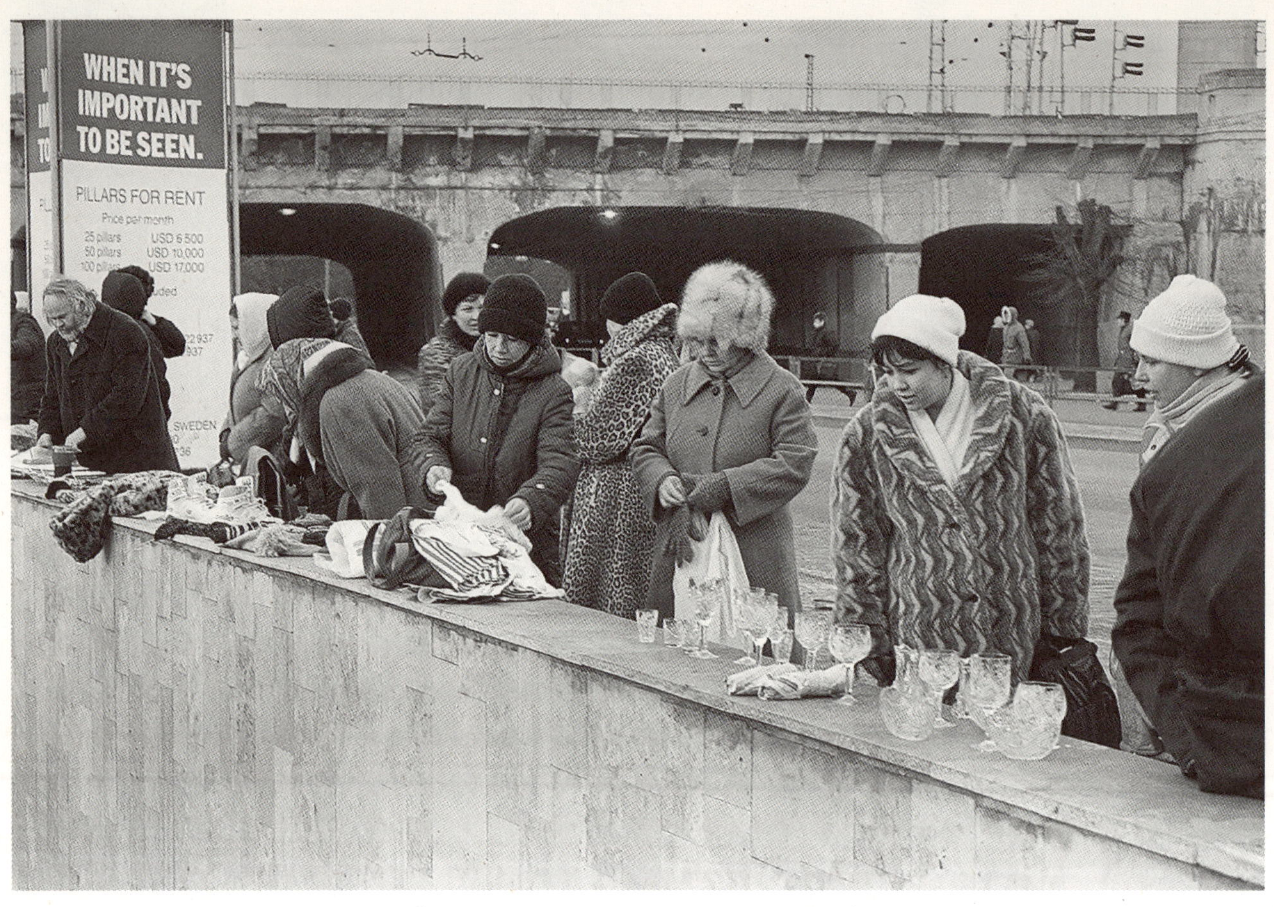

Free market in Gogola iela next to centrāltirgus (central market), circa 1992. Photo: Māra Brašmane

the local community, which is small in the Riga context, but also provide some creative tension, which certainly makes for a better project, helping to avoid the simplification of certain issues and potential pitfalls in the project. Thus, I wonder if a discussion that could still shape the actual event is planned soon, or if not, what is the reason for the decision not to organise these events before the biennial?

KG: It seems like an interesting and instructive approach to hear and gather the opinions of others when one organises an international art exhibition, especially when it is not on one's home territory. I have personally invested a lot of time in doing exactly that. We have also held a number of Think Tanks, where we gathered people who, exactly as you say, represent a diversity of opinions in the local community. But although holding an exhibition by collecting the various opinions that may exist about such an enterprise looks democratic, it is also the safest position to adopt. If it is all possible to do justice to the different sentiments and views, it would also end in a project without a specific point of view, a kind of tasteless soup, and the task of the curator would be just to provide a place for all the ingredients. That is not the way I work. I prefer to develop my own attitude towards a certain problematic, on the basis of all the relevant information that I can lay my hands on.

THE FACT THAT IT IS BACKED BY A PRIVATE FOUNDATION, IN FACT, ACTUALLY MAKES IT INDEPENDENT OF THE VALUABLE RESOURCES OF THE LOCAL ART SCENE.

IL: On one hand, the Riga Biennial brings to Riga a lot of resources (international attention, a proper production budget for artists, salaries for some local art managers etc), but on the other hand, of course, it also takes from the local scene (local private sponsors, the support of embassies, potential state spending on culture, employees from other institutions), since it clearly uses resources and relationships nurtured by local people over many years with the scarce means they have. From a local point of view, it shakes the fragile and scarce art ecosystem. What is your view on the relationship between the local art ecosystem in a city like Riga and the incoming body of a new biennial?

KG: The Riga Biennial is based on the principle of generosity: giving rather than taking. Let me explain, in order to dispel any misconception that the biennial is a kind of vampire, as you describe it in the second part of your question. The fact that it is backed by a private foundation, in fact, actually makes it independent of the valuable resources of the local art scene. First of all, we are not taking money from the state, or from embassies or other financing structures in Latvia.* In terms of local private support, we only have the support of Jānis Zuzāns, who has generously provided us with the

Zuzeum as a venue. In terms of the people we hired, most of them were working part-time or freelance, and so we were glad to offer them full-time work. There is only one person who has come from another institution in Riga, and she was planning to leave anyway. Considering all the above, I would hardly say that this 'shakes the local art ecosystem', or constitutes a threat to it.

IL: There is an inherent complexity in the relationship between Latvia and Russia, emerging from Latvia's occupation by the Soviet Union, and the fact that Russia has never acknowledged the fact, if we look at it from the perspective of recent history. Russia's constant aggressive reaction towards Latvia's political mistake in the early 1990s of not granting citizenship to everyone who was part of the reestablished country has just added insult to injury on both sides. Of course, this exposes only one small part of the complex and layered processes taking place between the countries, and the cohabitation of both ethnicities in Latvia. However, these issues immediately and inevitably come to mind, because the new biennial initiative comes as a private initiative from Russia. How do you plan to navigate this complexity?

KG: Since the end of the Second World War, the relationship between Russia and the free world in general has been complicated and tense, and I do not wish to ignore the fact that Latvia has been suffering from the Russian/Soviet occupation and its aftermath. However, although there are some works in the exhibition that touch on the issues you raise, the biennial as such is not about this. As I was assured total curatorial freedom, I thought this was an excellent opportunity to build more mutual trust, and work together with a Russian counterpart on this cultural project. I am not naïve, but I am also not very prone to conspiracy theories. If we want to achieve better bilateral relations, a cultural exchange project is probably the best way to open communication. While it is impossible to ignore linguistic and political questions, it is not my aim to base the biennial, which is, after all, international, on them. It is easy to demonise anything Russian, but that is a simplistic way of looking at things. I prefer to focus on the positive fruitful relationships that can emerge from such encounters. And one small correction: RIBOCA is not only a Russian initiative. Agniya Mirgorodskaya, the founder, is half-Lithuanian (on her mother's side). This provides her with a view from both sides.

WHEN SOCIO-POLITICAL AND CULTURAL RELATIONS CHANGE OVER THE COURSE OF TIME, AND ARE WEIGHED AND JUDGED DIFFERENTLY, ICONOCLASM SEEMS TO BE A LIBERATING WAY OF TAKING REVENGE ON AND GETTING RID OF A SHAMEFUL PAST.

IL: In a recent lecture in Amsterdam, you mentioned that one of the reasons why the younger generation in the Baltic countries does not know its history is because Soviet history has been erased, by uprooting, for example, monuments to Lenin and Marx. The historical amnesia that you mention, or the desire to revisit the past, has appeared in many artists' work in the Baltic since the 1990s, and has been a starting point for research projects by the Latvian Centre for Contemporary Art in Riga and the National Gallery in Vilnius, among others, trying to find emancipatory ways to speak about the Soviet heritage and history, starting by examining the artists Gustav Klucis and Karl Ioganson, or nonconformist artists from the 1970s, and looking at socialism as an ideology to be distinguished from its manifestation in the Soviet Union. In that light, I wonder if you could elaborate on your view of the monuments.

KG: Monuments, statues, memorials, buildings and the like reflect official historical events that were seen as important and decisive at the time. When socio-political and cultural relations change over the course of time, and are weighed and judged differently, iconoclasm seems to be a liberating way of taking revenge on and getting rid of a shameful past. But by physically destroying the testimonials of a discredited period, we are also erasing those historical moments from the collective memory. We should also consider keeping these monuments as warning signs, or even more importantly, contextualising them in the politics of the present day. Erasure and destruction contribute to historical amnesia, which is very, very dangerous.

** Even though funding has not been granted, an application has been made by the RIBOCA in 2017 to the State Culture Capital Foundation's open call for Cultural Events of State Importance. (Inga Lāce)*

P R

L

T

F

SHAHRYAR NASHAT'S PINK PORTFOLIO

Shahryar Nashat, *Mother on Wheels (Oro Grigio 1)*, 2016. Marble, powdercoated steel, castor wheel, 88×58×48cm. Courtesy of Rodeo Gallery, London.
Following spread: Shahryar Nashat, *Hard Up for Support*, 2016. Installation view, Schinkel Pavilion, Berlin, 2016. Marble, HD video, color / sound 9 min. 38 sec., 221×142×133.5cm. Courtesy of David Kordansky Gallery, Los Angeles.

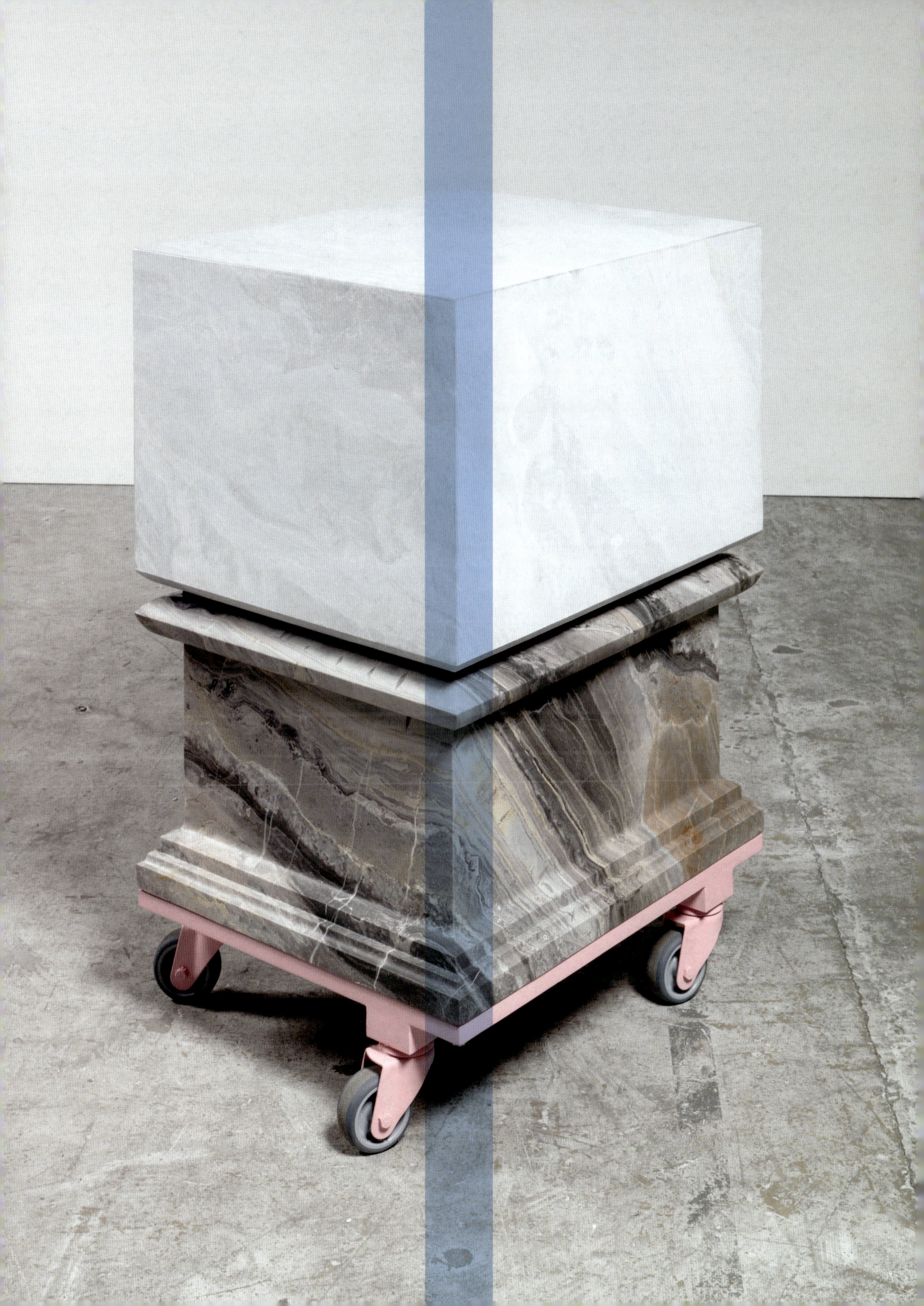

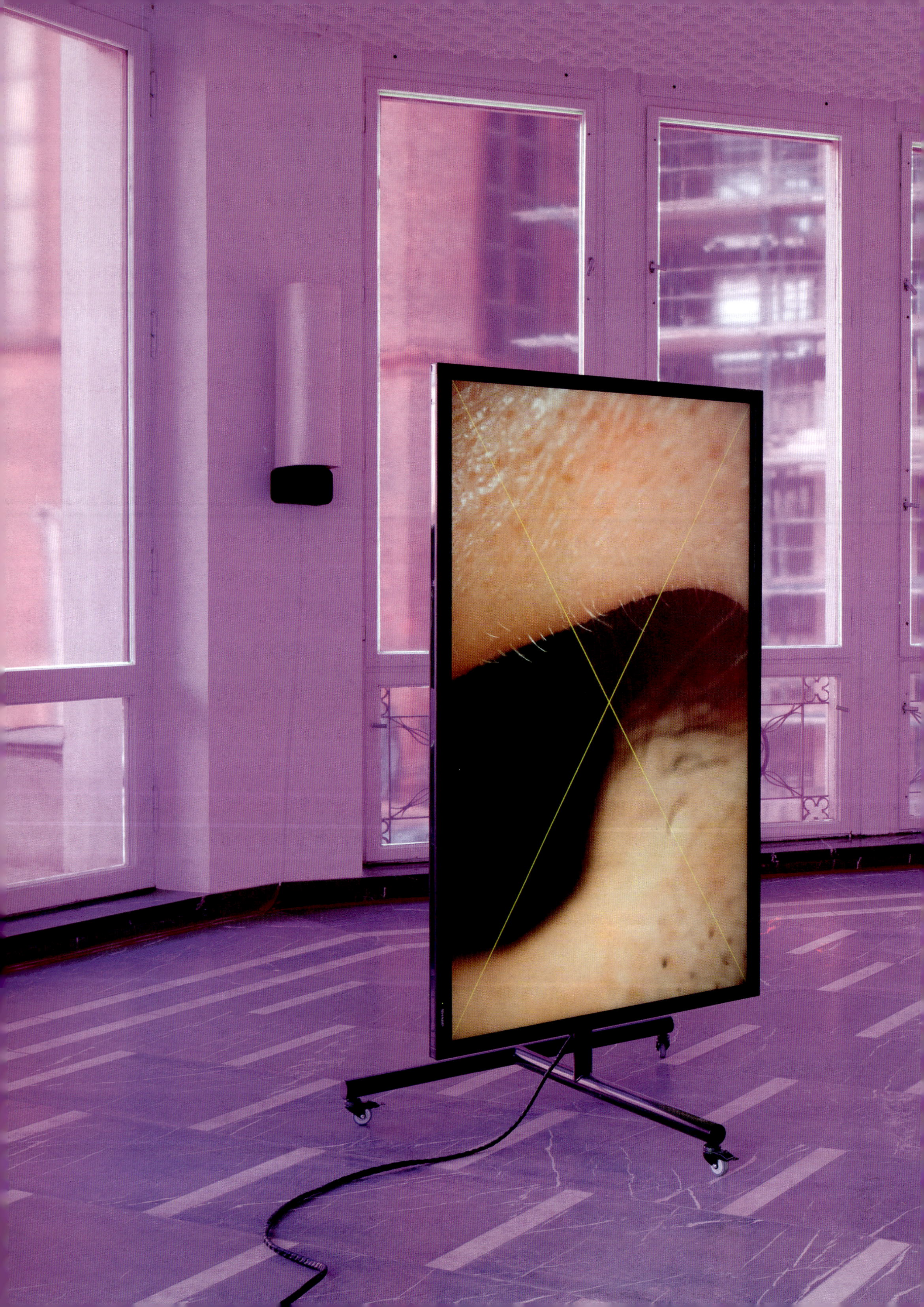

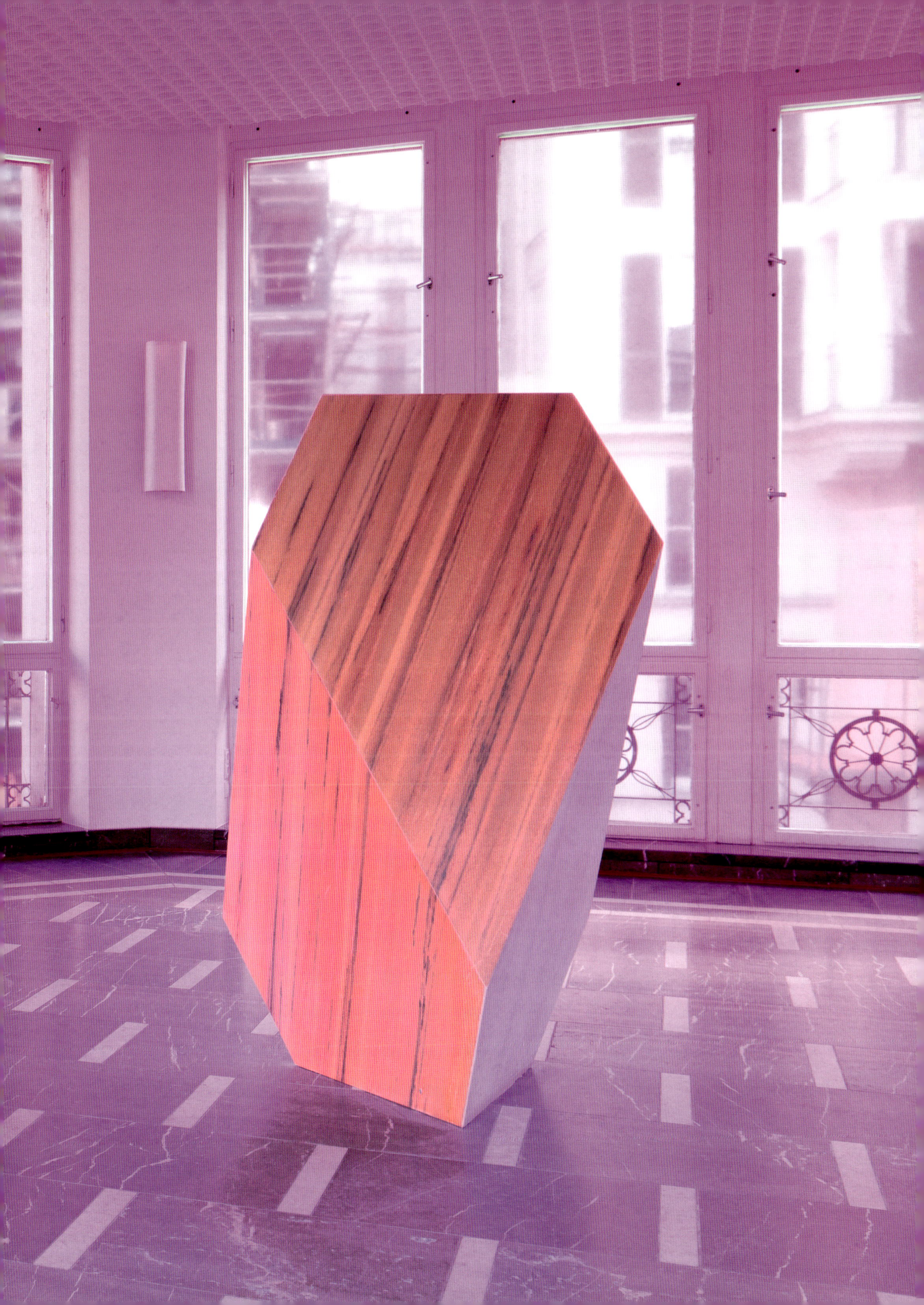

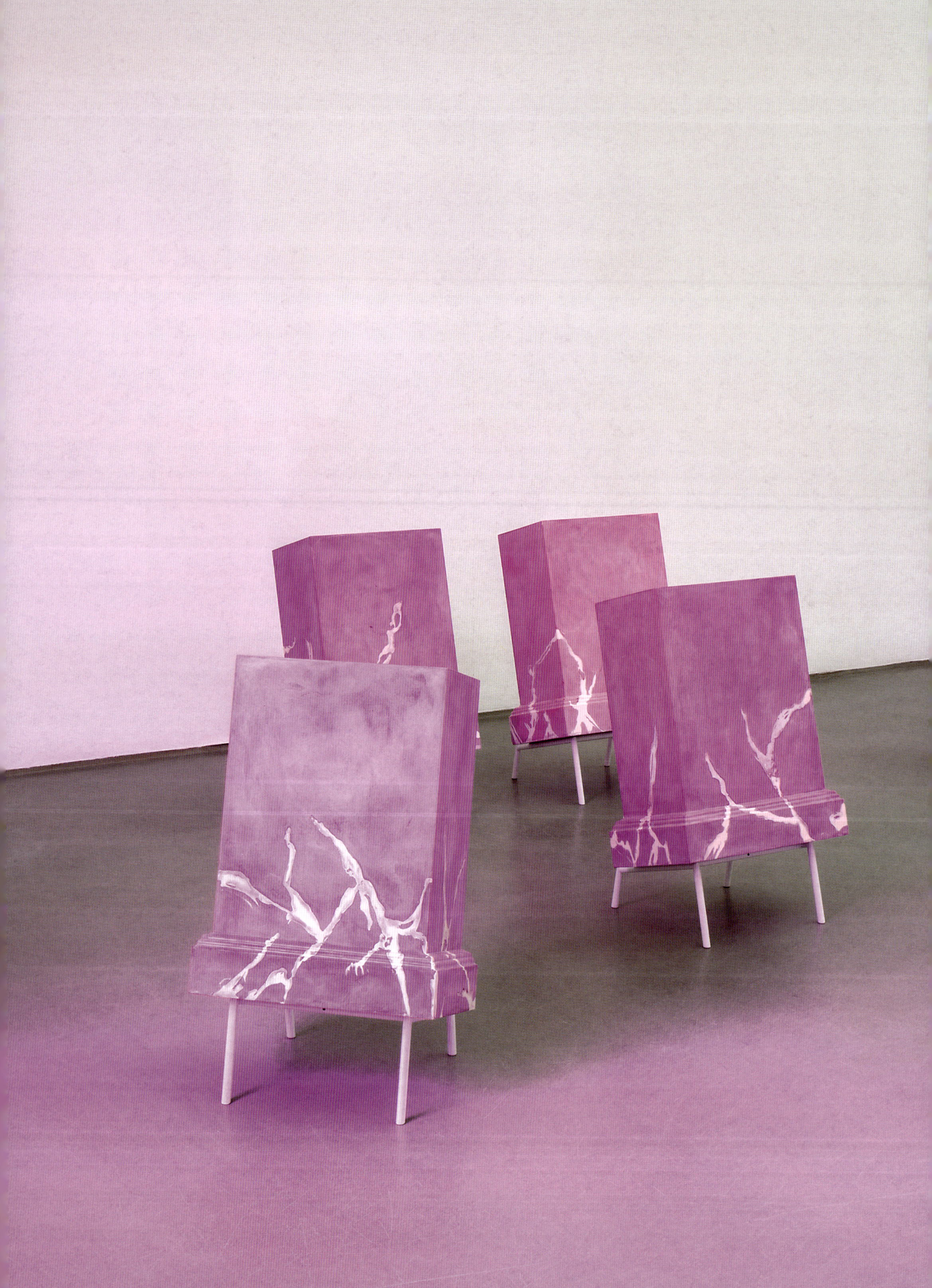

Left page: Shahryar Nashat, *Chômage Techique*, 2016. Hydrocal, fiber glass, pigment, oil, wax, 56×43×28 cm each. Installation view, Portikus, Frankfurt, 2016. Courtesy of Rodeo Gallery, London.
Shahryar Nashat, *Broken English*, 2018. Synthetic polymer, atomized acrylic, fiberglass, 38.4×31.1×30.8 cm. Photography: Jeff McLane. Courtesy of David Kordansky Gallery, Los Angeles, CA.

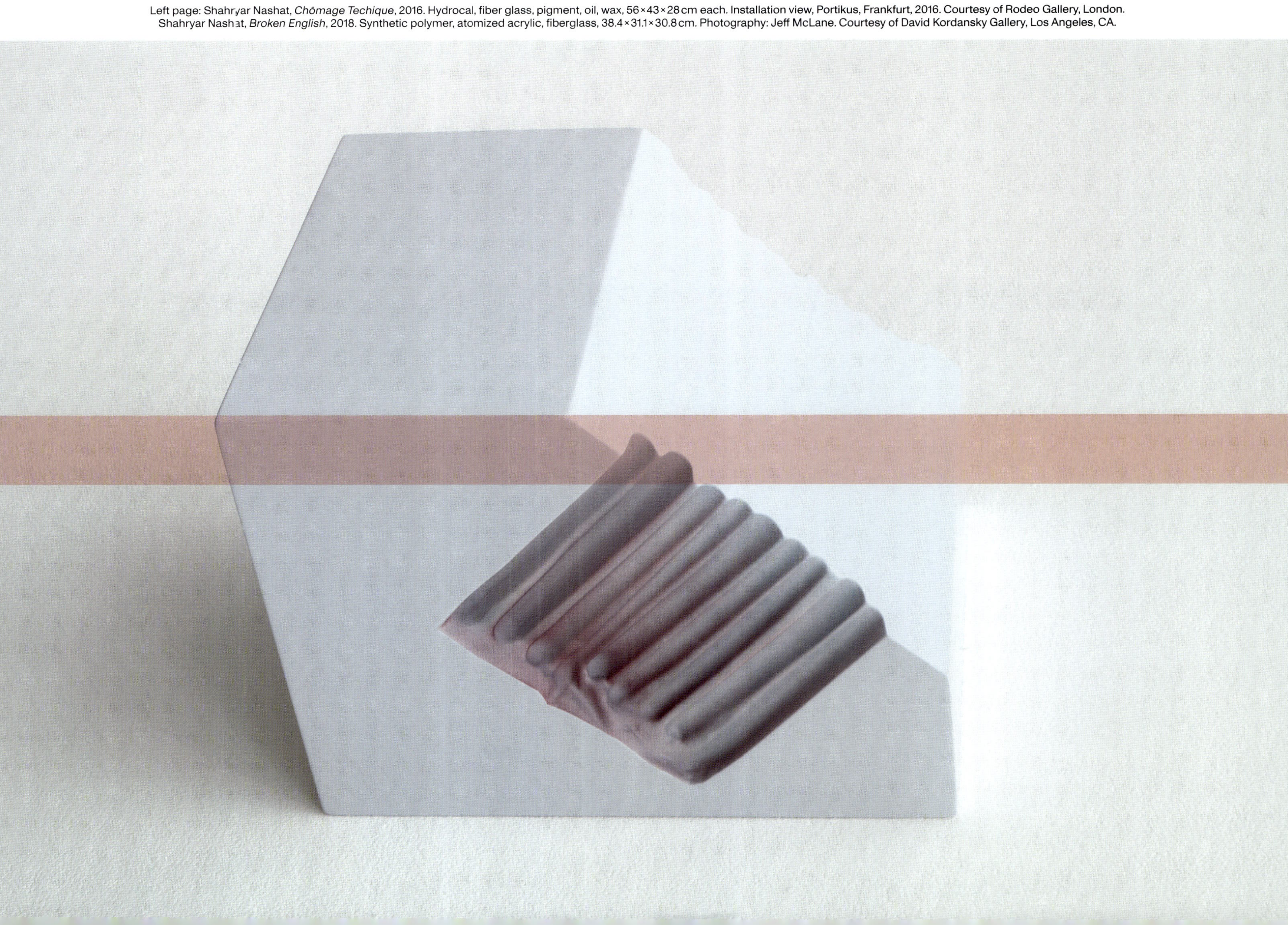

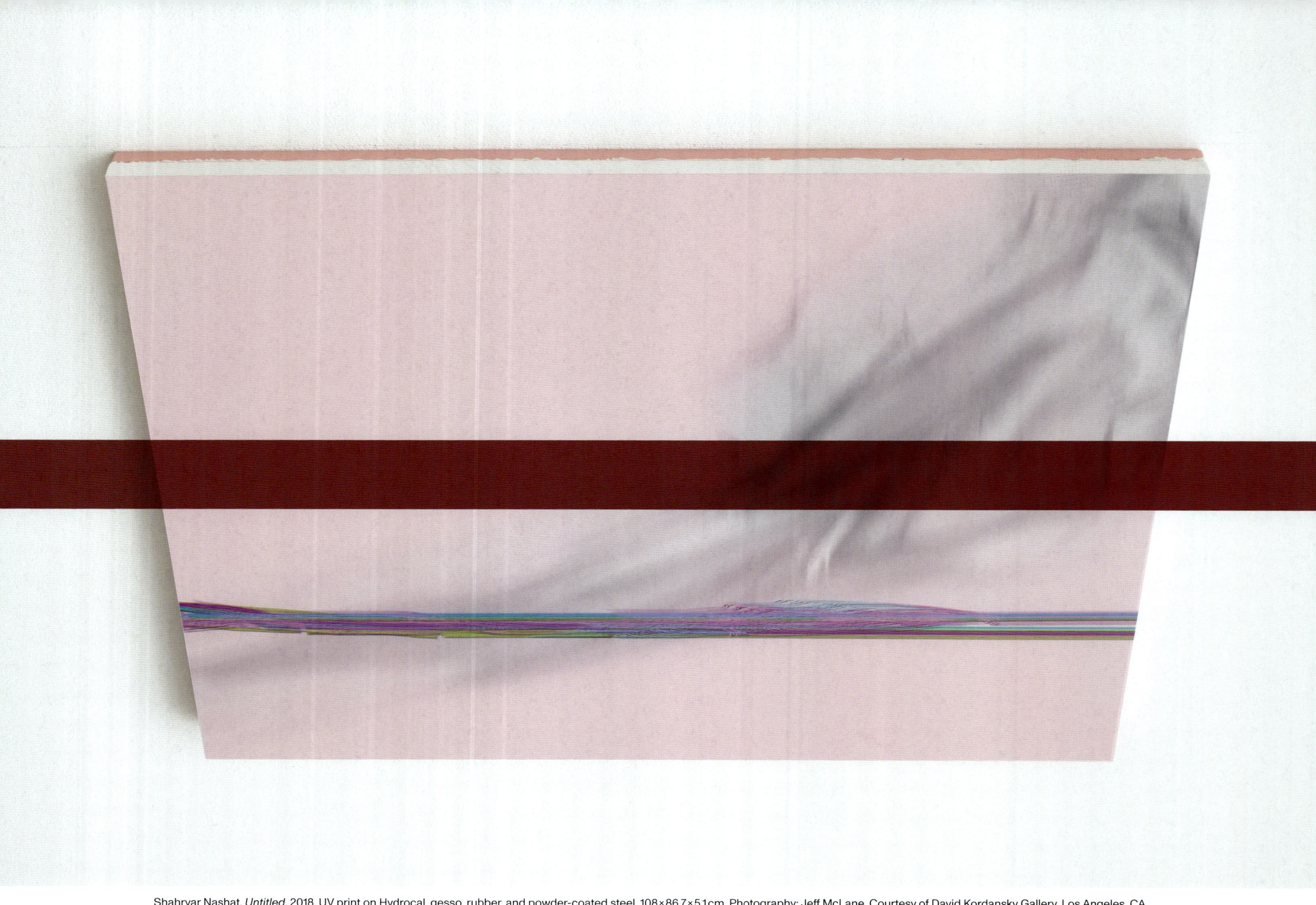

Shahryar Nashat, *Untitled*, 2018. UV print on Hydrocal, gesso, rubber, and powder-coated steel, 108 × 86.7 × 5.1 cm. Photography: Jeff McLane. Courtesy of David Kordansky Gallery, Los Angeles, CA.
Right page (top): Shahryar Nashat, *Cold Horizontal (BODY)*, 2017. Synthetic polymer, fiberglass, pigment, and powder-coated steel, 71 × 178 × 77 cm. Photography: Jeff McLane. Courtesy of David Kordansky Gallery, Los Angeles, CA.
Right page (bottom): Shahryar Nashat, *Cold Horizontal (GHOST)*, 2017. Synthetic polymer, fiberglass, pigment, and powder-coated steel, 80 × 178 × 46 cm. Photography: Jeff McLane. Courtesy of David Kordansky Gallery, Los Angeles, CA.

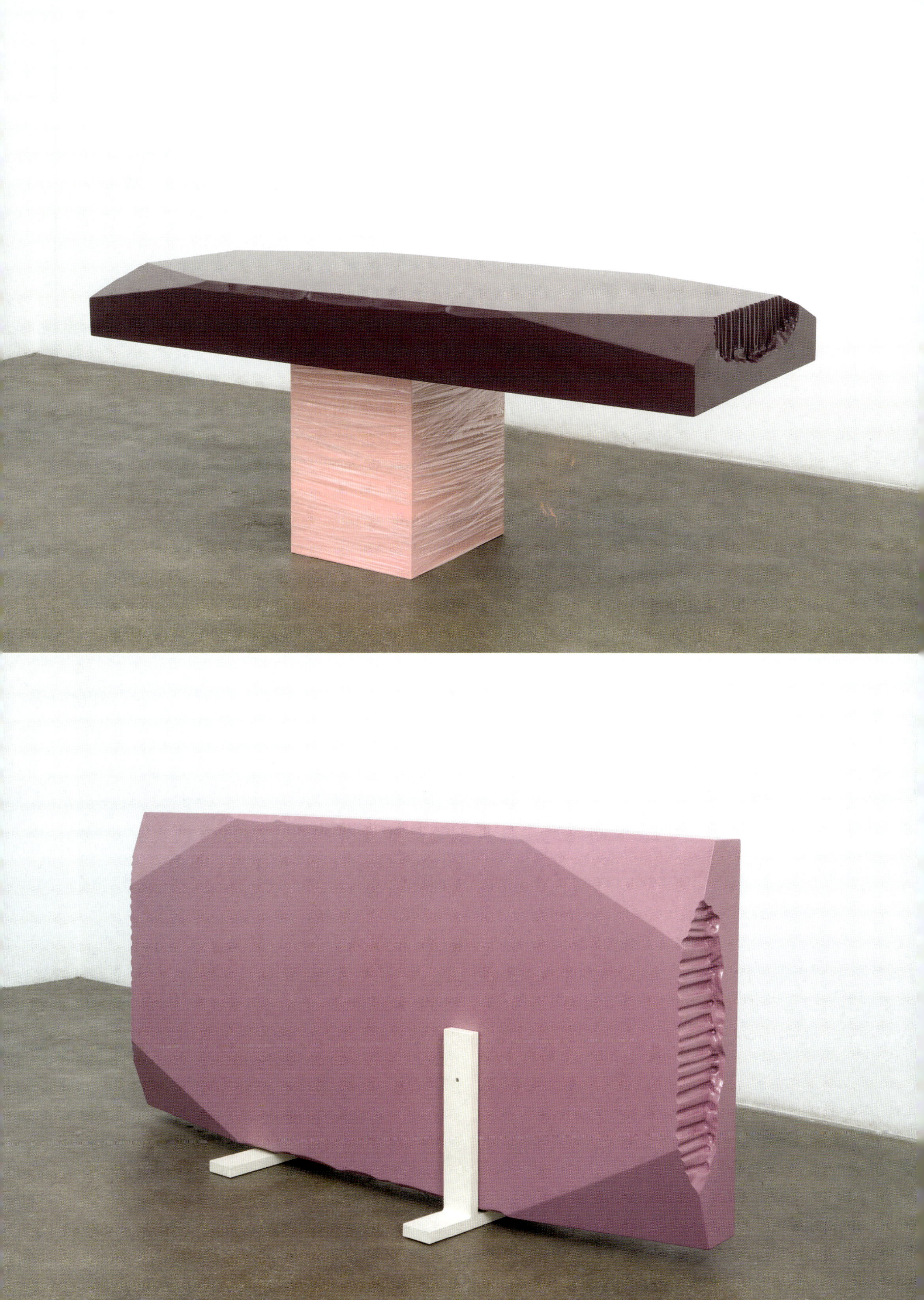

ARBEIT WAR DEIN LEBEN, LIEBE WAR DEIN TUN

Photography

Fashion
Models

Ilya Lipkin
Marc Asekhame
Ursina Gysi
Annina Herzer
Theresa Patzschke

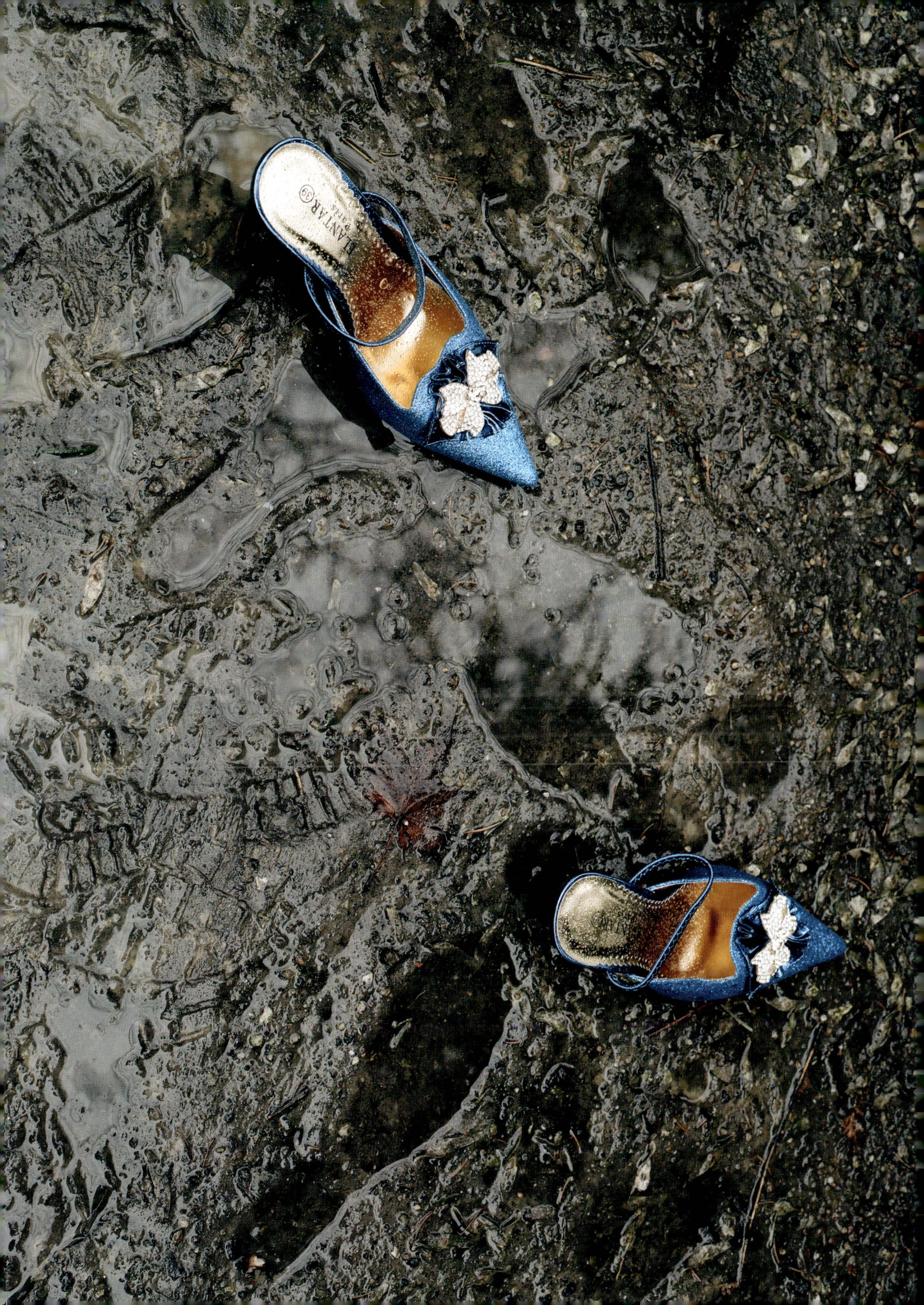

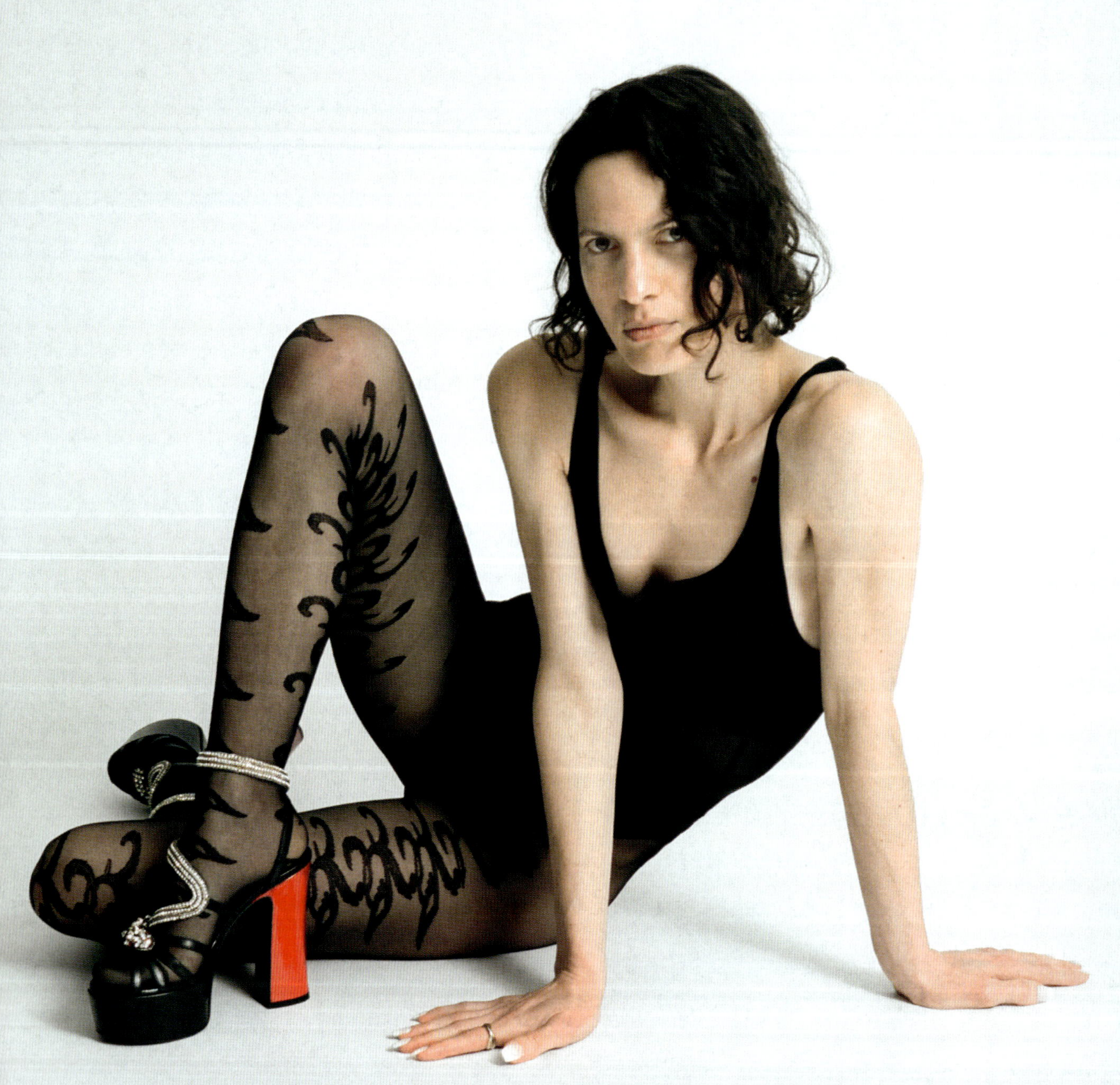

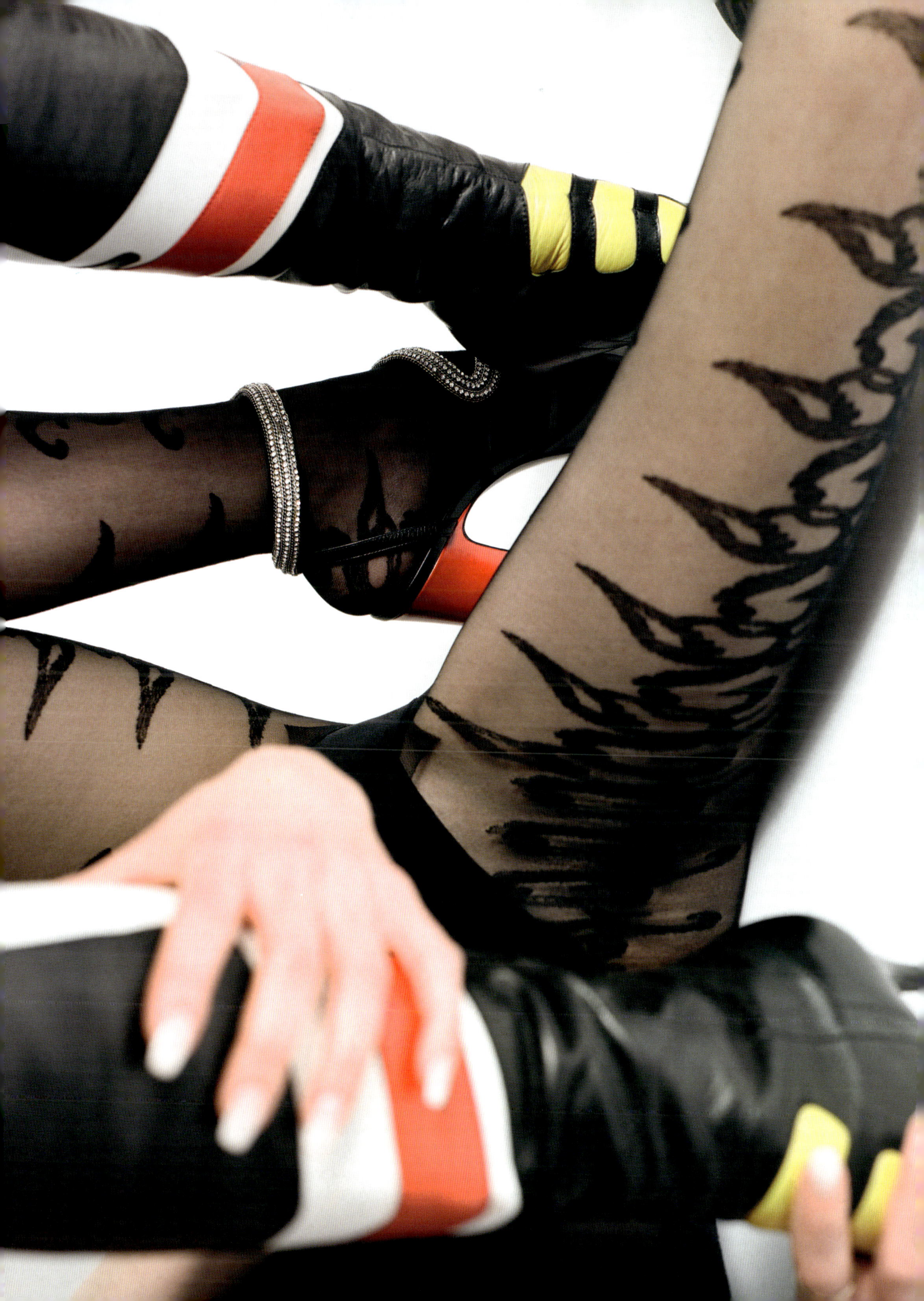

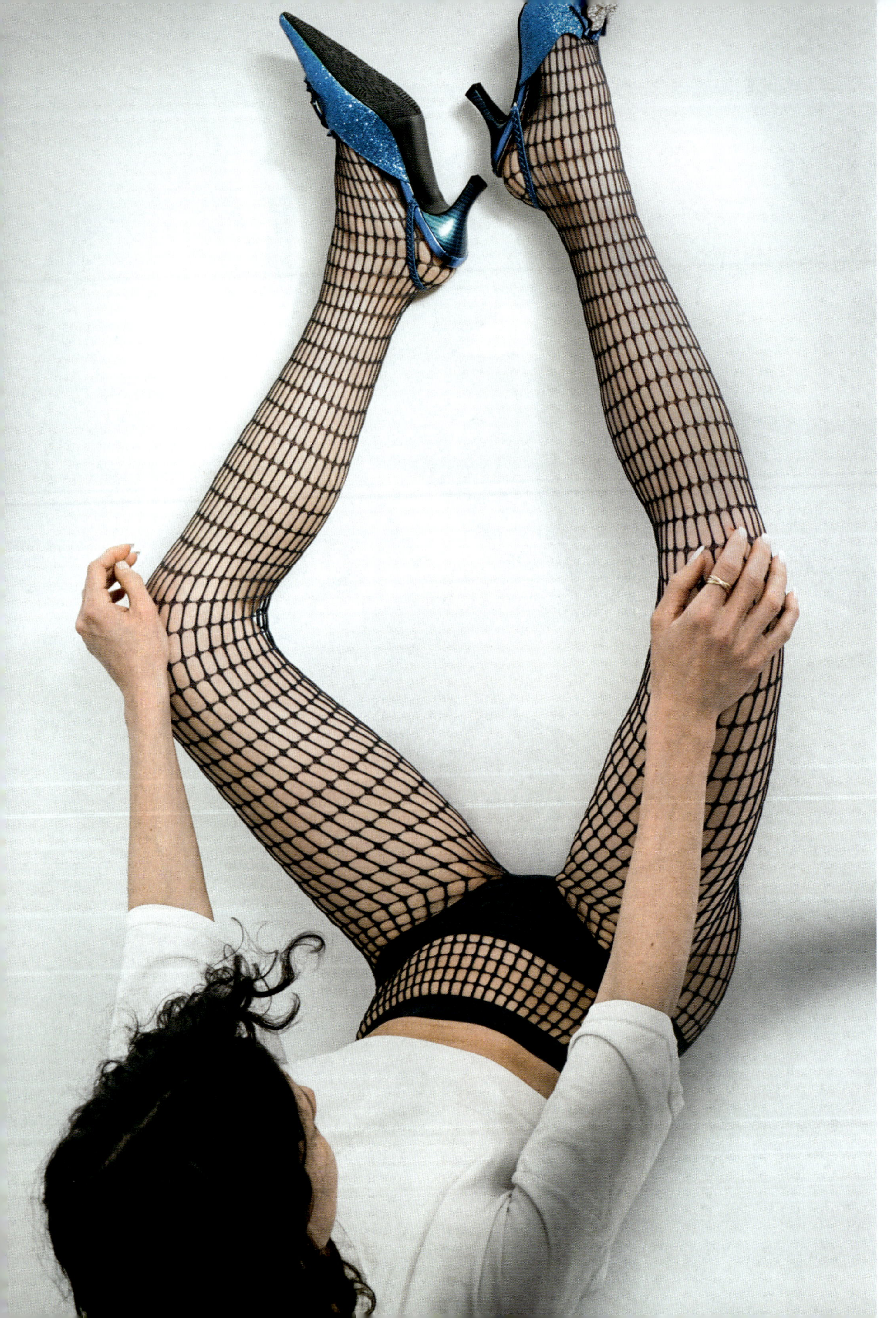

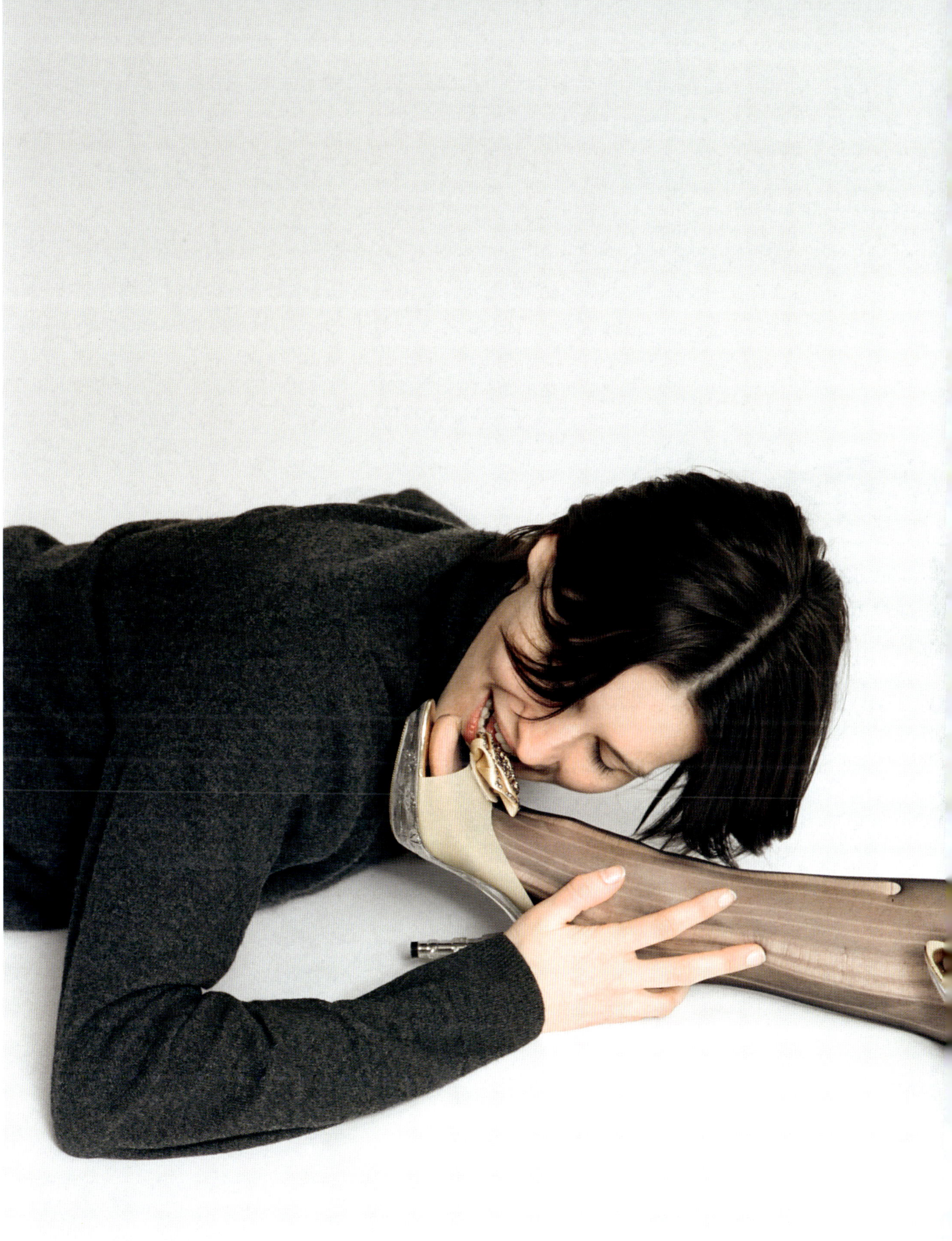

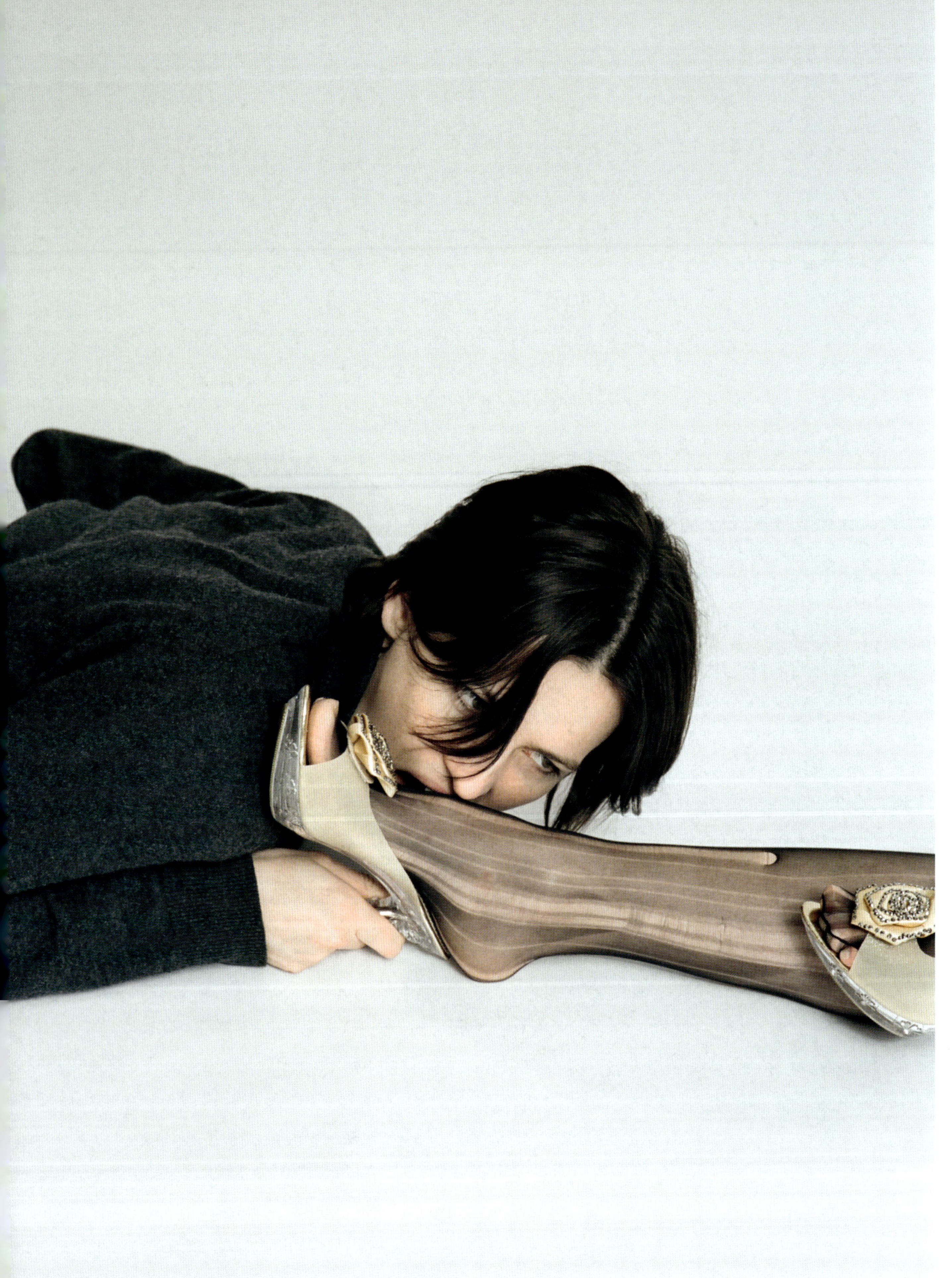

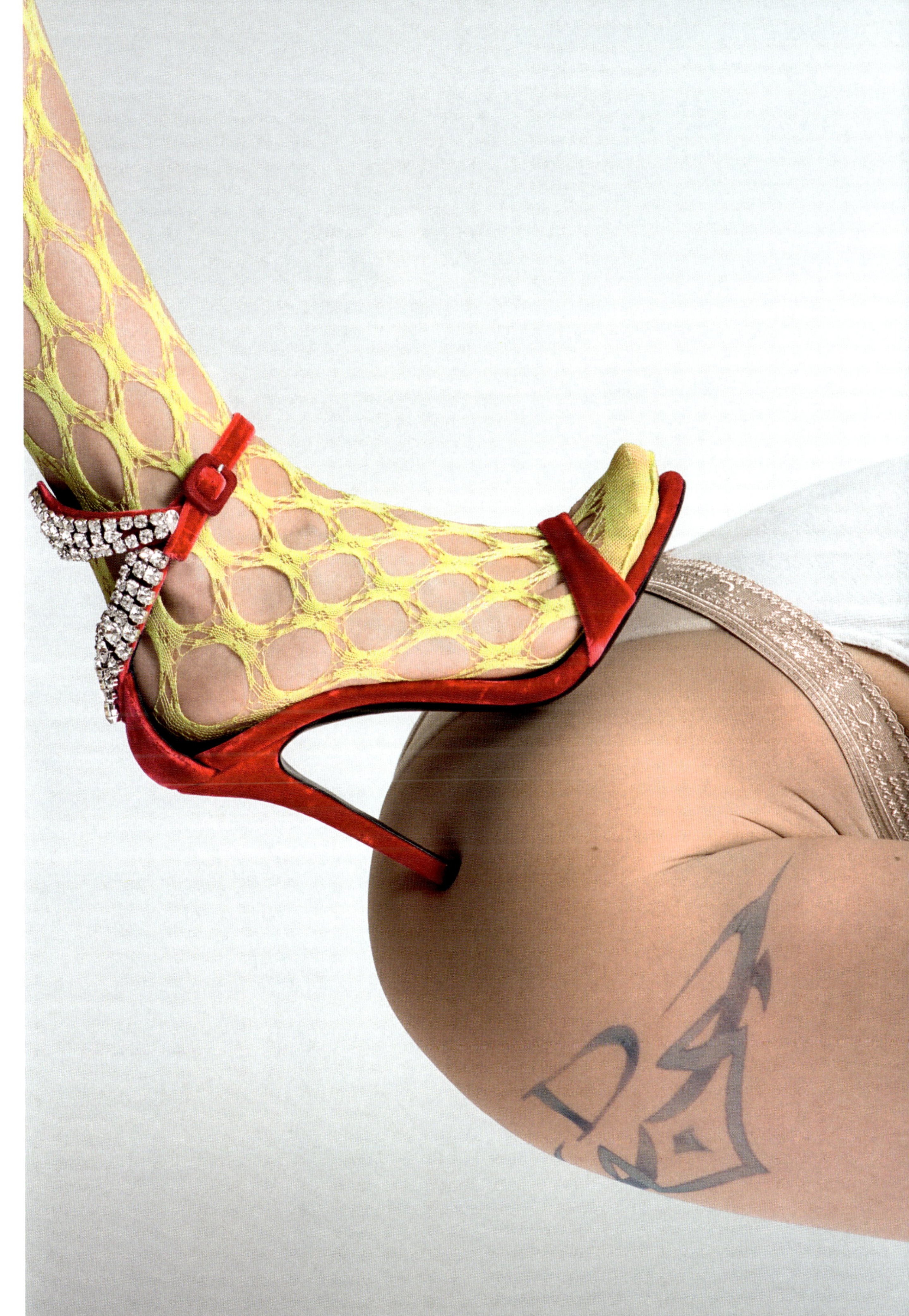

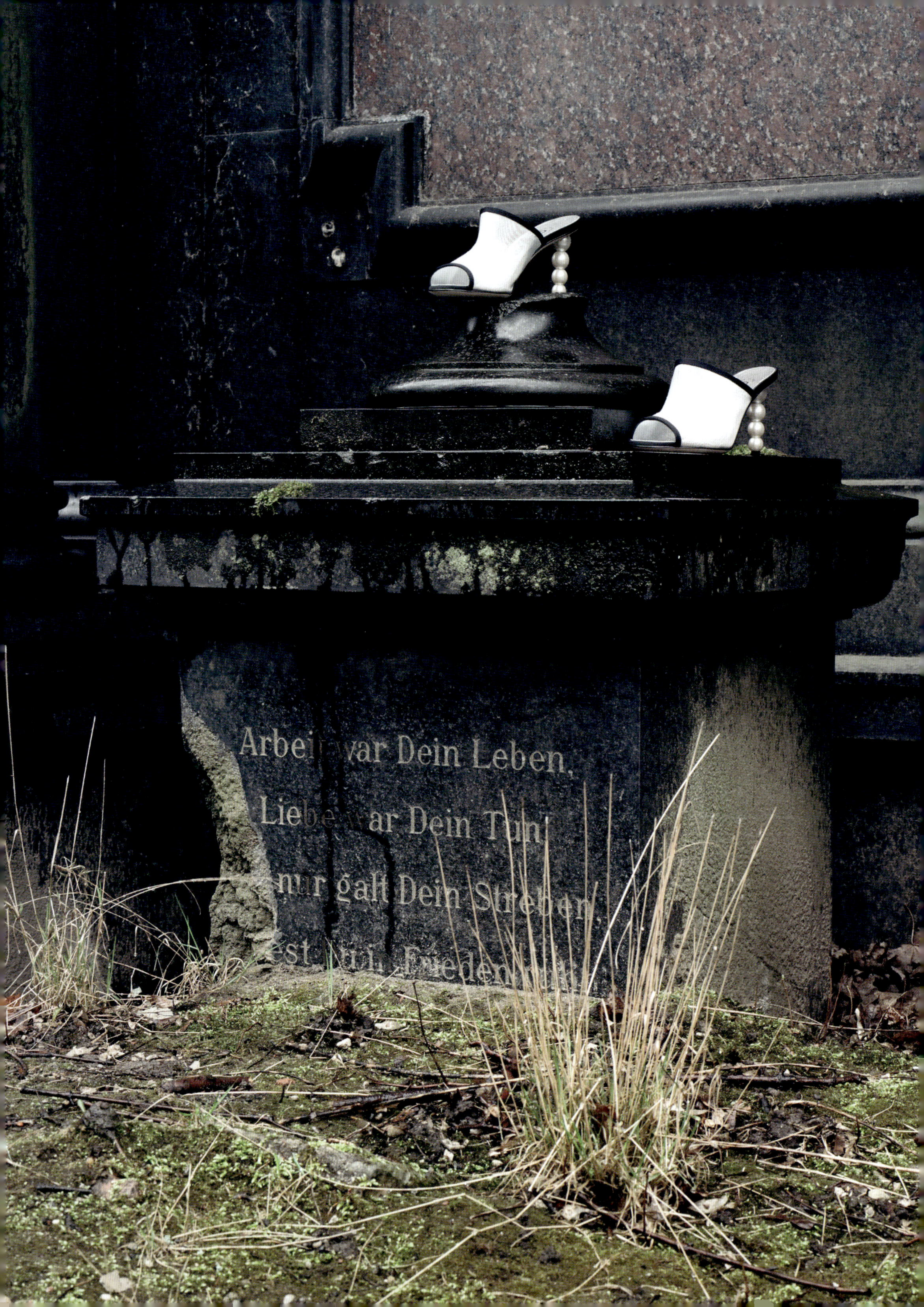
Dein Leben.
Dein Tun
galt Dein Streben

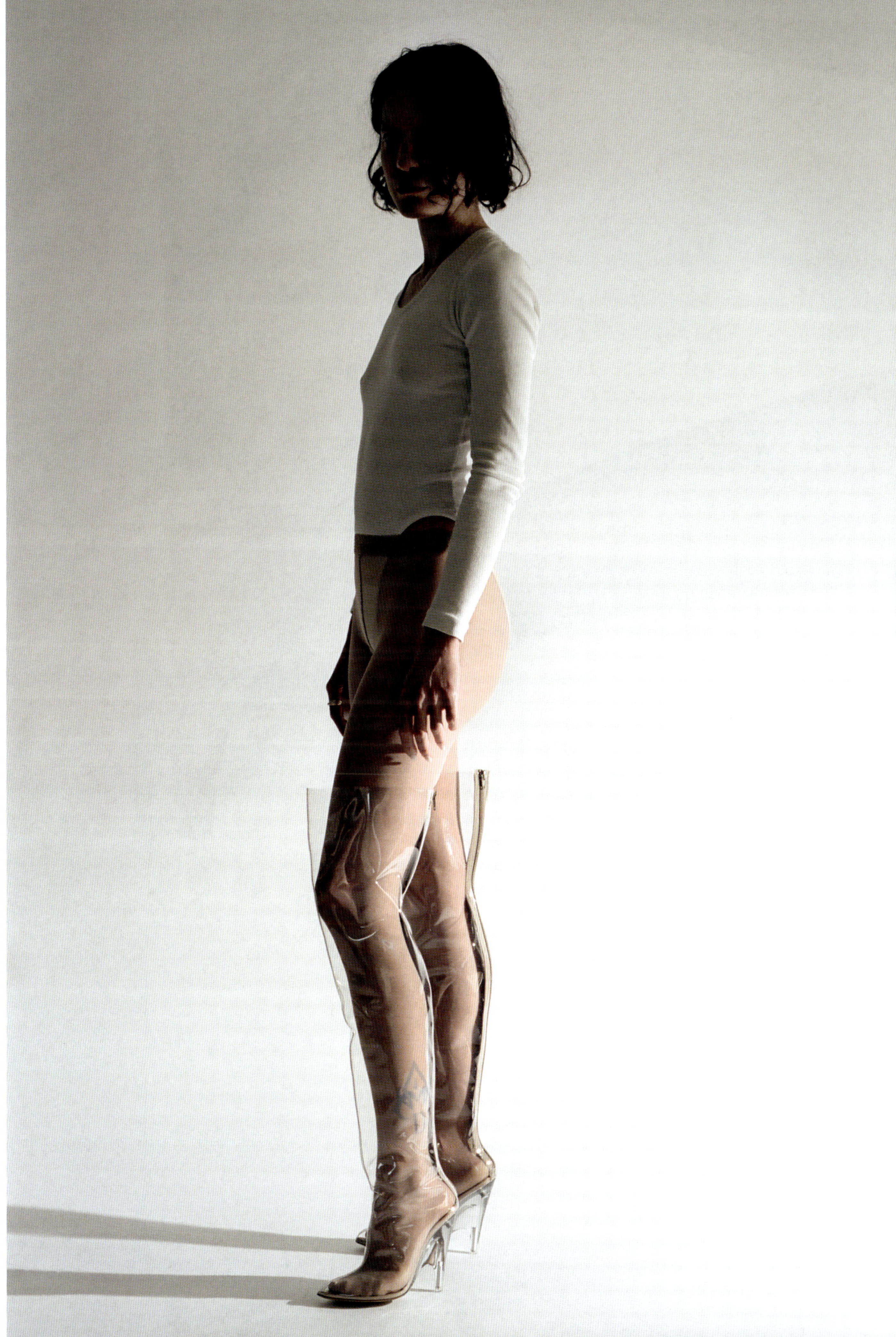

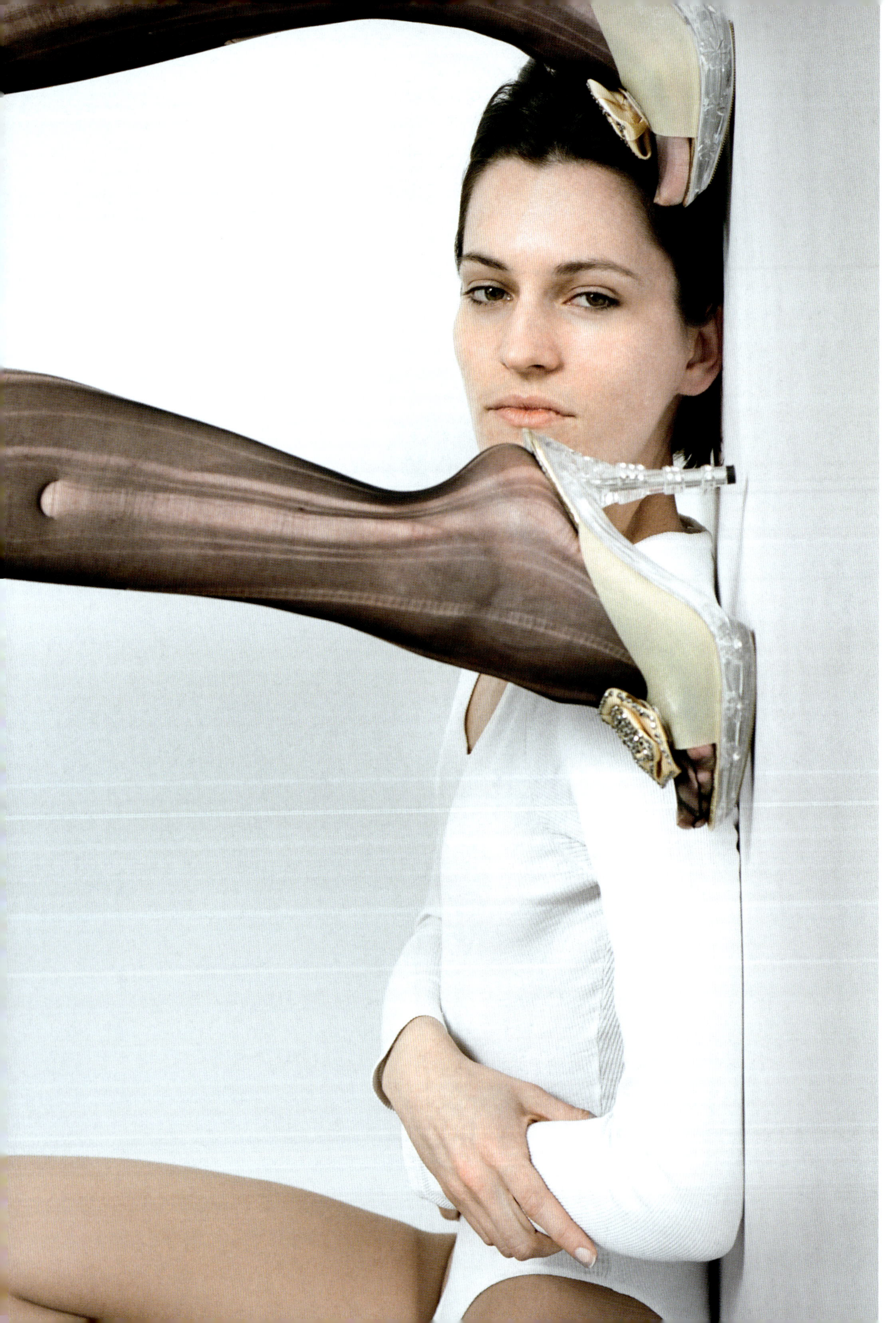

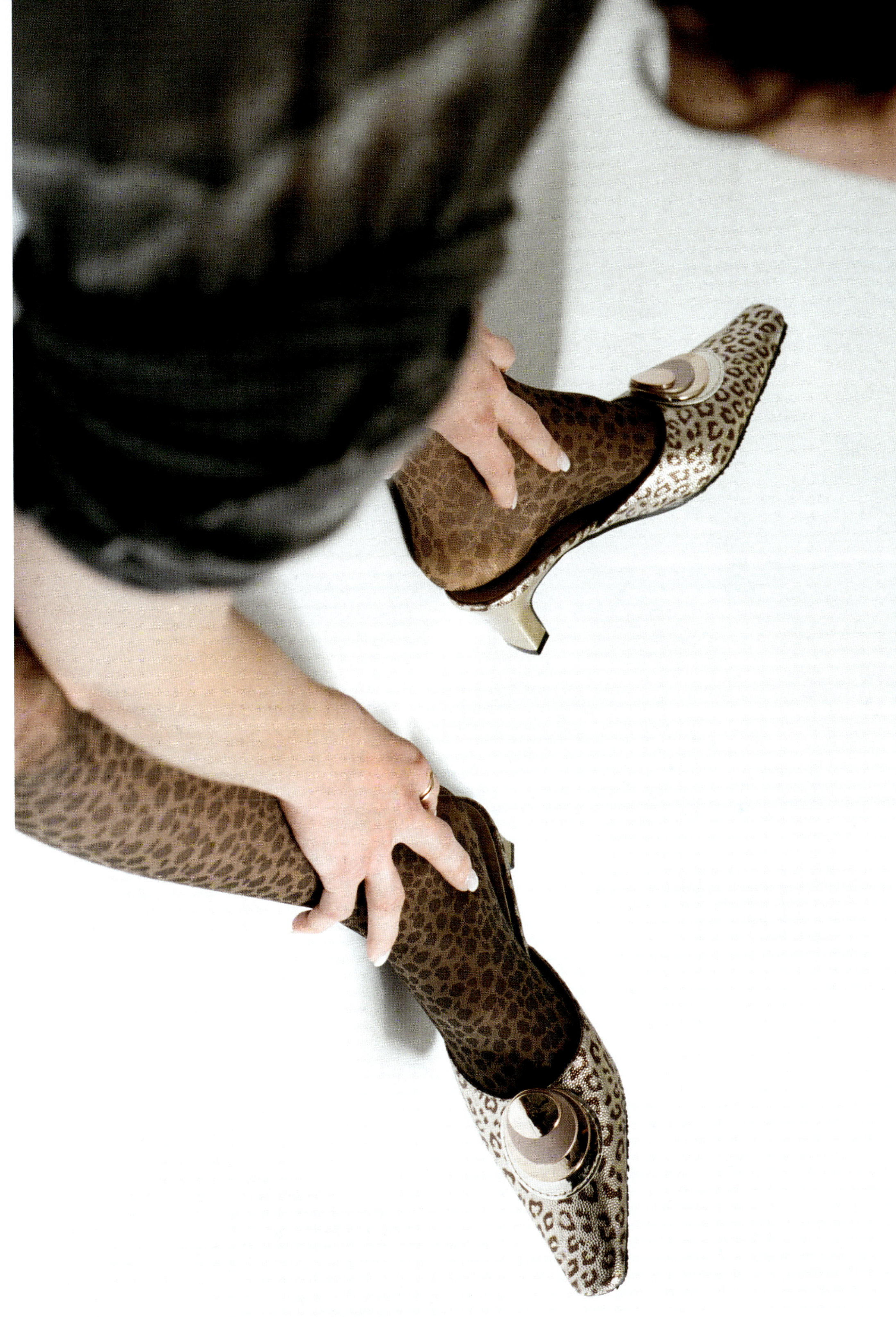

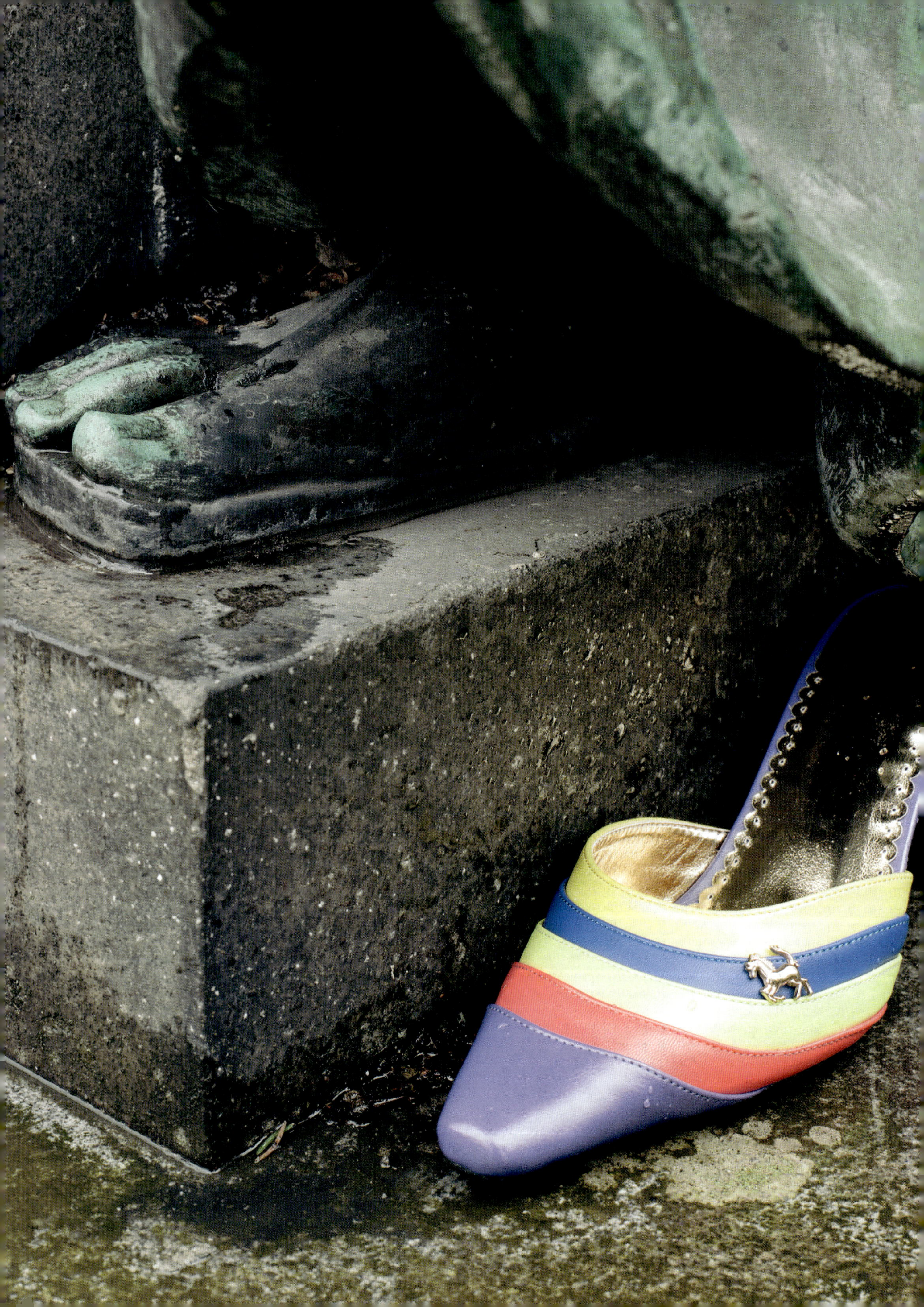

D P T

S

C H

CLOSED

The following gallery closing letters have been selected from numerous statements published by art dealers, gallerists, and others, collected from various media outlets such as Instagram, gallery websites, Facebook or the online platform of an art world magazine. State of the art.

MURRAY GUY
JANUARY 5, 2017

In celebration of 18 years of Murray Guy, we announce an exhibition with many of the artists whose work we have presented, with whom we have collaborated, and who have inspired us throughout this time.

This will be Murray Guy's final exhibition. It will be on view from Tuesday January 10th.

As we begin a new year, we look forward to future projects and conversations with the artists of the gallery, as well as with the colleagues, curators, collectors, and writers, whose enthusiasm and camaraderie has sustained and encouraged us over the years.

We will be continuing to work with the artists on current and upcoming exhibitions and can be reached by email as usual. As our separate plans advance they will be announced.

We look forward to seeing you all soon!

Janice Guy and Margaret Murray

ANDREA ROSEN GALLERY
FEBRUARY 21, 2017

I'm writing to you about some important information both regarding Felix Gonzalez-Torres and the gallery.

In my role as the executor of the Estate of Felix Gonzalez-Torres, I am excited to let you know that the work of Felix Gonzalez-Torres will be co represented by my gallery, the Andrea Rosen Gallery, and David Zwirner Gallery.

My greatest gift in life, after the privilege of having a daughter, is the ongoing honor to work with and for Felix. He is the backbone of my thinking, my constant inspiration, and his works are an astoundingly ever relevant blueprint of how to move forward each day of my life.

As one of the most influential and significant artists of our time, it simply makes sense that the work of Gonzalez-Torres deserves the attention and stewardship of more than one gallery providing a multi pronged support structure.

I find myself extremely interested in collaboration as well as encouraging and reigniting the spirit of our community working together. I am very much looking forward to both partnering with David, as well as for each of our individual strengths to benefit the legacy of Gonzalez-Torres. While I will continue to have the freedom to work with Felix's work as I always have, I am also looking forward to adding David's dedication to Felix's ideals. This also affords me the opportunity to work more with and in The Felix Gonzalez-Torres Foundation as I feel strongly that there is very significant work to be done in the Foundation specifically at this time. I approached David to co-represent Felix, as Zwirner Gallery is the obvious choice, as I very much respect the rigor of David's program and his gallery's focus on the holistic representation of artists.

Felix expressed that true equality meant that everyone has the right to be in the center of the discourse. I so often find myself recalling Felix speaking about his pending Hirshhorn exhibition in Washington D.C., like always he spoke with an amazing combination of rigor and optimism... It was 1994, the height of government censoring art and a few years after Jesse Helms had shut down the Robert Mapplethorpe exhibition at the Corcoran. Felix expressed to me how he was looking forward to Senator Stevens, who had spoken about going to preview Felix's show hoping to find reason to close it down. I remember Felix saying: I can't wait until he sees the two clocks touching, "Untitled" (Perfect Lovers), and it makes Stevens think of himself and his wife and at that moment there can be no recourse because his own ability to be moved by two clocks side by side, ticking together, will mean that my love is equal to his love.

I am always in awe of how Felix was able to pare his work down to the essence... to make objects that are universal, that have the ability to physically and conceptually transform themselves through time... to always be fresh and relevant and in and of the moment. And most of all, always moving and powerful.

When I approached David in November with the proposition, we were talking about quite a typical collaboration of two galleries and how that would unfold... What I did not expect was that over the course of our many weeks of conversation, that I found myself initiating a secondary internal dialogue. I privately came to realize, parallel to our discussion, that having David Zwirner Gallery share in the responsibility to the work of Felix Gonzalez-Torres or the idea of collaborating with other galleries, freed me to think about what is my true responsibility to our times. What is the most productive role that I can play, not only for Felix but for the role of my gallery, my role in the art world, and the world at large? My clarity evolved over the last few weeks.

I have come to realize that in order for me to be fearlessly open and responsive to our times and the future, requires mobility, flexibility and the willingness to change, and consequently, I have decided to shift my life, and the focus of the gallery, in a significant way. While the gallery will continue to exist, with selective activities, like the representation of Felix Gonzalez-Torres, I will no longer have a typical permanent public space and therefore no longer represent living artists. This transition will transpire over the next few months.

Of course my wish would have been to try to incorporate the depth of my growing intentions within my current immersive and beloved structure. As most people know, the gallery has been all consuming to me, always very happily, even when at the expense of much else. I have always felt that being open to the public and supporting artists was the perfect conduit for everything I care about. Yet I realized that the only way to be truly available and in order to set an example for my daughter of what it means to try to be an active, kind and connected citizen, or to try and live without ethical compromise requires time and the simplification of my life. While it will take a new form, I am one of those rare lucky people who loves and considers my work to be the vehicle for growth and contribution.

I am so very fortunate that the life and current structure of the gallery has afforded me the freedom to make this decision to shift, and I am so very aware of how grateful I am to so many, especially my team at the gallery, for their support and hard work and partnership in the gallery to date. Yet of course anyone who knows me will know that this shift could not be an easy decision as the representation of living artists has been my consuming focus and life-blood for the last 27 years. Above all, I feel most lucky to have had the honor to be immersed in dialogue with the artists I have the privilege to work with and to be in the presence of their work every day as conduits to deep insight and inspiration. It is impossible to express how extremely indebted I am to all of the incredible artists that I represent and I plan to stay connected with each of their careers as well as help in any way that I can in this transition. I believe deeply in the essential role of the public and the viewer and I am honored to have relationships with so many dedicated and impassioned collectors, colleagues in public institutions, and my community of fellow gallerists… whom I look forward to continuing my dialogue with. I look forward to balancing my responsibilities with yet unforeseen engagement and seeing my future structure both of the gallery and outside of the gallery evolve.

With all my warmest regards and gratitude,
Andrea

VILMA GOLD
MARCH 24, 2017

The nature of the art world has changed significantly in recent years. Where a gallery was once centred around a physical space where artists, collectors, and curators could engage directly with the exhibition programme, the focus has now shifted towards an endlessly accelerating global cycle of fairs which has impacted on the relevance of this traditional model.

I feel the time has come for me to step off this path, spend time with my family, and begin working towards a new model of collaboration with both living artists and estates—in the meantime, the office will continue to work on behalf of the gallery artists and the estates of KP Bremer and Stephen Dworkin for the foreseeable future.

Although this new direction is to some extent a walk into the unknown, I am also very excited about the possibilities presented by this new chapter, and I hope that I will continue to collaborate with the many friends and colleagues I have had the pleasure of working alongside for the past 18 years.

Rachel Williams, Vilma Gold

SILBERKUPPE
JUNE 28, 2017

Berlin's Silberkuppe gallery has closed its doors. Founded in 2008 by Dominic Eichler and Michel Ziegler, Silberkuppe staged more than seventy exhibitions in its space on Keithstrasse 12. The gallery's final exhibition was Win McCarthy's "Mister," which was chosen for a Critic's Pick by artforum.com contributor Kristian Vistrup Madsen. In a statement, Eichler and Ziegler say they are "very grateful to everyone who has supported [us] in the last nine years" and "remain committed to art, in particular art [that] doesn't shy from the political in all its guises."

The gallery represented Gerry Bibby, Michaela Eichwald, Margaret Harrison, Tobias Kaspar, Heinz Peter Knes, Laura Lamiel, Janette Laverrière, Adam Linder, Thomas Locher, Fred Lonidier, Shahryar Nashat, Anna Ostoya, Anne Speier, and Phel Steinmetz.

FREYMOND-GUTH
AUGUST 31, 2017

I've been advised to write a more neutral letter. But I find myself in the position, maybe as always before, not to be able to speak of something so dear to me in a more neutral way. Not at this point. Now that the gallery is closing the day after tomorrow.

I cannot remain objective in my choice of words, just as I could not be objective in my choices of which art to show and under which circumstances. Maybe my choices weren't always right. Possibly they were seduced by idealistic vision rather than commercial reality too often.

But those choices came from an urgency that initially sparked me to open Freymond-Guth Fine Arts, and that nourished every chapter of it so far. It is an urgency that is based on the belief in the value of sensation and reflection, a belief in creation and contextualization, a belief in collaboration and community.

Today, I dare to say I even believe in failure. As only by allowing failure to be part of a process, we allow experiment and from that true invention of thought, emotion or reality. Maybe, quite possibly, I paid my attention more towards process, rather than results. But if the provisional results of this process today might seem as failure to some who depend on its success, I do hope they are also reminded of our achievements in the past.

Much has been said about how the art world has changed in the last years. I will not repeat it here. The consequences for art in an increasingly polarizing society ultimately built on power, finance and exclusion are clear. What I would like to address though nevertheless is a sentiment closest described as alienation. Alienation in all relationships between all participants. Alienation in a climate where space and time for reflection, discussion and personal identification with form and content of contemporary art have become incompatible with the ever growing demand in constant, global participation, production and competition.

As described before, my motivation all throughout has been quite the contrary. The decision to end this chapter of Freymond-Guth Fine Arts thus is obviously a result of this conflict- on personal, conceptual and financial levels. It is however probably the hardest decision I have made as an adult. I fear the loss of friendship, community and recognition. I fear the results of the breakdown of a business, and the monetary loss my decision today causes some of my dearest collaborators. I fear the void that will replace the structure I have built with every element of my life in the last 10 years or more. When people asked me in the past years how I was, I used to joke: "Never been this old, fat and broke before!". Well, it's quite true now. And yet, my anxiety is comforted by my trust in the importance of what we have created in these past years, independently from momentary results or even my direct involvement. Despite the existential tremor those close to it and myself are experiencing now. I trust that every moment of Freymond-Guth Fine Arts is valuable soil for further inspiration, reflection and collaboration—and also very much the creation of values.

Today, I feel we need to urgently address questions to ourselves and our environments:

What are the circumstances and ideals we—artists, gallerists, collectors, curators, and writers—want to work in today? What are our reciprocal responsibilities and options? And more specifically: Why are we all supporting a system built in an entirely different market that today works only for a tiny amount of artists and galleries and for the rest is based on self-exploitation or privilege?

If we consider ourselves to be part of a free world and art being one of its great achievements, how can we accept structures that are so contrary to the idea of freedom on a most personal level? What is the difference between creation and entertainment? And for whom in a game where power and participation are spread so unevenly?

Though much has been said about the conflicts of a contemporary art world, little have there been proposals of alternative models for galleries to support artists in every stage of their career. I trust this current state of crisis and confusion bares an immense potential for invention. My personal decisions are certainly made around that. In that sense Freymond-Guth Fine Arts will continue its mission long after the current form.

Old ideas, new roads.

But, despite all beautiful words, I would like to express my deepest regrets for any losses my decisions have caused, also financial ones. I hope that both the values in the past and the potential for the future we have created together will produce relief, if I cannot personally do so at this point.

Ultimately, what I would like to share most of all is my gratitude to those people near and far I have been privileged to share a part of their life with. I want to thank you for your trust, support, and inspiration in the creation of what I see as fundamental aspects and values of our society that are unquestionably needed for a more differentiated experience of it.

Thank you. Jean-Claude

LAURA BARTLETT GALLERY
SEPTEMBER 5, 2017

Dear Friends and Colleagues,
this is to announce that after 12 years, Laura Bartlett Gallery is now closed.

I have had the pleasure to work with an incredible group of artists over the years and I am happy to announce that I will continue these collabrations as an advisor to international collections, working on private and public commissions and towards a more fluid exhibition programming model.

The gallery opened in 2005 with a performance by Japanese artist Sachiko Abe, and went on to stage the first solo gallery exhibitions of Cyprien Gaillard, Elizabeth McAlpine, Becky Beasley, Lydia Gifford, Nina Beier, Marie Lund, Beatrice Gibson and Sol Calero, as well as the first London shows of Simon Dybbroe Moller, John Divola and Alex Olson, as well as Margo Wolowiec and Ryan McLaughlin. I am grateful to the many other artists and curators who have contributed to our group shows and projects over the years as well as the countless colleagues in museums and galleries who we have collaborated with.

I would like to thank all the staff and co-directors over the years who I have had such pleasure working alongside. Please follow our instagram feed or website for current and upcoming artists news or contact our office for any enquiries at:

info@laurabartlettgallery.com

With many thanks for your visits, interest and support,

Kind regards, Laura Bartlett

MARC FOXX
FEBRUARY 23, 2018

Established 1994. Marc Foxx and Rodney Nonaka-Hill want to express their deep gratitude to all the artists, institutions, curators, writers, publications, colleagues, and collectors who have supported the gallery over the years and send best wishes and regards.

REAL FINE ARTS
APRIL 23, 2018

Real Fine Arts is closed.

PASSAGEWAYS

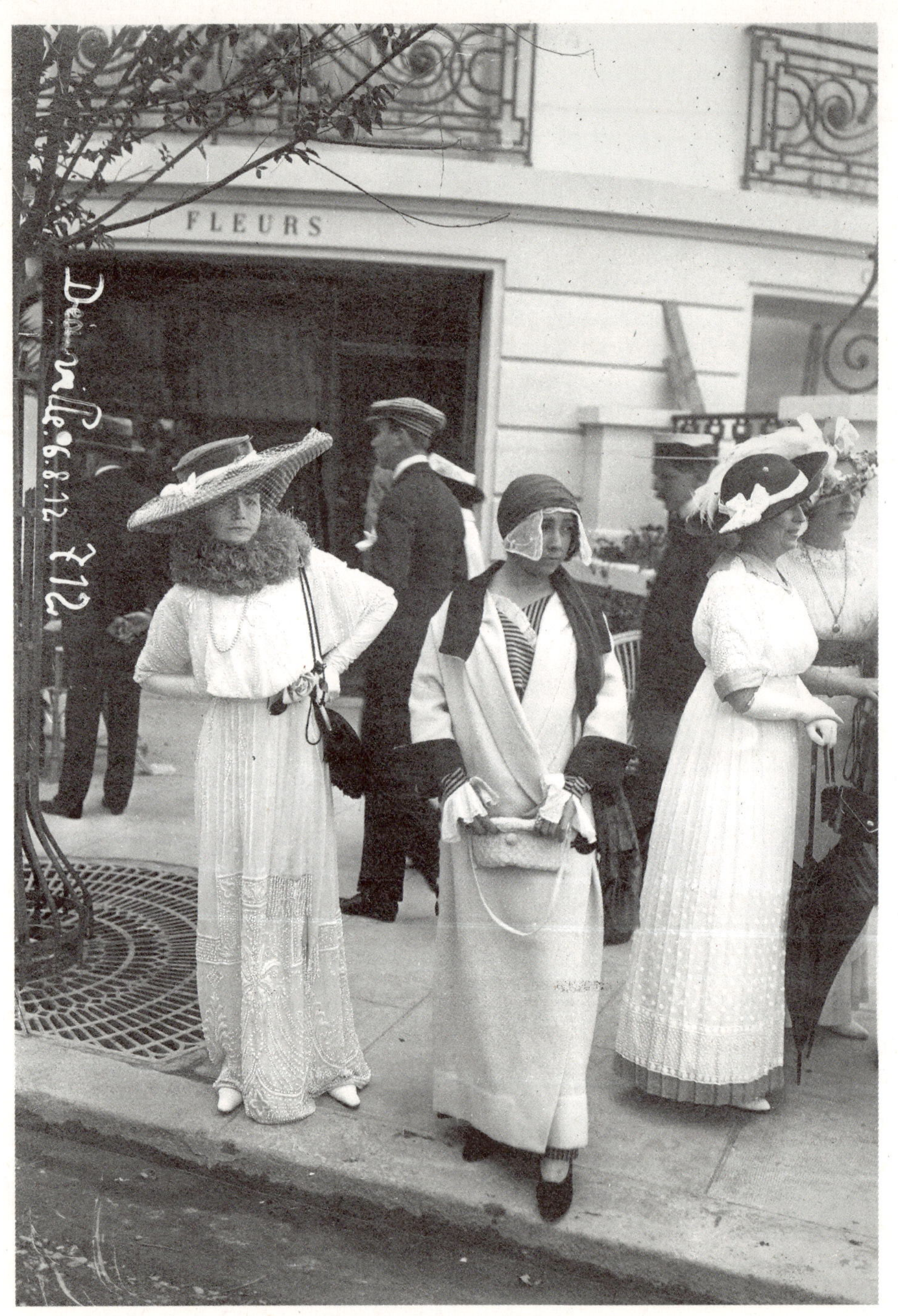

Text
Photos

Matthew Linde
Martin Kamer Collection

The *other* of art, fashion is an elusive discipline, an anxious aesthetic branch haunted by its relationship to mortality and time. From Hussein Chalayan's embrace to Rei Kawakubo's refusal, there is a tendency to turn to art as a recourse for unearthing or denying deeper truths of form. Yet art, as a contested and specialized discipline, can only offer shaky reflections that enforce dislocated histories upon fashion's own tempo. The origins of the fashion show themselves reveal the paradox of modern experience between standardization and abstract mutability. The fashion show, as a form of gestural modernism, illuminates culture in flux. While technological treatments of the fashion show have changed, its underlying performance remains intact; where commerce, leisure and the body converge.

NEW VELOCITIES

In *Adorned in Dreams* (1985), Elizabeth Wilson writes:

> "In the modern city the new and different sounds the dissonance of reaction to what went before; that moment of dissonance is key to twentieth century style. The colliding dynamism, the thirst for change and the heightened sensation that characterize the city societies particularly of modern industrial capitalism go to make up this "modernity," and the hysteria and exaggeration of fashion well express it."[1]

The fashion show first emerged in late nineteenth-century Europe, evolving out of antecedents such as dolls, miniature figurines donning new prototypes; and tableaux vivants, live acts involving a series of freeze frame poses mimicking postures in painting. One of the first innovations of the "show" entailed couturiers sending mannequins into the public square, shocking the public with new design lines and cuts and inciting photographed dispersal. After the Haussmannization of Paris, Charles Frederick Worth, commonly mythologized as the king of couture, sent his wife down the Champs-Élysées donning his designs in the 1860s. The racecourse too became a common cultural destination to watch the living mannequins sport new sartorial imaginations. This was practiced by other designers such as Jeanne Paquin, Jeanne Margaine-Lacroix, and Paul Poiret and during the 1900s it synthesized a powerful social marketing strategy for French couturiers. But more than trade, these mannequins and fashions embodied the new dynamics of city life. Walter Benjamin cites Charles Blanc:

> "Everything that could keep women from remaining seated was encouraged; anything that could have impeded their walking was avoided. They wore their hair and their clothes as though they were to be viewed in profile. For the profile is the silhouette of someone [...] who passes, who is about to vanish from our sight. Dress became the image of the rapid movement that carries away the world."[2]

If a society is deemed modern by its ability to produce and consume surplus images, the new phantasmagoric jolts of fashion were constitutive for a nineteenth-century unfolding. From 1852 to 1870 firms such as Worth, Virot, and Laferrière programmed private viewings for clients to view their new fashions, modelled on living mannequins, and by 1880 this was habitualized into twice a year. Thanks to the prosperity of a globalized press, shows were soon being covered by American newspapers and seared into the modern public consciousness. Presentations became elaborate affairs with specially crafted invites for exclusive clienteles and French couturiers begun to offer champagne and canapés for the event, adapting this socializing innovation from the English designer Lucile. The fashion show, from its inception, was tied to the production of spatial experience. Music and interiors were manipulated to illuminate the fantasy of bodily mutability and the fashion show encroached further into the sensorium. A report on Poiret's salon dating from 1912 describes in detail the walls (Nile Green, threaded with dark green and antiquated gold), carpet (raspberry), and curtains (also raspberry, made of taffeta): The very clear opposition of these two colors, the one neutral and the other hot, produced a bizarre atmosphere, at once soft and vibrant, and which must harmonize happily with the fresh and buoyant colors from which Poiret likes to take his effects.[3]

LUCILE PIONEERED THE FASHION PLAY, A SPECTACLE SITUATED BETWEEN A PARTY AND A THEATRICAL EVENT.

THE ENTERTAINMENT OF DREAMS

As fashion shows became more theatrical, they became fashionable occasions in themselves. It was Lucile who pioneered the fashion play, a spectacle situated between a party and theatrical event. Some of her shows lasted hours including highly stylized mannequins, accessories, dogs, and acrobatics. In fact, early couture houses often paralleled strategies in modern art. Nancy Troy remarks in *Couture Culture* (2002) that "historians of modern art have typically focused on avant-garde theatre, ballet or film as principal sites of artistic intervention," yet "remaining relatively unexplored are the more popular productions"[4] imagined by Poiret and Lucile. Unlike the manifestos of modernist art, these fashion shows located a hinge between modernism, the body, and commerce. Lucile deepened the complex eroticism of her theatrical spectacles when she removed the numbered taxonomy of the gowns and bestowed them instead with evocative titles such as *Passion's Thrall*, *Do You Love Me?*, and *A Frenzied Song of Amorous Things*—all performed as walk-abouts collectively titled as *Gowns of Emotion*.[5]

> The most elaborate had texts prepared by Lucile's sister, society novelist Elinor Glyn. The series culminated in 1909 [...] with the ambitious *Seven Ages of Women*, a stage piece in seven acts tracing from birth to death the dress-cycle of a society dame.[6]

In 1911, James Laver, writing for the New York Times, proclaimed that presenting the latest fashions on stage was "surely the most dramatic way of showing off splendid gowns that has ever been invented. [...] Such a spectacle is something well worth going to see, even if one does not buy the gown."[7] These events became so successful that, by the 1920s, Lucile's plays were touring Chicago, London, New York, and Paris. In America, department stores, fairs, and philanthropists initiated their own fashion plays, involving multiple designers and varieties of mannequins in daylong performances. One elaborate vaudeville was "The Fashion's Passing Show" at the Newport, Rhode Island, home of Mrs Hermann Oelrichs. The show featured society women in costume parading down grand stairs, mannequins running out in new bathing suit designs, as if appearing from nowhere, into fountains and others wearing golfing and tennis outfits in tableau enactments.

Back in France, Poiret also experimented in turning fashion shows into theatrical affairs. His most famous event, "The Thousand and Second Night" (1911), took the form of a highly staged party in the garden of his atelier, where three hundred guests arrived adorned in his new modish "orientalist" dress. As a fantastical evocation of the East, the event featured sartorial elements such as the harem trousers that dominated his following collection. Poiret's soirée behaved as a participatory advertisement that enjoyed abundant publicity. His exercise of orientalist sensibilities explored ideas of the *other*, specifically in modern gender masquerade where women were seen dressed in the masculine style. These PR tactics of surreal gestures have a remarkable similarity to the "experimental" designers of today, from the horrific dramaturgy of Alexander McQueen to the relational presentations by BLESS. In the early 1900s they caught the imagination of novelty and, more significantly, symbolized successional replaceability, reflecting a transition in fashion from idealized objects into dreams. As Anne Hollander explains, the figures in fashion photographs "came to resemble characters in small unfinished film dramas. These had no history and no future, they existed unsettlingly for an instant."[8]

IT WAS LUCILE WHO PIONEERED THE FASHION PLAY, A SPECTACLE SITUATED BETWEEN A PARTY AND THEATRICAL EVENT. SOME OF HER SHOWS LASTED HOURS INCLUDING HIGHLY STYLIZED MANNEQUINS, ACCESSORIES, DOGS, AND ACROBATICS.

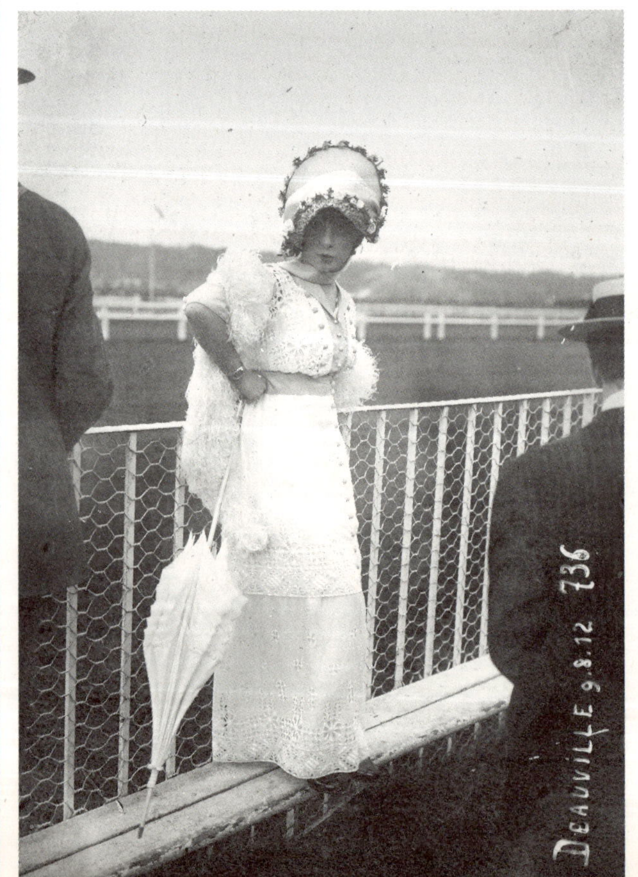

With a stamp by the Societé des nouveautes textiles, August 9, 1912

MATHEMATICAL ILLUSIONS

Caroline Evans writes in depth about the "rationalisation of the body" in her analysis of modernity and the fashion show, *The Mechanical Smile* (2013). The mannequin, as a live enactment of design, functioned in early fashion shows much the same as today—walking in mathematical configurations enacting stylized, repetitive poses made industrial. This rationalization of the body, however, was not unique to fashion. In dance, the women of the chorus line were distinctive in their effacement of individuality—Benjamin identified the chorus girl as a mass-produced article in the libidinal life of the big-city dweller. Military parades of the time also standardized bodies in uniformity, resembling the mechanized flow of modern life. When captured in images, these disciplines all share a concern: that of bodies in movement, fragmented and synchronous.

LIKE GLOBALIZED COMMERCE, THE MANNEQUIN WAS OPTICALLY RECONSTRUCTED INTO A MASS-PRODUCED COPY.

Complex systems of mirrors allowed the mannequin to be multiplied in salons and showrooms alike. In the fitting rooms of Paquin and Doeuillet, an arrangement of three angled panels reoriented the mannequin so that she was able to pose and look back at the client via the refracted image. Through the optical elision the client could forge a self-identification with the mannequin as a commodified figure. Other houses such as Redfern established fitting rooms as complete mirrored boxes. These dazzling optical devices became ubiquitous in presenting mannequins on stage, enabling effects of infinite recession, as if multiplying capital into the psyche. Like globalized commerce, the mannequin was optically reconstructed into a mass-produced copy. Chanel's salon, known for its magnificent mirrored interior, particularly its ascending staircase, had phantasmagoric effects. Evans argues that while analogies could be drawn with the modernist avant-gardes and their depictions of the fragmented body, Chanel's modernism was instead located in the rationalization of the body in the workplace.

The early fashion show also developed in tandem with techniques of the moving image. Emerging experiments with montage in film mimicked the displacement of the mannequin in movement. The start-stop nature of her image, reflected in paused poses and abstracted gestures suggested sensibilities shared with cinema's fragmentary modality. The paper L'Illustration detailed a 1910 Poiret show's filmic qualities as follows:

> "With a word, a gesture [...] Poiret directs the cortège [...] a sign from him, a syllable, throws them forward, halts them, then makes them start again, go, come back on themselves, cross over, mix, according to his fantasy, as if it were a ballet with lazy movements, [...] and return, suddenly, all of them, to show off for a moment the curve of their hips."[9]

If technologies alter ways of seeing, cinema and fashion articulated a world of moments, akin to how early writers of modernity characterized modern experience as ephemeral.

"THE COUTURIER DOES NOTHING DIFFERENT FROM THE PAINTER WHO CONSTITUTES A GIVEN OBJECT AS A WORK OF ART BY THE ACT OF AFFIXING HIS SIGNATURE TO IT"—WITH THE SIGNATURE BEING "ONE OF THE MOST ECONOMICALLY AND SYMBOLICALLY POWERFUL WORDS AMONG THOSE IN CIRCULATION TODAY."

MANUFACTURING THE ORIGINAL

It was Charles Frederick Worth who first offered "models"—as dress prototypes were known at the time—in order to enable the commercial distribution of couture to France and the world. As a complete product, his designs could be bought outright requiring only slight variations in fit and decoration. In standardizing dress, Worth predated the automobile industry by 30 years. This reproducible strategy was advanced by offering American buyers models designed to be copied. As cheaper counterfeits ensued, Worth's signature was introduced in the 1860s to distinguish the genuine from the fraudulent. Couture had been created as a fantasy for exclusive novelty, yet it was equally oriented as a commercial enterprise for market expansion into America. In managing this contradiction, couturiers delivered two consecutive shows to two distinct audiences; an elaborately sensorial show to French clients, followed by a truncated presentation to overseas buyers. While this preserved the soul of Parisian fashion, upon his visit to America in 1913, Poiret discovered the true extent of counterfeit dresses. Reconciling the predicament three years later, he planned a transatlantic line of inexpensive designs suited for the economic demands of the American woman. In a strange psychosis of inversion, fashion offered the promise of unique experience through mass-produced readymade clothing.

Nancy Troy expounds how this ambiguous relationship between art and industry was simultaneously taking place with Duchamp. Indeed, in art's readymade the same dilemma of the original and the authorial subject were being questioned vis-à-vis a booming industrial capitalism. Bourdieu reflected on the auratic collusion between the two disciplines: "The couturier does nothing different from the painter who constitutes a given object as a work of art by the act of affixing his signature to it" and described the signature by both as "one of the most economically and symbolically powerful words among those in circulation today."[10] The authorized reproductions of both Poiret and Duchamp's industrialized objects cast a type of black magic on form. In erasing the existence of the original, they function as simulacra.

MODERNITY & MODERNISM

The danger of canvassing modernity and modernism so interchangeably is that their definitions can collapse altogether. "Modernity," as a process of modernization, refers to the technological, economic, scientific, and political transformation associated to the industrialization of 18th and 19th century. "Modernism" refers to the artistic avant-garde who reflected these new societal sensibilities. If the two occupy an unstable relationship, scholarship regarding Charles Baudelaire and Benjamin has thrown fashion into the ring. It was Baudelaire who appreciated the etymological wedding of *la mode* and *modernité*. In his writing on modernity, the poet-critic located art's epistemological gain within the ephemeral, where fashion was the visual manifestation par excellence. Evans develops on the value of ephemerality by arguing a possible type of gestural modernism, located within the performance of everyday life. She quotes from Michael Levenson's *Modernism* (2011):

> "Men in capes, women on bicycles, workers in the square, suffragettes in the street, audiences in the theatre. The increased visibility, not only of modernist artworks but of modernist bodies, was central to the cultural milieu. [...] We need to acknowledge the special character of gestural Modernism, a major lineage within the period constituted by unrepeatable spectacles. The performances were not offered as texts, nor were they made permanent in paint. If they survive at all, and this was not their aim, it is only in half-reliable newspaper reports or memoirs. But the unrepeatable event and the evanescent gesture that 'takes the place of poetry' were crucial to adversary culture."[11]

EPILOGUE

What is often overlooked in the endless repeats of fashion media roundtables discussing the epistemological seesaw of "fashion/art" is that the artistic strategies deployed in fashion shows today parallel those developed in its inception. The emergence of the fashion show constituted a critical constellation that embodied, as Benjamin saw it, the new velocities of life. This relation to modernity is more profound, for its investigation of fashion's fugitive nature, than the idea that any recent designer has brought fashion closer to the epistemological truth of "art."

WHAT IS OFTEN OVERLOOKED IN THE ENDLESS REPEATS OF FASHION MEDIA ROUNDTABLES DISCUSSING THE EPISTEMOLOGICAL SEESAW OF "FASHION/ART" IS THAT THE ARTISTIC STRATEGIES DEPLOYED IN FASHION SHOWS TODAY PARALLEL THOSE DEVELOPED IN ITS INCEPTION.

1 Elizabeth Wilson, *Adorned in Dreams: Fashion and Modernity* (New Brunswick: Rutgers University Press 2003), 10.

2 Charles Blanc, "Considérations sur le vêtements des femmes," Institut de France (October 25, 1872): 12–3, cited in Walter Benjamin, *The Arcades Project* (Cambridge: Harvard University Press, 1999), 74.

3 "Poiret: Une silhouette Parisienne," in: *Le miroir des Modes* 64, no. 6 (June 1912): 242, cited in Nancy Troy, *Couture Culture* (Cambridge: MIT Press, 2003), 69.

4 Troy, 2003, 81.

5 Joel H. Kaplan and Sheila Stowell, *Theatre and Fashion: Oscar Wilde to the Suffragettes* (Cambridge: Cambridge University Press, 1994), 119.

6 Ibid.

7 "Drecoll and Beer Show Conservative Styles," in: *New York Times* (October 15, 1911): pt. 8, 4.

8 Anne Hollander, *Sex & Suits: The Evolution of Modern Dress* (Kodansha America, Inc.: New York 1995), 159.

9 Gustave Babin, "Une Lecon d'elegance dans un parc," in: *L'Illustration* (July 1910): 21–2.

10 Pierre Bourdieu and Yvette Delsaut, "Le couturier et sa griffe: contribution à une théorie de la magie," in: *Actes de la recherche en sciences sociales*, vol. 1, no. 1 (January 1975): 7–36, 21.

11 Michael Levenson, *Modernism* (New Haven: Yale University Press, 2011), 247.

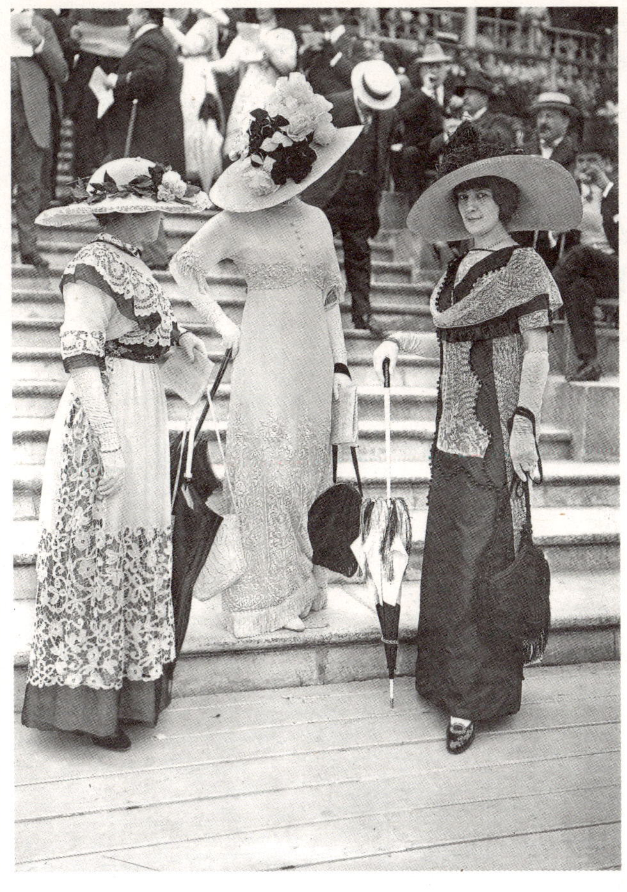
Stamp by Design & Sampling Dept., June 16, 1911

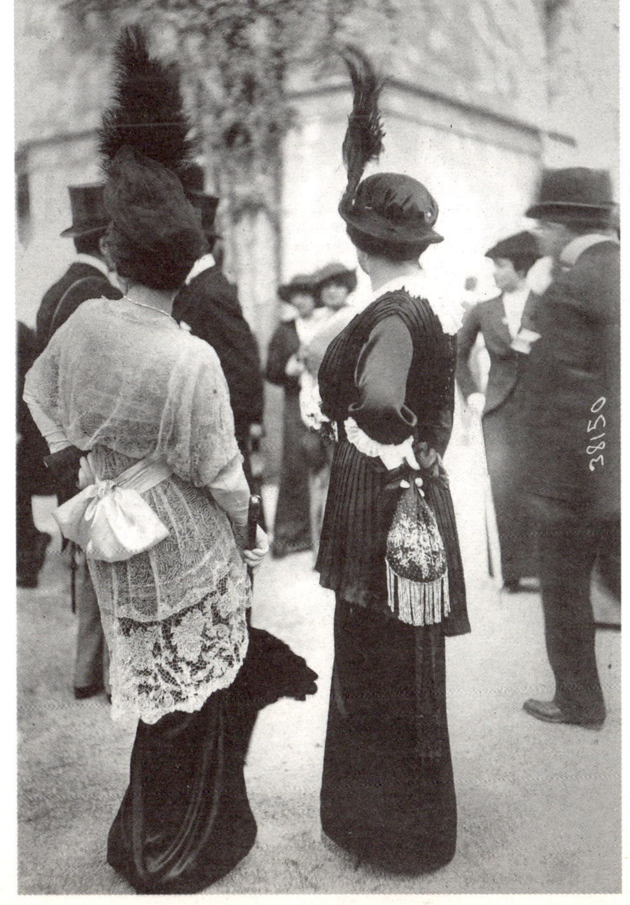

Stamp by Design & Sampling Dept., French subscription library room, 541, May 31, 1913

PASSAGEWAYS: ON FASHION'S RUNWAY

Kunsthalle Bern, Oct 13 – Dec 2, 2018
Opening: Friday Oct 12, 6 pm
Curated by Matthew Linde

The origins of the fashion show reveal a constellation where the body, commerce, and modernity converge. Described as a theatre without narrative, fashion's runway illuminates the paradox of fugitive desire and mechanical standardization. The "first" runway could be understood as the practice of couturiers sending live mannequins (what we now call models) into the public boulevard sporting new designs, eliciting shock and photographic dispersal. This animation of bodies performing novelty in urban life foregrounded the format we know today: models passing along a strip flanked by their consuming onlookers. They are, like ancient palimpsests, the formaldehyde of a culture in flux. While technological treatments of the runway have modified since its emergence at the turn of the 19th century, its underlying edifice has remained largely intact. Despite this ongoing scenographic sameness, various designers have explored the runway as a discursive site to interrogate the mechanics of fashion's circulation. These runway experiments reconfigure the relations between audiences, arrangements of space, the carnivalesque body and the haunting of its commodity form. Leaping from Paul Poiret's epic 1911 "A Thousand and Second Night," the designers exhibited in "Passageways: On Fashion's Runway" at Kunsthalle Bern have approached the runway-as-medium, using it twofold to extend and challenge the ideas within their own practice as well as the fashion system at large.

Just as these designers have tested the fashion show, runways themselves test the uncanny allegory for the passage of history as labyrinthine time that folds back onto itself. As a style of dress vanishes into the exiled *démodé*, our willingness for sartorial being requires revising. But in this "revising" fashion always arrives with quotations of its prior selves. Motifs and themes from previous periods are recycled from the refuse of progress and made proximate to each other. This discontinuous upheaval of the past into the present expresses our eternal reworking of history. Fashion-time then is not simply a series of chronological temporalities, but an audacious conception of history of ideas that breaches the continuum. So, it is the task of the fashion runway to embark on a speculative future in order to recover the now.

"Passageways" curates over thirty videos of runway shows by designers that have reimagined the catwalk as an exploratory performative tool to produce fashion. Also exhibited are specific outfits from six fashion designers of these selected runways, alongside a series of commissioned replicas that rewrite new histories of the runway as a suspension of fashion-time.

YUICHIRO TAMURA'S SUKAJAN BOMBER JACKETS

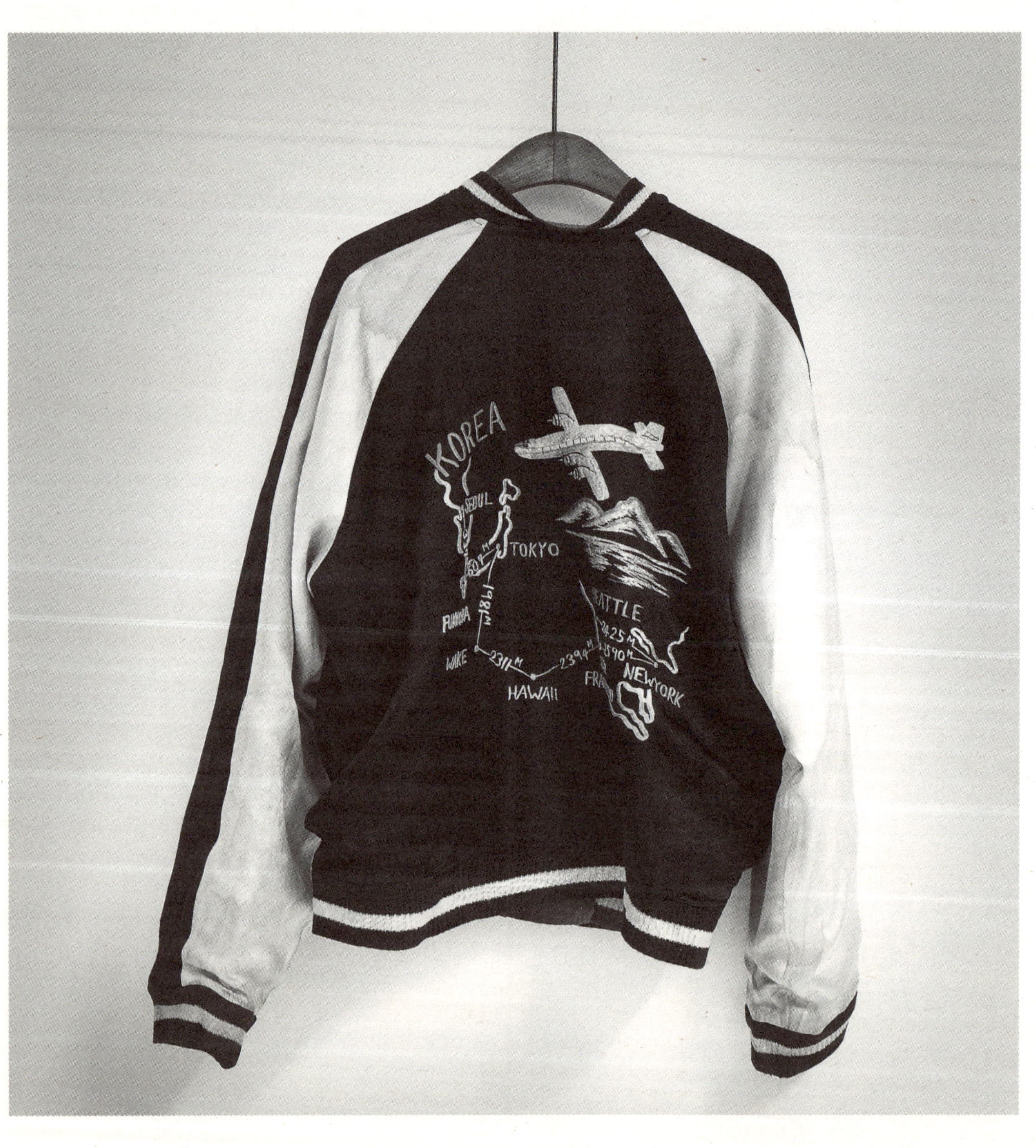

Hey Daddy, Hey Brother, 2017. Jackets in different sizes
Courtesy Yuichiro Tamura, KADIST

Sukajan is a style of bomber or baseball jacket embroidered with East Asian symbols, which is said to have been a popular souvenir among the United States military stationed in postwar Japan during the Korean War in the 1950s and 1960s. The garments gained popularity in Japan where they were first introduced and then predominantly became associated with the symbols of Japanese Yakuza gang members in the 1970s and 1980s. Since then, the popularity of Sukajan-style jackets has spread worldwide to become the commercial street fashion item it is today.

Embroidered on Sukajan jackets of the Cold War period are images and symbols that would have had particular appeal to returning US troops, including the mythological symbols of East Asia such as the valorous tiger and dragon, or the mystical Mt. Fuji. Commemorative maps of Japan and Korea, air raid routes, the serial numbers of US troops, and the exotic imagery of women from the 1950s and 1960s have also inspired the imagery embroidered on Sukajan. Others take the pictorial style of kimonos, Korean womenfolk washing clothes on the riverbank, etc.

According to Tamura, who has collected such jackets for many years, Sukajan represents a cultural and temporal nexus that collapses the borders, both between traditional and popular culture and the East and West. It is an intriguing example of pastiche with a variegated backdrop: the war in East Asia, the pervasion of US military forces, the rebellious codes of the Yakuza as well as subculture, the youth, and globalism.

PROVENCE: Where and when did you purchase this bomber jacket?

Yuichiro Tamura: I bought it in the fall of 2015 on an internet auction site.

PROVENCE: What does the motif of the jacket depict? What was its original meaning? And what's the connotation today?

YT: It is speculated that it was made by the US military in the 1950s. The route and distance of the flight from the New York to Korean Peninsula via Hawaii and Japan are shown. The airplane depicted is probably a bomber. The war itself is serious, but such an illustration drawn from the side of the US military is a somewhat comical impression. The design of other jackets made at the same time also has an innocent impression. This jacket has been made about 70 years ago. Given the present political situation between the United States and Korea, the topic is still fresh and didn't fade.

THE AIRPLANE DEPICTED IS PROBABLY A BOMBER. THE WAR ITSELF IS SERIOUS, BUT SUCH AN ILLUSTRATION DRAWN FROM THE SIDE OF THE US MILITARY IS A SOMEWHAT COMICAL IMPRESSION.

PROVENCE: Did you wear the jacket yourself?

YT: Just once or twice.

MIRRORED GARDENS

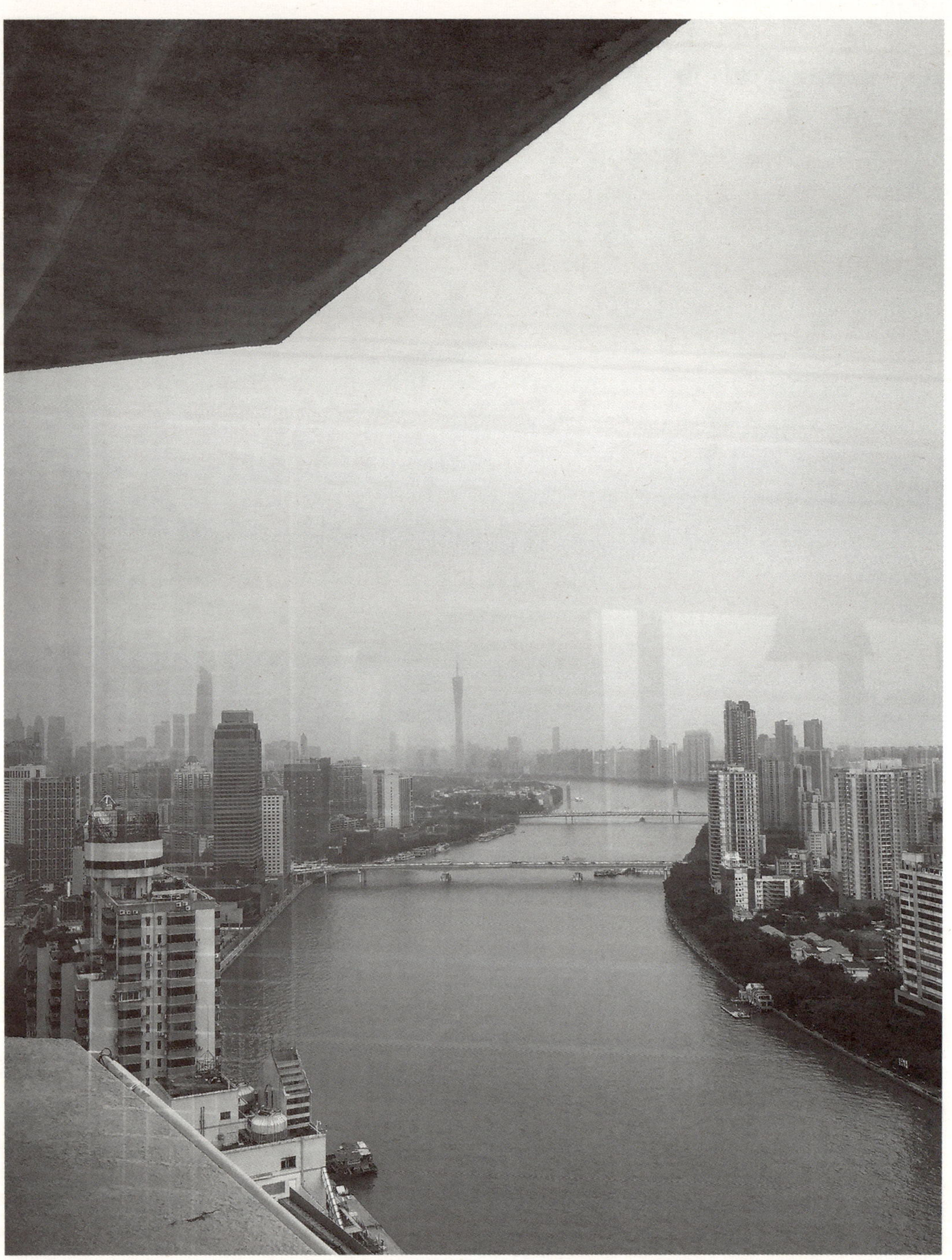

View of Guangzhou's Pearl River from Landmark International Hotel, January 2018

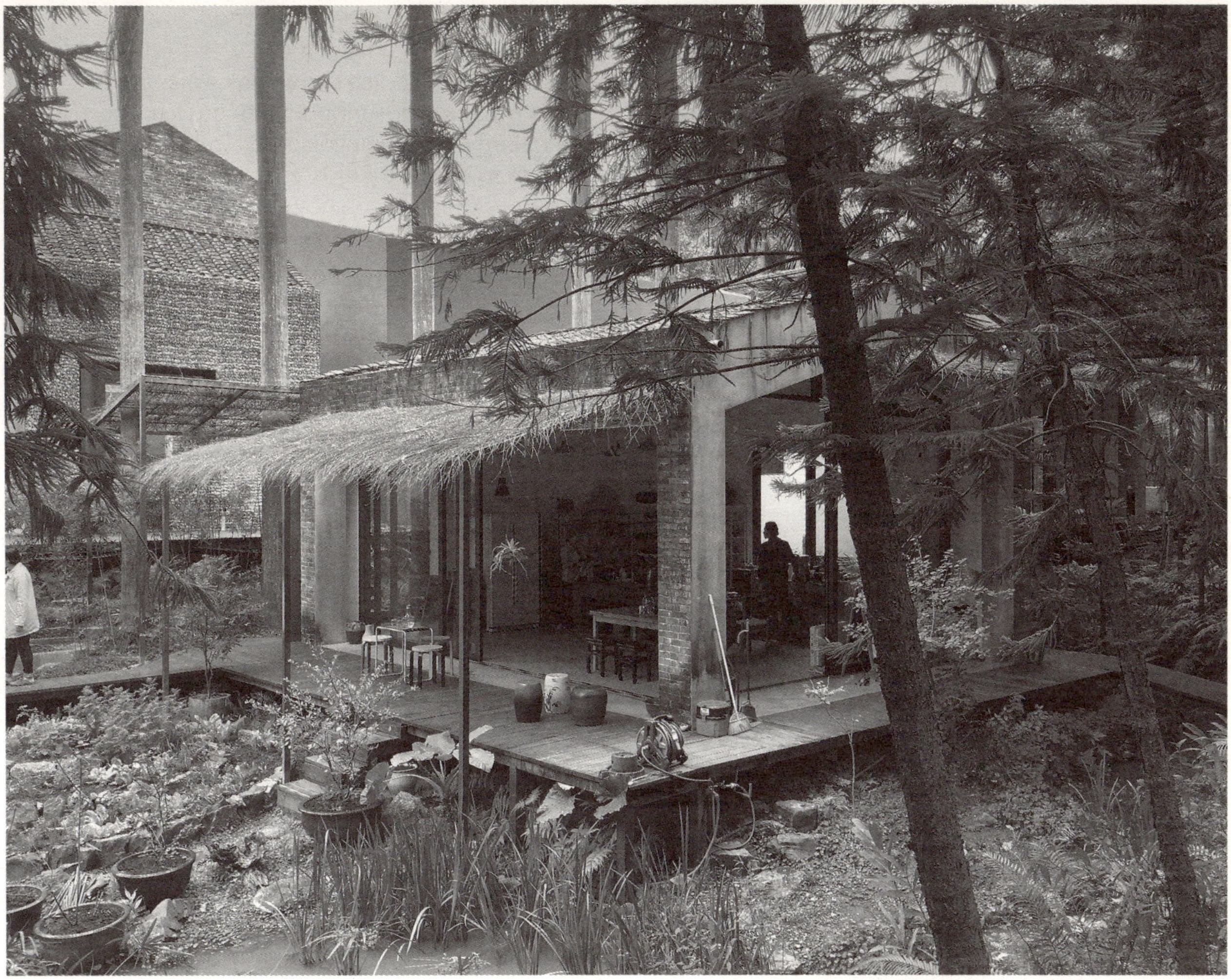

View of kitchen pavilion at Mirrored Gardens, January 2018

Mirrored Gardens in Guangzhou is an independent art space initiated by Vitamin Creative Space in 2015 and is dedicated to coupling global art economies with local farming-oriented life.

This gallery model is unfolded through the wide array of material published by Vitamin Creative Space including an introductory video that mixes Chinese proverbs with footage from daily garden activities—featuring a captivating slow-motion shot of Hu Fang flipping a pancake.

Their publication *Towards A Non-intentional Space Vol. 1* (2016) presents the diverse source material that informed the design of Mirrored Gardens through essays, poetry, and architectural blueprints by Sou Fujimoto Architects.

Skip Art Basel Hong Kong and visit Mirrored Gardens on a day-trip or go to their online shop at

http://shop57284870.world.taobao.com

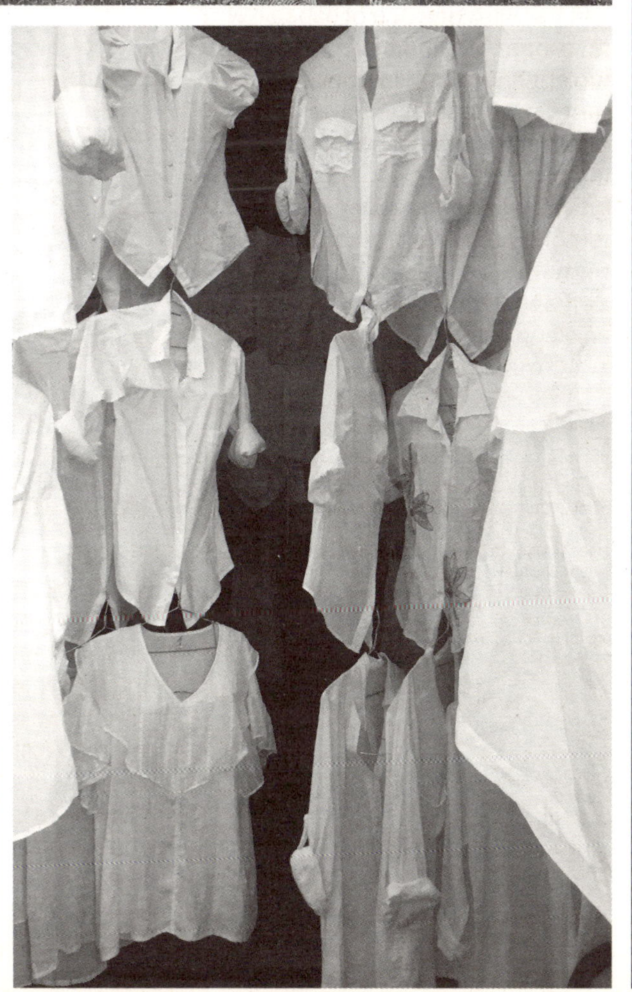

Store selling exclusively white shirts and dresses, Guangzhou, January 2018

ACTOR'S LEG

ERNST JÜNGER WATCHING SEINFELD

Text

Edgars Gluhovs

ON ALBERT SERRA'S *LIBERTÉ* AT VOLKSBÜHNE

The most memorable moment of Albert Serra's play *Liberté*, which premiered at the Volksbühne in Berlin earlier this year, takes place moments before the play begins. Just as we enter to take our seats, a bearded, jeans-wearing stage-hand rushes across the stage to help push a lone leg into a sedan, from where it is dangling awkwardly—rather like Goethe's leg in the famous Tischbein picture. The play takes place shortly before the French Revolution, roughly around the time Goethe wandered around Italy and had his preposterous picture painted. Dressed in the fashion of Ancien Régime's twilight years—white knee-length stocking, black leather shoe—the leg looks in fact just like Goethe's. Meanwhile, the bearded stage-hand gently but resolutely grabs the leg by its heel and calf, places it inside the sedan and shuts the door. After he leaves, the play begins. Throughout the evening, the exit door clacks four or five times, marking the premature flight of some spectators potentially confused by the absence of tinsel, pop-songs, and references to post-Fordism. The sedan door mostly remains closed. The leg makes an appearance a few more times. Propped by a cane, it emerges and even shuffles offstage at one point, only to return shortly after. "La bellezza porta alla morte," slowly intones the voice from within the sedan. The leg appears one last time for the death-scene in the end, and is helped up to take a bow. Without waiting for the applause to subside, the leg retreats backstage.

Ernst Jünger died, aged 102, in early 1998—the year the final season of Seinfeld aired on US television.

Living in the forester's house of the Stauffenberg's castle in Wilflingen, Upper Swabia, taking long walks in the woods, dusting off his vast beetle collection and no longer writing much except for irregular entries into his journal, the centogenarian author of *Storms of Steel* and *On The Marble Cliffs* spent his twilight years as an avid fan of Jerry Seinfeld and Larry David's show.

It remains a bit of a mystery how Jünger came across the TV series, and one can only guess what it was exactly that first piqued his interest, which soon gave way to unbridled enthusiasm.

The German TV started broadcasting the dubbed episodes in 1994, but Jünger preferred the original, undubbed versions. His publisher Ernst Klett would send him tapes of the US show, which Jünger would watch repeatedly on his VHS player, an antique opium pipe laying next to the TV set (symbolizing its addictive qualities).

One would think that it would be the neat, detached figure of Jerry that Jünger would most identify with. Both possessed an aloof manner, something Jünger had, years before, expanded on in his writings on *désinvolture*. But it was Kramer who quickly became Jünger's favorite character on the show. So much was Jünger engrossed with Jerry's eccentric neighbor that he even took to "kramering" into the rooms of his own house. The still springly Jünger would swing open the door and burst in, once even knocking down his wife Liselotte in the process.

His final years ticked by. Incidentally, there wasn't a single ticking clock in the house—Jünger had a phobia of clocks, and the only clock he owned was an alarm by his bedside, encased in its original protective styrofoam casing, muting the alarm's ticking sound. In that silence, the dry Jüngerian "ha-ha" salvos echoed from the TV room and across the house, chiming off his old war-helmet and muffled by the piles of books, furniture, snake skins, and tortoise shells.

S C

R

N

TRANS ON TV

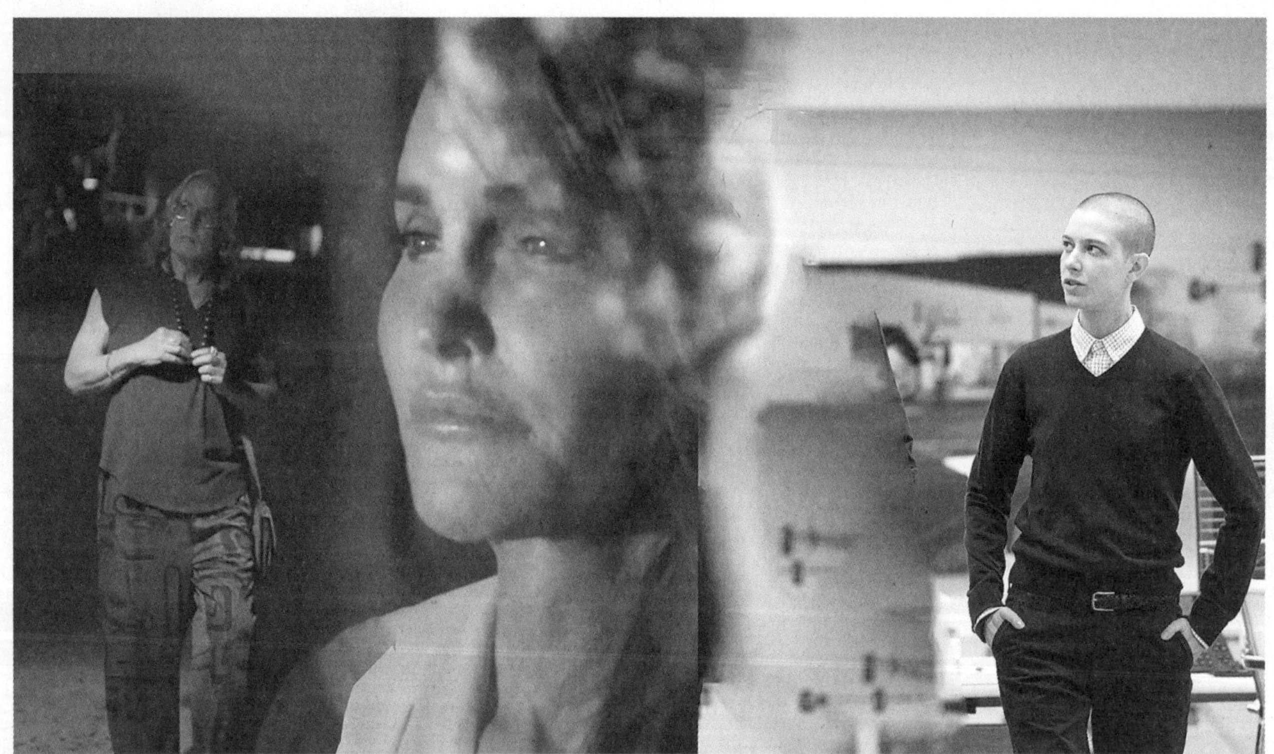

On Television: Jeffrey Tambor in *Transparent*, Caitlin Jenner in *I am Cait*, Asia Kate *Dillon in Billions*, Collage by Anke Dyes

TV column by Anke Dyes

She speaks about her responsibility, about giving the right image, projecting the right things, and how she has a voice while so many others do not. She is concerned. However, watching the nightly cold open of the reality TV series "I am Cait" (2015/16), we see Caitlin Jenner's mood has changed, we decide that her self esteem has been restored. And indeed the massive impact her appearances have, as related (via phone) by her step-daughter Kim Kardashian speaks for itself. This image of Jenner must be real and true if so many people have retweeted it. In the performative act that is both Caitlin Jenner's transition and her PR construction, likes and followers seem to validate Jenner's projected sense-of-self as a positive influence. Since at least her Vanity Fair cover, people have questioned the image of Jenner's femininity, which she reproduces and claims as an emanation of her "true self," a self in which she can finally live, and via which she can finally express herself. But what, after all, is an unquestionable female identity? Hair and make up? Being emotional? Jenner's choice of how to express femininity predate gender debates, go back further in time than difference feminism and threaten to make a long held feminist anxiety true, where trans somehow stabs the anti-sexist, anti-gender struggle in the back.

Yet as TV, "I am Cait" plays into one of the most successful (and common) contemporary TV/streaming tropes: the pursuit of becoming who/what one "truly" is. And the truth of Jenner's true self, here, lies in the material body. Jenner presenting her transition on TV makes this becoming visible, gives it an unmistakable form; and her "becoming" is much more radical than getting a make-over or gaining self esteem, visibly only in the set of your shoulders. Of course there is a distinct difference between the becoming-yourself narrative and being trans—as only one of these comes with an actual political debate and emancipatory struggle. But this also means that there is a different authenticity being transferred, too.

I AM NOT TRYING TO ARGUE ABOUT HOW "REALISTIC" CAITLIN JENNER'S REALITY TV SHOW IS.

Via the criticism of Jenner's representation in particular, something else about this narrative of transition has come to light: that the state of becoming has to have a true core, an anchor in the endless possibilities of metamorphosis, something that is unchanging and by that deserves to be understood as an identity. That this self might stem from patterns that are learned, from the reactions that one experiences as either positive or negative, bringing out a sense of self as much as "what women want," is replaced with the idea of a female (or other) self, that is assumed to be located in the brain, the stem cells, the bio-chemistry of how deep your voice gets. Of course, the daily experience of people that identify as trans* or inter* or even cis-gendered transcends this pattern easily. But I am not trying to argue about how "realistic" Caitlin Jenner's reality TV show is, but rather that somehow her transition gains traction with the way TV works, with how lives, identities, and ambitions are narrated today.

THE ONLY WAY THESE IDENTITIES CAN SEEM TO COME TOGETHER IS IN A QUALITY OF QUESTIONABLE REVOLUTIONARY POWER—I.E., VISIBILITY.

One cannot just be anything one feels, as Rogers Brubaker shows in his recent analysis and comparison of the "cases" of Caitlin Jenner and Rachel Dolezal, *Trans: Gender and Race in the Age of Unsettled Identities* (2018). For Brubaker, the idea of transgenderism is strongly related to the idea of the self-made person, which is to say to a particularly American strand of individualism. And even if race and gender are understood as foremost socially constructed categories, gender is—by now, by many—seen as something you can chose voluntarily, as it is not "inherited" the way race is, even if the physical change between say Jenner and Dolezal is much more severe in Jenner's case. And because the claim of being "transracial," yet widely unacceptable within the American public, threatened the state of acceptance that transgender had already gained, commentators and critics took up the "if Jenner then Dolezal"-rhetoric as a moment to distinguish between the cases, not least because it was in fact a political slogan used by anti-trans Christians and other right-wing conservatives. So a case for their distinction had to be made, that, again, produced a performative discourse of what a true self is, underlining yet again the double meaning of performance as speech-act as well as dramatized actions.

For trans as a dramatic action, it seems, some form of physical consequence has to be made visible, some suffering has to be had. Until Rachel Dolezal gets kicked out of a Starbucks for just sitting around while being black, she'll remain SNL weekend update source material, not someone celebrated for living their truth. Even if Jenner's position (both on- and off-screen) seems less controversial, she was subject to a similar critique with commenters questioning how one can voluntarily claim a gender role, or as one critic wrote: if you've never, say, gotten your period on the train or been otherwise shamed and inconvenienced by your female biology in a sexist environment, how can you claim to be a woman, let alone be qualified to speak for women? It appears, in some kind of over-estimation of the juridical within the performative, the suffering has to be true to change the legislature.

Adding to that the intrinsic quality of a trans perspective, agency takes shape as some form of super power: In season 2, episode 2 of "Billions," Asia Kate Dillon plays a brilliant non-binary analyst named Taylor who makes said billions for their boss, Bobby Axelrod (Damien Lewis). In the bro-y atmosphere of hedge-fund management, relating the speculative to one's own identity is to become one with the job. Taylor are really good at their job, they don't have any private life, they are, very likely, "on the spectrum." Yet, they are somehow also like the unquestionably manly main character Axelrod. They are the part of him that is an outsider, that feels alienated by his world, but can make this feeling of being alien work for himself: In episode 4 of season 2, we get to the core of this quality, that both Taylor and Bobby supposedly share. In a dialogue that reminds both in tone and message strongly of the identity politics of the TV series "Glee" (2009–15), Taylor are told, that their somehow distanced perspective is an asset and are advised, quite literally in this case, to capitalize their difference.

"Transparent" (2014–) also treats transitioning as becoming one's true self, but in this case it is not solely a matter of performance enhancement, but rather a coming to terms with one's heritage, with upbringing as well as with the family history. Arguably the series is less about "Mo-Pa's" transition, but about her kids, and how they do or do not find themselves, not least in terms of identification, attraction, preferences. "Transparent" too, uses gender transition as a *chiffre* for finding one's true self, but also hinting at the contradictions: replaying a conflict that any feminist scene must have had in the last 15 years, Soloway, in season 2, episode 9 ("Man on the Land"), lets Maura (born Morton) go to a women's music festival with her daughters, where her difference to the surrounding is one of class but also one of being trans in a scene of cis-gender women, who don't want a trans-women as a "man on the land" attending their festival. Again, the truth comes down to the body and its parts. But also the episode, somehow performatively, plays out how the discourse of trans identities threatens to monopolize feminist debates and spaces. Leaving open how much cis-male entitlement is in Maura's (Mo-Pa's) indignation of being excluded, the episode gives an idea of the current debate about competing claims and individualist struggle in its complexity.

The only way these identities, that each stand for their own story, for their own struggle, can seem to come together is in a quality of questionable revolutionary power—i.e., visibility. Visibility, in a somewhat butchered version of performativity, is, when "seeing someone like yourself on TV," comes to be understood as a form of empowerment, because it is assumed, that you are more able to relate to a character, that is more like yourself. This logic somehow overlooks, and in doing so sadly undermines, the fact that there is something inherently queer about projection. In theory, one could feel for the trans women what one feels for the macho man, if it is told to you in the right way. But of course, the realists of trans representation are not the only ones to overlook this, otherwise the mandatory white cis protagonist in the center of most stories would have ceased long ago. As we are reading industry truths about abusive behavior (even in the series mentioned here) coming to light these days as well, one can appreciate the change in the lookism of contemporary TV, without mistaking it for a feminist breakthrough. As one can see with "I am Cait," trans is good for TV, even if TV might not yet be the best for trans.

IN THE BRO-Y ATMOSPHERE OF HEDGE-FUND MANAGEMENT, RELATING THE SPECULATIVE TO ONE'S OWN IDENTITY IS TO BECOME ONE WITH THE JOB.

Next up: *Intelligence as a TV Trope*

LT

D

T R

T

T H I

T R

HISACHIKA TAKAHASHI BY YUKI OKUMURA

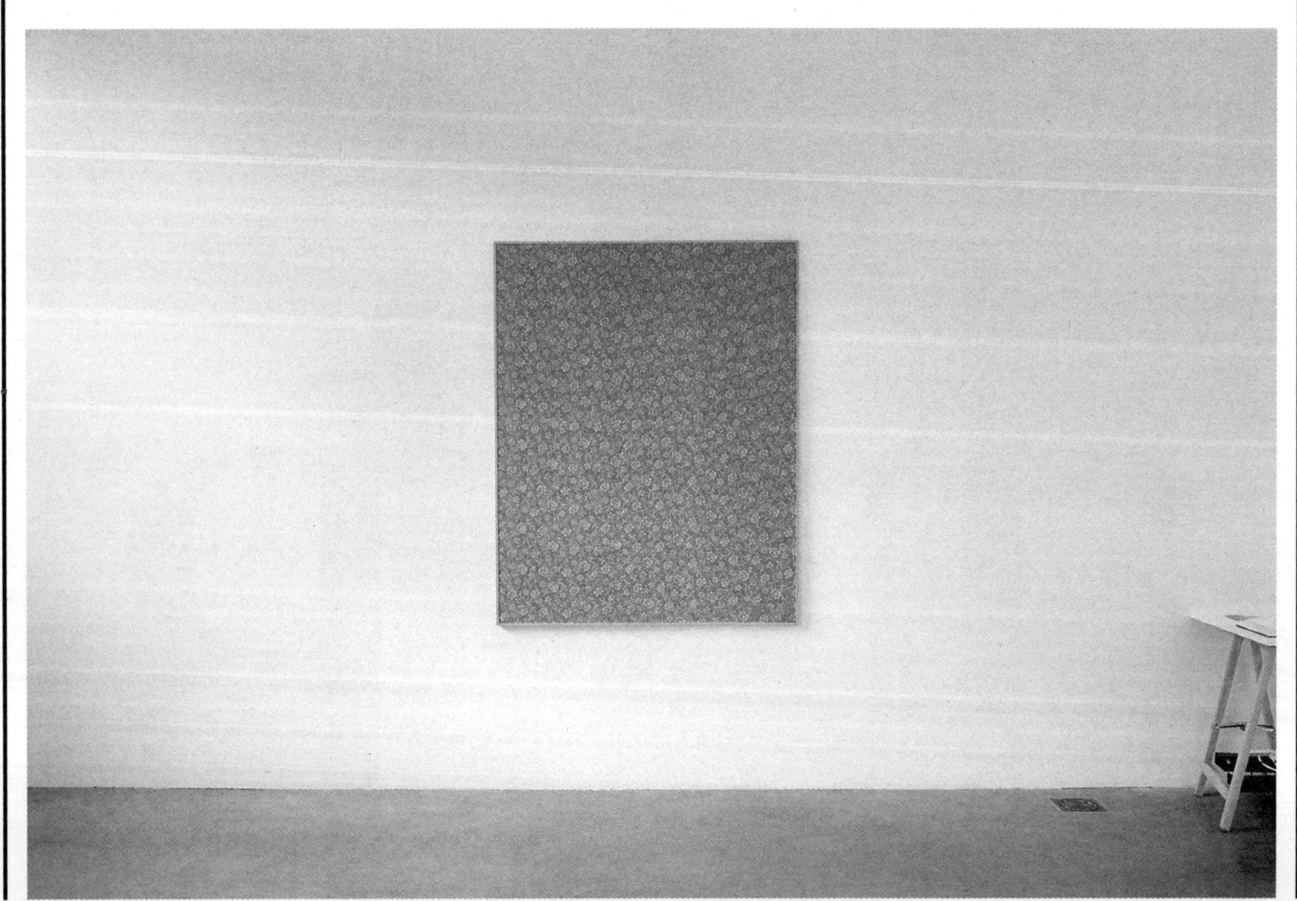

Hisachika Takahashi, *Untitled*, 1966, synthetic paint on canvas, 160×130 cm; installation view at Project Room, WIELS, Brussels, 2013, photo by Shogo Matsushiro; from Yuki Okumura, *Hisachika Takahashi: From Wide White Space, Antwerp, 1967 to Project Room, WIELS Contemporary Art Centre, Brussels, 2013*, 2013, mixed-medium installation at Mori Art Museum, Tokyo, dimensions variable. Courtesy the artists and MISAKO & ROSEN, Tokyo.

Letter to the reader by the legendary Japanese artist Hisachika Takahashi by much younger Brussels-based artist Yuki Okumura.

DEAR READER,

My name is Hisachika Takahashi. I was born in 1940 and grew up in Tokyo. I went to an art university to study sculpture, but found it too conservative and left the country to Milan in 1962.

There I served as an assistant to Lucio Fontana, who called me *Chacha*, while working on my own pieces such as a series of patterned paintings. Using readymade embossed rubber rollers for home wall decoration, I applied a combination of repetitive forms all over the canvas with fluorescent and phosphorescent acrylic paints—something no one was doing back then. For me it was a collaboration, with each roller being a collaborator. But I also did a human-to-human collaboration; In 1966, in response to my invitation, Fontana made a cut to an already completed flower-patterned painting of mine. Swish!

In 1969 I met Bob Rauschenberg in New York and soon became his assistant. Through the community of artists around Bob, who called me *Sachika*, my own practice also became more collaborative with more focus on memory as the subject—as something that is personal yet shareable beyond individuality.

Inspired by how Bob had approached de Kooning for his "erased" drawing, I knocked the doors of various artists, asking them to draw a map of the United States only from their memory. Twenty-two artists including Bob, Jasper Johns, Joseph Kosuth, Gordon Matta-Clark, and Cy Twombly responded to my instruction. In 1972, based on the idea that a mirror might have memory of the people it has reflected, I collected and presented various mirrors from friends, and in 1973 I collaborated with my favorite red hunting hat, using frottage and polaroids to document my past, present, and future memories with it. In the end I worked for Bob for nearly 40 years until his passing in 2008. Bob's family gave me a small container, engraved with the initials "R.R.", filled with the ashes of his bones. Since then I have taken him with me for each of my exhibition openings.

In 2013, a young Japanese artist named Yuki Okumura called me. He said that he had encountered a Japanese name in a book about Wide White Space, the legendary gallery active in Antwerp from 1966 to 1976, and had started to research this artist because there was no photographic documentation of his 1967 show at the gallery. Of course, this artist was me, and thanks to Yuki, I reunited with Anny de Decker, one of the co-directors of the gallery, and my paintings, which she had stored for 45 years.

Yuki and I then decided to reactivate my original exhibition and make it tour from Antwerp 1967 to Brussels in 2013 and to Liverpool and Rotterdam in 2014. In Rotterdam, the Tokyo gallery Misako & Rosen sold all the paintings, which was such a great ending for our time-traveling exhibition project.

The collaboration between Yuki and me went on and in 2016 we built a large-scale exhibition called "Hisachika Takahashi by Yuki Okumura" at Maison Hermès Le Forum in Tokyo.

I was very happy to finally show my map project in its entirety to a Japanese audience. Yuki's exhibits were all about my work and life, including a video where he presented himself as me, talking to the Swiss curator Daniel Baumann, who had seen my work in an old catalogue and wanted to get to know who I really was. Yuki answered his questions, drawing from his memory of my memory! This entire exhibition was perhaps a single work of Yuki's, which conceptually incorporated all my exhibited works as its components, perhaps like the way my map project consisted of works by other artists. It felt a bit uncomfortable, but I enjoyed his attempt, despite his imperfect recollection. After all, it was his way of paying homage to my practice—his version of dealing with memory and collaboration.

Some visitors doubted if I ever existed. Maybe Yuki made me up as a fictional artist and even the maps were his own creations drawn under all those now famous names. That would be funny! No wonder, as I once almost disappeared from art history. Anyway, it is not a big deal if I am real or fictitious—in the end, all artists are mere names, whether physically active or not, remembered only with links to their work. That is who we are!

Hisachika Takahashi
(Ghostwritten by Yuki Okumura)

BOB'S FAMILY GAVE ME A SMALL CONTAINER, ENGRAVED WITH THE INITIALS "R.R.", FILLED WITH THE ASHES OF HIS BONES. SINCE THEN I HAVE TAKEN HIM WITH ME FOR EACH OF MY EXHIBITION OPENINGS.

THE LAST "NEW YORK LETTER"

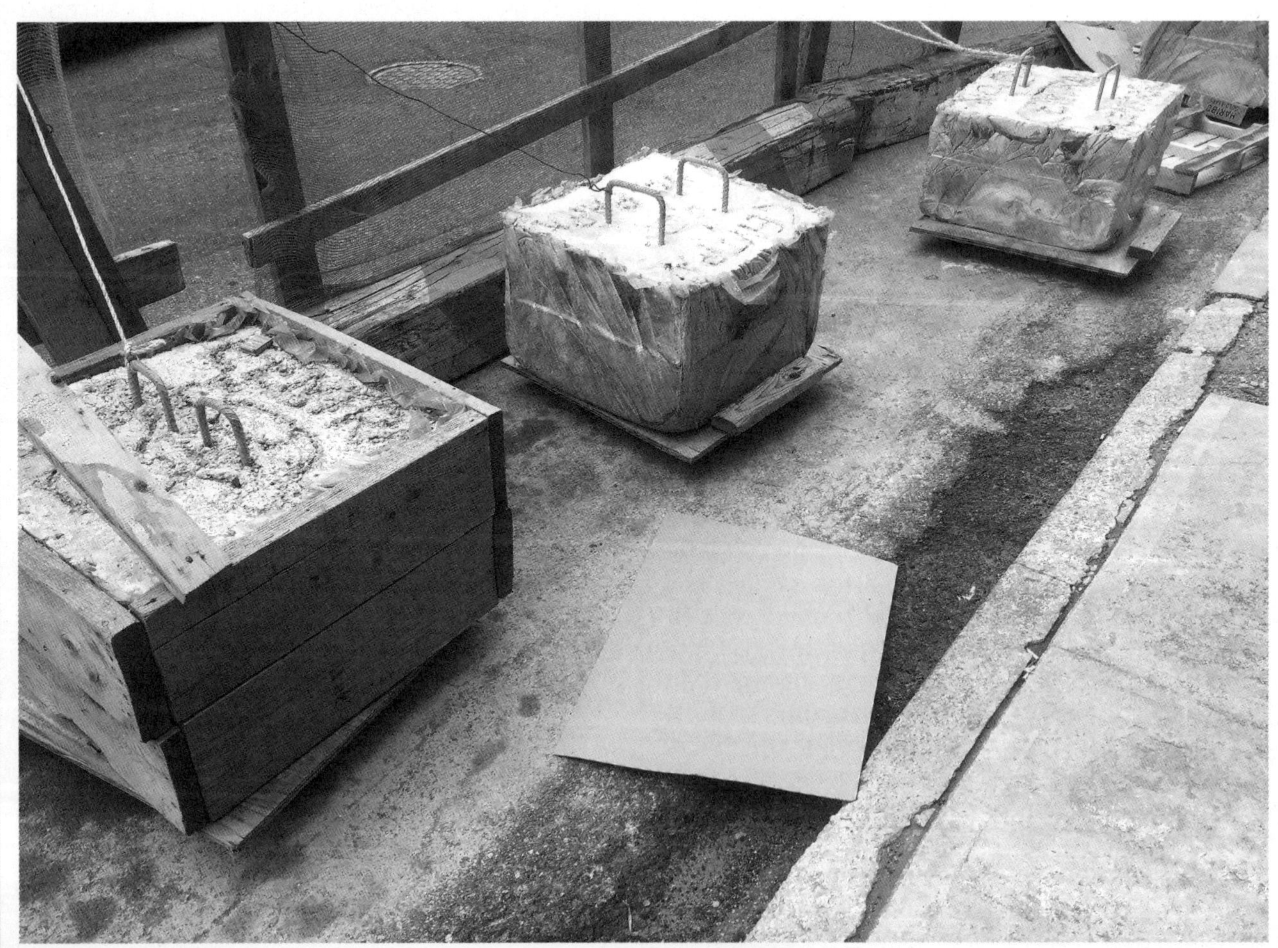

Text / Photos Simone Roberta

Thursday, May 10, 2018

I clearly remember a series of reports from New York City, *New York Briefe*, in a German art magazine. The letters were written by an artist acquainted with the magazine. This was at a time when NYC still was interesting and news travelled slower than today. I also remember a couple of artists commuting between NYC and Berlin—creating a great deal of capital by simply travelling back and forth between the cities, carrying news and superior insight in their hand luggage.

WHITE CASTLE

Last autumn, the NYC-based fashion label Telfar, known in the art world since its 2013 runway show at NY's Artists Space, designed gender-neutral uniforms for the American burger chain White Castle. Liberian/American fashion designer Telfar Clemens—after whom the label is named—is less connected to the fashion of Ivy League art students (in contrast to Eckhaus Latta), and has stronger ties to the music scene, clearly audible in this years spring presentation. Telfar extended his work with the White Castle uniforms by using the White Castle logo for an entire collection, merging the burger chain castle logo with his own logo. Here we have an emerging NY label championing a bargain burger chain to reclaim a certain amount of autonomy after having worked in their service as a designer. Or put another way: instead of hiding the fact that he redesigned the White Castle uniforms, he brings it to the forefront by building an entire collection around the White Castle brand. That is a big difference to fashion label Vetements, that didn't work—or not that we know of—in the service of DHL, but just made Vetements DHL T-shirts purely for the style. In Telfar's case a minimum degree of transparency is involved by letting everyone know, through the promotional campaign, videos, and lookbooks, that he worked for the oldest burger chain in the US.

RUINS OF ANOTHER WHITE CASTLE

A couple of weeks ago, the NY-based artist, Gedi Sibony showed a large-scale installation in one of the powerhouse galleries in Chelsea. I forgot the title. It's the facade of an entire White Castle building, placed in the gallery, fit to size. You see, it's a huge gallery space. The press-release doesn't mention White Castle at all, but refers to Sibony's minimalistic practice and how this show, and the works in it, mark a huge departure within the artist's practice. A small note in The New Yorker mentions the sculptures origins and further states: "The structure's modularity may invite thoughts of Donald Judd's stacks; its reconceptualization of architecture recalls Michael Asher and what jargoneers call 'institutional critique.' But the institution in Sibony's crosshairs isn't the art-industrial complex for which the term was coined—it's that derelict white fortress, America itself." Apparently all the white enamel painted facade panels are from a former Brooklyn location of White Castle, perhaps close to Sibony's house or studio? Is the artist aware of Telfar? White Castle? And consider how extreme the name of the burger chain reads in 2018. Apparently White Castle is being associated with working class and super low-income communities. Clemens stated in an interview that White Castle stayed in the neighborhoods McDonalds left. Business would not be worth it. Therefore Clemens grew up going to White Castle after a long night out and not to any other fast food chain.

THE PROMOTION OF ARTHUR JAFA BY KAHLIL JOSEPH

The next day I briefly attended an opening of Wade Guyton at another Chelsea White Castle. I was meeting a dear friend who gave me the keys to her room because I had to leave someone else's house. Finding a bed in NYC is always a hustle. Before this I was in Harlem at an opening; Arthur Jafa at Gavin Brown. White Castle is moving on up. Jafa first rose to prominence for his work on *Daughters of the Dust* (1991). This seminal film made by Julie Dash, Jafa's wife at the time, earned him a "Best Cinematography" award at the 1992 Sundance Film Festival. In the early 2000s he left Hollywood behind and made his first steps into the art world. After participating in Hans Ulrich Obrist's Mediacity Seoul and the Whitney Biennal, both in 2000, he quit and returned to Hollywood. In an interview he stated that he wasn't ready to deal with all the pressure, meeting collectors and everything, and felt more comfortable working for other film-makers.

Kahlil Joseph was born 1981, and his dad was a lawyer for the Williams tennis sisters. A young filmmaker from Seattle, Joseph is known in the art world for his blockbuster shows at the Tate, the New Museum and, to a larger audience, through his music videos for Kendrick Lamar and Beyoncé. Joseph saw Jaffa's recent new film, titled *Love Is The Message, The Message Is Death*. Joseph, smart and eager, immediately grasped Jafa's qualities and must have been searching for an artist to admire: an artist he could refer to. Jafa—born 1960—is much older and does not have the same visibility as Joseph. As the story goes, whenever Joseph had a film screening of his own, he simply slipped in Jaffa's *Love Is The Message, The Message Is Death* beforehand—and audiences who saw it would not know what it was or who made it. This is apparently exactly how gallerist and dealer Gavin Brown got introduced to Jafa's work. Brown called Jafa up and screened his film the day after Trump got elected. NYC was traumatized and found moral shelter in Brown's gallery. I am making it sound a bit ridiculous, while I do think Joseph's "promotion" of Jaffa's work is very unique and great (and a bit sneaky), also Gavin Brown's sense for timing is almost uncanny. And this could be all wrong, since I'm writing it all down after having skimmed interviews, read texts online, and listened to recordings from panel discussions dealing with Joseph and Jafa.

THE UNDERGROUND MUSEUM

Joseph's older brother by two years, Noah Davis, sadly passed away in 2015, suffering from a rare cancer. He was a painter based in LA, who initiated, in a working class neighborhood, the Underground Museum, where, amongst other things, he produced his project "Imitation of Wealth." The museum imitated, redid, and restaged famous artworks from Duchamp's bottle rack to a Jeff Koons vacuum cleaner. No museum would loan anything to them—and this was actually also not necessary, as he was interested in deciphering these artworks and the power and White Castles they represent. It's also at this museum that Joseph (actually his brother Davis started with the "Jafa screenings") screened Jafa's film for the first time. Today, after Davis' untimely death, the MOCA LA is somehow involved in maintaining The Underground Museum, loaning them works from their collection.

Recap: White Castle, Telfar, Gedi Sibony, Kahlil Joseph, The Underground Museum, Arthur Jafa

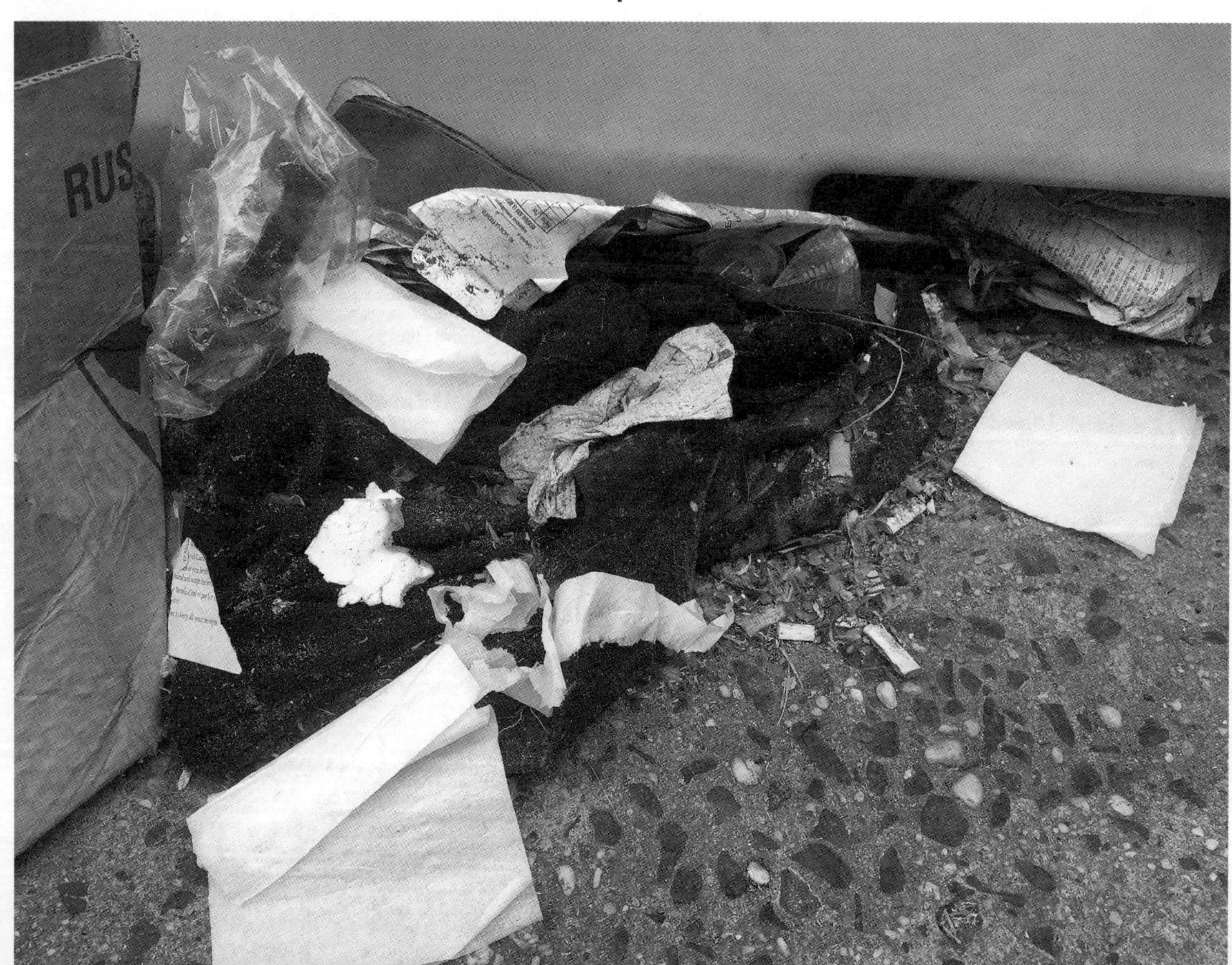

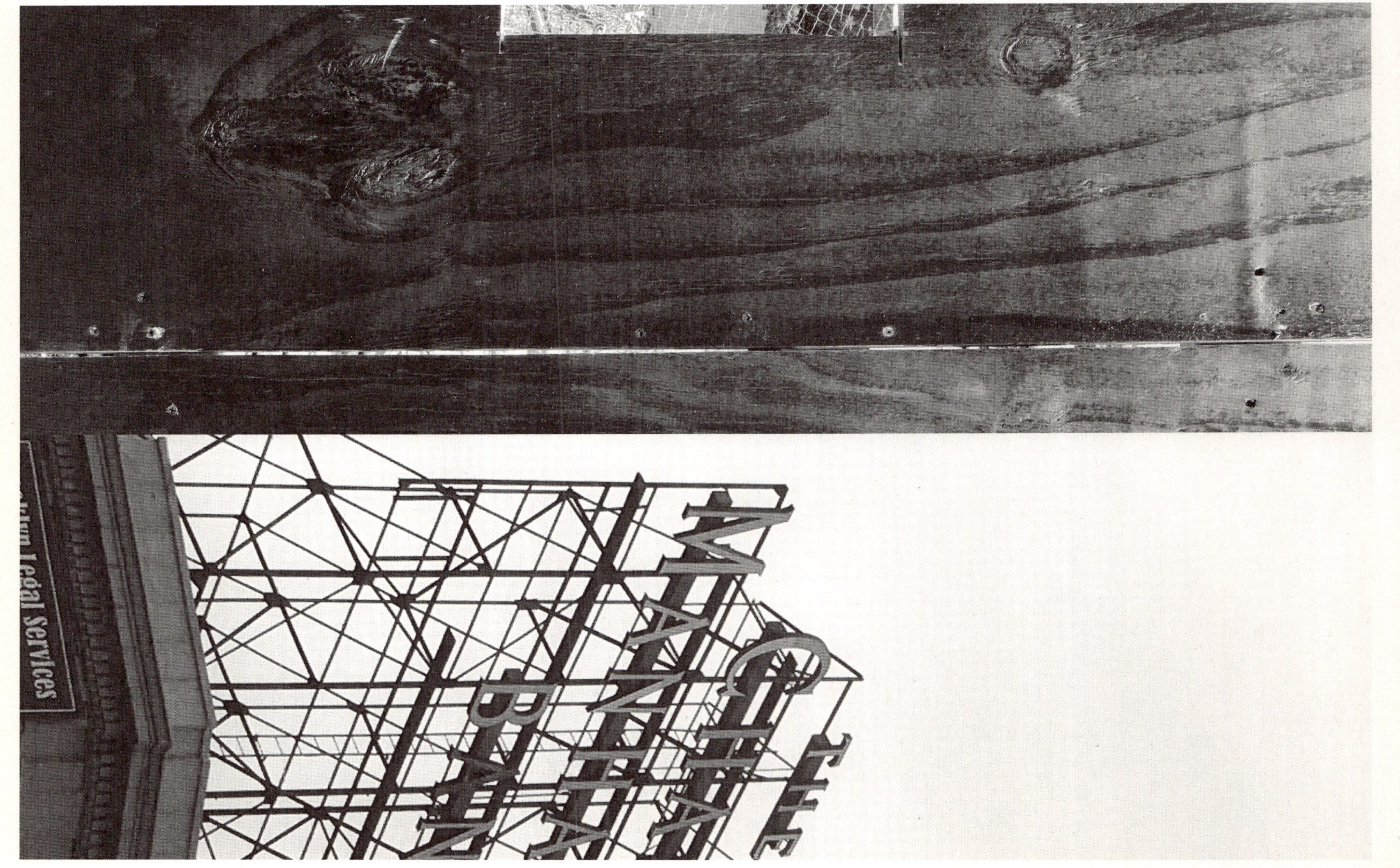
THE
CHA
MANHA
BAN
Legal Services

T

L

K

FALL / WINTER 2018 COLLECTION OF CELESTIAL ADVICE AND TERRESTRIAL INSIGHTS

Text

Miss Needle

ARIES (MARCH 21–APRIL 20)

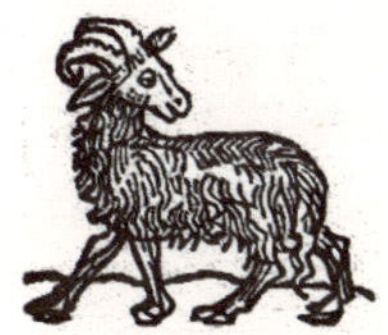

House of the self, appearance, and ego drive. Ruled by Mars.

In the coming fall, you may experience a steady continuation of what 2018 has generally offered: a deepening commitment to love and collaboration. Use it to turn the strong, internal energy that burns within your sign away from your self-haunting anxiety and towards constructive sabotage: you are charming, smart and fun—perfect traits for seducing enemies. Finally you'll feel aligned with your abilities and activities, and through this you will grow.

TAURUS (APRIL 21–MAY 21)

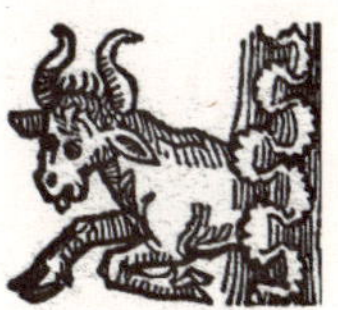

House of personal values and finances. Ruled by Venus.

In the Scots language spoken in Lowland Scotland, a watergaw is a fragmented rainbow that appears between clouds. A skafer is a faint rainbow that arises behind a mist, presaging the imminent dissipation of the mist. A silk napkin is a splintered rainbow that heralds the arrival of brisk wind and rain. Use these as power symbols for the rest of 2018. Pack your bags with integrity—these borderlands are tricky—and remember; things are what they seem. Look closely.

GEMINI (MAY 22–JUNE 21)

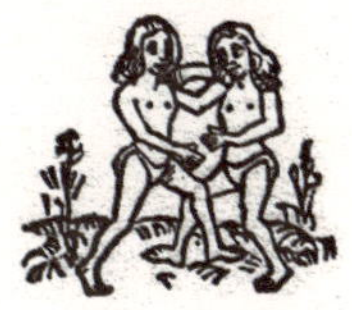

House of communication and local culture. Ruled by Mercury.

An old astrological omen tells us that a great gathering of individuals of a particular sign from all nations and layers of respective societies can eliminate altogether one fellow sign member per decade in whom the Big Three—capital, capital, and capital have turned utterly destructive and whose actions threaten the World Peace. This is your call, tribe of Gemini. Reflect and communicate wisely while spreading and perceiving this message. You're a bunch of dual selves with a lot of practical energy to be channeled...

CANCER (JUNE 22–JULY 22)

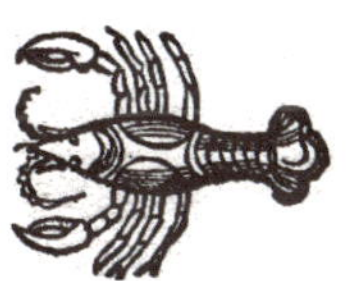

House of identity and roots. Ruled by the Moon.

You are a wonderfully conflicted parcel sent with special delivery, Cancerian, for no-one knows if you can break or not; no-one knows how to handle you. I advise you to remain as unpredictable as possible—violent tenderness is a solid feature when calling out everyday harassment. Through the last part of the year, your bulboid corpuscles will be more sensitive than usual, and your soul, too, will have a heightened capacity to receive and register delight. Blossom on!

LEO (JULY 23–AUG 21)

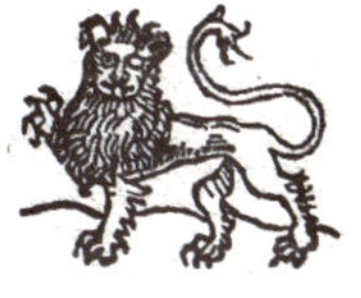

House of children, creativity, and gambling. Ruled by the Sun.

Your whole being is permeated by an indomitable, bubbling energy—quickly categorized by the surroundings as anger. This discrepancy between energy drive and reception thereof is a tough, general challenge for you, Leo, that got you categorized ever so often as harasser—which you probably got used to by now. But just because you've accustomed to this certain trouble doesn't mean you should stop searching for relief. In late 2018 you can finally track down the practical magic necessary to accomplish a thorough healing of that trouble and pain.

VIRGO (AUG 22–SEP 23)

House of work and ritual. Ruled by Mercury.

The pure, deep, and obedient are traits of yours, are traits you pass on. With conflict cooking in an innocent belly, you are easy to hurt. Your wounds heal to clean, white scars, your body's soon full of them. You are the proof that the chipped bowl's glued reparations serve enrichment of the object rather than loss. Your wounds are beautiful, and we trust you. Your most interesting successes of late 2018 could come from using things as they're not supposed to be used.

Zodiac signs from the 16th century (Source: Wikipedia; PD)

LIBRA (SEP 24 – OCT 23)

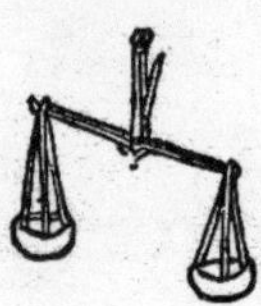

House of partnerships. Ruled by Mercury.

You are intact, Libra, trembling and threateningly intact. With the triangular sail of the caravel that enabled it to sail against the wind before the fifteenth century, here, in the end of 2018, you stand with similar abilities: you sail safely into the wind. You own your desires from the sacred to the profane, which allows your creativity to grow. In this last part of the year, you can rise to powerful new heights if you stick with yourself and don't get lost in other people's (lack of) decisions.

SCORPIO (OCT 24 – NOV 22)

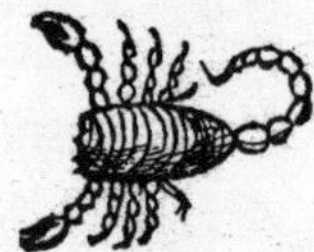

House of sex, death, and other people's money. Ruled by Mars and Pluto.

It is with stinging mystery and sensuality you seduce—even yourself. In the spectrum of your subconscious you are sly and hot with great healing powers. You speak the language of plant medicine, and in late 2018 your tribe will be extra skilled at clearing blocked passageways: heavy doors, treasure boxes, buried secrets, shy eyes, guarded hearts, and insular minds. In the last part of the year, you might start clicking with an avant-garde group of people.

SAGITTARIUS (NOV 23 – DEC 22)

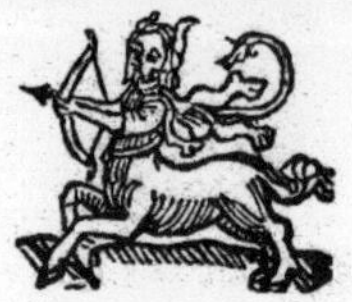

House of adventure, travel, and learning. Ruled by Jupiter.

Anchored in your being is an ability to shoot far—and strike. By October of 2018 you will have become as smart a gambler as you may have ever been. You fearlessly (sometimes naïvely) venture into foreign territory and quickly know how to read its coordinates, which makes you an excellent hacker—be it structural or emotional. Be mindful, though, of how you use people, things, and institutions as containers for the parts of yourself that you judge critically.

CAPRICORN (DEC 23 – JAN 20)

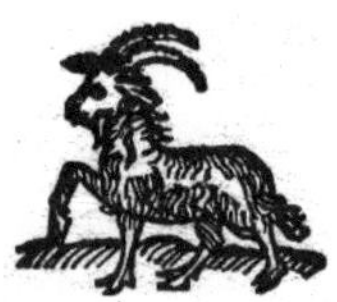

House of career and public persona. Ruled by Saturn.

Beauty was always a topic for you —skin-deep, expensive, or glamorous beauty. Now, get ready to rebuild. Your ruling planet, structured Saturn, arrives in Capricorn for the first time since 1991, which is an excellent opportunity for you to gain interest in a deeper, more provocative kind of beauty—a soulful beauty! Don't miss out on growing wilder and wiser. This is how your relationship to money and sex, by the end of the year, will get makeovers, too.

AQUARIUS (JAN 21 – FEB 19)

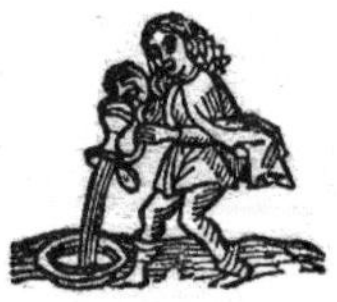

House of gatherings and crowds. Ruled by Saturn and Uranus.

Your sign is lounging around, encapsulated in its element. On one side, immersion is strengthening for any process; on another it prolongs and postpones endings. This might have kept you an apprentice in your field, rather than the professional you could have become. Now is the time for your maturation, Aquarius. 2018 is the year of stepping out of your element (and your over-sensitivity) not to abandon it, but to develop from it a wise, generous empathy.

PISCES (FEB 20 – MARCH 20)

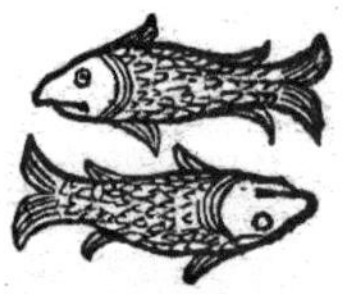

House of mystery and intuition. Ruled by Jupiter and Neptune.

2018 has been your year of liberation. You've finally found a path you find worthy for your talented, restless, generous being. You've always had a tail of fire running after you and a—at times greedy—need for stimuli and knowledge, while now you seem to settle with what you're doing. You have great potential for mobilizing big groups of people—and making them aware of the metaphysics of their actions. This is one of the most important universal tasks—please continue!

LADINA STEINEGGER

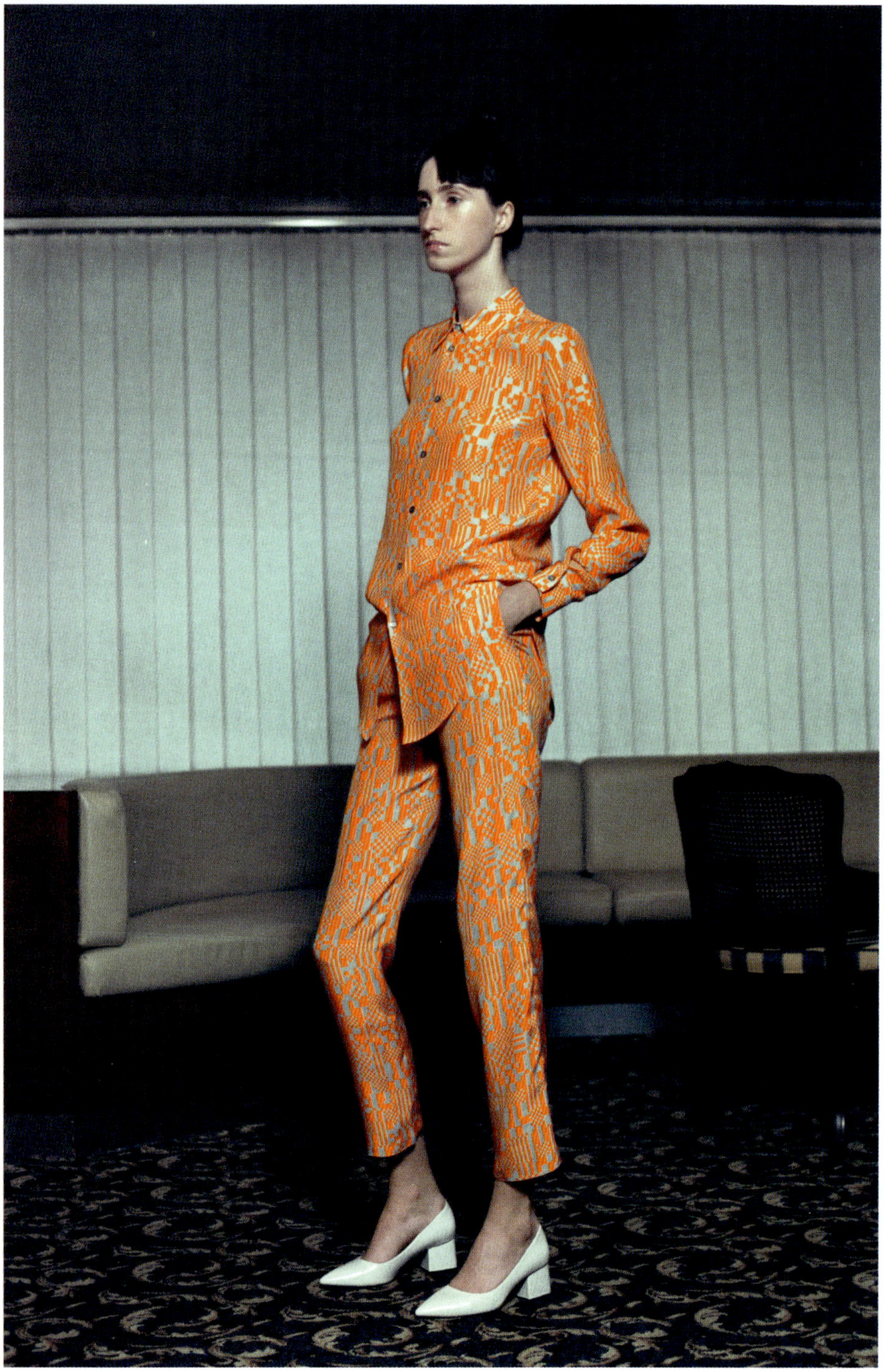

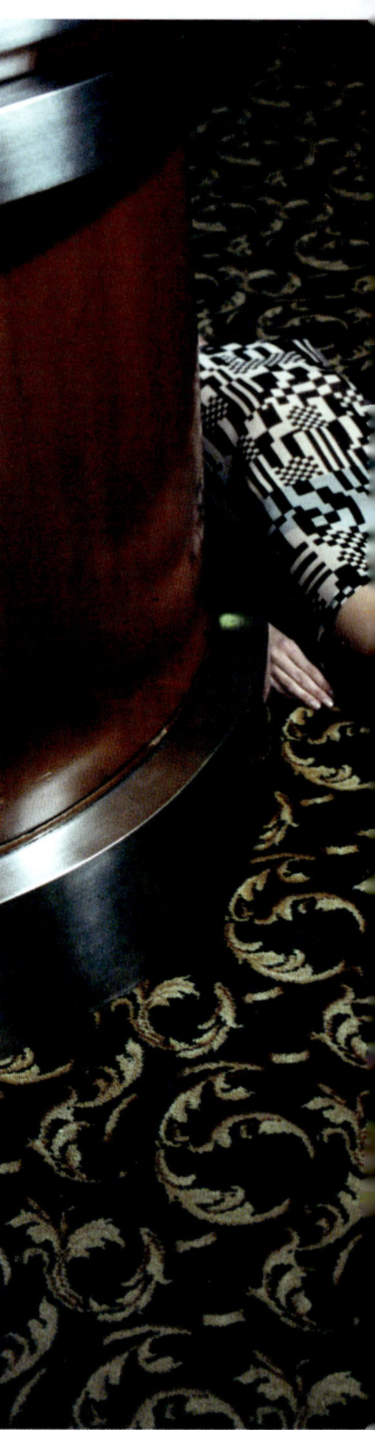

Textile Designer: Ladina Steinegger
Photographer: Arno Nollen
Location: York Hotel, Rome

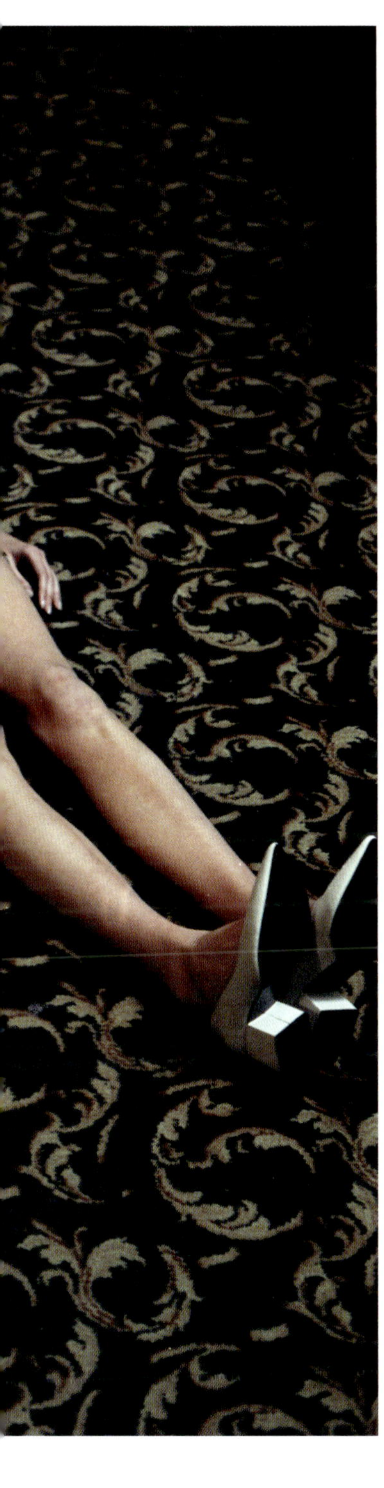

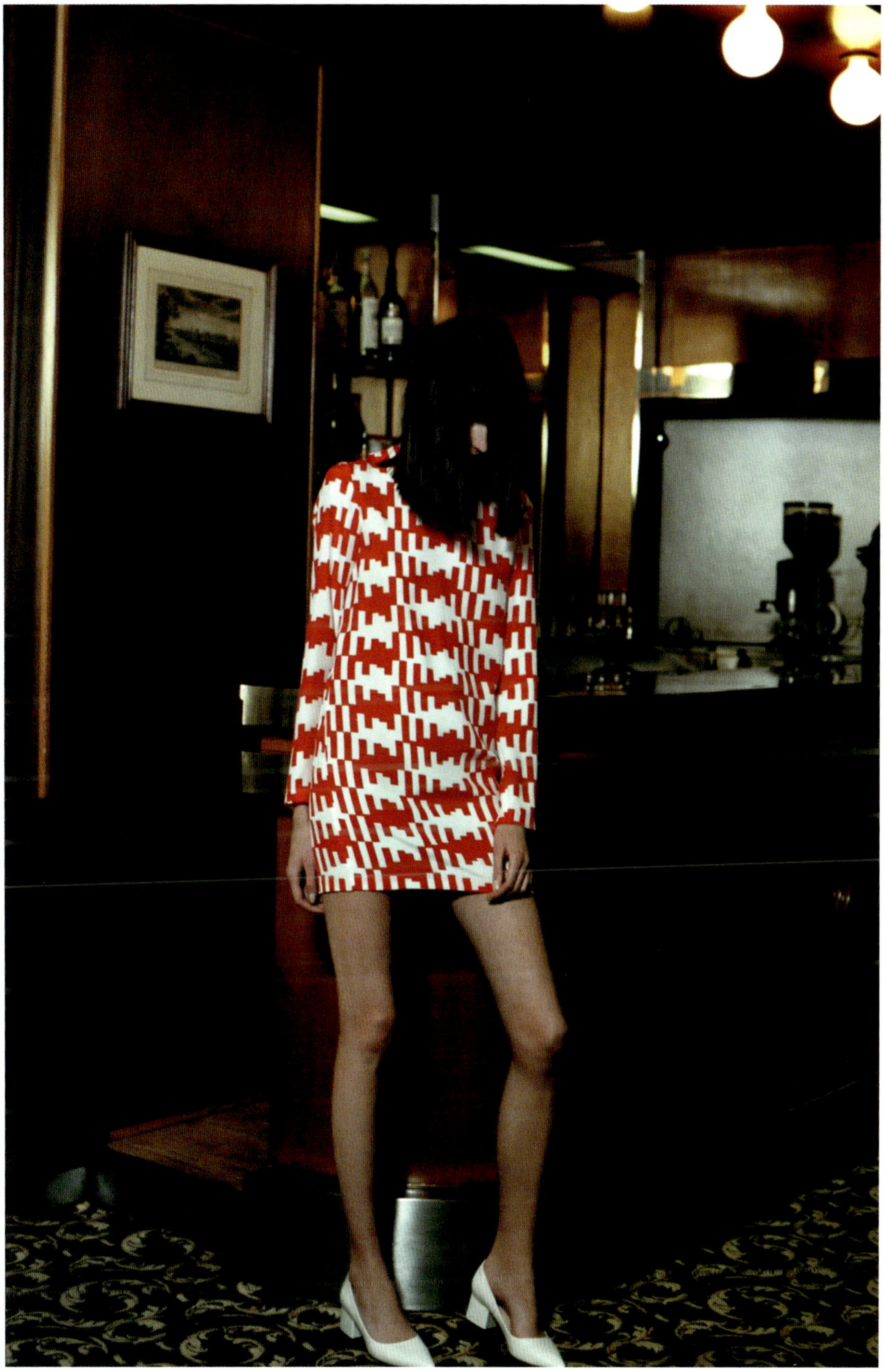

WWW.LADINASTEINEGGER.COM

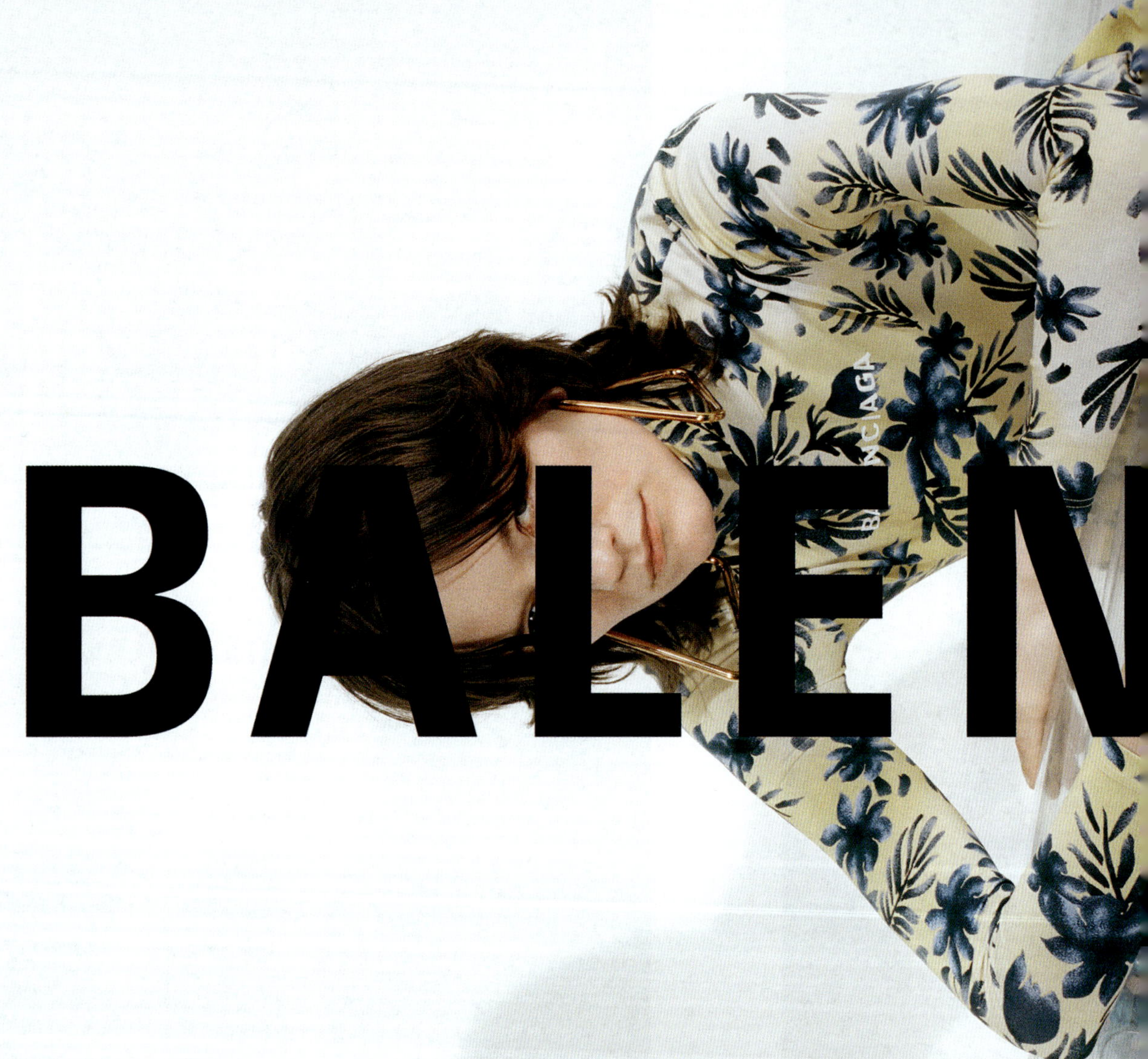
BALEN

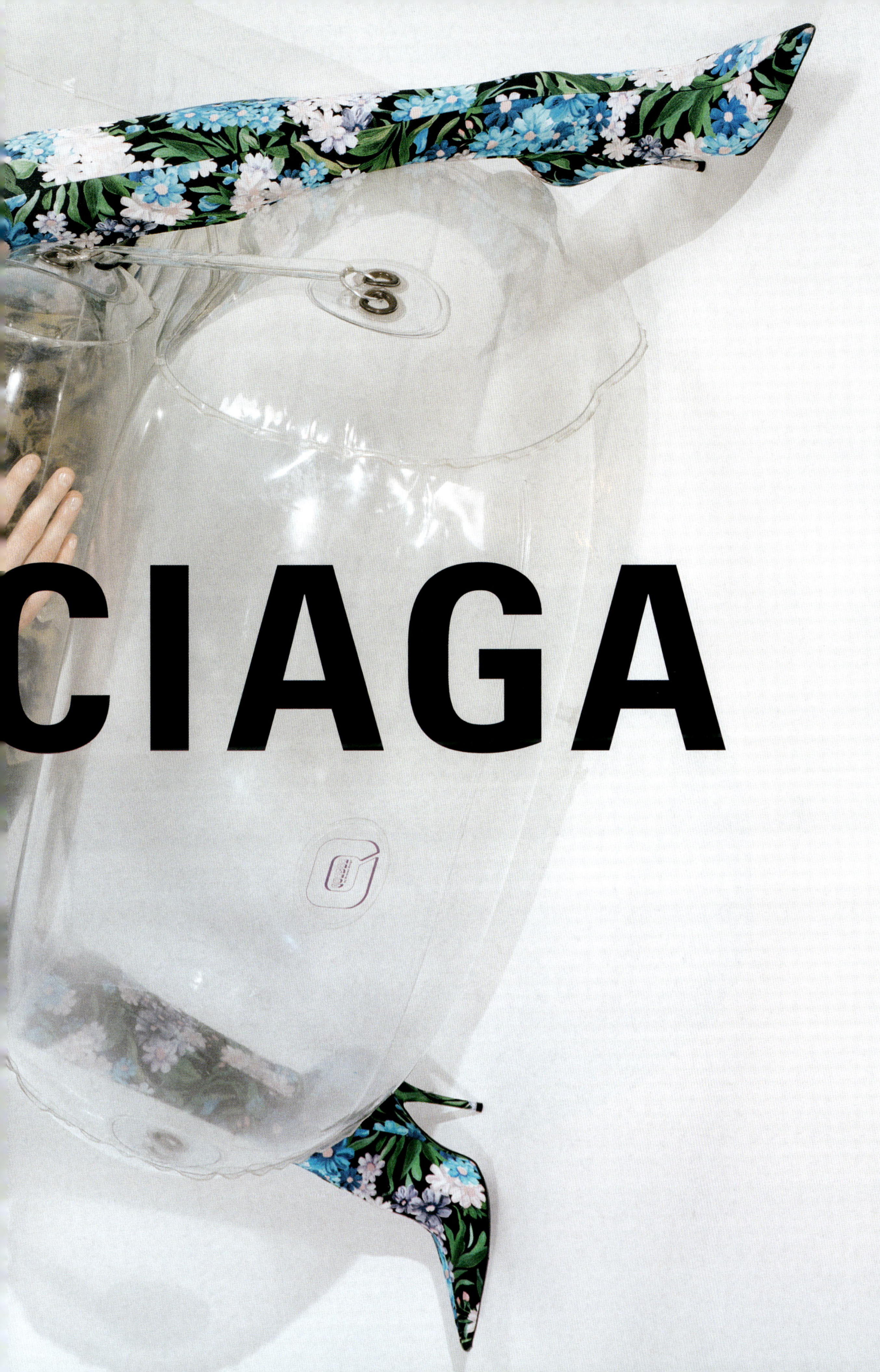
CIAGA

23H30–5H

CARTES D'IDENTITÉ OBLIGATOIRES
NAVETTES À DISPOSITION

Disease of the Eyes

31.8. – 11.11.18

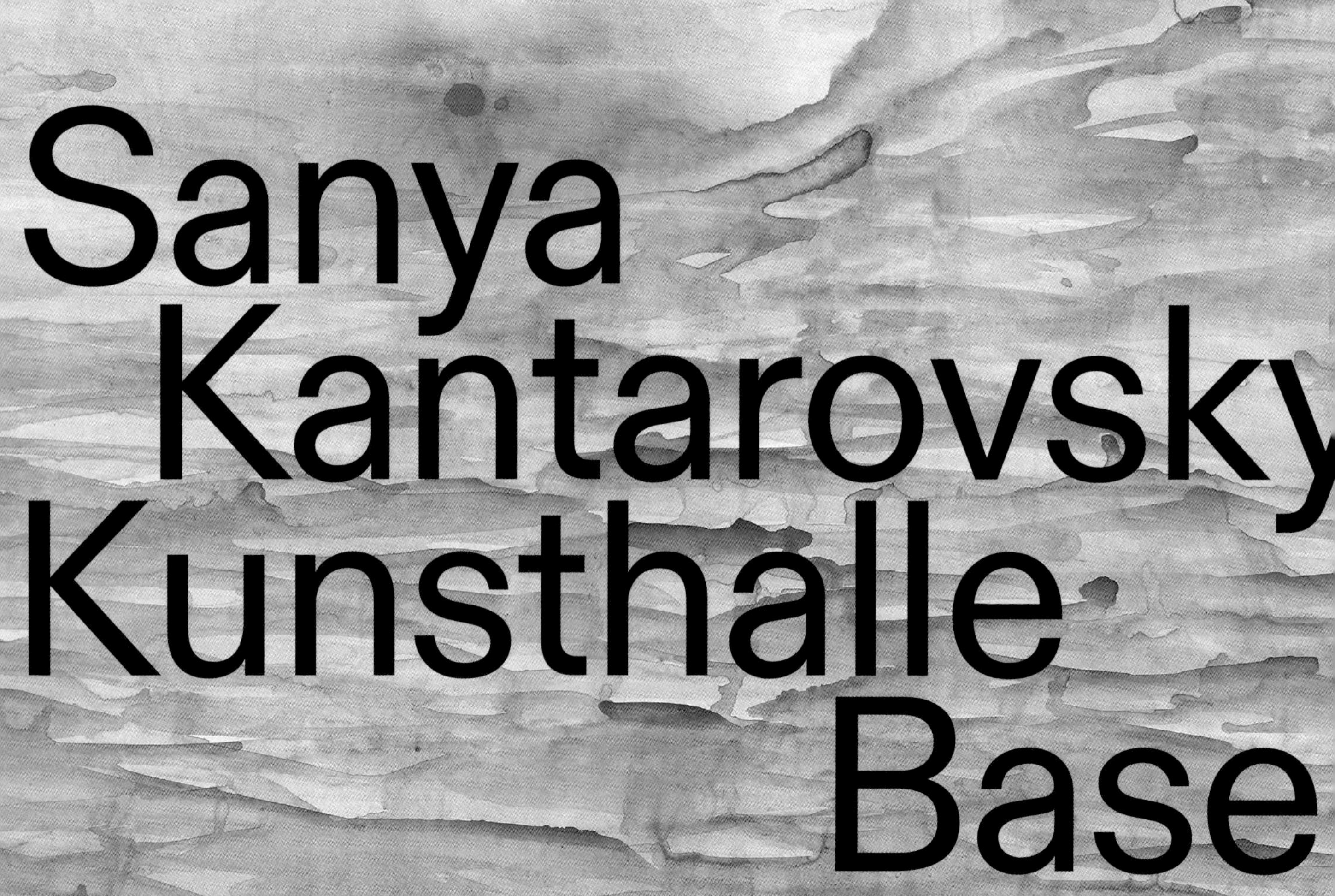

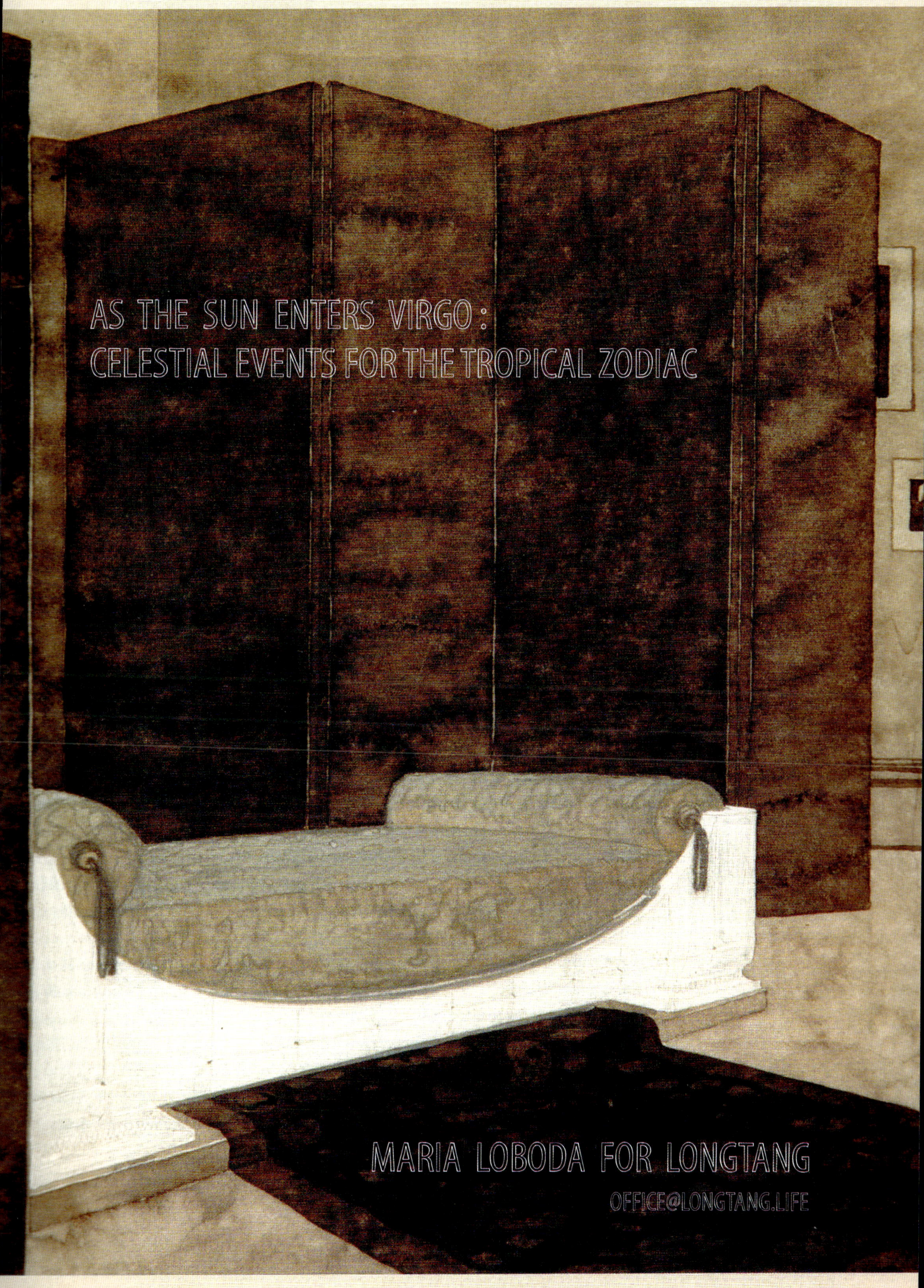
AS THE SUN ENTERS VIRGO:
CELESTIAL EVENTS FOR THE TROPICAL ZODIAC
MARIA LOBODA FOR LONGTANG
OFFICE@LONGTANG.LIFE

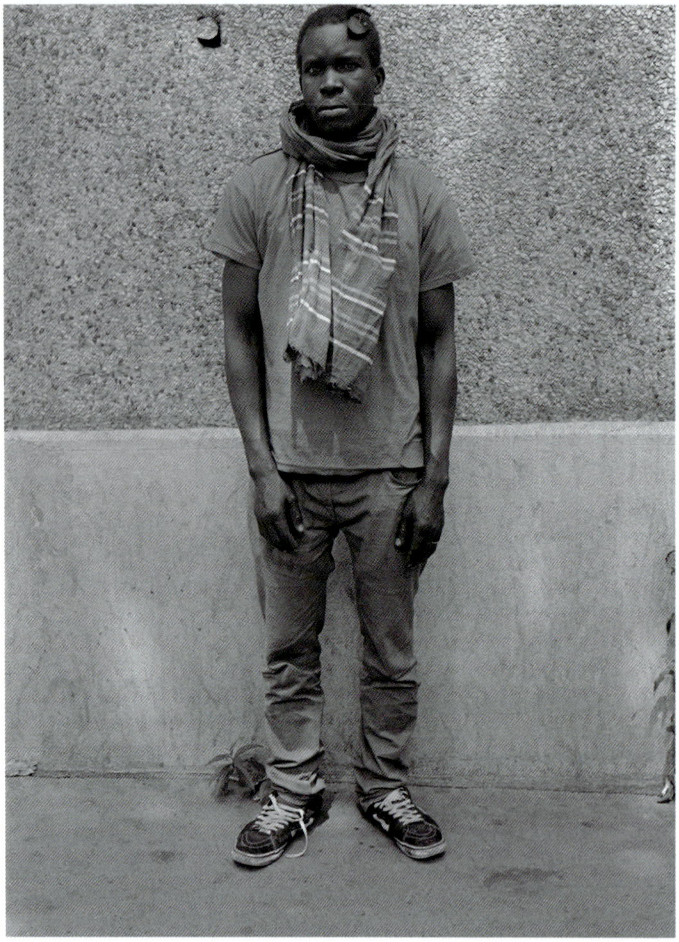

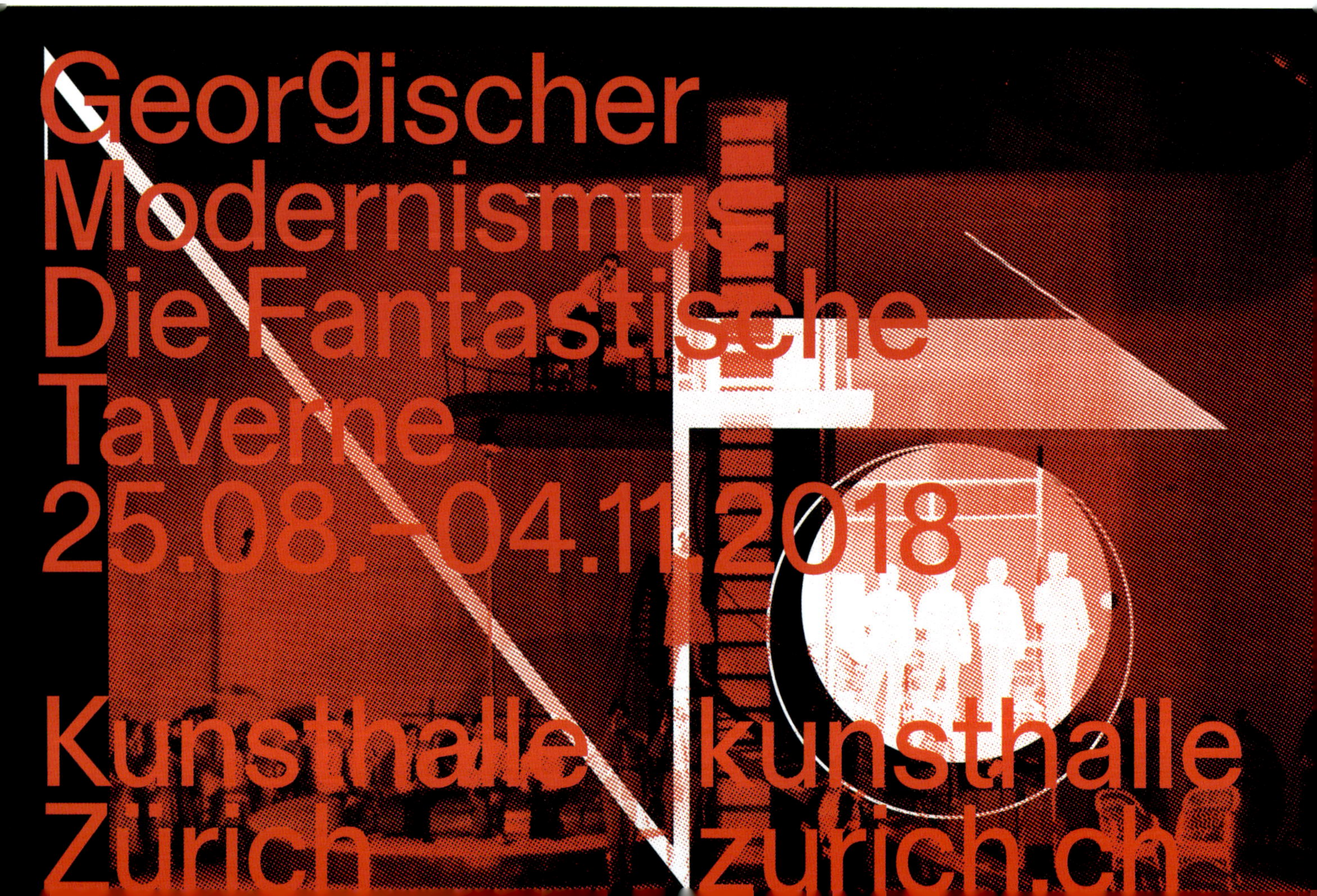

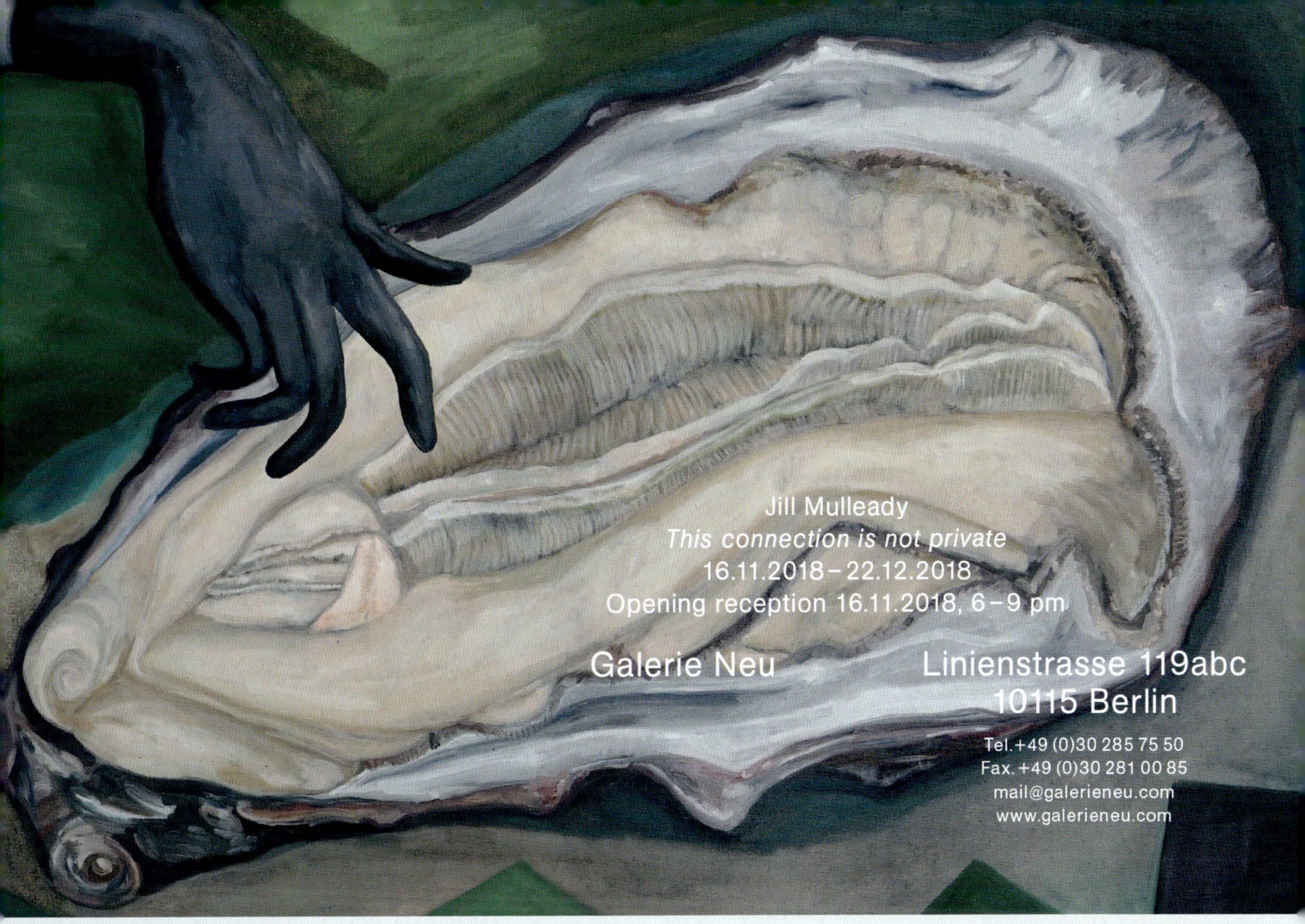

Jill Mulleady
This connection is not private
16.11.2018 – 22.12.2018
Opening reception 16.11.2018, 6 – 9 pm

Galerie Neu

Linienstrasse 119abc
10115 Berlin

Tel. +49 (0)30 285 75 50
Fax. +49 (0)30 281 00 85
mail@galerieneu.com
www.galerieneu.com

ERESA BURGA
6.05 – 12.08 2018

OKI TANAKA
5.08 – 11.11 2018

MARIA EICHHORN
0.11 2018 – 3.02 2019

tstrasse 270 CH–8005 Zurich
smuseum.ch migros-culture-percentage.ch

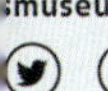
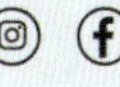

MIGROSMUSEUM
für Gegenwartskunst

AN INSTITUTION OF THE MIGROS CULTURE PERCENTAGE

Hauptstraße 97
D – 69117 Heidelberg
www.hdkv.de
hdkv@hdkv.de

Heidelberger Kunstverein

Tel +49 – 6221 – 184086
Di, Mi, Fr 12 – 19 Uhr
Do 15 – 22 Uhr
Sa – So 11 – 19 Uhr

Eröffnung
Freitag 30.11.
19 Uhr

1.12. 2018 – 17.2. 2019

H Halle

Raumblüte

Kerstin Stoll
Friedrich Kiesler

S Studio

Sharing as Caring #6

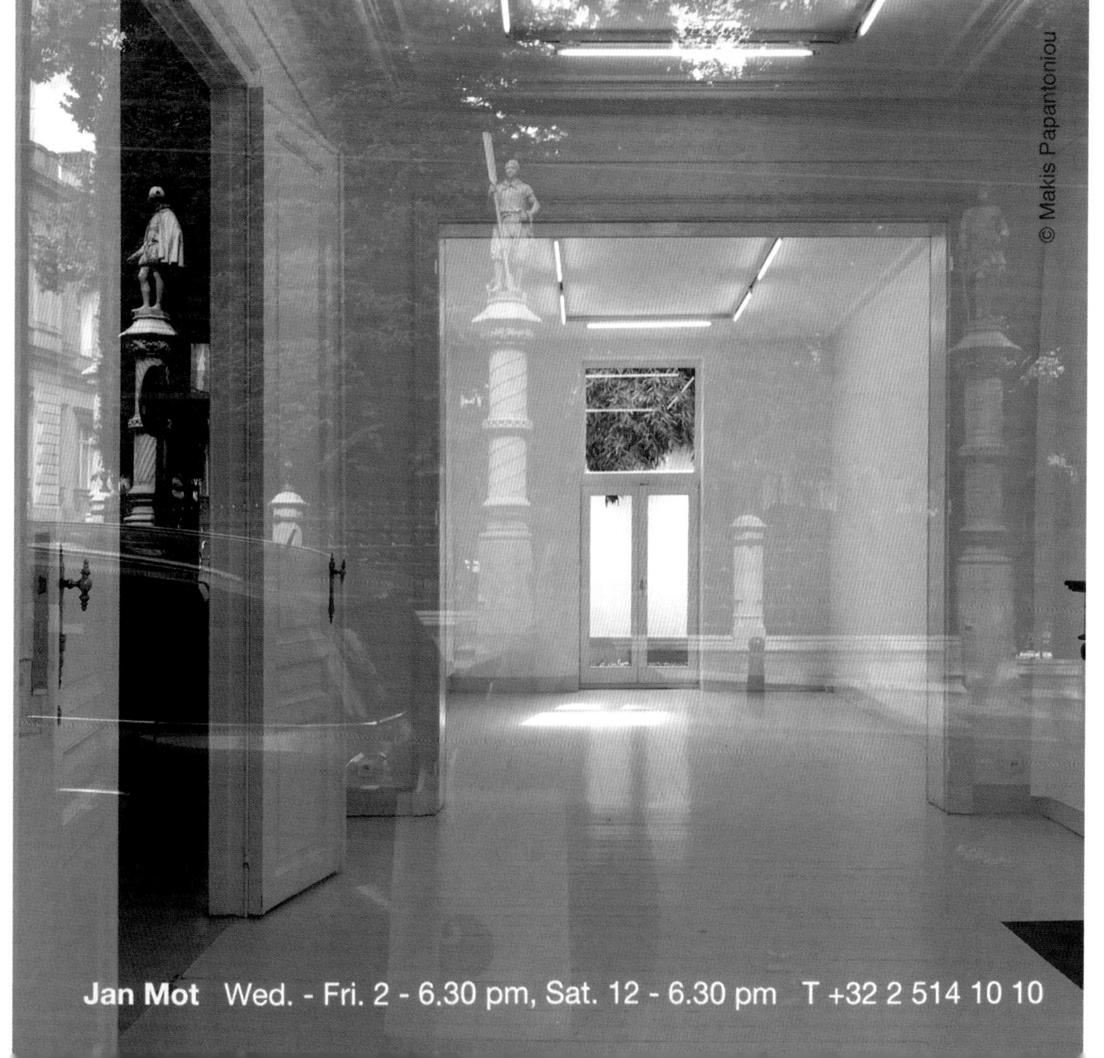

Midway
Contemporary
Art

Julia Haller
Sept 7 – Oct 27, 2018

Jean-Michel Wicker
Nov 10 – Dec 22, 2018

www.midwayart.org

ANDREA
BÜTTNER

*SHEPHERDS
AND KINGS*

24.8.–28.10.

No. 5: Tony Cokes
24.8.–28.10.

BERGEN KUNSTHALL

www.kunsthall.no

Halle f. Kunst
Lüneburg eV

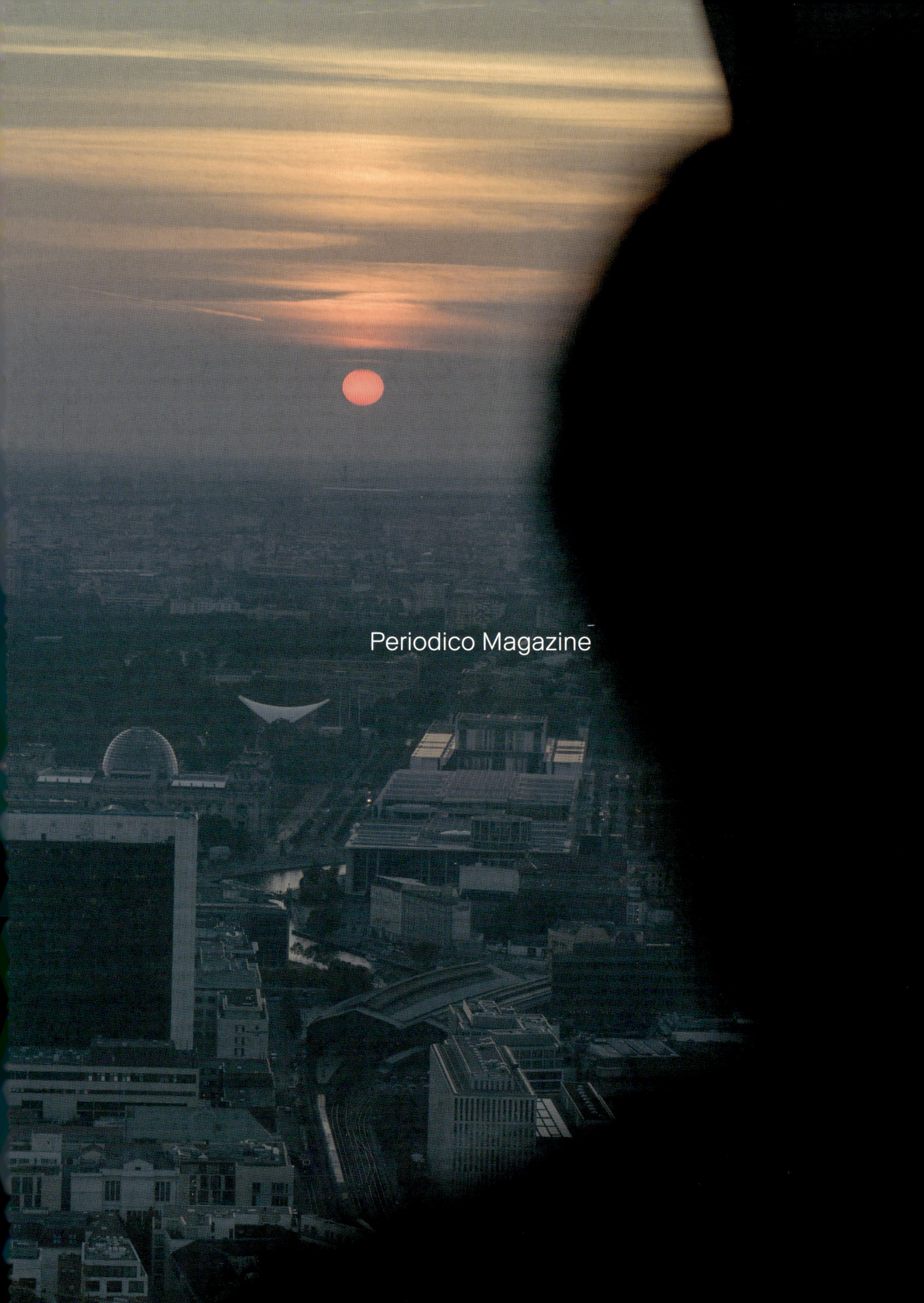
Periodico Magazine

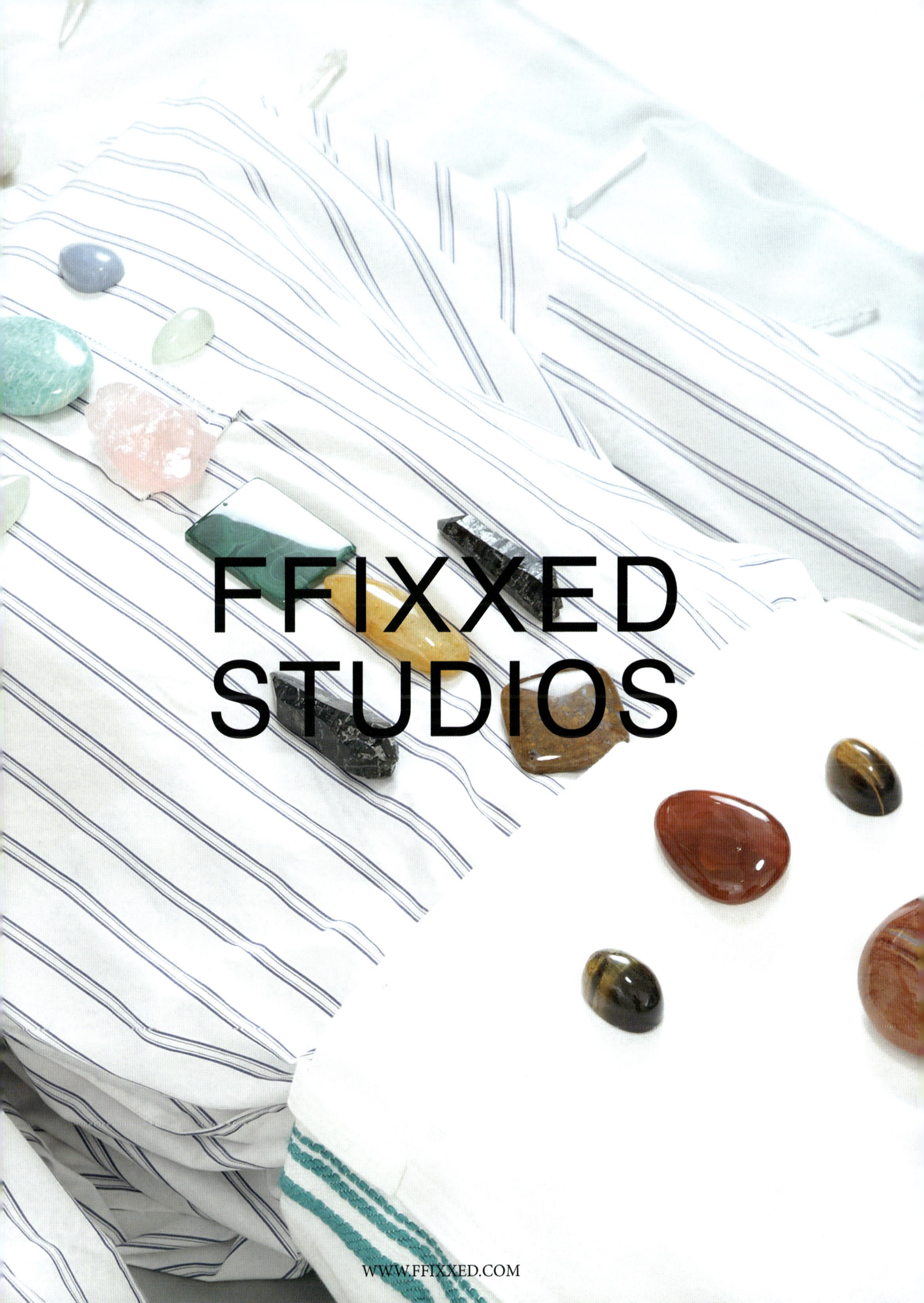

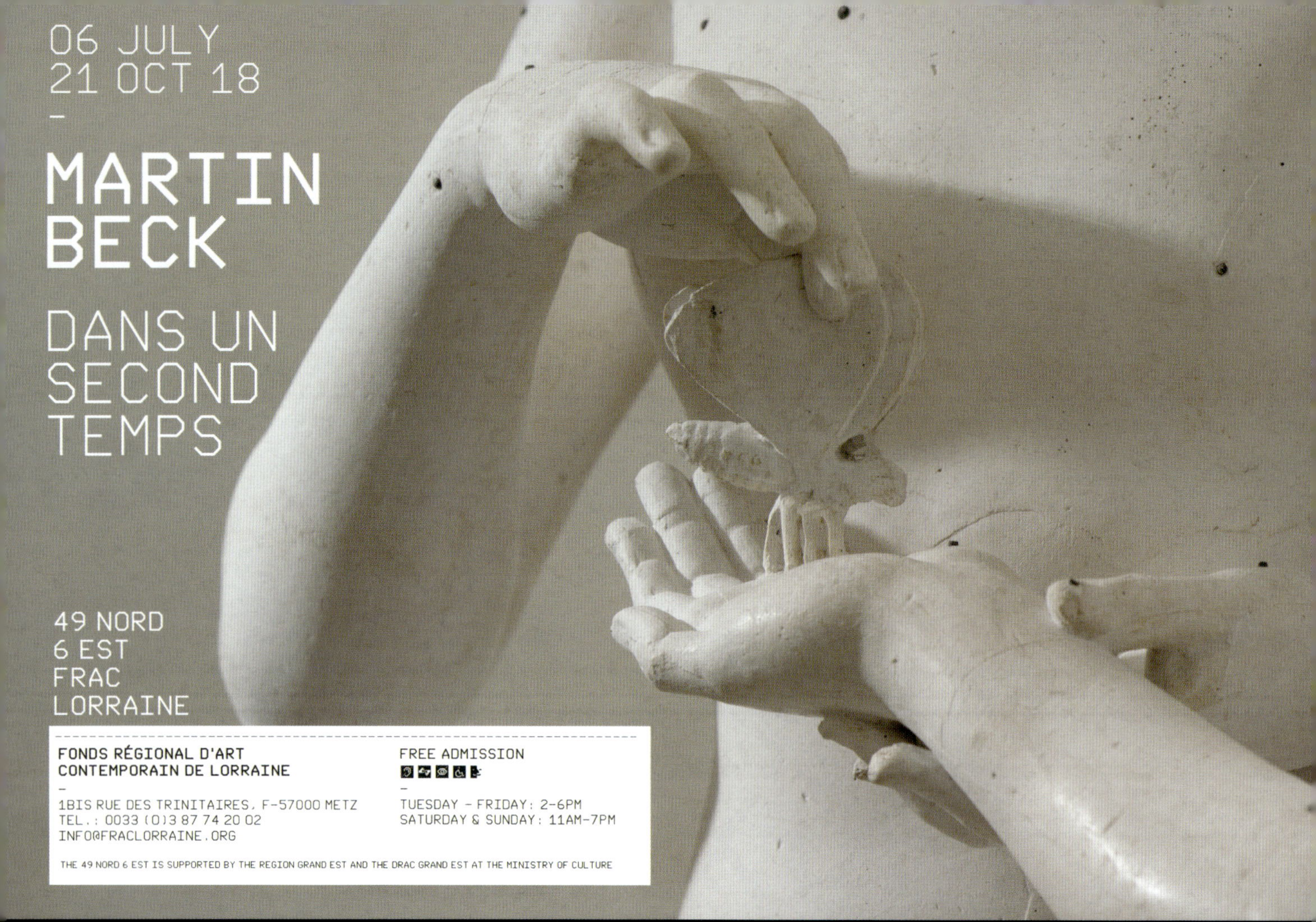

06 JULY
21 OCT 18
-

MARTIN BECK

DANS UN SECOND TEMPS

49 NORD
6 EST
FRAC
LORRAINE

FONDS RÉGIONAL D'ART
CONTEMPORAIN DE LORRAINE
-
1BIS RUE DES TRINITAIRES, F-57000 METZ
TEL.: 0033 (0)3 87 74 20 02
INFO@FRACLORRAINE.ORG

FREE ADMISSION
-
TUESDAY - FRIDAY: 2-6PM
SATURDAY & SUNDAY: 11AM-7PM

THE 49 NORD 6 EST IS SUPPORTED BY THE REGION GRAND EST AND THE DRAC GRAND EST AT THE MINISTRY OF CULTURE

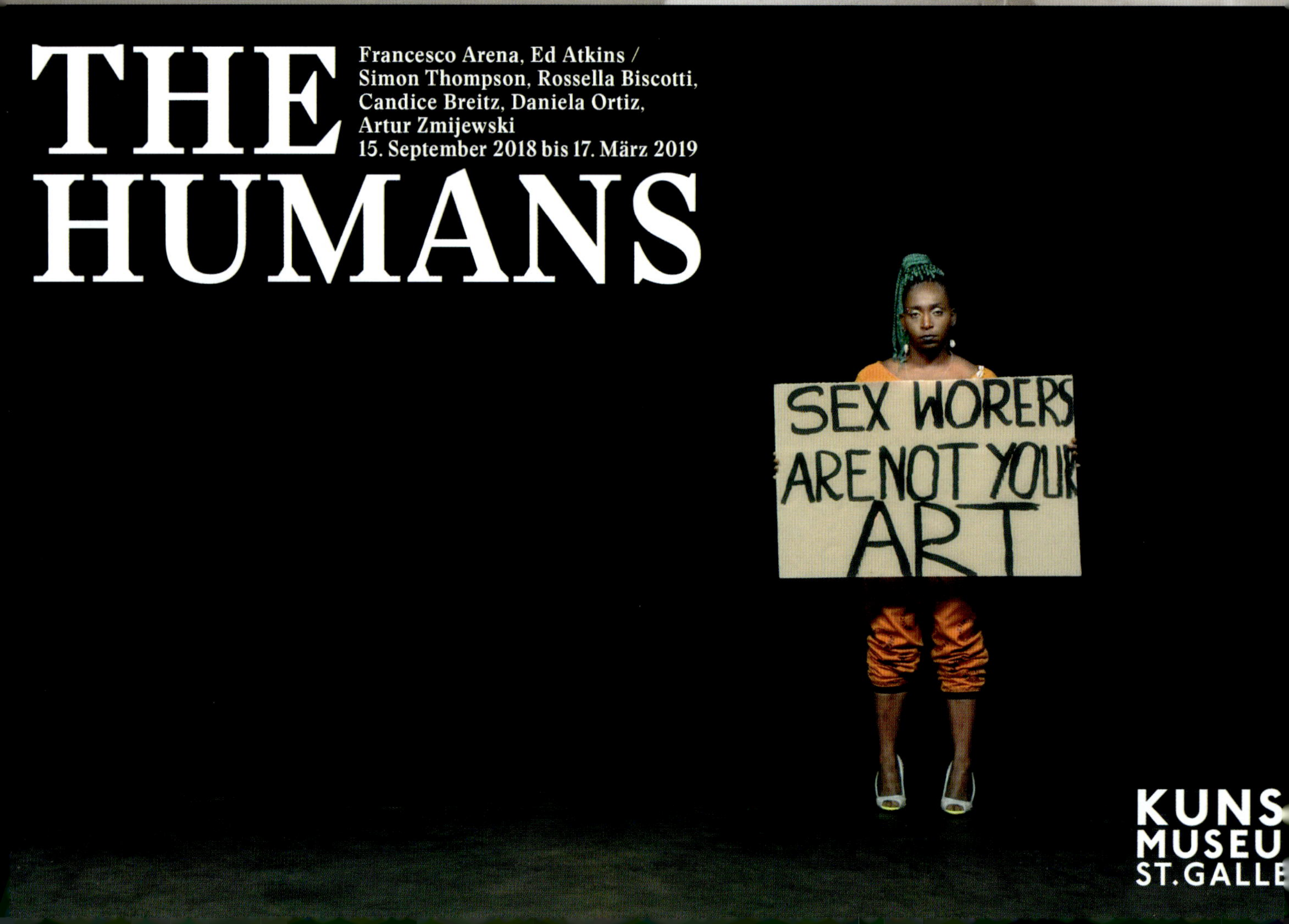

THE HUMANS

Francesco Arena, Ed Atkins / Simon Thompson, Rossella Biscotti, Candice Breitz, Daniela Ortiz, Artur Zmijewski
15. September 2018 bis 17. März 2019

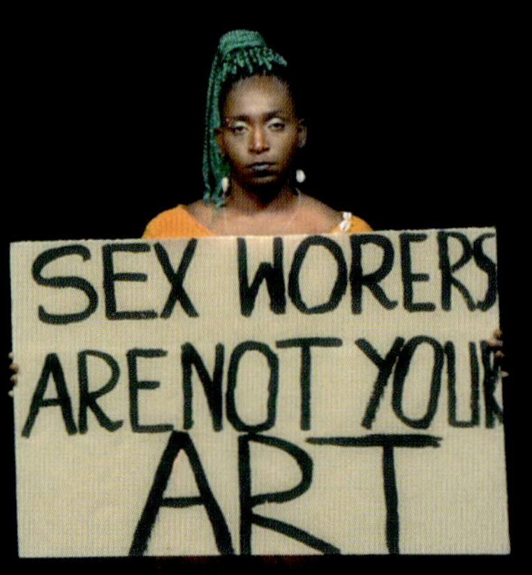

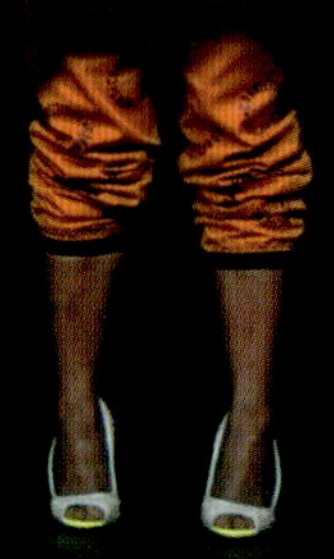

KUNS
MUSEU
ST.GALLE

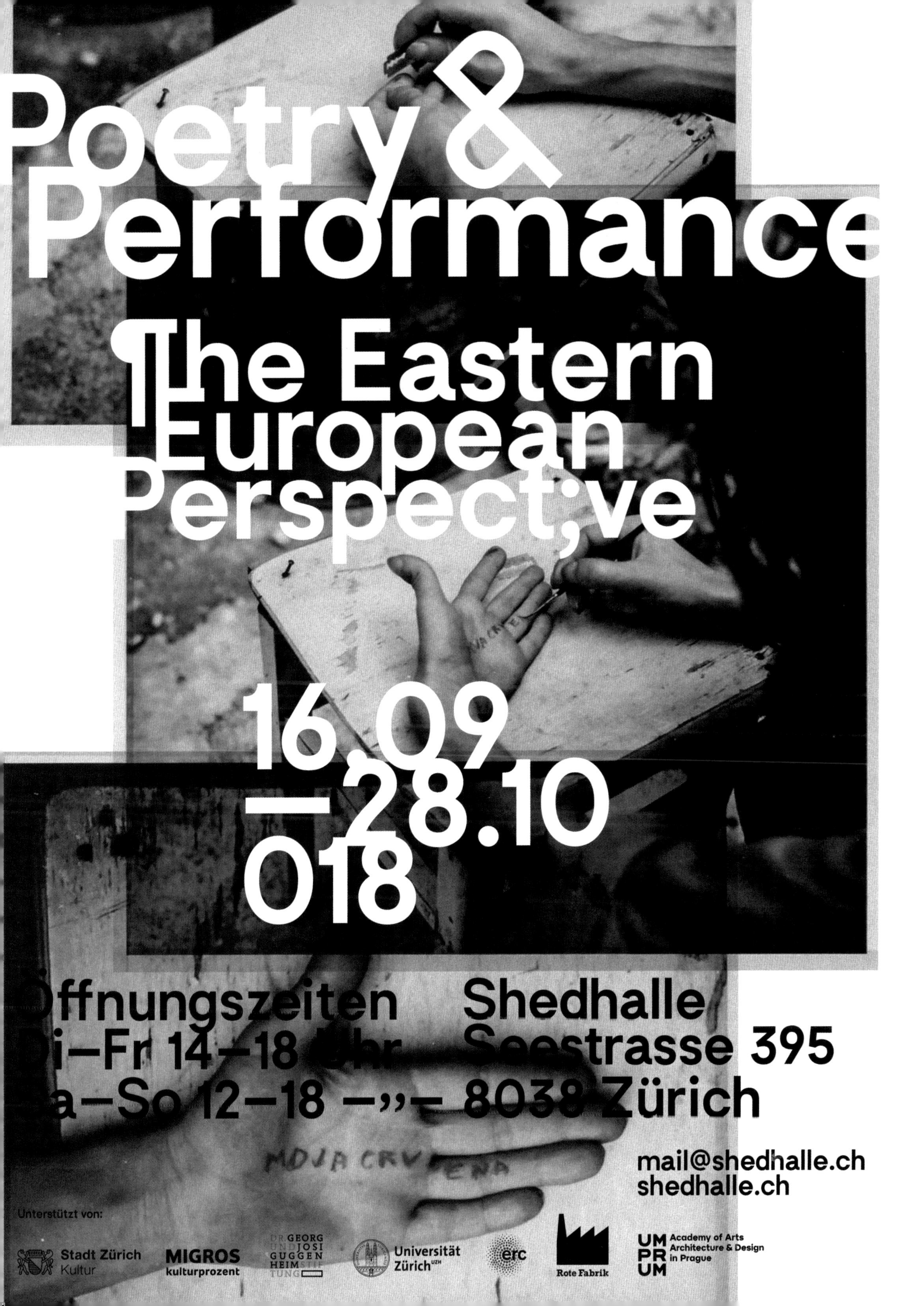

Poetry & Performance

The Eastern European Perspect;ve

16.09 – 28.10 018

Öffnungszeiten
Di–Fr 14–18 Uhr
Sa–So 12–18 –„–

Shedhalle
Seestrasse 395
8038 Zürich

mail@shedhalle.ch
shedhalle.ch

Unterstützt von:

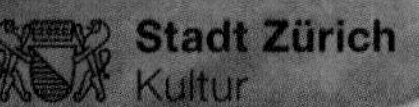

MIGROS kulturprozent

DR. GEORG UND JOSI GUGGENHEIM STIFTUNG

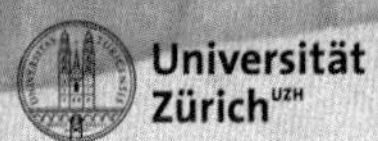

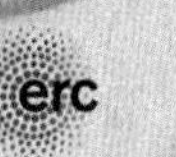

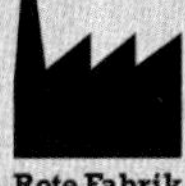

UM PR UM Academy of Arts Architecture & Design in Prague

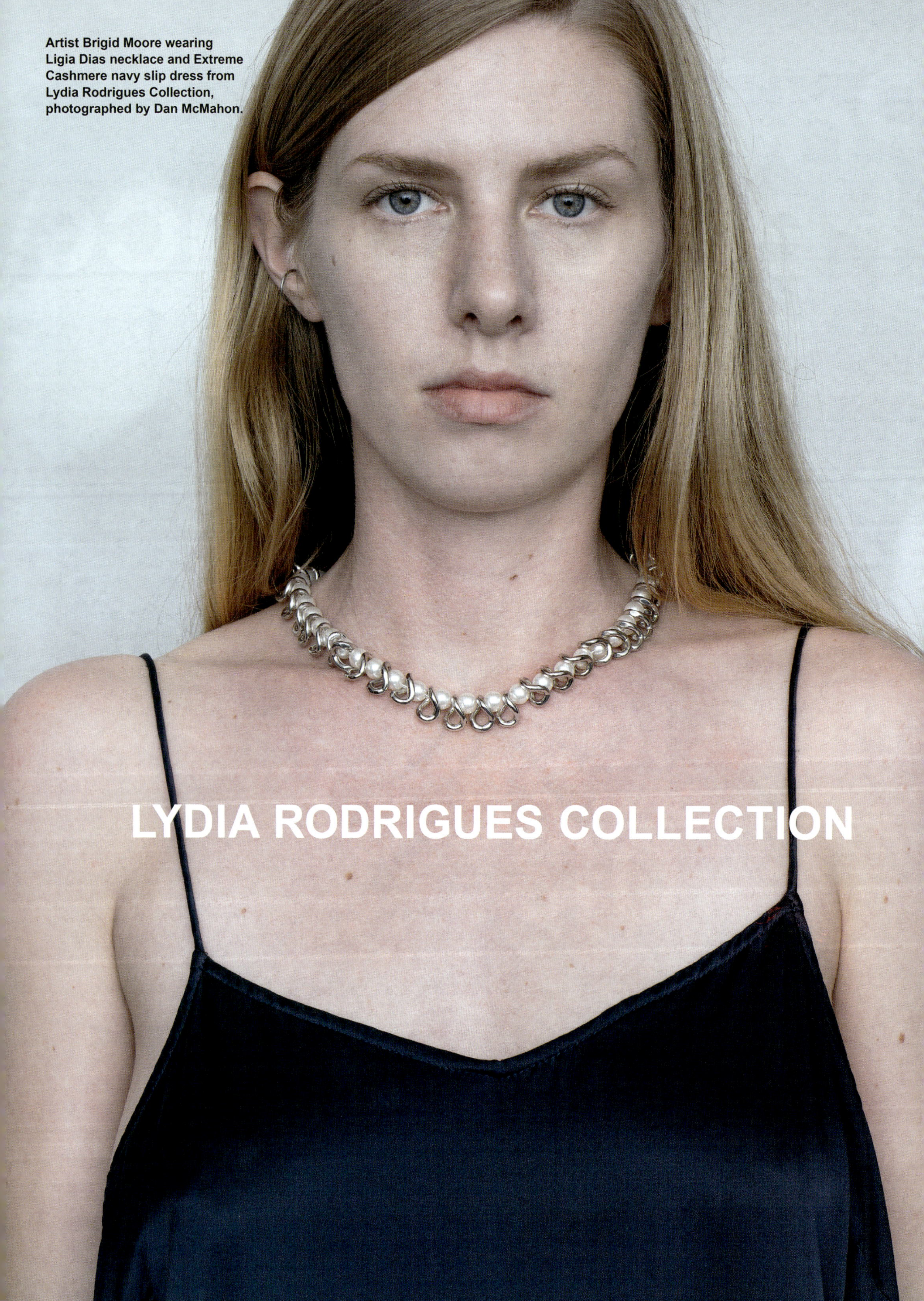

Artist Brigid Moore wearing Ligia Dias necklace and Extreme Cashmere navy slip dress from Lydia Rodrigues Collection, photographed by Dan McMahon.

PROVENCE REPORT AUTUMN / WINTER 2018/2019

Copublished by
PROVENCE, Spector Books

Conceived by
Tobias Kaspar,
Hannes Loichinger

Editor
Hannes Loichinger

Editorial assistant
Philip Pilekjær

Advertisement
Jean-Claude Freymond-Guth,
Philip Pilekjær

Art direction
Tobias Kaspar, Pascal Storz

Design
Pascal Storz, Fabian Bremer

Image editing
Georgs Avetisjans

Printing and binding
Studio RBB, Rīga

Proofreading and copy-editing
Ruth Buchanan (Isabel Mehl and Lynne Tillman; Silvia Simoncelli), Vincenzo Latronico (Nina Hollensteiner), Mme B (Preface; Edgars Gluhovs; Nina Hollensteiner; Jac Leirner and Tobi Meier; Adam Linder and Hannes Loichinger; LaKela Brown and Inka Meißner; Julia Moritz; Cecilie Norgaard and Karsten Pflum)

ISSN: 2624-7682
ISBN: 978-3-95905-264-1

Made possible by the generous support of Stadt Zürich Kultur.

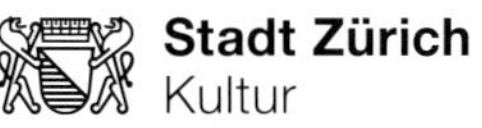

Publishers

PROVENCE
Genossenschaftsstrasse 11
8050 Zurich
Switzerland
www.provence.st
mail@provence.st

Spector Books
Harkortstrasse 10
04107 Leipzig
Germany
www.spectorbooks.com
mail@spectorbooks.com

Distribution

Germany, Austria
GVA, Gemeinsame Verlagsauslieferung Göttingen GmbH & Co. KG, www.gva-verlage.de

Switzerland
AVA Verlagsauslieferung AG, www.ava.ch

France, Belgium
Interart Paris, www.interart.fr

UK
Central Books Ltd, www.centralbooks.com

USA, Canada, Central and South America, Africa, Asia
ARTBOOK | D.A.P.
www.artbook.com

South Korea
The Book Society, www.thebooksociety.org

Australia, New Zealand
Perimeter Distribution, www.perimeterdistribution.com

For subscriptions and back issues

Bruil & van de Staaij
Postbus 75
7940 AB MEPPEL
The Netherlands
(T) +31-522-261303
www.bruil.info/provence
info@bruil.info

Acknowledgments

APRA Foundation Berlin, Elisa Barrera, Caroline Busta, Heinz Emigholz, Olamiju Fajemisin, Sally Schonfeldt

Many thanks to all the authors and collaborators for their contributions.

Credits

Cover: *Arbeit war Dein Leben, Liebe war Dein Tun*, 2018. Photography: Ilya Lipkin and Marc Asekhame. Fashion: Ursina Gysi. Models: Annina Herzer and Theresa Patzschke.

Flap: Fashion editorial for PROVENCE REPORT, 2018. Art direction: Nina Hollensteiner. Photography: Nadine Fraczkowski. Model and styling: Éric Remba. Foreground: Gabriel Shields and Lionel Deng.

P. 40–49: The text by Raphael Gygax is a reprint from: Raphael Gygax, *Extra Bodies. Über den Einsatz des 'anderen Körpers' in der zeitgenössischen Kunst* (Zurich: JRP|Ringier, 2017), 63–74. With the kind authorization of the author and JRP|Ringier. Translated for PROVENCE REPORT by Gerrit Jackson.

P. 56–65: Silvia Simoncelli's text is a revised version of “The Price of Art and Value of Artists' Labour,” initially presented at the conference *Artists on the Market* (Berlin, November 13–14, 2015), fourth workshop of the Forum Kunst und Markt / Centre for Art Market Studies, TU Berlin and first published in *I will work for you for one hour, but someone else should pay for it*, ed. by Emanuele De Donno and Juan Sandoval (Foligno: VIAINDUSTRIAE, 2016), 35–51.

P. 118–25: The contribution on RIBOCA is a shortened version of “Inga Lāce in conversation with Katerina Gregos,” which was first published on April 24, 2018 at http://echogonewrong.com/inga-lace-conversation-katerina-gregos/, just a few weeks before the Riga Biennial opened.

P. 162–63: *Yuichiro Tamura's Sukajan Bomber Jackets* is based on an email conversation between Yuichiro Tamura and PROVENCE in June 2018 and includes rewritten excerpts taken from the material published on the occasion of the exhibition “2 or 3 Tigers” (2013) at HKW, Berlin.

P. 190–91: Ilya Lipkin, *In any case, each photo must include the following credit: “Ilya Lipkin – Balenciaga – Fall 18 Advertising Campaign”*, 2018; Inkjet print, aluminium frame; Courtesy Ilya Lipkin and Galerie Lars Friedrich, Berlin.

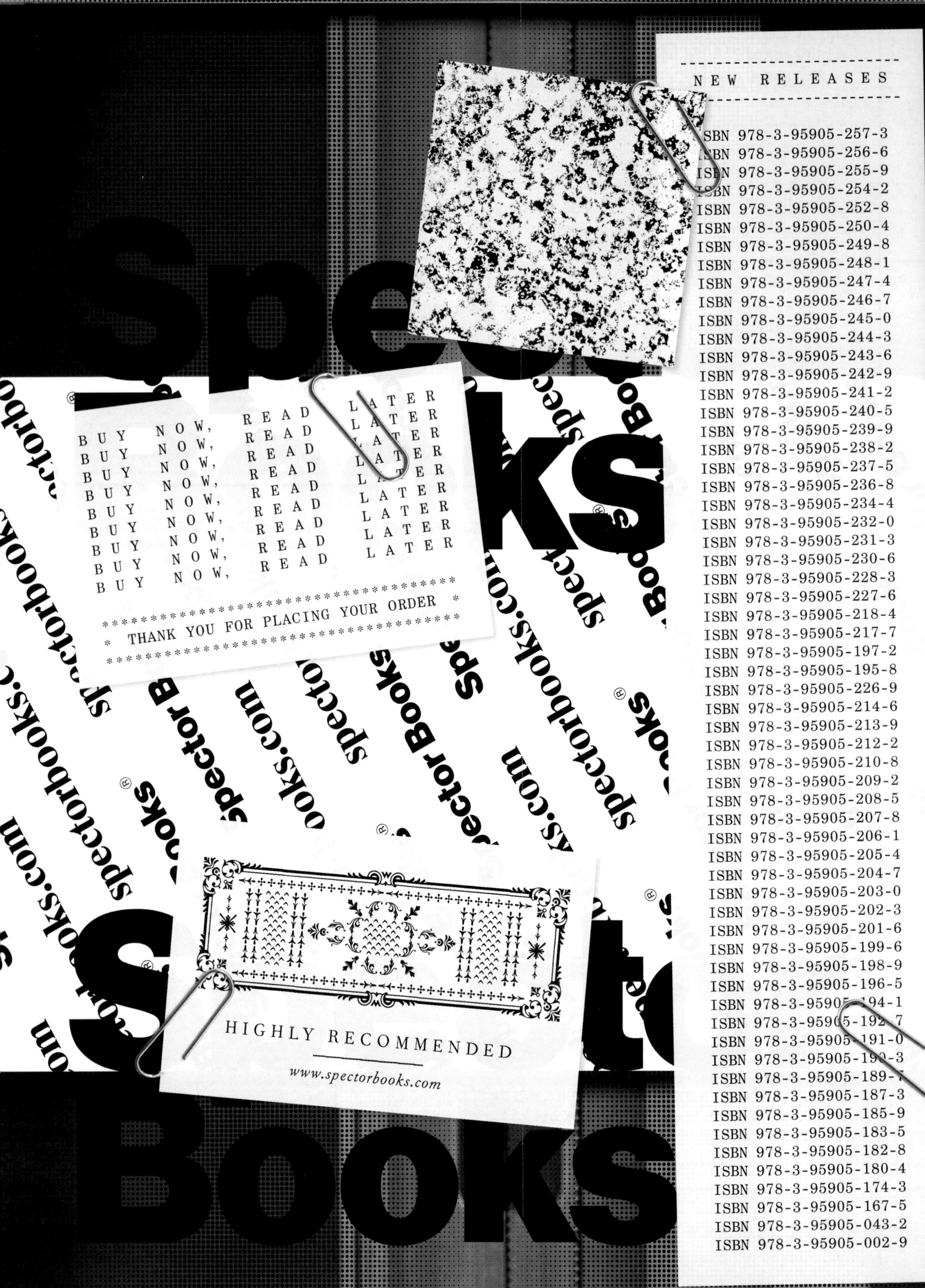
Spector Books
NEW RELEASES
ISBN 978-3-95905-257-3
ISBN 978-3-95905-256-6
ISBN 978-3-95905-255-9
ISBN 978-3-95905-254-2
ISBN 978-3-95905-252-8
ISBN 978-3-95905-250-4
ISBN 978-3-95905-249-8
ISBN 978-3-95905-248-1
ISBN 978-3-95905-247-4
ISBN 978-3-95905-246-7
ISBN 978-3-95905-245-0
ISBN 978-3-95905-244-3
ISBN 978-3-95905-243-6
ISBN 978-3-95905-242-9
ISBN 978-3-95905-241-2
ISBN 978-3-95905-240-5
ISBN 978-3-95905-239-9
ISBN 978-3-95905-238-2
ISBN 978-3-95905-237-5
ISBN 978-3-95905-236-8
ISBN 978-3-95905-234-4
ISBN 978-3-95905-232-0
ISBN 978-3-95905-231-3
ISBN 978-3-95905-230-6
ISBN 978-3-95905-228-3
ISBN 978-3-95905-227-6
ISBN 978-3-95905-218-4
ISBN 978-3-95905-217-7
ISBN 978-3-95905-197-2
ISBN 978-3-95905-195-8
ISBN 978-3-95905-226-9
ISBN 978-3-95905-214-6
ISBN 978-3-95905-213-9
ISBN 978-3-95905-212-2
ISBN 978-3-95905-210-8
ISBN 978-3-95905-209-2
ISBN 978-3-95905-208-5
ISBN 978-3-95905-207-8
ISBN 978-3-95905-206-1
ISBN 978-3-95905-205-4
ISBN 978-3-95905-204-7
ISBN 978-3-95905-203-0
ISBN 978-3-95905-202-3
ISBN 978-3-95905-201-6
ISBN 978-3-95905-199-6
ISBN 978-3-95905-198-9
ISBN 978-3-95905-196-5
ISBN 978-3-95905-194-1
ISBN 978-3-95905-192-7
ISBN 978-3-95905-191-0
ISBN 978-3-95905-190-3
ISBN 978-3-95905-189-7
ISBN 978-3-95905-187-3
ISBN 978-3-95905-185-9
ISBN 978-3-95905-183-5
ISBN 978-3-95905-182-8
ISBN 978-3-95905-180-4
ISBN 978-3-95905-174-3
ISBN 978-3-95905-167-5
ISBN 978-3-95905-043-2
ISBN 978-3-95905-002-9
BUY NOW, READ LATER
BUY NOW, READ LATER
BUY NOW, READ LATER
BUY NOW, READ LATER
BUY NOW, READ LATER
BUY NOW, READ LATER
BUY NOW, READ LATER
BUY NOW, READ LATER
BUY NOW, READ
THANK YOU FOR PLACING YOUR ORDER
spectorbooks.com
Spector Books
HIGHLY RECOMMENDED
www.spectorbooks.com
Books